SPAIN AND THE MEDITERR

BOOKS OF RELATED INTEREST

In the Shadow of the Holocaust and the Inquisition: Israel's Relations with Francoist Spain
by Raanan Rein

The New Mediterranean Democracies: Regime Transition in Greece, Spain and Portugal
edited by Geoffrey Pridham

Politics and Policy in Democratic Spain
edited by Paul Heywood

Israel, Turkey and Greece: Uneasy Relations in the East Mediterranean
by Amikam Nachmani

Jews, Christians, and Muslims in the Mediterranean World after 1492
edited by Alisa Meyuhas Ginio
(new in paperback)

Intercultural Contacts in the Medieval Mediterranean
edited by Benjamin Arbel

Latins and Greeks in the Eastern Mediterranean after 1204
edited by Benjamin Arbel, Bernard Hamilton and David Jacoby

Spain and the Mediterranean since 1898

Edited by

RAANAN REIN

FRANK CASS
LONDON • PORTLAND, OR

First published in 1999 in Great Britain by
FRANK CASS AND COMPANY LIMITED
Newbury House, 900 Eastern Avenue, London IG2 7HH, England

and in the United States of America by
FRANK CASS
c/o ISBS
5804 N.E. Hassalo Street, Portland, Oregon 97213-3644

British Library Cataloguing in Publication Data

Spain and the Mediterranean since 1898
1. Spain - History - 20th century 2. Spain - Politics and government - 20th century
3. Spain - Foreign relations - Mediterranean Region - 20th century
I. Rein, Raanan, 1960-
946'.08

ISBN 0 7146 4945 7 (h/back)
ISBN 0 7146 8004 4 (p/back)

Library of Congress Cataloging-in-Publication Data

Spain and the Mediterranean since 1898 / edited by Raanan Rein.
p. cm.
Includes index.
Contents: Spain on the Threshold of a New Century: Society and Politics before and after the Disaster of 1898 / Octavio Ruiz – Between Europe and the Mediterranean: Spanish-Italian Relations, 1898-1922 / Fernando García Sanz – Spanish Colonialism during Primo de Rivera's Dictatorship / Susana Sueiro Seoane – The Mediterranean in the Foreign Policy of the Second Spanish Republic / Nuria Tabanera Garcia – Spanish Morocco and the Second Republic: Consistency in Colonial Policy? / Shannon E. Fleming – Fascist Italy and Spain, 1922-45 / Stanley G. Payne – Fascism and Empire: Fascist Italy against Republican Spain / Ismael Saz – The International Policy of the Second Republic during the Spanish Civil War / Ricardo Miralles – The Spanish Civil War and the Mediterranean / Michael Alpert – Franco's Bid for Empire: Spain, Germany, and the Western Mediterranean in World War II / Norman J.W. Goda – In Pursuit of Votes and Economic Treaties: Francoist Spain and the Arab World, 1945-56 / Raanan Rein – Spain's Input in Shaping the EU's Mediterranean Policies, 1986-96 / Alfred Tovias – Spanish Foreign and Security Policy in the Mediterranean / Antonio Marquina.
ISBN 0-7146-4945-7 (hb). – ISBN 0-7146-8004-4 (pb)
1. Spain – foreign relations – Mediterranean region. 2. Mediterranean Region – Foreign relations – Spain. 3. Spain – relations – 20th century. 4. Mediterranean Region – Foreign relations – 20th century. I. Rein, Raanan, 1960- .
DP86.M38S6 1999
327.4601822–dc21 98-45229
CIP

This group of studies first appeared in a Special Issue of *Mediterranean Historical Review* (ISSN 0951-8967), Vol.13, No.1/2 (June/December 1998), [Spain and the Mediterranean since 1898].

Printed in Great Britain by Anthony Rowe Ltd., Chippenham, Wiltshire

Contents

Introduction

The year 1898 is considered a watershed in Spanish history, and some have even gone to the extreme of giving it the same weight as the pivotal 1492. The 1898 centennial, recently observed with various congresses and events, has further inflated the already extensive bibliography on the subject.[1] Yet, hyperbole aside, the military defeat Spain suffered at the hands of the United States did in fact mark, to a considerable extent, the beginning of a new era in Spanish history. The Disaster of 1898 had far-reaching repercussions on the Spanish political system. It helped undermine the constitutional monarchy, which functioned on the basis of a peaceful rotation of power between the two dominant parties. Even General Miguel Primo de Rivera, who seized power in September 1923, and General Francisco Franco, who led the Nationalist uprising against the Second Republic in July 1936 and ruled Spain as its dictator until November 1975, linked their own victories with the naval defeat at the end of the nineteenth century. The loss of Cuba, which had been the main market for Catalan industry, also sharpened criticism of Madrid and accelerated the development of Catalan nationalism.

Certainly the events of 1898 had powerful long-term consequences for Spain's position and role in the international system. The loss of the Caribbean islands of Cuba and Puerto Rico (in addition to Spain's defeat in the Philippines) meant the loss of the last vestiges of the Spanish empire in the New World. That immense enterprise, begun at the end of the fifteenth century, thus came to an end politically and militarily, although not culturally, at the end of the nineteenth century. From that time on, Spain focused its attention on the European arena, particularly the Mediterranean basin – a change of course that, according to the Spanish historian Salvador de Madariaga, represented a return to Spain's 'natural' foreign policy objectives, which had been sidetracked by the 'discovery' of the New World in 1492 and the accession to the Spanish throne of the Hapsburg King, Charles I.[2]

The ruling elites' inability to give up the imperial myth and the fact that the loss of the Spanish empire had come just at a time when other European powers were at the height of their colonial competition on the African continent encouraged Spain to try to carve out a mini-empire for itself in North Africa as compensation for losing its American dominions. As the historian David Woolman wrote,[3]

> National pride demanded that something be done to regain a certain measure of prestige. Where were there greater possibilities of glory

> than in Morocco? One had merely to look across the Straits of Gibraltar to see plainly the peaks of this unexploited land. The two presidios planted on its shores had been Spanish for over three hundred years; and moreover, the Spanish Army had easily won the recent brief military excursions. Now was surely the moment … to rebuild the glory of Spain.

To Spain's rulers in the first third of the twentieth century, the Spanish presence in Morocco was essential if Spain was to enjoy any measure of prestige and influence in the international sphere. As the liberal Prime Minister of the time, Conde de Romanones, wrote in his memoirs, 'Morocco was for Spain her last chance to keep her position in the concert of Europe'.[4]

The rhetoric concerning Spain's special relationship with Spanish America continued throughout the twentieth century – particularly during periods when Spain's relations with the European powers were rocky – and served the efforts of various regimes to enhance their prestige at home and abroad. Whatever the regime, however – civilian or military, monarchic or republican, tyrannical or democratic – most of Spain's attention and resources now went to Europe and the Mediterranean countries. This tendency has grown stronger since Spain's admission to the European Community in 1986.

The present collection of articles examines diplomatic, strategic, economic, and cultural aspects of Spain's relations with the Mediterranean countries in the past 100 years. The opening essay, by Octavio Ruiz, analyses the difficulties, tensions, and internal contradictions that characterized Spanish society and politics at the end of the nineteenth century and the beginning of the twentieth under the renewed reign of the Bourbons. That liberal monarchy's increasing difficulties with the challenges of urbanization and industrialization and the resulting acceleration of social radicalization and pressures for political democratization all contributed to the institution of the military dictatorship in 1923.

Fernando García Sanz's article studies the relations between Spain and Italy from the end of the last century up until 1922, when the Fascists took power in Rome. It shows how economic ties between the two countries were hampered by competition for the same agricultural markets in Europe and by conflicting interests in North Africa, particularly with respect to France. Decision makers in Rome and Madrid always hoped that their counterparts would help maintain the balance of power in the Mediterranean by curbing French aspirations in North Africa without becoming too friendly with Paris.

Susana Sueiro shows how Primo de Rivera, Spain's dictator from 1923 to 1930, managed to end the Rif war, which, encouraging political and social ferment on the Iberian Peninsula, had been something of a nightmare for the constitutional government that had preceded the dictatorship. The article assesses Primo de Rivera's achievement in the context of the struggle among the European powers, which sought to maintain their influence in the western Mediterranean in general and in North Africa in particular.

The Second Republic, established in Spain after the fall of the dictatorship, had trouble implementing the new, different foreign policy it envisioned both because it was busy coping with the internal political problems that plagued its short life (1931–36) and because its rule coincided with a world economic depression and growing tension in the international sphere. Nuria Tabanera García focuses on the principal points of reference for the Republic's foreign policy, namely the League of Nations and the Anglo-French axis. The Republican leaders' primary concern was to maintain stability in the western Mediterranean at a time when the collective system of security was falling apart. The same concern has led Spain to participate in successive regional efforts to draw up a 'Mediterranean pact'.

Shannon E. Fleming discusses the evolution of the Second Republic's colonial policies in Spanish Morocco from April 1931 to July 1936. He argues that despite the frequent administrative and personnel changes in the protectorate during this period, the Second Republic's policies remained fairly consistent. They included most notably a commitment to the colonial ethos, the replacement of the military administration with a civil one, and continuing efforts to isolate the protectorate from the political and social issues that engaged the Peninsula.

Stanley G. Payne provides a broad view of the ups and downs that characterized the relations between Rome and Madrid during Benito Mussolini's rule. The first phase of the relationship (1923–30) produced friendly ties between the two dictators, Mussolini and Primo de Rivera, but no decisive changes. During the second phase, under the Second Republic, relations were adversarial but Mussolini had no significant influence on Spanish affairs, which were a comparatively low priority for Italian diplomacy. The third phase encompassed the Spanish Civil War (1936–39), during which the Italian dictator provided more support to the Spanish Nationalists than Hitler did, both absolutely and proportionately. During the fourth phase, spanning most of World War II (1939–43), relations remained very close, though they were less significant than Spain's relations with Nazi Germany.

Ismael Saz's essay analyses Hispano-Italian relations during the second and third phases mentioned above. During the Second Republic, Mussolini tried to influence Spanish politics through a combination of diplomatic activity and covert support for monarchist conspiracies. However, it was not until the outbreak of the Civil War that he became seriously involved in events on the Iberian Peninsula. Saz examines Mussolini's motives for intervention, which included his wish to block Communist influence and to eliminate the democratic challenge represented by the Republican government, as well as the desire to increase the regime's prestige at home and abroad as a means of achieving Italian hegemony in the Mediterranean.

The non-intervention policy adopted by France and Britain during the Civil War contributed to the Nationalists' overthrow of the Republic. Both countries were worried that events in Spain might drag them into an international war and therefore tried to remain aloof from the hostilities. Ricardo Miralles's article examines the diplomatic moves the Spanish Republic made to counteract the effects of this policy.

The Mediterranean as a scene of conflicted interests and naval battles is the subject of Michael Alpert's article. The Spanish Civil War came at a time when the British navy did not consider itself strong enough to fight Italy in the Mediterranean while continuing to defend Britain's widespread empire. Italy, however, was heavily rearming and resented Britain's refusal to respect Italian rights in the Mediterranean or to extend total recognition to Italy's conquest of Abyssinia. The Spanish Civil War gave Italy an opportunity to challenge the security of British and French sea routes and to undermine British power and prestige. Although Britain ultimately kept the Italian navy from dominating the entire Mediterranean, it could not break the Italians' control of the western part of the sea. The Spanish Republican fleet in the Mediterranean was unable to challenge the Nationalist insurgents or to blockade their ports, and the sea routes by which supplies and food were shipped to Republican Spain became increasingly hazardous. The USSR, now the Republic's sole friend, maintained no presence in the Mediterranean. By 1938, Nationalist warships strategically based at Palma (Majorca) and aided by German and Italian aircraft, had the Spanish Republic effectively blockaded, and they were to be an important factor in its defeat.

Norman J.W. Goda argues in his article that Spanish foreign policy during World War II must be understood within the context of Madrid's aims in the western Mediterranean, particularly in French Morocco. Although the Franco government had been unwilling to enter the European war when it erupted in 1939, it changed its policy when it saw France facing defeat by the Germans (in June 1940). Reluctant to subordinate Spanish aims to those of the Axis powers, Franco initially tried to obtain French colonial territory without consulting the Germans or the Italians by negotiating with the new Vichy regime. Only after this attempt failed did Madrid offer to enter the war on the Axis side, hoping in this way to gain the territory it coveted. Hitler's competing aims in Northwest Africa, however, ultimately helped keep Spain out of the war.

At the end of World War II, Franco's regime found itself isolated in the international sphere and confronting profound economic distress at home. As a strategy for expanding trade and ending the diplomatic boycott imposed on it by the United Nations, Spain began to cultivate its relations with the Arab world. Raanan Rein examines Francoist Spain's systematic campaign to woo the Arab countries in the late 1940s and early 1950s, a campaign in which even the regime's failure to form diplomatic relations with the state of Israel became a vehicle for improving Spanish ties with the Arabs. However, Franco's hopes that displaying hostility towards the Jewish state and fostering political and economic ties with the Arab countries would allow him to maintain Spain's control over northern Morocco proved illusory.

The last two essays in this volume focus on the evolution of Spain's Mediterranean policy since 1986, when the country joined the European Community. Alfred Tovias emphasizes Spain's role in the European Union, especially with respect to Spanish policies concerning Mediterranean non-member countries. According to Tovias, these policies underwent a rapid change, shifting from an emphasis on unilateral trade preferences in favour of those countries to a focus on financial aid, reciprocal trade concessions, and such non-economic issues as political dialogue, cultural cooperation, and horizontal cooperation between non-governmental organizations. However, other European policies, such as the institution of a borderless Europe, have called upon Spain to serve as gatekeeper of the south in order to restrict the entry of immigrants from North Africa into the European Union labor market by way of Spain.

Antonio Marquina's essay concentrates on Spain's efforts to achieve stability in the Mediterranean by making the United States, the European Union, and NATO aware of security problems there. The Euro-Mediterranean Conference of Barcelona (November 1995) was one notable manifestation of such efforts.

All in all, this collection fills a vacuum in English-language historiography relating to Spain's international relations. In the past ten years important work has been done on this subject in Spain itself, where academic activity has been characterized by growing openness and vitality since Franco's death. It is therefore no wonder that about half of the contributors to this volume are Spaniards.

I should like to thank the editors of the *Mediterranean Historical Review*, Irad Malkin and Ron Barkai, for their support and encouragement; the authors of all the essays, particularly Stanley Payne for his advice and encouragement; and Lorenzo Delgado Gómez Escalonilla and Florentino

Portero for their help and goodwill. Finally, I should also like to thank Tal Agmon for the work put into producing this book and Barbara Metzger for her diligent copy-editing.

Raanan Rein

NOTES

1. According to Sebastian Balfour, '1898 looms almost as large in Spanish historiography as that other fateful and much more trumpeted year of 1492'. See Sebastian Balfour, *The End of the Spanish Empire, 1898–1923* (Oxford, 1997), p.v.
2. Cited in Gerie B. Bledsoe, 'Spanish Foreign Policy, 1898–1936', in J.W. Cortada (ed.), *Spain in the Twentieth-Century World* (Westport, CT, 1980), p.3.
3. David Woolman, *Rebels in the Rif: Abd el-Krim and the Rif Rebellion* (Stanford, 1967), p.35.
4. Cited in Raymond Carr, *Spain 1808–1975*, 2nd edn. (Oxford, 1982), p.518 n.2.

Spain on the Threshold of a New Century: Society and Politics before and after the Disaster of 1898

OCTAVIO RUIZ

The military defeat of Spain at the hands of the United States in July 1898 has always been a reference point in the collective memory of Spaniards. It goes far beyond the actual consequences – military, economic, colonial and political – of a disaster which, to anyone with a modicum of information, always seemed inevitable, given the extraordinary inequality between the opponents and the diplomatic isolation of Spain. In fact, historical writings of recent years agree that, apart from the enormous symbolic significance of the loss of the last colonies of a once-great empire, the effects of the war, both economic and political, were relatively limited. At the same time, one writer[1] *has pointed out that, faithful to a tradition common to the European political culture of the time, the date 1898 was used as a rhetorical device to increase awareness of the need for a profound political transformation. French intellectuals had done the same after the defeat at Sedan in 1870. It is as well, therefore, to set out in greater detail the chronological framework of these reflections with which we shall try to develop the idea that the colonial disaster of 1898, far beyond its intrinsic importance, serves to illustrate the disorder from which the Spanish political system was suffering at the end of the nineteenth century and the subsequent attempts to transform it and adapt it to new demands.*

At the end of the nineteenth century Spain was still markedly agricultural in character, that being the occupation of two-thirds of the working population. This ratio had remained constant since the beginning of the century and, since the great majority of these agricultural workers were only hired hands and had very little job security, the most obvious result was a society with extraordinary inequalities in which the aristocratic ideals characteristic of the *ancien régime* prevailed. The country's large agricultural landowners came from the ranks of the Spanish nobility and continued to enjoy extraordinary prestige, as is attested by the almost 300 titles which were created in the last quarter of the century.

Although the years after 1875 – a period known in Spain as the *Restauración* (Restoration) – were years of moderate economic growth, on the whole that growth was insufficient to sustain a population which was also increasing moderately but steadily (from 16.6 to 18.6 million between 1877 and 1900). This meant that living conditions did not improve appreciably. This helps us to understand the reasons for the great wave of migration to Spanish-speaking American countries – it is calculated that more than one million left in the last 20 years of the century[2] – and the marked concentration of people in the main cities. The latter process, although far less important in actual numbers, would have powerful repercussions on the nature of the political system.

The main cities of the country expanded in the final years of the century, but those who came to the cities were, for the most part, illiterates who lacked professional training. However, the first timid steps towards industrialization meant that the cities would offer better wages and greater employment opportunities than the countryside. At the beginning of the twentieth century almost two-thirds of the total Spanish population were illiterate, and this made them extraordinarily dependent on those who had money or education. The situation was the same for the great majority of those who lived in small centres of population with fewer than 5,000 inhabitants as for those who had preferred the precarious way of life and the overcrowding suffered by the common people in the big cities. The most elementary education reached little more than half of Spanish children, and only a tiny proportion of those went on to secondary and higher-level studies, which were beyond the reach of the common people and of women. Gloria Giner de los Ríos, niece of Francisco Giner de los Ríos, who was one of the great educational reformers of modern Spain, had to pursue her secondary education in a Barcelona school sitting next to the teacher, since it was considered improper for her to share benches with boys. In fact, the first secondary school for girls was not set up until 1910.

In general, as the nineteenth century gave way to the twentieth, Spanish society appeared to be a backward one in which, despite a marked process of urbanization, most of the population seemed to be confined to small, isolated centres to which it was difficult to bring advances in education and culture. This was a time of confident optimism which was, however, enjoyed by very few. The construction of a liberal state had been a slow process and had produced very limited results. The crisis at the end of the century could only point up those imbalances.

A LIBERAL SETTING

Since the 1830s society had been trying to develop a form of political organization based on the principles of liberal ideology. The process had been a faltering one, and the dysfunctions of the system had provoked years of political paralysis. These years (1868–74) had witnessed the overthrow of Queen Isabella II, the introduction of a constitutional monarchy with a new dynasty (that of the Italian Savoys), and the establishment of a republic in which experiments in federalism gave way to centralism presided over by the military. This collection of experiments, which Spanish historians call the *Sexenio Democrático,* had as its guiding theme the democratic principle of universal suffrage. However, as had happened in France in 1848, the experiment turned out to be premature, and practical difficulties inherent in converting country folk into city dwellers manifested themselves.

The *dénouement* of these years was brought about by means of a military insurrection which cleared the way for the return of the traditional Bourbon dynasty in the person of a young King, Alfonso XII, son of the deposed queen. It was the key event in the Spanish Restoration, a distant echo of what other European states had experienced since the defeat of Napoleon.

Spain's Metternich was Antonio Cánovas del Castillo (1828–97), a doctrinaire liberal of conservative background who had tried to devise formulas of consent which would open up the political game and allow changes of party in the formation of government. He had accumulated political experience in the years before the *Sexenio Democrático*, in which he had been minister several times, and he was sympathetic towards the Liberal Union, a moderate faction between the extreme conservatives and the liberal progressives. All this, as well as the deep sense of historical continuity gained from his studies of the decadence of the Spanish monarchy, led him to establish a political structure which united traditional interests with liberal political forms aimed at bringing about stability and consensus based on a constitutional monarchy. In order to do this, he solved the problem of sovereign authority, exercised jointly by the King and by the representatives of the nation, in accordance with what he called the internal constitution of the country. It was a question of ploughing the old furrow of Spanish history, to use his own expression, and the result would be, as has been pointed out by an expert on the period,[3] the most stable and lasting system in Spanish contemporary history.

Although political artifice dictated the construction of a national state based on traditional values, Cánovas was especially careful to separate the new regime from two institutions which could have threatened the credibility of a system affirming the primacy of secular and civil values: the army and the Roman Catholic Church.

THE ARMY AND THE CATHOLIC CHURCH

The experience of the middle years of the nineteenth century had shown that the commitment of a large number of army chiefs of staff to the liberal cause ended in a complete reversal of attitude. This reversal reached a point where the military stopped being the guarantors of liberal institutions and involved themselves – perhaps because of the weakness of civil society and, more specifically, the weakness of the political class – in political decisions which were imposed through insurrections. This had been the procedure which led to the overthrow of the Bourbon dynasty and, with it, the delegitimation of the first Spanish liberal system.

Cánovas looked for a way of neutralizing this militarism by stressing the role of the King as supreme commander of the army. As the new King was still an adolescent, it was an easy task to create the image of the soldier-king and his first appearances were on the battlefronts of the civil war then being waged against absolutist elements in some areas in the north of the country. These appearances were so successful that they led to the recreation of the soldier-king figure whenever another male heir acceded to the throne. However, this formula was not always effective in containing the danger inherent in the military interests which, in fact, all the male monarchs of this period exhibited. Referring to the display of such tastes by Alfonso XIII, Miguel de Unamuno sharply criticized tendencies which were evident from early on. In 1904, when the King had been little more than two years on the throne, he commented:[4] 'People are not amused to see him walking around forever dressed in the uniform of a field marshal.'

Relations between the Roman Catholic Church and liberal politicians were always very strained, and the church was forever thought to view favourably those political solutions which might lead to a restoration of the values of the *ancien régime*. These values were represented in Spain by the Carlists, who denied the legitimacy of the accession to the throne of Isabella II, daughter of Ferdinand VII, and supported the supposed right to accession of Don Carlos, his brother.

As in other European states, the church had emerged from the revolutionary turmoil of the early years of the nineteenth century in a stronger position and maintained intact its power to shape opinion, particularly in the small rural centres scattered throughout the country. At the end of the nineteenth century, ecclesiastical institutions exercised almost total control over matters of public welfare and had established a strong presence in the primary and secondary education system, having particular influence on the children of the better-off social classes.

THE ACHIEVEMENTS OF *CANOVISM*

Cánova's achievements project were more apparent than real. His attempt to set up a civil political system was forced to suffer the humiliation of having to accept that it was a military coup which had initiated the Restoration.

Although such coups did not proliferate in the years which followed, with the passage of time it became ever clearer that the Spanish army was the victim of structural problems which made it ineffective while at the same time remaining a threat to the stability of the political system. The tensions at the end of the century were clear evidence of this.

As for the church, the relative integration of its leaders did not prevent the institution as a whole from demonstrating an almost congenital incapacity to assimilate liberal principles. Mutual distrust increased as the years went by, and the contemporary movements of clericalism and anti-clericalism were an essential element in the nature of the relationship between religion and politics from the moment the liberal system was initiated in Spain.

For all that, a willingness to contain the pressures that might be exerted by both the army and the church was evident from the very beginning. In early December 1874, when the restoration of the monarchy was only a possibility, the future King Alfonso XII published a manifesto signed – with some significance – at the British military academy of Sandhurst. In it he promised a civil society which would not – he also promised – mean any lack of consideration for traditional values as represented by the church or the army. He concluded: ‘I will not cease to be a good Spaniard or, like all my predecessors, a good Catholic or, as a man of this century, a true liberal.’

The monarch with whom the Restoration started, Alfonso XII, was an adolescent of conservative upbringing. He had military and authoritarian inclinations, but these did not interfere with the respect he showed for the liberal ideas which the new regime was encouraging. Indeed, he collaborated quite sincerely with the steps being taken to broaden the political base of the system and helped to overcome the purely personal confrontations which lay at the root of these pressures.

The same could be said of his second wife, María Cristina of Hapsburg-Lorraine, who would succeed him as regent in 1885. She was an Archduchess of mature years who showed great care in the fulfilment of her constitutional duties, just as she had embraced the task of producing children with seriousness and dedication – the male heir, Alfonso XIII, would be born in 1886, after the death of his father. The figure of this widowed queen evokes direct parallels with Victoria.

TO GOVERN IS TO COMPROMISE

The most significant feature of the new political structure was a constitution, enacted in June 1876. It was strongly conservative in origin but offered wide scope for forms of consensus because of its essentially open nature and because of the ambiguity of many of its formulations. The recognition of many individual rights and the possibilities for their expansion brought it close to the democratic constitution of 1869.

The regime was a constitutional monarchy in which sovereignty was shared between the monarch and a two-chamber parliament (*Cortes*). 'The power to make laws', stipulated article 18 of the constitutional text, 'lies with the Cortes and with the King.' In any case, the text appeared to be directed more to the question of the exercise of sovereignty than to resolving the old question of where the ultimate basis of power actually lay.

The difficult question of the relations between Church and State, a touchstone for the credibility of the Spanish liberal system, required the introduction of article 11. This recognition of Roman Catholicism as the state religion and of its monopoly of public religious manifestations was tempered with a recognition of the tolerance due to the religious preferences of every citizen. 'No one in Spanish territory will be discriminated against for his religious opinions or for exercising his particular form of worship, except that respect is shown for Christian morality.'

This was not, of course, an unconditional recognition of religious freedom. However, once again, the constitutional text offered a step forward that might satisfy those, both within and outside Spain, who were anxiously awaiting a response to the old call for freedom of religious opinion. A visit to the present civil cemetery in Madrid is still extraordinarily revealing, for the names on the headstones represent the Spain which refused to accept the idea of a Catholic unity.

The constitution signified a renewal of the revolutionary path trodden in 1868. However, the democratic experience of the years that followed had permeated the political culture of many Spaniards, and the advances gained during the six democratic years remained in the programmes of the republican parties and more progressive liberal groupings. In setting up the constitutional framework, Cánovas left the door open for these achievements to be reincorporated into the system. 'This statesman from Málaga might well have spoken the words which Ganivet put into the mouth of his hero Pío Cid: "It was for me without question that a Restoration could not be complete if it did not accept something of what had been done during the period of non-legitimate government. To govern is to compromise."'[5]

AN ENFORCED TWO-PARTY SYSTEM

One particularly effective way to make clear this willingness to compromise was the consolidation of a political system similar to the much-admired British one, that is, a system whereby various parties (but preferably only two) could peacefully succeed each other in government without having to pin their hopes of gaining access to power on insurrection or revolution.

This was something which the liberal Spanish regime had not achieved before the revolution of 1868.

In short, the intention was to ensure that the country could be governed. The parties which were integrated into the system had to continue with a political tradition whose normal area of existence was that of parliamentary life alone. It was impossible for party leaders to seek support from an electorate which could hardly ever be mobilized. The oligarchies which headed the parties had as their main objective access to government and, with it, access to the resources of the budget. With such resources they could set in motion a process which would assure them of victory in the elections. Then, with a safe parliamentary majority, they could establish a network of relationships which would guarantee them permanent power for as long as this support remained strong. Only the loss of this homogeneous support – the exhaustion of the situation – would make it appropriate for the monarch to consider passing the responsibility for government to the other party.

Large party organizations were not, therefore, needed, nor was there any need for an excessively complicated organizational structure. Party life was settled in parliament, and party supporters received sufficient news of what was happening from what was published in the newspapers. The press was, in fact, strongly politicized. Newspapers were read frequently in *casinos* – a type of political club – where they were freely passed from one person to another in spite of the heavy bar used to bind the pages together. Reading a particular newspaper was a clear indication of one's political leanings, and the novelist Benito Pérez Galdós repeatedly used the technique of identifying his characters according to which newspapers they carried under their arms. It did not, therefore, appear at all strange to find newspaper editors occupying the places of honour at assemblies of the political parties which their newspapers supported.

It is worth mentioning here that the press also offered one of the liveliest forums for political debate. Both professional politicians and intellectuals agreed on this. It was in the newspapers that it was easiest to appreciate the various elements of this debate and that attitudes less clearly formulated in the formal atmosphere of professional politics were more precisely expressed. In the case of Spain, this means that the press continues to be an essential reference source for historical research. Apart from the fact that many books were simply compilations of what had previously appeared in the newspapers, it is only by consulting the latter that one can gain an exact picture of the conditions leading to the adoption of particular positions.

THE CONSERVATIVE AND LIBERAL PARTIES

To achieve the desired alternation of the parties in government, Cánovas counted on placing his own party, a party composed of the most conciliatory elements of the old moderate party, in the most moderate area of the political spectrum. These were elements that originated in what was called the 'puritan' sector, went on to the *Unión Liberal*, and ended up as members of what had been the conservative liberal opposition in the Cortes elected in 1869.

Although the majority of those conservative liberals had taken part in political life during the reign of Isabella II, they also accepted the 1869 constitution, just as they had proved willing to collaborate during the monarchist experiment of the brief reign of Amadeus I (1871–73). The failure of this experiment, culminating in political isolation during the republican period which followed (1873–74), led them to place their hopes in a restoration of the Bourbon dynasty in the person of the crown prince, who would have to rely heavily upon strong parliamentary support. In this sense, the insurrection of General Arsenio Martínez Campos on 29 December 1874, which set in motion the process leading to the Restoration, seemed initially to be a reversal, since, yet again, it seemed to rely on the power of the army. And there were many who thought that this insurrection made possible a return to the situation which obtained before the revolution, true to the traditional counter-revolutionary mentality of those who had forgotten nothing and learned nothing.

Cánovas, however, did not accept this interpretation and his Conservative Liberal – or simply Conservative – Party became the voice of those with integrative attitudes, who were channelling their efforts towards making alternate succession easy. Their political actions showed a high degree of pragmatism, which their rivals sometimes condemned as mere opportunism. This pragmatism made possible successes such as that of the incorporation into their party in 1884 of Alejandro Pidal y Mon (1846–1913), who headed the neo-Catholic sector pledged to bring about the Roman Catholic unity of Spain. This was the Spanish version of the 'rallying' of Catholics to the liberal regime inspired by Pope Leo XIII, and which entailed, in the Spanish case, the neutralization of the Carlists, who had already provoked two civil wars in their eagerness to impose an absolutist dynastic solution.

The alternate succession of two major parties became possible with the final consolidation of the Liberal Fusionist Party – or simply Liberal Party – in which a great many of the scattered leading supporters of the system during the *Sexenio Democrático* found a home. The process was a complex and detailed one and could not be considered complete until the second half of the 1880s.

An outstanding role in the success of this enterprise was played by the pragmatism of Práxedes Mateo Sagasta (1825–1903), a highly experienced politician who had encouraged the founding of the Constitutional Party in

1871. His capacity for compromise was enormous and he allowed elements from the old liberal progressive party and from the Constitutional Party of the *Sexenio Democrático* to join the Liberal Party. These were later to be joined by elements of the Dynastic Left, among whom figured the old radicals of the former democratic period. All of these set their political sights initially on the reinstatement of the 1869 constitution, with its individual political freedoms, although ultimately they would come to accept the 1876 constitution.

Although there were many similarities in the way the two major parties functioned and despite the fact that their programmatic differences were very slight, they reflected widely differing traditions of Spanish liberalism. Stability and alternate succession were achieved at the expense of representing popular interests, and the names of Cánovas and Sagasta became symbolic of the functioning of the system.[6]

OUTSIDERS TO THE SYSTEM

Outside the system were the supporters of the *ancien régime* monarchy (Carlists) and those who rejected the monarchic state (republicans). There were also some small labour movements determined to bring about profound social transformation as a first step towards some kind of political change. Without the shadow of a doubt, the solidest of these groups was the Carlists, who had emerged from a dynastic dispute over the legitimacy of female succession to the throne which had led to confrontation between supporters of liberalism and those who defended the *ancien régime*. The strength of the Carlists lay in the popular support they enjoyed and the complicity of a large part of the Catholic clergy, who saw them as a possible way of bringing about Catholic unity in Spain.

At the beginning of the Restoration, the Carlists conducted an intense debate over the advisability of integration into the system as opposed to withdrawal until a very considerable sector of their possible support, that of the Catholic fundamentalists, decided to join Cánovas' party at the end of the 1880s. Although this did not harm Carlist politics definitively, it took away from them the sole right to represent Catholics politically. It also dispelled the spectre of a Carlist triumph, whether by insurrection or by the weight of votes when universal suffrage was implemented.

Throughout those years the republicans were almost like fossils, living proof of a past political experiment which no-one wanted to see return. The precautions necessary for the exercise of many individual rights and the distrust fomented by France's Third Republic forced them initially into a policy of mere survival, where very few placed any trust in a popular uprising or a military coup. From the beginning of the 1880s, in any case, and increasingly as the liberals strengthened their ties with the left, the republicans began to find room for themselves in the new situation and even benefited from corrupt practices within the system. The result of this was that, although they never lost their established reputation for having rejected institutional monarchy, they never constituted a true and effective political opposition. As for Alejandro Lerroux, a rising figure in intersecular republicanism, a writer of the time had no hesitation in representing him as a tamed lion who always roared magnificently at his master's command. Example after example leads us to the conclusion that republicanism entered the new century without offering a true alternative to the political system.

It was also impossible to find that alternative among the labour movements, which had to face extraordinary obstacles to their organization. All this was in addition to the fact that it was difficult for them to get on with the working classes, whose rough-and-ready political culture was often more receptive to republican political speeches. At the end of the century, socialist membership was negligible, while the anarchists, forced underground, devoted most of their efforts to terrorist attacks and to proving themselves innocent of the attacks falsely attributed to them by the police.

ELECTORAL GERRYMANDERING

In practice, the efficiency of the system would be related to a great extent to its ability to meet society's demands and especially to the methods of selecting the political class, which in turn depended on various electoral procedures. The need to consolidate power when public opinion was non-existent led the political class to take a very active part in the electoral processes and to practise all possible kinds of corruption.

As political succession could not be based on the decisions of a public opinion which did not exist, the system had to create substitute mechanisms, which reached as high as the monarch himself. It was he who had to decide the opportuneness of a political change which could not come about through a parliamentary defeat, given that every government in advance ensured a parliamentary majority great enough to guarantee its survival as long as there were no deep divisions at the heart of this majority. Once the other political party was charged with the formation of a government, the first task of the new team was to call for new elections, which had to produce the parliamentary majority necessary for smooth government.

There was no true electoral body, nor had there been one during the previous experiment of the *Sexenio Democrático*, and the political leaders had no option but to feign its existence in order to legitimate the changes in government. It fell to the Minister of the Interior to select a number of deputies, who would have to be elected by a series of districts which were totally obedient to the government, whatever party was in power. This list was known as the *encasillado*. But the electoral contest was also very limited in most of the other districts in which the name of the candidate was thrown up as a result of negotiation between the government and prominent local political personalities (*caciques*). The situation, of course, changed over the years, and it was clear to everyone that, as society matured, the practice of electoral corruption would cease to be a mere substitution device to offset the lack of citizens who could vote, and become a straightforward abuse of power.

Although universal suffrage had been established by decree in November 1868, the political weariness which made the triumph of the Restoration possible also made it easy for Cánovas to re-establish limited suffrage – limited to those registered and eligible to vote – by means of the electoral law of December 1878. This gave the right to vote to only one out of five adult male Spaniards. This law also incorporated a few significant modifications to the traditional system of one-candidate districts. Some multi-candidate districts were allowed in urban areas and it became acceptable for some parliamentary seats to be allotted by means of an accumulation of votes for the same candidate in different districts.

Far more important was the reintroduction of universal male suffrage in June 1890. Although the territorial division of the districts remained unchanged, the electoral roll multiplied six-fold, and this produced a notable effect in the cities. In any case, the Spanish parliament continued to bear a strongly agrarian stamp, since rural districts accounted for more than 70 per cent of parliamentary seats. This law did not demand serious transformation in the political parties, nor did it change the sociological profile of members of parliament in subsequent years. The electoral practices continued unchanged, and it could be said that corruption and arbitrariness undermined the credibility of the system in the final decades of the nineteenth century.

IMPLEMENTATION OF THE SYSTEM

References to corruption and to political fictions do not, however, mean that the political system was a failure. On the contrary, it had been capable, during the first quarter-century of its operation, of ensuring a stability which was translated into a longing for survival, as shown by the degree of harmony between the monarchist parties, which had been ferociously opposed before 1868. Further proof of this desire for continuity was the widening of the political spectrum through the legalization, in the 1880s, of all the political groupings outside the system, from the Catholic fundamentalists to the anarchists. Liberal values were widely shared in end-of-century Spain, while traditional and conservative attitudes, despite being strongly supported in the Catholic world, had moved to a marginal position, along with organizations which tried to mobilize the working classes.

At the same time, the desire for peace was satisfied when the civil wars which had devastated the country at the beginning of the Restoration were ended by the establishment of a strong law-making force and the recognition of basic freedoms in the Law of Freedom of Association of 1887 and the Electoral Law of 1890. Not without reason, as a law historian has pointed out, do declarations of rights, constitutions, and codes of laws constitute the backbone of the bourgeois liberal world.[7]

It is possible that these formal extensions of democracy did not substantially affect the system and, for that reason, could not have contributed to its effective transformation. José María Jover pointed out some time ago[8] that one of the characteristics of contemporary Spanish history is the unusual durability of the moderate state and the durability of 'facades of power' which concealed archaic political structures. The crisis of 1898, in any case, did not reveal anything new, but rather pointed up some deficit which made the need for regeneration (to use a catch-word of those times) particularly urgent.

THE DISASTER: A TIME FOR RHETORIC

The immediate circumstances of the crisis were a result of the rapid ending of the Spanish–American War of 1898, which culminated in an unavoidable defeat. The events were the predictable outcome of a colonial situation in which the peak of Cuban nationalism combined with the intense penetration of the island by American capital. In reality, Cuba had entered the sphere of influence of the American economy and Spanish interests had no place to hide except in nationalist rhetoric and the defence at all costs of colonial pride.

At the same time as American sympathy was warming towards the independence-seeking Cubans who had revived the war in 1895, the fragility of the Spanish position and the diplomatic isolation in which the country found itself, were becoming ever more apparent. The concentration of more than 200,000 Spanish soldiers on the island did not significantly alter the look of things. Spain had no option but to speed up the process of autonomy or accept certain defeat.

Strictly speaking, the war was over in less than three months in the Philippines and Cuba, and the annihilation of the Spanish fleet made it very clear that any resistance offered by the army would be useless. Talks began at the peace conference in Paris in the second half of October and less than two months later Spain had to sign a peace treaty bowing to the American demands. It lost all the colonies related to the conflict and was obliged to pay compensation and to honour all existing economic agreements. The least sign of a defeatist attitude previously would have brought the threat of revolution to the mother country, which is why many historians have viewed the war, which was very short-lived, as a defeat both assumed and calculated.

The defeat, in any case, opened the vein of rhetoric in a country that had already spent many years listening to the so-called *literatura de la regeneración* (literature of regeneration). Before the Spanish–American War had even started, Unamuno had referred to the impact that the defeat at Sedan had had on French politicians: 'The thrashing inflicted in '70 was like a shower which made the corruptions of the Second Empire break out and then wither. It had a similar effect to that of the French invasion on us.'[9] The events of 1898 therefore offered a new opportunity to build an argument for reconstruction, although the defeat had already been rationalized by the ruling classes and had come as no surprise to them. However, the movement in favour of regeneration noted how pens were being filled for the task of describing the nation's ills. To this end, perhaps no one made such explosive statements as Joaquín Costa (1846–1911), a self-made man and an extraordinarily vigorous publicist. It was he who put into circulation the expression '*oligarquía y caciquismo*', and his role as spiritual mentor for many intellectuals of the time is very clear.[10]

However, this literature of regeneration usually contained an important anti-liberal and anti-parliamentary element which the defeat only served to increase. It reached the point that Spanish political culture came to include the concept of the providential emergence of a leader who, invested with special authority, would impose the measures necessary for reform. These authoritarian appeals, which were not unlike the intellectual currents running throughout Europe at the time, represented an invitation to dictatorship. Many judged this to be disastrous for a society deeply in need of creating a new social morality. José Ortega y Gasset refers to this danger in a letter to Miguel de Unamuno in January 1904:[11]

> One of the honourable deeds that must be done in Spain, where all foundations are lacking, is to banish, to prune from the collective soul the expectation of the genius who will appear like a manifestation of the spirit of the national lottery and to encourage the steady and measured footsteps of talent. Were we France, we would be talking of another deed. I prefer for my homeland the work of a hundred men of average intelligence, but honourable and tenacious, to the appearance of this genius, this Napoleon for whom we are waiting.

LIMITED ECONOMIC EFFECTS

It is a commonly accepted view that the loss of the colonies did not cause Spain any great economic loss. The Cuban economy had been drawn into the orbit of the US economy many years before and the importance of the Philippines for the metropolis was very slight.[12]

Commercial relations with Cuba had, in fact, been declining throughout the second half of the nineteenth century, while at the same time the Spanish foreign sector was going through a process of reorienting its markets, particularly towards Europe. This helps to explain why the loss of the colonies had little impact on the principal economic order and, of course, was in no way similar to the bankruptcy that struck the economy and the public treasury with the emancipation of the South and Central American colonies at the beginning of the nineteenth century.

The Spanish foreign sector showed signs of recovering quickly, and the interests of Spanish subjects in the former colonies hardly suffered at all from the defeat. Most companies continued in business without being affected in any way, and the flow of emigrants from the Spanish mainland picked up again with unusual speed. Capital flowed into the Spanish financial system and led to the creation of some of the banks (Vizcaya and Hispano Americano) which have been most important in Spanish life in the present century.

Although its impact was very limited in strictly economic terms, it is possible that the defeat contributed to the strengthening of a nationalist perspective reasoning which accentuated the projectionist and autarchic trends in some quarters, thus distancing Spain from liberal European economies.

NEW LEADERS

In order to understand Spain after the Disaster one must take another factor into account. In the ten years following 1898 there was a notable series of changes in political leadership which radically transformed the appearance of the system. Cánovas del Castillo was assassinated by an anarchist in August 1897, and after him the following disappeared from the political scene: Emilio Castelar (1899), Francisco Pi y Margall (1901), Práxedes Mateo Sagasta (1903), Francisco Silvela (1905), Francisco Romero Robledo (1906) and Nicolás Salmerón (1908). All those who had set in motion the system of the Restoration vanished.

Of those who then moved into key positions one must, of course, single out the new King, Alfonso XIII, who acceded to the throne in May 1902. Once again, Spanish political life had as its central element an adolescent faced with a difficult task. It was difficult because of the calculated ambiguities of the constitutional text, the lack of any public opinion and, of course, a political tradition hardly weakened at all despite the efforts made to educate the prince in constitutional matters. As he was only 16, there was a clear generation gap between him and even the new generation of politicians, which became evident at the first ministerial cabinet meeting. For all this, the arrival of the new monarch breathed life for more than ten years into the hopes for renewal, although his response to the inducements he received was luke-warm. Right up to the eve of World War I he was being encouraged to take the lead in renovating the liberal regime. 'We want the word "monarchic"', wrote Ortega,[13] 'to lose its passive restorative associations and acquire the meaning of fertile and risk-taking dynamism, as in 1840.'

Historians have always taken opposing positions when it comes to assessing the monarch's responsibility for the political collapse of the system and, in particular, the establishment of the Primo de Rivera dictatorship in 1923. The debate was initiated by Raymond Carr, and, although it is far from being resolved, later research has emphasized the fragile nature of the constitutional resources to which the monarch had access.[14]

REFORMS FROM WITHIN

In the two governing parties the change of political leaders provoked serious internal tensions when it came to deciding who would remain as leader of each group. The choice of Francisco Silvela, who appeared to be making his way in the Conservative Party, although with serious internal pressures, vanished with a rapidity that would further increase the tensions in the heart of the party.[15] He did, however, leave behind the idea of dignifying politics through the mobilization of public opinion, administrative reform, and an increase in state intervention to correct social inequalities. His government of 1899 made half-hearted moves in these directions, though the results were far from encouraging. The baton was then passed to Antonio Maura, and with him the party seemed assured of stable government and integrated policies; into the Conservative Party came large sectors representing Catholic fundamentalism, attracted by his call for a strong state.

His programme of reforms, however, followed an authoritarian line. In a very short time it led to a kind of reactionary *Maurism* incompatible with even the minimum requirements of a liberal system, from which he would choose to exclude himself after 1913. María Jesús González Hernández has described[16] his state project as one of conservative socialization directed towards strengthening of the liberal institutions of the Restoration system and a gradual transition from oligarchic liberalism to democracy. With this came confirmation of the notion of a strong state cherished in large conservative sectors of Spanish life. But there were serious risks when the reform proposals were distanced from the assumptions of the liberal tradition.

The leadership crisis unleashed in the Liberal Party after Sagasta's death in 1903 was worsened by the doctrinal exhaustion evident since the end of the previous century. The last great political victory of liberalism had been the introduction of universal male suffrage in 1890, but the Liberal Party had proved incapable of implementing it, and its members incapable of revitalizing its programme. It was, in fact, the Liberal Party which attracted most of the criticism directed against the old parties, especially in intellectual quarters. The situation changed very little under José Canalejas' government (1910–12), which seemed to be searching for a way towards a new liberalism close to the radical French model[17] in which the affirmation of civil power against ecclesiastical interference would be decisive and in which there would be greater government intervention in social affairs and labour relations. The brief Canalejas government has been viewed with extraordinary sympathy by the most recent historians, who have seen its measures as an attempt to nationalize the monarchy by means of a truly democratic programme. The fleetingness of this attempt, however, meant that it went unnoticed by its contemporaries.

It could be said that in early 1913 the departure of Canalejas and the distancing of Maura, who refused to comply with the solution offered by Alfonso XIII, represented the culmination of the long process of delegitimation of the system. It is not therefore surprising that 'extra-mural' negotiations were initiated, such as the palace visit made by intellectuals – Gumersindo de Azcárate, S. Ramón y Cajal and M. Cossio – with clearly republican sympathies. Ortega, who must have been party to the preparations for the audience, had written some days before[18] 'We have to carry out the experiment with the monarchy. And in an experiment those who are conducting it are the ones who must offer the first assurance. Those who are already well known offer no such guarantee to the people. But new men arise and are ready to carry it out with love, with sadness, with discipline and with competence.' 'Azorín' (José Martínez Ruiz), for his part, would refer in later years[19] to the expectations created by that visit: 'There was one moment, marked by the visit of the venerable Azcárate to the palace, when it seemed as if all the intelligentsia … were going to unite with a majestic personality who would realise their hopes; but the hoped-for union came to nothing. And the Spanish nation continued on its way independent of the monarch.'

NEW FORCES PRESENT

Although unsuccessful, the visit to the palace of those representatives of republicanism led to a recognition that the republican solution, though it did not offer sufficient consistency to be a viable alternative, had became a permanent point of reference in the Spanish political panorama. From the beginnings of the Restoration the republicans had alternated between very different positions. They had maintained a presence, although perhaps only a token presence, which represented a line towards a possible regeneration of political life. This offered sporadic moments of hope, such as that awakened some years earlier by the Lerroux movement or that of the Republican Union of 1903 and, later on, the Reformist Party of Melquíades Alvarez.

Spanish republicanism had alternated between hope for a revolutionary insurrection and a search for victory through universal suffrage. The decade of the 1890s had witnessed a clear increase in the republican vote. However, apart from the fact that this increase was very limited, the persistence of corrupt electoral practices made it possible to dismiss any likelihood of a republican triumph. Furthermore, indications that republicanism had decided to adapt to the system and even benefit from it were ever more frequent.

The republicans were in need of a radical renewal of their leaders and programme. The men of 1873 vanished from the scene in the first years of the twentieth century and most of the planned aims were limited to recovering the achievements of the *Sexenio Democrático*. However, the 'generational changing of the guard of 1900', to which Alvaro de Albornoz referred,[20] appeared to involve only a few individuals. He himself was part of this generation, together with Lerroux, Marcelino Domingo, and some others. Republicanism itself experienced only half-hearted radicalization, for the most part governed by opportunism. The intellectuals who allied themselves with republicanism, such as Pío Baroja and Ortega, did not have to wait long to experience the fragility of the project, as had happened earlier to Joaquín Costa. As Ortega would say several years later:[21] 'We have never been republicans – or if we have been, it was only as many of our fellow countrymen have: for a passing moment when we were in a bad mood.'

In this context the Reform Party of Melquíades Alvarez, launched in April 1912, unquestionably represented innovation, for it offered a new formulation distancing itself from the populist republicanism which Lerroux had headed since 1901. 'Reformism', Manuel Azaña[22] would write, at the beginning of 1915, in agreement with Ortega, 'should aspire to the formation of a great radical party within the monarchy. Failure would be for Melquíades to find himself within the monarchy but without having created this party.' The references to the models of French radicalism and British new liberalism were clear. All of this contributed to its conversion, initially, into the most suitable, although not ideal, channel – through which to direct the political projections of many intellectuals. Among these were those connected with the world of the Institución Libre de Enseñanza.[23] Many others had been awarded grants by the Junta de Ampliación de Estudios for study abroad and on their return to Spain felt the need for a political vehicle which echoed their yearnings to modernize the country through science. Ortega was the figure who best embodied these points of view.

After 1913, however, the new party launched itself in the direction of what was possible, placing itself closer to the monarchy. This caused it to lose a great deal of support, but at the same time confirmed that the republican offer remained a remote option for those who were thinking in terms of a profound reform of the political system. 'This move', Ortega would write,[24] 'I consider to be a mortal blow to reformism and thus to the immediate future of national politics, for it is only within this new party that an effective instrument can be fashioned for public revival.'

Nor did the Socialist Party appear to be prepared to promote reform from outside the political system. Although its foundation date (1879) made it one of the oldest parties, and although it had joined the Second International at the first opportunity in 1889, the Spanish Socialist Workers' Party was slow to achieve political significance in comparison with its western European counterparts. It was not until 1910 that its first deputy, Pablo Iglesias, was elected to parliament and its parliamentary influence was always very limited throughout the whole of the period of the constitutional monarchy. The limitations and the dogmatic nature of the first nucleus of Madrid socialism have often been pointed out,[25] and these helped give the party a certain narrow-minded image that discouraged those who placed their hopes for a reform of the system on socialism.

Socialist ideas were notably attractive to Spanish intellectuals looking for alternative formulas to replace a set of liberal ideals that seemed to be worn out. This did not, however, lead to significant political affiliations. An essential element of the proposals of the intellectuals was the search for a new liberalism with greater interest in social reform and a focus on well being rather than wealth and on distribution rather than production. It was therefore not surprising that critics of Spanish political life fixed their eyes on the reform politics of Lloyd George. The writer who appears to have best reflected this interest in reconciling liberalism with socialism was Ramiro de Maeztu, who followed British politics at close range through his work as a press correspondent. For Maeztu: 'The liberal idea is everything, and the socialist idea is only a part of it and, more than a part, a route.'[26]

THE NATIONALIST OPTION

Other currents which were exerting pressure from outside the system were the nationalists, present but with very different intensity and characteristics in Catalonia and in the Basque Country. The political movement for Catalan separatism was the strongest of all the nationalist movements of the new century. To a certain extent it can be understood as the collective projection of the national Catalan revival crystallized in a nationalist doctrine from the 1890s. As a result of the Disaster it achieved political identity in the Regionalist League, founded in 1901, which could already be considered a modern conservative party in the European mode, disposed to implant nationalist ideals through the procedures of the liberal system. 'All the strength of the Regionalist League', said an editorial written in Catalan in 1910 in the most notable Catalan newspaper,[27] 'lies with this: when somebody joins the League he is not asked if he is monarchist or republican, liberal or conservative. All that is expected is a profession of Catalan faith and an acceptance of the evolutionary process.' In practice, the League lacked the social support to transform the political system, but it did contribute to a great extent to revealing the obsolescence of that system. In this respect, Catalan nationalism, although in this particular version conservative by nature, was unquestionably a force for modernization.

THE INTELLECTUALS CENTRE-STAGE

The successive offers to reform the system, from both within and without, clashed with the forces of inertia and were totally spent by 1923. In that year a military dictatorship put an end to the constitutional monarchy, and not surprisingly intellectuals quickly leapt to the front-line of political criticism. These intellectuals were in perfect harmony with the Spanish liberal tradition, and they saw this tradition betrayed by the political fictions created by the Restoration and, more specifically, by the absence of a truly liberal party prepared to carry out a programme of radical reforms. Ortega, in one of his earliest writings, shared this view when he characterized Spanish political life as a barren wasteland: 'In political Spain there are only conservatives, which is the same as saying that there is none.'

The vacuum caused by the demise of the Spanish Liberal Party resulted in the virtual paralysis of one of the two parties necessary for the system to operate. 'English political life', Maeztu had written, 'suffers, like the Spanish, from paralysis. But in England it is the conservative masses which fail to produce activists, whereas in Spain it is the radical masses.' The failure of Spanish liberalism had resulted not so much from an abandonment of the political scene as from the inability of the liberals to distance themselves from the conservatives' positions.

Throughout these years the intellectual world remained attentive to the situation and attempted to cooperate in the task of finding a remedy through diagnosis and appropriate treatment. Such proposals would come both from the rationalist tradition and also from currents of opinion which centred their attention on nationalist sentiment. The intellectuals alternated between the possibility of revitalizing the parties from within and the creation of a 'party of intelligence'. Both options were tried, but with a certain timidity. Neither could definitively alleviate the profound crisis of legitimacy in which the regime was seen to be immersed – a crisis which had become more acute as a result of the Disaster of 1898. The crisis led to the collapse of the regime and the monarchy and later to the social and political bankruptcy of the Spanish Civil War. Spain after the Disaster was not inevitably headed towards civil war, but the events of 1898 led virtually everyone to agree that any official way of fully understanding Spain was showing an increasing lack of legitimacy.

NOTES

1. V. Cacho Viu, *Repensar el 98* (Madrid, 1997), p.94.
2. V. Pérez Moreda, 'Evolución de la población española desde finales del antiguo régimen', in *La nueva cara de la historia económica de España, Papeles de Economía Española*, 20 (Madrid, 1984), pp.32–8; and B. Sánchez Alonso, *Las causas de la emigración española 1880–1930* (Madrid, 1995), p.13.
3. C. Dardé, *La Restauración, 1875–1902* (Madrid, 1996), p.5.
4. M. de Unamuno, *Cartas inéditas* (Santiago de Chile, 1965), p.334.
5. V. Cacho Viu, *Las tres Españas de la España contemporánea*, (Madrid, 1962), p.9. Also, the essay on the First Republic in J.M. Jover Zamora, *Realidad y mito de la primera república. Del 'Gran Miedo' meridional a la utopía de Galdós* (Madrid, 1991).
6. Despite all this, Seco has suggested that, if one leaves aside the effectiveness of the Cánovas-Sagasta binomial in representing the functioning of the system, then the real confrontation in the political debate was between Cánovas and the moderate republicanism of Castelar. C. Seco Serrano, 'Introducción', in A. Figueroa, *Epistolario de la Restauración* (Madrid, 1985).
7. J. Baró Pazos, *La codificación del Derecho Civil en España 1808–1889* (Santander, 1993).
8. J.M. Jover, *Historia de España*, Vol.34, *La era isabelina y el sexenio democrático* (Madrid, 1981), p.xxi.
9. The reference is to the Napoleonic invasion of 1808. 'En torno al casticismo', *La España Moderna*, Feb. 1895.
10. *Oligarquía y caciquismo como la forma actual de gobierno en España: Urgencia y modo de cambiarla* (Madrid, 1901). There is recognition of Costa, despite his excesses, in J. Ortega y Gasset, 'Sencillas reflexiones II', *El Imparcial*, 6 Sept. 1910; J. Pijoan, *Mi don Francisco Giner* (Madrid, 1932), p.44; and M. de Unamuno, 'Sobre la tumba de Costa', *Nuevo Mundo*, March 1911.
11. *Epistolario completo Ortega – Unamuno* (Madrid, 1989), p.31.
12. L. Prados de la Escosura, *La independencia americana y sus consecuencias económicas* (Madrid, 1993).
13. Letter published in *El País*, 27 March 1914, in a collection by Béatrice Fonck, 'Tres textos olvidados de Ortega sobre el intelectual y la política', *Revista de Occidente*, 156, May 1994, p.131.
14. For a recent comprehensive view of Alfonso XIII, see C. Seco Serrano, *Historia de España Menéndez Pidal*, Vol.38, *La España de Alfonso XIII; El Estado y la política (1902–1931). Vol. 1: De los comienzos del reinado a los problemas de la posguerra, 1902–1922* (Madrid, 1996).

15. F. Portero, 'Francisco Silvela, jefe del conservadurismo español', *Revista de Historia Contemporánea*, 2 (1983), p.163.
16. *El universo conservador de Antonio Maura. Biografía y proyecto de Estado* (Madrid, 1997), p.2.
17. S. Forner, *Canalejas y el Partido Liberal Democrático* (Madrid, 1993), p.38.
18. 'Sencillas reflexiones', *El Imparcial*, 10 Jan. 1913.
19. 'La responsabilidad de la derecha', *Crisol*, 18 June 1931.
20. A. de Albornoz, *El Partido Republicano* (Madrid, 1918).
21. Lecture 'Vieja y nueva política', Madrid, 1914.
22. M. Azaña, '*Cuaderno de apuntes*', in *Obras completas* (Madrid, 1990), Vol.3, p.819.
23. A. Jiménez-Landi, *La Institución Libre de Enseñanza y su ambiente* (Madrid, 1996), Vol.4, p.56.
24. 'Más literatura resignada', *España*, 4 June 1915.
25. For recent general view of these opinions, see S. Juliá, *Los socialistas en la política española, 1879–1982* (Madrid, 1997).
26. R. de Maeztu, 'El liberalismo socialista', *Heraldo de Madrid*, 12 Dec. 1909. Published in E.I. Fox (ed.), *Ramiro de Maeztu. Liberalismo y socialismo (textos fabianos de 1909–1911)* (Madrid, 1984). On Maeztu's British period and his relations with Ortega see R. Santervás, 'Maeztu y Ortega. Dos formas de regeneracionismo: el poder y la ciencia', *Revista de Occidente*, 96 (May 1989), pp.80–102.
27. *La Veu de Catalunya*, 25 April 1910.

Between Europe and the Mediterranean: Spanish–Italian Relations, 1898–1922

FERNANDO GARCÍA SANZ

The history of relations between Spain and Italy during a decisive period for both countries is here examined not simply from a bilateral perspective but in terms of two external points of reference. The first is the influence of the strongest powers in Europe on their politics, ideology, and economic and foreign policy, and the second is their perception of the Mediterranean area, their guarantees of each other's national interests, and the enduring link between developments in the Mediterranean and the evolution of international relations in the rest of the European continent. This analysis reveals the different answers given by Spain and Italy to a complex set of problems that is broadly European in nature: the crisis of the liberal system, the crisis represented by World War I, the economic crisis, and the crisis of the international role of the old European powers. The two countries' participation in Mediterranean affairs was the sole basis for their participation in the development of international relations during this period.

Europe and the Mediterranean are historically linked in the international relations of Spain and Italy. To say that it is within this Euro-Mediterranean reality that the economic and political systems of the two countries find their points of reference and meaning is to state the obvious. The problem is that until a few years ago the research on the Mediterranean was driven by the search for an explanation for what has been considered an anomaly: the delay if not the failure of both the industrialization process and the adaptation of the liberal and political social systems to the changes occurring at the national and the continental level.

At the turn of the century Spain and Italy were dual economies in which agriculture was clearly predominant, but even then there were signs of the industrial development that would launch both countries on the road to modernization in the first two decades of the twentieth century. The pace of this economic development was different in the two countries, however. There is some consensus among economic historians about the possibility of defining a model of delayed industrialization for the Mediterranean. They agree that it is more appropriate to compare the factors which slowed the industrial take-off than the achievements, since these latter were more rapid and more evident in the case of Italy.[1] Differences in the pace of development between the two economies are said to have been recognizable since the 1880s,[2] and whereas Italy approached European standards of development by the turn of the century, Spain had achieved this level only by the 1920s.[3] The gains made during World War I had placed it in a position to undertake the final move towards industrialization.[4]

According to recent studies, agriculture was not the dead weight it was traditionally considered to be, but also had begun to adapt to changing social, political, and economic circumstances, gradually modernizing without major structural changes.[5] Spanish and Italian agricultural products invaded European markets, with large-scale sales of citrus fruits joining the traditional exports of wine and olive oil. The biggest obstacle to Spanish–Italian trade relations was found here,[6] first, because it was impossible for the two countries to compete in each other's domestic markets and, second, because they were selling the same products in the international market. At the beginning of this period there was no commercial treaty between Spain and Italy but only a provisional agreement, a so-called *modus vivendi*, signed in 1892 and valid until 1914, when a real treaty was finally established. In 1905 the governments of Spain and Italy signed a new *modus vivendi* which restored most-favoured-nation status and did not exclude wine from the products favoured by the new conditions of commerce. In December of that year the government of Alessandro Fortis introduced the agreement to a parliament conditioned by the protests of the largest wine producers. The authorities knew that their fears were unfounded, because, except for specialities such as Marsala and Malaga, neither Spanish nor Italian wine had ever found a place in the other country's market. The issue became a political one and turned into an instrument for toppling the government. From this time onward wine was symbolic of the commercial distance between the two countries. Taking into account Fortis's experience, only a few Italians were prepared to raise the issue of commercial relations with Spain, and any initiative in this direction was interpreted not in economic but in political terms.

Quantitatively speaking, Spanish–Italian trade was not very important, but it was highly relevant from a social point of view because it did involve a whole range of traditional products, a large proportion of which went to the other country. When Spanish commerce stagnated at the turn of the century, in a period of expansion of international trade, the sales to Italy did not suffer and even increased. The result was a favourable balance of trade.[7] During this period, except for World War I, trade focused on a very limited set of products. Three-quarters of Spain's sales to Italy were of fishing products, olive oil, and cork, with small variations depending on the harvest in the case of the olive oil. Barrels, dry vegetables, charcoal, hemp, silk, marble, and sulphur made up the majority of Italy's sales to Spain.

However, from an early date the Spanish market was important to Italy because of its possibilities for expansion, that is, the substitution of Italian industrial products for those of other countries. It was assumed in Italy that Spain had yet to reach its own level of development. Italy was a power and Spain was not, but it could be on its way to becoming one. The images of Italy and Spain that prevailed in the two countries had their most important roots in economics. Italy's achievements seemed enormous when compared with those of Spain, a country rich in raw materials but unable to take the first steps towards industrialization. The 1898 war against the United States had revealed Spain's backwardness and inferiority, too many of its traditional values and practices being useless in an era of technology. To Italy, Spain was also an exotic country – the Far East of the West, as it was once called, or the Western Turkey, as it was known during World War I.[8] It was said over and over again that Spain's degree of civilization had nothing in common with that of the major European powers. Its image in Italy in 1909 was determined by a number of enduring stereotypes, old and new. The execution of Francisco Ferrer y Guardia, founder of Modernism, who was accused of being the instigator of the events of Barcelona's Tragic Week, generated protests throughout Europe, with wide repercussions in Italy. The Spain of the Inquisition was back again – backward and cruel, under the obscurantist power of religion, and possessor of a way of thinking which Europeans had long since abandoned.[9] Spain was the only European country in which the Pope's views on the Roman question still produced a response and even dominated occasional debates in parliament, although without interfering in the relations between the two states.

Spain was not like Italy, although their political regimes had many resemblances. Both countries had oligarchic systems based on manipulation of elections, and both had many problems in absorbing social and economic change. Italian liberalism was much more developed and more democratic than the Spanish version, and the political regime was more open to forces in opposition to the system. Profound reforms were required to provide stability for economic development. This new way of understanding the political system, once embodied by Giovanni Giolitti, largely failed because of a basic contradiction: the reform of the system was designed within its own conservative orientation. The crisis of *Giolittism* symbolized a crisis for Italian democratic liberalism, because the efforts by Antonio Salandra and Sydney Sonino did not seem a real alternative given the profound changes the country had experienced since the beginning of the century. The outbreak of World War I intensified the crisis and left liberalism to face the avalanche of Fascism alone. In Spain, the 1898 Disaster did not bring any apparent changes in the political system created by the 1876 constitution. The rotation of political parties in the government (conservatives and liberals shifting in power) worked in a monotonous and extraparliamentary fashion. Despite all the reform initiatives[10] – all of them failed – being constantly at risk became a characteristic of the system, and this is why it responded as it did to the proposals for political reform in 1917. At this stage in the century, Spain was also able to show a significant degree of economic development and its inevitable social consequences. The unrest over the persistence of a system which was less and less representative increased after the war. This tension, combined with the economic crisis of the postwar period, the military setbacks in Morocco, and the consent of Alfonso XIII, gave way to the successful *coup d'état* by General Miguel Primo de Rivera in September 1923.

Although it is tempting to compare the two Mediterranean dictatorships (Mussolini's and Primo de Rivera's), they did not have much in common.[11] However, it is possible to identify an element of continuity in the relations between Spain and Italy throughout these years, one that was adopted both by Fascism and Primo-Riverism – the roles that the two countries assigned to each other in the Mediterranean scenario. Up till the first postwar period, Europe was more than ever the owner of the world. It translated the principle of the European balance of power to all scenarios outside the Continent, interconnected as it was by a delicate network of international alliances. The Mediterranean – in its wider geographical sense – was no exception. Its historical role in European events did not come to an end at this point when imperialist expansion was lending a global dimension to the commitments and the cultural, social, and political schemes of the Continent. More than in any other region, the crisis in the Mediterranean (Morocco, the Straits question, the Balkans, and so on) presented the threat of a European war.

In 1898 Spain's historical overseas framework dissolved. From then on the state could count on foreign action only on a regional scale confined to the Iberian Peninsula, the North African territories, and the Balearic and Canary Islands. Europe's perspective (which to a contemporary eye was the epitome of self-centredness in its attitude towards the crisis between Spain and the United States) seemed far from the concerns of Spanish officials and focused on the threats of a diminished crown, particularly if this institution were to enter into the game of international alliances. The territorial shrinking suffered by Spain since 1898 had affected the way in which the Spanish politicians viewed their country, the international sphere, and the possibilities of development available to a defeated country with limited resources. In the past Spain had entertained the possibility of seeking refuge in a European alliance. Now, it was looking primarily for an international *guarantee* that would preserve its territory from further losses.

In the course of these years, Spain's views on Mediterranean issues became very well defined. The Mediterranean had very specific geographical limits for Spain because of the nearly complete lack of imperialist ambitions in political circles. It did not reach beyond the Balearic Islands to the east, but to the west it extended to the Canary Islands and a line whose axis was in the Gibraltar Strait and the North African territories, Ceuta and Melilla. The destiny of the Moroccan empire was dependent more on security and defence considerations than on colonial aspirations. Spain believed that it had *historical rights* to the Moroccan issue which 'ought to be taken' into consideration by the international community. Once the unavoidable break with the *status quo* had occurred (as agreed by the powers at the Madrid Conference in 1880), Spain expected to be recognized as a main actor in the search for a solution to any problems that might arise. This position had advantages and disadvantages. As for the former, Spain could have a presence in Morocco without wasting any forces and without facing the dangers inherent in any international alliance. The disadvantages were that its interests remained at the mercy of foreign ones and, of course, of any changes in the international situation, since it lacked the strength and the initiative to play a major part in international arrangements. Its international role did not give it the capacity to act as a great power. Its presence was useful, however, in removing some of the obstacles to greater understanding between France and Britain. Morocco was practically its only link to the international system of this period.

One historical feature that Italy had and Spain lacked was its central location: Italy met Spain only on foreign policy issues which affected the western Mediterranean. Until the 1898–1902 period, Italy's interest in the international position of Spain arose from its participation in the Triple Alliance's challenge to France and its desire to curb any expansionist action by the latter in the western Mediterranean. The secret Spanish–Italian agreement reached in May 1887 and prorogued until 1895 provided support for both objectives. This is not the place to reconstruct the history of this commitment, but it is necessary to highlight some of its features to understand the change in the relations between the two countries after 1898. In 1897 Spain had become part of a kind of Mediterranean Triple Alliance in which Italy was central and that was concerned with the eastern Mediterranean and the situation in the Balkans, and in North Africa from Egypt to Morocco.[12] Spain, following the line of the most powerful international arrangement in Europe (it is important not to forget Britain's consent), was taking part in the planned siege of Morocco to guarantee the *status quo* proclaimed at the Madrid Conference. The 'Secret Pact' named France explicitly and established Spain's unilateral commitment to refrain from signing any agreement with the neighbouring republic that could affect the North African territories, among others, and that might be contrary to the interests of the powers of the Triple Alliance together or singly. The Mediterranean remained closed to Russia and to France. Spain obtained the pact's renewal in 1891, and also persuaded Italy and its allies to allow it more freedom of action by recognizing some rights which gave a Moroccan orientation to the agreement. The commitment to refrain from signing agreements with France was made reciprocal. Spain managed to include the rights acquired through the 1860 Treaty of Wad-Rass maintaining the Moroccan *status quo* and freedom of action to provide security for its North African possessions, Ceuta and Melilla.

The agreement was limited to four years and was not renewed in 1895, by which time the international situation had significantly changed. France was no longer isolated, and Britain no longer had the friendly relationship with Germany which had characterized it in previous years. Italy's demands, motivated by its own interests and by German pressure, were rejected by the Spanish government, which allowed the agreement to die, but the secret had been revealed and France had sent a serious warning.[13] No one in Italy was unaware that Spain had very little room for manoeuvre with respect to France, given its proximity, its financial and commercial dependence, and the asylum provided by France to the Carlists and the republicans. The foreign policy options available to Spain on this issue were very limited, and breaking off relations – as was done in Italy when Francesco Crispi came to power – had no advantages. However, the Spanish card was always there for Italy as a counterbalance to the power of France in the Mediterranean. It was a constant of Spanish–Italian relations that the international role of Spain was anti-French. The value of Spain for Italy depended much more on the progress of French–Italian relations than on Spain's capacity for international action.

From the failure of Italy's first colonial effort in 1896 until 1902, the direction of Italian foreign policy became more flexible. Crispi's attempt to turn the Triple Alliance into a full and active alliance which would cover even strategic scenarios such as East Africa failed completely. It became evident that a broad continental alliance did not satisfy the most basic Italian needs in the Mediterranean and in North Africa in particular. A *rapprochement* with France demanded a solution to the serious and unresolved conflicts which had created tension in the relations between the two countries – the issues of Tunis and trade relations.[14] Both problems were settled between 1896 and 1898, establishing the basis for the 1900 and 1902 agreements which changed the balance of power in North Africa. France recognized the priority of Italian interests in Tripolitania and Cyrenaica in exchange for Italian recognition of French priority in Morocco. In addition, a link was established between the actions the two powers would take if it were impossible to defend the *status quo*. Only if France disrupted the balance in Morocco could Italy pursue its interests in Tripolitania.[15] Thus the new foreign policy designed by Théophile Delcassé achieved its first successes: the withdrawal of one of the states traditionally interested in Morocco and Italy's commitment not to support any unprovoked attack by Germany against France. The French interest in deactivating the chain of the Triple Alliance by breaking its weakest link became increasingly clear. From now on, Italy would be more consistent in its foreign policy, but it would have to pay much more attention to the limits set by its international commitments. The objective was to increase as much as possible its scope for action without giving up the possibility of developing 'an independent point of view of the diplomatic interests of Italy'.[16]

Spain came out the worst in all this international activity, since it lost once and for all the mediating and pressurizing roles on the Moroccan question that it had always assigned to Italy. Delcassé also sought an agreement with Spain to settle the North African issues in France's interest as a dominant power, counting on two initial advantages to achieve this: the rise to power of Francisco Silvela and the failure of his foreign policy options and the effect on the Spanish authorities of the agreement between France and Italy on the distribution of strategic areas in North Africa.

Before the war against the United States, Francisco Silvela had publicly criticized the foreign policy of Antonio Cánovas del Castillo, which he considered dangerously isolationist. When he came to power in March 1899 he tried to implement a new foreign policy project that would guarantee the security of the Spanish territory, including the islands, the Peninsula, and North Africa, through international agreements. The alternative attempted by the liberals since August 1898, a security agreement with Britain, had failed.[17] Silvela directed his efforts towards the enemies of the great sea power, pursuing a continental alliance which would include Russia, France, and Germany.[18] The failure of these efforts caused him to point out in 1901, when he had been already replaced in the presidency by Práxedes Mateo Sagasta, that an alliance with France was the only possible solution: 'Since it is impossible to resolve the Moroccan question with just one European power, without an international agreement, the place where we will find the most natural intelligence and the greatest support not for war but for reasonable and equitable participation is France.'[19] It seemed clear that the Moroccan situation was proving more and more indefensible, but it was also evident that Spain, lacking a fleet and significant coastal defences, had not yet resolved its security problems.[20] The pursuit of a solution to both problems through the same international initiative encouraged the liberals to begin conversations with France. In his memoirs, the Spanish Ambassador to Paris, Fernando León y Castillo, says that he took the initiative in the negotiations and adds that it was very hard for him to convince Sagasta, who finally gave in with the famous aphorism, 'It is impossible to make an omelette without breaking eggs'.[21]

All doubts were finally dispelled in December 1901, when the agreement signed between Italy and France the year before was made public. This created much more concern than has generally been accepted. The Minister of State himself, the Duke of Almodóvar del Río, wrote to the Spanish Ambassador:[22]

> Whatever the future scope of that intelligence and its effects on general policy, it is of extraordinary importance for us, since one of the most important supports of the Moroccan status quo was lost as the domain of S.M. Scherifana was abandoned by Italy under French influence. The seriousness of the matter would be even greater if the agreement, instead of being negative in content (each party declaring that it has no expectations in the sphere of influence of the other), had a positive component, an agreement on common action to implement their respective rights, or forsaw a certain event as the time for legitimately attempting to achieve their aspirations.

The threat would be greater, he said, if Italy's allies were to honour its agreement with France, since in this case Spain would be in danger of being isolated in its efforts to contain the Moroccan situation or forced to 'take sides with one of the major powers which fought for predominance in the Magreb'.

The treaty with France was finalized in the first days of November 1902, pending ratification by the liberal government, but that government was overthrown in December, and the conservative government which followed left it to die. Liberals and conservatives later accused each other of having been responsible for this, but all of them feared that Britain would not approve the division of Morocco between France and Spain. The warnings of León y Castillo about a foreseeble solution to the problems that confronted France and Britain were useless, as was his suggestion that Spain follow the example of Italy, which had not hesitated to negotiate individually with France 'in the same conditions and at the same time as Spain'.[23]

This attitude cost Spain not only a favourable distribution of the old empire but also the opportunity to appear in the international arena as playing the main part in the destiny of North Africa. Finally, what was being rejected was a foreign policy project which called for Spain to be linked to the enemies of the Triple Alliance. But if there were many people in Spain who had already decided to pursue international commitments, there were only a few who were ready to take what was widely considered too great a risk, that is, to seek to control the destiny of Morocco without abandoning the other important objective of foreign policy since the defeat by the United States, the security of national territory.

The events of 1902 gave rise to the attitudes that France, Britain, Italy, and Spain would maintain until the outbreak of World War I. The attitude of Spain served to show France that the shortest line between Oran and Fez passed through London.[24] This translated into the Anglo-French agreements of 1904 and the later negotiations between France and Spain (concluded in October of the same year) in which the reduction of the Spanish area of influence in Morocco – in a hypothetical distribution – reflected the subordinate role that Spain had adopted. Britain obtained freedom of action in Egypt and a French commitment not to occupy northern Morocco, which was important for the balance around Gibraltar. This forced France to negotiate with Spain. Italy achieved the dominant role in Tripolitania and Cyrenaica by negotiating individually with France and Britain (in 1902), although it linked its possible conquest of these territories to France establishing its dominance in Morocco.

With regard to the relations between Spain and Italy, the events of 1902 were decisive because for the first time since the 1880s the Moroccan issue, which had been the meeting point of the foreign policies of the two countries, disappeared. From then on Spain would be able to count on Italy only to moderate French aspirations in Morocco. Italy's position was determined only by its own interests, which were committed to the agreements with France. An example of all this was found in Italy's attitude towards the agreements of 1904 and its role in the Algeciras Conference and in the French–German conflict of 1911. In relation to the Algeciras Conference, the attitude of Italy was less openly pro-French than the press in Paris and Berlin portrayed it.[25] More than ever before, Algeciras made clear to the Italian officials the difficulties of trying to maintain an independent foreign policy between the Triple Alliance and the commitments needed to protect its interests in North Africa. Algeciras avoided a European war. It revealed once again the secondary role of Spain, which, however, was very useful in resolving the international conflict. It highlighted France's interest in weakening the Triple Alliance and Germany's determination to destabilize the new Anglo-French friendship. For the first time since the Cuban war, Spain had a chance to show that it had its own foreign policy line. The Algeciras Conference confirmed the commitments of 1904 and, consequently, Spain's *rapprochement* with France and Britain.

Spain's value to Italy did not disappear completely, although with regard to the Moroccan issue their interests no longer converged. Too close an alignment of Spain with French interests would worry a basically Mediterranean power like Italy. For that reason, the so-called Cartagena agreements (named for the city where Edward VII met with Alfonso XIII in April 1907) interested Berlin, Vienna, and, especially, Rome. An exchange of identical notes between the governments of Spain and Britain (Villa Urrutia and Grey) and between Spain and France (León and Castillo-Pichon) took place on 16 May and was complemented by an oral agreement between the governments of France and Britain which recognized the exchange of notes and their shared acceptance of the guarantees included in both. The notes guaranteed the maintenance of the territorial *status quo* and the rights of the three powers in the Mediterranean and in their territories on the Atlantic coast, both African and European. This international act represented the high point of relations between Spain and the *entente*, and political circles in Spain gave it greater value than it really had.[26] But the negotiations and the intentions behind them could not conceal the inferiority of Spain. Although Spain was far from showing an independent personality, however, one objective of Spanish foreign policy since 1898, the protection of the national territory by France and Great Britain, seemed to have been achieved.

The Spanish negotiators were limited to clarifying the wording of the agreements in order to avoid as much as possible terms which revealed the unequal position of Spain. There were three basic changes: the removal of the term 'guarantee', although it was recognized that the intention of the three governments was precisely that; the removal of the description of all the territories which remained under the protection of the agreements, since this would have implied the recognition of British sovereignty over Gibraltar; and, finally, the replacement of the term 'not to cede' by the positive 'maintaining' the territories under the sovereignty of each country.[27] But not even the 'guarantee' offered to the Spanish possessions could be taken literally, since there was no mention whatsoever of the mechanisms the states would use in the case of an attack by a third power. This term was replaced by a euphemism in order not to offend any sensibilities: 'new circumstances that could change or contribute to change the present territorial status quo'. Communication among governments was not mandated, even in the case of such danger of territorial modification. The diplomat Manuel González Hontoria wrote that the pact of May 1907 was basically a moral commitment, determined only by the circumstances of the moment of its enforcement.[28]

Francesco Tommasini, perhaps the Italian scholar who devoted most attention to the Cartagena agreements, took a very negative view of them. His judgement was somewhere between the chronicler and the politician, since he was a career diplomat and held the post of Tommaso Tittoni's personal secretary in 1907. He considered the agreements unnecessary in that they did not bring any 'effective' advantage to the parties involved while disturbing the international atmosphere.[29] Analysing the position of Spain, he argued that the agreements were basically concluded between Britain and France against Spain, that is, to reduce the danger of Spain's becoming the tool of potential enemies of those two powers, namely Germany.[30] The Spanish-Anglo-French agreements left Spain in a 'confusing and humiliating' position.[31] Tommasini's judgements may be linked to the assessments of Tittoni or his entourage from an Italian perspective.

Some days after the interview between Edward VII and Alfonso XIII in Cartagena, the former met with Victor Emmanuel III in Gaeta on 18 April. Was this about attracting Italy to a major Mediterranean alliance? According to the available evidence it is possible that they did not discuss political issues, but it does seem that during the month of April the governments of France and Britain had considered the possibility of inviting Italy to the negotiations. We also know that Edward VII expressed his desire for a meeting between the kings of Italy and Spain.[32] Spain might have been a good vehicle for drawing Italy towards the Anglo-French orbit, as Italy itself had done for Spain with regard to the Triple Alliance. The Cartagena agreements were received calmly in Rome. They were considered a model of vagueness, and it was only if they had secret clauses or if the concept of 'Mediterranean' included the area of interest to Italy – as the Ambassador in London, the Marquis of San Giuliano, thought – that Rome might become worried about them. The Under-Secretary of the Foreign Office, Charles Hardinge, dispelled the Ambassador's fears by assuring him that the bilateral commitments were still valid and that the concept of 'Mediterranean' which appeared in the agreements was simply poorly expressed.[33]

Spain had reason for concern, because a short time after the signing of the agreements of 1907 it was demonstrated that they did not protect it from French ambitions. In February 1909, France and Germany signed an agreement on Morocco which insisted on the provisions of the Algeciras Conference in order to 'avoid any disagreements between them'. France guaranteed economic equality in the Moroccan empire, while Germany declared that it had only economic interests there, recognized the 'specific political interests of France', and committed itself not to be an obstacle to Morocco's development.[34] Their signing of an agreement on Morocco without Spanish participation damaged Spain's prestige. This French foreign policy initiative indicated the role that would thenceforth be assigned to Spain in North Africa. The diplomatic effort to achieve for

Spain an agreement similar to the Franco-German one was especially humiliating.[35] As for the Italian government, the Franco-German agreement was cause for concern to the extent that it might mean a change in the European balance affecting its relations with Germany and Austria-Hungary at a key moment for its interests in the Balkans. It was no surprise to Italy that Spain had been left out of the Franco-German negotiations, since the Italian diplomats increasingly accepted the idea that Spain, with its policy of inaction, was allowing itself to be exploited by France in Morocco.

The events of the spring–summer of 1911, the incident at Agadir, and new Franco-German negotiations put an end to the relative enthusiasm over the agreements of 1907. The French occupation of Fez was an excuse for Germany to threaten direct intervention in Morocco, under the umbrella of a violation of the Algeciras agreement. Germany saw no reason to allow France to occupy Moroccan territory without paying for it. Paris and Berlin prepared to negotiate, knowing from the start that they would have to exchange territorial compensation. Once again, Spain was left out, with the promise that its interests would not be affected.[36] The Spanish government resigned itself to wait and hope that the Franco-German negotiations would cause the least possible damage and soon be concluded, leaving it to resolve its differences with France later, during the second half of the match. These events were debated in the Italian Chamber of Deputies, where the government was criticized for having allowed Italian interests in the Mediterranean to be sacrificed to the boundless ambition of France – its first victim was, of course, Spain.[37] San Giuliano pointed out in diplomatic circles that respect for the agreements of 1902 was no obstacle to remaining alert to the possible repercussions of these events on the Mediterranean balance.[38] The Franco-German agreement of 4 November 1911 gave France freedom of action in Morocco in exchange for part of the French territories in Congo.[39] France had yet to negotiate with Spain in accordance with the 1904 agreements. These negotiations began in December 1911 and ended only on 27 November 1912 with the establishment of the Spanish protectorate over the zone agreed upon with France in 1904 – except for some territories as payment for the cessions made by France to Germany and France's establishment of its own protectorate on 30 March 1912.[40]

The Spanish government tried to win the support of Italy during the Franco-German negotiations, but this was a poorly calculated move. It was still September when Tittoni, then Ambassador to Paris, informed his Spanish colleague Pérez Caballero that the events in Morocco could 'force the king of Italy to intervene in Tripoli'.[41] He said that his country ought to learn from the Spanish experience – it had been excluded from the Franco-German negotiations – 'how little treaties can be trusted'. A month later Pérez Caballero was ordered to discover Tittoni's opinion on his possible intervention with the French government in support of the interests of Spain. To think that Italy, which was involved in a war against Turkey and had part of international public opinion against it, would intercede on behalf of Spain was a mistake that made Spanish weakness even more evident. Tittoni answered that it was impossible to do what they were asking.[42] The Spanish Ambassador to Rome, Ramón Piña y Millet, was ordered to ask San Giuliano to postpone his recognition of the Franco-German agreement until the Franco-Spanish negotiations had been concluded. The presence of Italian troops on the coast of Tripolitania became the final payment of the debt contracted with France, and San Giuliano limited himself to reminding the Spanish Ambassador of this situation and repeating it whenever the Moroccan issue was mentioned.[43]

The reasons the Italian government, headed once again by Giovanni Giolitti since March 1911, was forced to occupy Tripolitania and Cyrenaica after declaring war on Turkey are above all political and international in nature: the 'solution' of the Moroccan question. The long diplomatic effort that led to the military occupation of the territory that would now resume its old name of 'Libya' did not envision a set date for it; that had depended entirely on the evolution of the international situation.[44] Giolitti considered domestic and foreign policy as two different worlds. The international issues had variables which went beyond the parliament and the government.[45] Neither finances, investments, nor trade were reasons to declare war on Turkey.[46] The foreign policy of Italy accepted the basic rules of international relations and sought its own way of adapting to those rules.[47]

There was no lack of incidents in Spanish–Italian relations during the military campaign. This was due in part to the dependence of the Spanish press on foreign news agencies, in part to rumours of a possible trade agreement between Spain and Turkey which would replace Italian products in the Turkish market, and in part to an alleged network for transporting arms and Turkish officials from France to Tripolitania through Spanish ports.[48] But the biggest problem appeared at the time of recognizing the Italian conquest sanctioned by the Treaty of Lausanne in October 1912. Spain was the last European state except Switzerland to offer that recognition, and when it finally did so it expressed reservations with regard to the possible consequences 'for the Spanish zone in Morocco, an agreement that is being negotiated between Italy and France regarding that empire'.[49] Spain and Italy initiated negotiations once the agreement between those two countries was known.[50] The agreement was not signed until 4 May 1913. The murder of Spain's President, José Canalejas, and the numerous objections raised by the ministers in Giolitti's cabinet with regard to the possible economic consequences of applying most-favoured-nation treatment to Libya, which had no trade agreement with Italy, turned a negotiation that had seemed easy into a lengthy diplomatic process. San Giuliano had to remind his colleagues in the cabinet that there were political reasons for speed in concluding the Libya–Morocco agreement with Spain.[51] Italy was more Mediterranean than ever since 1912, and its new presence had caused enough problems to raise the question of modifying the Mediterranean balance of power from east to west. Spain could not be forgotten. More than that, it had acquired a new perspective for Italy.

The Italian–Spanish agreement on Libya and Morocco[52] was used as a tool for reactivating the relations between the two countries. From the beginning of the negotiations to the end the climate of Spanish–Italian relations had substantially changed. The trade negotiations which had begun off the record in February 1912 finally acquired official status in April 1913. From February onward the press in both countries began to publish articles in support of the *rapprochement*, reflecting political interests which moved through diplomatic channels. The Triple Alliance and Italy in particular might be affected by the attitude of Spain in case of armed conflict between alliances. This new climate must be interpreted in the context of European attempts to reach a global agreement on the balance of power in the Mediterranean,[53] in which the role of Spain would be important.

Once Spain and France seemed to have put an end to the Moroccan problem, Spain was in the position to accept other commitments in relation to strictly European issues within the *entente*. The statements of some Spanish politicians supported this possibility.[54] The Spanish government made the first step in suggesting to the Italians the possibility of giving the agreement on Libya and Morocco – which was being negotiated at the time – 'a wider, more political scope'.[55] This suggestion interested San Giuliano, although he believed that the Libya–Morocco agreement should be only a first step towards other commitments separate from the current negotiations.

What kinds of political agreements might be signed with Spain? This question was on the table for the Minister of Foreign Affairs until World War I. The limits seemed clear at least: Spain could not sign anything against France or Italy against the Triple Alliance.[56] Until Giolitti[57] there were two starting points: getting closer to Spain and keeping an eye on French–Spanish relations. There was agreement on these objectives in Rome, Berlin, and Vienna, but there were three possible options for achieving them. The Germans, who for the first time admitted their mistakes in their relationship with Spain, believed that the best formula was to go back to the model of the secret agreement of 1887,[58] even though it had been impossible to implement for many reasons. Italy's Ambassador to Madrid, Lelio Bonin de Longare, believed that there was just one way: to get Italy to join the agreements of Cartagena. This was a difficult option because it was incompatible with the Treaty of the Triple Alliance.[59] Finally, it was suggested that the links with Spain should be tightened – without thinking about any specific agreement – in order to prevent it from abandoning its neutrality in the event of armed conflict to the detriment of Italy. The government of Madrid needed to know that Spanish territory was not at risk.[60]

In the midst of this speculation two events took place that, on the one hand, made sense of Bonin's pressure and, on the other, increased the interest of the Triple Alliance and Italy in the development of Spain's international position. The first one happened during the visit of Alfonso XIII to Paris in May 1913, right after the opening of the Institut Française d'Espagne in Madrid. The Minister of State, Juan Navarro Reverter, proposed to Bonin the possibility of using the agreements on Libya and Morocco as a first step towards other agreements on the Mediterranean. He assured the Italian representative that Italy's commitment granted it complete freedom of action on Mediterranean issues. This initiative did not go any farther, and the minister was soon replaced.[61] The second event took place in October during the visit of Prime Minister Raymond Poincaré to Spain and his meeting with Alfonso XIII in Cartagena accompanied by the British vessel *Invincible*. The commitments of 1907 were revisited. Romanones informed Bonin that he had defended before the Council of Ministers the need to craft the trade agreement with Italy – which was being negotiated at the time – from a political perspective. He suggested the possibility of reaching an agreement on the Mediterranean and, in an attempt to give more force to his words, even mentioned how useful it would be for the two monarchs to meet on Italian soil.[62] These statements coincided with the final moments of Poincaré's visit and the beginning of negotiations between France and Italy with regard to a French initiative for an agreement on the balance of power in the Mediterranean. Romanones's initiative seemed to complement the conversations between Paris and Rome and to have the same objective: to lure Italy towards the Mediterranean policy of the *entente*. The proposal of the liberal leader evaporated because he was replaced by the conservative Eduardo Dato at the end of October. At this time, San Giuliano said that it was necessary to increase the links with Spain and to monitor 'the more than friendly relations that currently exist between France and Spain'.[63]

From the end of 1913 onward, the possible bilateral commitment remained frozen, waiting for the international and political obstacles to disappear. Meanwhile, the two states increased their 'spiritual and moral' links as well as their commercial ones. An Italian–Spanish committee was created in Rome on 6 June 1913, and the corresponding Spanish–Italian committee was born in Madrid on the last day of November 1913. A commerce and shipping treaty was signed on 30 March 1914 and ratified on

13 July. The political character of the agreement received more attention than the economic one during the parliamentary debate both in Italy and in Spain.[64]

The outbreak of World War I put the brake on these initiatives. The relations between the two countries during the war are unknown.[65] Until May 1915, when Italy declared war on Austria–Hungary, Spain and Alfonso himself conceived the possibililty of the two countries leading a peace initiative among the contenders. But the King did not entertain any false expectations, and he knew that the most likely option for Italy was to go to war against Austria. Spain's persistence in asking Italy to remain neutral might be interpreted as an expression of self-pride, according to Bonin. If Italy went to war, Spain would be the only European state of any importance outside the conflict, which 'would make it all the more evident how little influence Spain had on the general policy of Europe'.[66]

Spain became an important ally to the Italian war effort, and this help increased as the hope for peace disappeared. But it was also a country under constant suspicion. The freedom of action attributed to enemy propaganda, the incidents with German submarines, and the increasingly frequent sinking of merchant vessels near the Spanish Levant made the Italian government take Spain seriously after 1916. First, it made an effort to create a surveillance network on the Peninsula, and second, it pressed the Spanish government to make good on its words of friendship by entering the war. The alternative represented by Sonino was very clear to the Spanish government: if Spain did not support anyone it could not expect any support after the conflict on the most important issue, Morocco, and specifically on Tangier. The alternative was the immediate signing of a bilateral political agreement to counterbalance the anticipated expansion of France after the war.

In fact, France tried to monopolize Morocco, including Tangier, in 1919. Only British determination was able to stop this attempt.[67] From then on the *rapprochement* initiatives of the prewar period began to be revisited, this time supported by the anti-French feeling that had appeared in Spain, especially since the Annual disaster. Was Italy ready to commit itself to Spain knowing that its interest lay in Tangier, one of the points of conflict with France? The optimism in Italy at the time of the departure for Spain of the new Ambassador, Carlo Fasciotti, in 1919, carrying the possibility of a political agreement, had cooled a year later.[68] The Spaniards – with less enthusiasm on the part of the politicians than of the press – were the only ones to consider the possibility of an agreement with Italy to counterbalance French power. The years before the triumph of Fascism in Italy and the dictatorship of Primo de Rivera in Spain were spent in pursuit of a new trade agreement, study of a new and massive penetration of Italian industry to

Spain, and preparations for a new and eagerly awaited royal meeting in Rome.

NOTES

1. On comparative economic history, see G. Tortella, 'Las causas del atraso económico en la economía: Un ensayo bibliográfico sobre la España del siglo XIX con algunas comparaciones con los casos de Italia y Portugal', in A. Grohmann (ed.), *Due storiografie economiche a confronto: Italia e Spagna (dagli anni '60 agli anni '80)* (Milan, 1991), pp.189–228; L. Prados and V. Zamagni (eds.), *El desarrollo económico de la Europa del Sur: España e Italia en perspectiva histórica* (Madrid, 1992); N. Sánchez Albornoz, 'La integración del mercado nacional: España e Italia', in *Jalones en la modernización de España* (Barcelona, 1975).
2. R. Vaccaro, 'Industralization in Spain and Italy (1860–1914)', *Journal of European Economic History*, 3 (1981), pp.709–51.
3. L. Prados, 'Crecimiento, atraso y convergencia en España e Italia', in Prados and Zamagni, *El desarrollo económico de la Europa del Sur*, pp.27–55. Against this thesis, A. Carreras, 'La producción industrial en el muy largo plazo: Una comparación entre España e Italia de 1861 a 1980', in Prados and Zamagni (eds.), *El desarrollo económico de la Europa del Sur*, pp.173–210, presents some results which show the Spanish industrial sector ahead of the Italian until the 1940s.
4. S. Roldán and J.L. García Delgado, *La formación de la sociedad capitalista en España: Contribución al análisis de la influencia de la I Guerra Mundial sobre el capitalismo español* (Madrid, 1973).
5. G. Pescosolido, *Agricultura e industria nell'Italia unita* (Firenze, 1983); R. Garrabou *et al.* (eds.), *Historia agraria de la España contemporánea*, Vols.2 and 3 (1850–1960), (Barcelona, 1985–86).
6. Regarding the commercial relations between Spain and Italy, which have been covered very briefly in these pages, I refer to my work F. García Sanz, *Historia de las relaciones entre España e Italia. Imágenes, comercio y política exterior (1890–1914)* (Madrid, 1994).
7. A. Tena, 'Protección y competitividad en España e Italia, 1890–1960', in Prados and Zamagni (eds.), *El desarrollo económico de la Europa del Sur*, pp.321–55.
8. On the exchange of images between Spain and Italy, see García Sanz, *Historia de las relaciones entre España e Italia.*
9. F. García Sanz, 'Tra strumentalizazzione e difesa del liberopensiero: Il caso Ferrer nella opinione pubblica italiana e nei rapporti Madrid/Roma', in *Stato, chiesa e società in Italia, Francia, Belgio e Spagna nei secoli XIX–XX* (Foggia, 1993), pp.251–86.
10. M. Suarez Cortina (ed.), *La Restauración, entre el liberalismo y la democracia* (Madrid, 1997).
11. J. Tusell and I. Saz, 'Las relaciones políticas y diplomáticas de dos dictaduras mediterráneas', *Boletín Real Academia de la Historia* (Sept.–Dec. 1982), pp.413–83.
12. These agreements were signed successively between February and May of 1887 by Italy with Germany, Austria-Hungary, Britain, and Spain. All of them had a defence orientation – maintaining the *status quo* in the Mediterranean. In the event that this was not possible, the priorities were underlined: Tripolitania and Cyrenaica would go to Italy, Egypt to Britain, Austria and Italy in the Adriatic, and so on. On the agreement with Spain, see Federico Curato, *La questione marocchina e gli accordi italo-spagnoli del 1887 e del 1891* (Milan, 1964); F. García Sanz, 'La guerra de Cuba, las alianzas de España y el equilibrio Mediterráneo', in *La nación soñada: Cuba, Filipinas y Puerto Rico, 1898* (Madrid, 1996), pp.755–66. For a sketch of Italy's international commitments until 1915, see E. Serra, *L'Italia e le grandi alleanze nel tempo dell'imperialismo: Saggio di tecnica diplomatica, 1870–1915* (Milan, 1990).
13. Antonio Cánovas was the head of the government. He had never liked the pact signed by Sagasta's liberals, but in 1891 he had accepted its renewal because of the events in Portugal which threatened the monarchy and the outside support provided by Britain. On the

government's motives for renewing the pact in 1891 and the reasons it failed in 1895, see García Sanz, *Historia de las relaciones entre España e Italia*, pp.54–83.

14. E. Serra, *La questione tunisina da Crispi a Rudinì ed il colpo di timone alla política estera dell'Italia* (Milan, 1967).
15. E. Serra, *L'intesa mediterranea del 1902* (Milan, 1957); and *C. Barrère e l'intesa italo-francese* (Milan, 1950).
16. E. Di Nolfo, 'Préface', in M. Petricioli, *L'Italia in Asia Minore: Equilibrio mediterraneo e ambizioni imperialiste alla vigilia della prima guerra mondiale* (Florence, 1983), p.7.
17. J.M. Jover, 'Gibraltar en la crisis internacional del '98', in *Política, diplomacia y humanismo popular* (Madrid, 1976), pp.431–88, and Rosario de la Torre, 'La crisis de 1898 y el problema de la garantía exterior', *Hispania*, 162 (1986), pp.115–64.
18. In addition to the titles reviewed, see H. Hallmann, *La Spagna e la rivalità anglo-francese nel Mediterraneo (1898–1907)* (Milan, 1942), in particular 'La Spagna fra l'Inghilterra e un'alleanza continentale (1898–1899)', and R. de la Torre, *Inglaterra y España en 1898* (Madrid, 1988), pp.286–92.
19. F. Silvela, *Artículos, discursos, conferencias y cartas*, Vol.3 (Madrid, 1923), p.115.
20. In December 1901 Maura reminded Sagasta: 'We are totally defenceless; it is possible to blockade us with fishing boats; it is possible to interfere with the communication with our islands. Nothing; not only we do not have anything but also we have something that is an obstacle and that it is urgent to demolish.' A. Maura, *Treinta y cinco años de vida pública: Ideas políticas, doctrinas y campañas parlamentarias* (Madrid, 1953), p.129.
21. F. León y Castillo, *Mis tiempos* (Madrid, 1978), Vol.2, p.204. The main role in the negotiations was played by a man from the Ministry of State, Juan Pérez Caballero. See F. García Sanz, 'Juan Pérez Caballero y Ferrer, una nueva diplomacia en la estela del '98?', *Historia Contemporánea*, 15 (1996), pp.53–76.
22. Archivo General de la Administración (AGA), Asuntos Exteriores-Archivo Embajada Quirinal (AE-AEQ), legajo Marruecos: Varios, *Real Orden Muy Reservada*, No.12, 11 Feb. 1902.
23. Cited in R. Gay de Montella, *Valoración hispánica en el Mediterráneo* (Madrid, 1952), p.161.
24. R. Raynaud, *Les relations franco-spagnoles et le Maroc* (Paris, 1913), p.113.
25. E. Decleva, *Da Adua a Sarajevo: La politica estera e la Francia* (Rome andBari, 1971), in particular pp.288 ff.; F. Tommasini, 'La Conferenza di Algesiras e l'Italia', in *Nuova Antologia*, 379 (1935), pp.427–47; García Sanz, *Historia de las relaciones entre España e Italia*, pp.289–312.
26. 'In a few months Spain, following Maura's initiative and with the agreement of all political forces, made much more international policy than in previous years.' Conde de Romanones, *Notas de una vida*, Vol.2 (Madrid, n.d.), p.216. For a historical perspective, see E. Rosas Ledezma, 'Las "declaraciones de Cartagena" (1907): Significación en la política exterior de España y repercusiones internacionales', *Cuadernos de Historia Moderna y Contemporánea*, 2 (1981); R. Gay de Montellá, *Diez años de política internacional en el Mediterráneo, 1904–1914: Ensayos de historia política moderna* (Barcelona, n.d.); R. de la Torre, 'Los acuerdos anglo-hispano-franceses de 1907: Una larga negociación en la estela del 98', *Cuadernos de la Escuela Diplomática*, 1 (1988), pp.213–29; F.García Sanz, 'De Cartagena a Gaeta: España, Italia y el *statu quo* en el Mediterráneo', in *Historia de las relaciones entre España e Italia*, pp.312–27.
27. J.M. Allendesalazar, *La diplomacia española y Marruecos, 1907–1909* (Madrid, 1990), pp.53–5.
28. 'Cartagena is simply what many international law authors call "pseudo-guarantee agreements".' Cited by A. Mousset, *La política exterior de España, 1873–1918* (Madrid, 1918), pp.182–3.
29. F. Tommasini, *L'Italia alla vigilia della guerra: La politica estera di Tommaso Tittoni* (Bolgona, 1934–38), Vol.3, p.288.
30. Ibid., pp.288–9.
31. Ibid., p.289.
32. Tommasini, *L'Italia alla vigilia della guerra*, p.278.

33. Archivio Ministero Affari Esteri Roma (AMAER), Serie Politica (SP), SPAGNA, Busta (B) 75, rapporto riservato No. 966/392, Embajador de Italia en Londres a Ministro de Asuntos Exteriores, Londres, 26 June 1907.
34. The text of this agreement can be found in M. Gómez González, *La penetración en Marruecos (Política europea de 1904 a 1909)* (Zaragoza, 1909), pp.267–8.
35. It consisted of a German declaration that the agreements with France did not prejudice the political interests of Spain in Morocco. Allendesalazar, *La diplomacia española y Marruecos*, pp.200–203; cf. M. González Hontoria, *El protectorado francés en Marruecos y sus enseñanzas para la acción española* (Madrid, 1915), pp.248–9.
36. M. González Hontoria, *El protectorado francés en Marruecos*, pp.249 ff.
37. Atti Parlamentari, Camera Deputati, 5 July 1911, pp.16.845–16.848.
38. AMAER, SP, MAROCCO, B. 220, minuta de telegrama in partenza No. 2546, 8 July 1911.
39. The agreements were translated into two covenants, one for Congo and one for Morocco. See González Hontoria, *El protectorado francés,* pp.18 ff. E. Ghersi, in *La questione marocchina nella politica europea (1830-1912)* (Florence, 1939), pp.84 ff. says that this underlines the inferior position in which Spain was placed by France's treating Morocco as undivided territory.
40. González Hontoria, *El protectorado francés*, pp.20-27; on the Spanish–French negotiations and the Spanish protectorate, see pp.251–63.
41. Archivo Ministerio Asuntos Exteriores Madrid (AMAEM), Serie Política (SP), ITALIA, legajo 2533, telegrama reservado, Embajador de España en París a ministro de Estado, Paris, 27 Sept. 1911.
42. AMAEM, SP, legajo 2533, telegrama. cifrado, Embajador de España en París a Ministro de Estado, Paris, 27 Oct. 1911.
43. AGA, AE-AEQ, 'Despachos, 1911', Minuta de d. No. 127, Embajador de España en Roma a Ministro de Estado, Rome, 4 Nov. 1911.
44. We should remember the agreements with France (1900 and 1902), the recognition by both Germany and Austria-Hungary (1902), the Anglo-Italian agreement (1903), and the Russian acquiescence (Racconigi, 1909). See A. Torre, 'La preparazione diplomatica dell'impresa libica', *Rassegna di Politica Internazionale* (Dec. 1936–Jan. 1937); and L. Peteani, *La questione libica nella diplomazia europea* (Firenze, 1939).
45. Giolitti, *Memorie*, pp.213 ff.; cf. B. Vigezzi, 'Politica estera e opinione pubblica in Italia dal 1870 al 1914: Orientamenti degli studi e prospettive della ricerca', *Opinione Publique et Politique exterieure* (Rome, 1981), pp.75–123; S. Romano, *Giolitti* (Milan, 1989). On the war in Libya in general, see S. Romano, *La quarta sponda: La guerra di Libia, 1911–1912* (Milan, 1977).
46. R. Mori, 'La penetrazione pacifica italiana in Libia dal 1907 al 1911 e il Banco di Roma', *Rivista di Studi di Politici Internazionali*, 1 (1957), pp.103–18; L. Di Rosa, *Storia del Banco di Roma* (Rome, 1982–83); cf. M. Petricioli, *L'Italia in Asia Minore*, pp.15–42. On the debate over the causes of Italian imperialism see B. Vigezzi, 'L'imperialismo e il suo ruolo nella storia italiana del primo novecento', *Storia Contemporanea* (Feb. 1980), pp.29–56; cf., in line with Vigezzi, the contribution by D. Grange, *L'Italia et la méditerranée (1896–1911)* (Rome, 1994), Vol.2, Ch.26–8.
47. Vigezzi, 'L'imperialismo', p.42.
48. On all these issues, see F. García Sanz, 'España y la guerra de Libia', in *Historia de las relaciones entre España e Italia*, pp.411–24.
49. AMAER, Archivio Riservato Di Gabinetto (ARDG), telegrama in partenza, Ministro de Estado de España a Embajador en Roma, Madrid, 26 Oct. 1912.
50. AMAER, SP, Marocco, B. 223, Pro-Memoria entregada por el embajador de España en Roma al ministro de Asuntos Exteriores de Italia, Rome, 7 Nov. 1912. According to Orden Real, No.9, 17 Feb. 1913, a text proposal for the agreement was sent to the ambassador in Rome. In general, it was similar to the French–Italian one: a commitment not to be an obstacle to Italy's action in Libya and Spain's in Morocco, as well as most-favoured-nation status.
51. AMAER, SP, MAROCCO, B. 223, No.15915/230, Nota diretta dal Ministro degli Affari Esteri ai Ministeri delle Colonie e delle Finanze, Rome, 16 March 1913.

52. Text in García Sanz, *Historia de las relaciones entre España e Italia*, p.430. The agreement confirmed the freedom of action in their zones and most-favoured-nation treatment.
53. G. Andrè, *L'Italia e il Mediterraneo alla vigilia della prima guerra mondiale: I tentativi di intesa mediterranea (1911–1914)* (Milan, 1967).
54. Romanones made clear that 'Spain is very close to entering a completely new period in its international life. The principle 'With everyone and with no one' is nonsense today, an idea which has nothing to do with the examples we see everywhere'. AMAER, ARDG, B. 13, fasc. 81, r. No.780/315, Embajador de Italia en Madrid a Ministro de Asuntos Exteriores, San Sebastián, 17 Sept. 1912.
55. This is a statement made by the Spanish ambassador, Piña y Millet, to San Giuliano on 25 Feb. 1913. AMAER, ARDG, legajo 27, fasc. 315, ibid. telegrama partenza No.102, Ministro de Asuntos Exteriores de Italia a embajadores en Viena, Berlín, Madrid y París, Rome, 26 Feb. 1913.
56. AMAER, ARDG, legajo 27, fasc. 315, telegrama No.114, Embajador de Italia en Madrid a Ministro de Asuntos Exteriores, 28 Feb. 1913.
57. AMAER, ARDG, legajo 13, fasc. 81, letter, riservata alla Persona, San Giuliano a Giovanni Giolitti, Rome, 18 July 1913. San Giuliano insisted on the need to cultivate the Spanish friendship beginning with the signature of a trade agreement as a basis for political commitments and to reduce the likelihood of agreements with Italy's adversaries.
58. Gottlieb von Jagow and Alfred Zimmermann admitted that Germany was to blame for the demise of the 1887 agreements. AMAER, ARDG, legajo 27, fasc. 351, telegrama No.115 and No.122, Embajador de Italia en Berlín a ministro de Asuntos Exteriores, Berlin, 3 and 6 March 1913.
59. Ibid. telegrama No. 121, Embajador de Italia en Madrid a Ministro de Asuntos Exteriores, Madrid, 6 March. On 4 March, with telegrama in partenza No.113, San Giuliano had informed Bonin about the telegram from Bollati in which he asked for his opinion about this.
60. AMAER, ARDG, legajo 13, fasc. 81, letter, Bonin a San Giuliano, Madrid, 9 March 1913, and letter, San Giuliano a Bonin, same date, and minuta d. s/n del Ministro de Asuntos Exteriores de Italia a Embajador en Berlín, Rome, 21 March 1913.
61. AMAER. ARDG. legajo 13, fasc. 81, letter, Bonin a San Giuliano, Madrid, 14 May 1913. Regarding the motives and consequences of this ministerial exchange, ibid., letter, Bollati a San Giuliano, Berlin, 27 June 1913, and letter, Bonin a San Giuliano, Vicenza, 20 July 1913.
62. AMAER, ARDG, B. 13, fasc. 81, d. riservato No.974/352, Embajador de Italia en España a Ministro de Asuntos Exteriores, Madrid, 18 Oct. 1913. About the royal meeting, both men knew it was impossible unless the Spaniards accepted Rome as the place.
63. AMAER, SP, SPAGNA, B. 79, r. circular riservato, No.62040, Ministro de Asuntos Exteriores de Italia a Embajadores en París, Berlín, Viena, Londres y San Petersburgo, Rome, 14 Nov. 1913, and ARDG, B. 13, fasc. 81, r. riservato No.3306/797, Embajador de Italia en Berlín a Ministro de Asuntos Exteriores, Berlin, 6 Dec. 1913.
64. García Sanz, *Historia de las relaciones entre España e Italia*, regarding the committees, pp.457–64, and the parliamentary debates on the treaty, pp.475–83.
65. My current research involves the relations between Spain and Italy during the war.
66. On 15 May 1915, in a private audience, Alfonso XIII insisted before Bonin on the advantages of neutrality and the consequences that Austria's defeat would bring to the Mediterranean balance. AMAER, SP 'Spagna', B. 79, r. (s/n), riservato, Embajador de Italia en Madrid a Ministro de Asuntos Exteriores, Madrid, 14 May 1915.
67. S. Sueiro, *España en el Mediterráneo. Primo de Rivera y la 'cuestión Marroquí', 1923–1930* (Madrid, 1992), pp.14–16.
68. AMAER, Affari Politici, 1919–1930, B. 1586, letter, Fasciotti a Sforza, San Sebastián, 4 July 1920.

Spanish Colonialism during Primo de Rivera's Dictatorship

SUSANA SUEIRO SEOANE

In September 1923, when Miguel Primo de Rivera became dictator, the Moroccan problem was the crux of Spanish foreign policy and the catalyst for political and social domestic problems, as it had been for constitutional governments during the reign of Alfonso XIII. The gruelling Rif war against the traditionally warring tribes that in 1921 had come together under the leadership of Abd el-Krim was consuming the country's human and material resources and becoming a nightmare that aggravated all other conflicts. It was, however, Spain's presence in Morocco that provided its only chance of playing any sort of role in the international arena. This article tackles the complex process that led to the resolution of the Rif conflict, undoubtedly the greatest success achieved by the Primo de Rivera dictatorship.

In 1923, when Miguel Primo de Rivera became dictator, the 'Moroccan question' was the main issue of Spanish political life. Spain found itself confronting serious difficulties in the territory it had been assigned during the colonial distribution. On acquiring an area of influence in Morocco[1] during the first years of the century, Spanish leaders had managed to achieve the goal they had set themselves: participation among the major powers after a long period of international isolation that many considered one of the principal causes of the 1898 Disaster.[2] However, they had also taken on a heavy burden, the human and material costs of which were far greater than its economic benefits. Some clearly saw from the start that Morocco was not going to be an easy colonial enterprise, but even the most pessimistic forecasts fell short of the reality. The Moroccan venture turned out to be not only troublesome and costly, as some had predicted, but a veritable national cancer. In the rugged Rif mountains the Spanish leaders found themselves confronted with a war that had no end in sight. Presence in Morocco was required for Spain to play an international role, but it represented an intolerable drain of men and money. The impotence of the Madrid governments stemmed from the impossibility of avoiding the colonial task they had undertaken and from the evidence that this task was unprofitable and, even worse, poisoning national politics.

Trapped in a apparently unresolvable dilemma – the imperative of being in Morocco versus the almost unbearable tension deriving from that gruelling colonial mission – successive governments followed an inconsistent and contradictory policy, opting now for warmongering, now for 'pacifism', which in most cases meant nothing more than bribing tribal chiefs in exchange for a cease-fire. In fact, despite public opinion's clear opposition to the war on Moroccan soil,[3] the governments found themselves increasingly involved in military action. It has often been said that the strong influence of the army on Spanish politics, and particularly the pressure exerted by the Africanist military, was the reason for Spain's decision to impose a military protectorate in Morocco rather than a civil one. The praetorianism or militarism of Spanish politics and certainly of its Moroccan policy has repeatedly been pointed out.[4] However, regardless of military pressure, one should keep in mind that 'pacific penetration' – an attempt by a colonial power to ingratiate itself with the indigenous population by developing the country – was undoubtedly difficult in Spanish Morocco. The Rif was a very turbulent territory, inhabited by warlike Berber tribes with aspirations to independence and a strong spirit of resistance not only to any attempt at colonial penetration or foreign occupation but also to the *Makhzan*, the Moroccan central government; to assert his authority and to collect taxes the sultan had always needed to send armed troops. Moreover, this was a complicated and tortuous territory ideally suited to the guerrilla warfare tactics that these tribes had come to master. The Spanish troops, in contrast, lacked knowledge of the land they were crossing because of the absence of maps and topographic information, and all too frequently found themselves the victims of ambushes and surprise attacks.

The characteristics of Spanish Morocco left little room for a non-military solution. Without making light of the undeniable difficulties of colonizing the territory, however, the truth is that there was much to find fault with in the organization of the protectorate, which in turn was basically a reflection of the serious defects afflicting an army with an overabundance of officers which diverted most of the budget to the paying of salaries rather than to the modernizing of equipment or the improvement of training. The flaws in Spain's policy in Morocco became dramatically evident during the summer of 1921, when through a combination of circumstances it suffered a humiliating defeat at Annual and Mount Arruit.[5] The recklessness of General Manuel Fernández Silvestre, General Commander of Melilla, had much to do with this. He enjoyed a tremendous autonomy of action because of his relationship with the King and his previous capacity as commanding officer of the High Commissioner, Dámaso Berenguer, who did not dare to restrain him. In a few weeks all the efforts of the earlier years were destroyed. In the face of Rif assault, the Spanish retreat turned into a general scattering of troops, a desperate flight, absolute chaos, leaving the corpses of some 10,000 Spanish soldiers strewn on the battlefield.

While there had long been anti-Spanish sentiment and opposition to colonization in the Rif, it had been unorganized and fragmented because the tribes were also fighting among themselves. After Abd el-Krim's spectacular victory over the Spaniards at Annual, his power and prestige among the tribes of northern Morocco increased tenfold. His considerable aptitude for leadership and political intelligence helped him achieve control over a constantly expanding territory. He managed to centralize his political authority through a government made up of family and friends from his native village Axdir, near the bay of Alhucemas, and he moulded his men into a highly disciplined army that was well organized and well armed. By the start of 1923 he had proclaimed a Rif Republic and had even given it its own flag.[6]

Thus the picture in Morocco darkened considerably for the Spaniards from 1921 onward. The exhausting Rif war had turned into a nightmare that aggravated all other conflicts. The impotence and frustration caused by colonial failure aroused a sense of fatalism, but also profound rancour towards France, Spain's protectorate neighbour, which was seen as seeking to expel Spain from the African continent. It was at this time that the treaties dealing with Morocco signed between 1904 and 1912 began to be interpreted as a chain of abuses on the part of ambitious France, which had progressively snatched lands away until Spain was left with only 'the bone of Djebala', 'the thorn of the Rif' – the poorest and most ungovernable area – while France had the best and most fertile lands of the empire. Moreover, Spain had also lost its most important enclave, the city and port of Tangier; Spaniards considered it the 'jewel' of their zone and its loss a 'mutilation'. Without Gibraltar and without Tangier Spain had no control over any of the Gibraltar Strait's strategic points.[7]

It must be said that Spain had not benefited from the international negotiations that decided the distribution of Morocco. In each of these negotiations, Spain had not only seen its assigned territory diminish by thousands of square miles, but also suffered increasing subordination to France.[8] Curiously, however, at the moment of their signing these treaties had been considered a diplomatic success, 'a sort of international recognition'[9] – proof that the end of international isolation had come. Spain was becoming integrated into the group of the major powers, even if only as a junior partner. Despite the fact that its leading classes feared that the advance of France was unstoppable, they harboured the hope that their area of Morocco could be beneficial to Spain. It is evident that they were preparing to imitate the French model, seeking inspiration in the colonial ideas being tried out in French Morocco by Marshal Hubert Lyautey. Spain's leaders appeared to be delighted to have the rest of Europe consider their country indispensable to Mediterranean equilibrium, and they were grateful for being allowed to become part of the system. All in all, the first two decades of the century proved to be a period of confidence, hope, and optimism in which Spain aspired to become a responsible colonial power together with its partner in Morocco.

By 1923, at the beginning of the dictatorship, that feeling of hope had definitely disappeared, making way for deep discomfort. Antipathy towards the neighbouring republic was so strong that the French Ambassador in Madrid referred repeatedly in his reports to an anti-French psychosis that permeated Spanish public opinion and even went so far as to describe as 'unhealthy' the disposition towards France that could be felt in 'all spheres of political discussion'.[10] Some voices could even be heard blaming France for the Annual disaster, claiming that the Rif had followed a plan designed by the French, using military strategy which they had practised during the European war. The tendency to attribute this failure to external aggression – to a foreign conspiracy – can be explained by the difficulty of accepting the discredit involved in the fact that a nation equipped with the instruments of war created by European science should have suffered a spectacular defeat at the hands of backward mountain tribes. Given the psychological necessity of pointing to an external culprit, the theory of the 'Machiavellian manoeuvre', the international confabulation, spread during that period; in most cases a French origin was attributed to the plot.

However, many factors other than psychological ones contributed to this Francophobic sentiment. Spain had long since lost all hope of cooperating with its protectorate partner. Toasts to the fulfilment of common objectives had come to nothing. France, with more or less hidden expansionist aims, had made use of its evident superiority and developed a policy that excluded rather than concurred with Spain.[11] This French policy of non-cooperation became much more evident after Annual. The Rabat authorities – particularly the almighty Resident General, Marshal Lyautey – clearly recognized the new situation created by Abd el-Krim's appearance on the scene, but the Rif leader had made it very clear that his fight would be directed solely against Spain. From Lyautey's point of view, the Rif movement was a localized conflict with the caliph of the Spanish zone that did not appear to threaten the sultan's authority. In his reports he claimed that the reason for this was not only that this institution signified submission to Spain, the hereditary enemy from the time of the reconquest, but also that it was a creation alien to the country's traditions and a symbol of the arbitrary division of the empire.[12] Thus, France's disassociating itself from Spain did not appear to pose serious risks, especially if it responded to the good will expressed by the Moroccan leader. The Resident General defined his policy regarding the Spanish–Rif conflict as 'neutrality', but the truth is that at the very least this neutrality would have to be described as 'benevolent' towards the Moroccans. While the Spanish charges of massive military smuggling supported by France were groundless,[13] there is no doubt that Rif emissaries and agents had complete freedom of movement across French territory and that the Rif's inhabitants were able to obtain merchandise (including rifles) in the markets both in the French zone and in Algeria, where thousands of them went every year to work during harvest time; this gave a huge advantage to tribes living in a poor country with a primitive economy.

PRIMO DE RIVERA'S MOROCCAN POLICY: THE MYTH OF THE STRATEGIST

The Spaniards, therefore, were not only not given any help from their protectorate neighbours in coping with the war in the Rif, but quite the opposite: the attitude adopted by Rabat made matters even more difficult. The truth is that – especially after Annual – no leader dared to take radical or decisive action of any sort in Morocco. An out-and-out military offensive, which would imply carrying out the often discussed landing at Alhucemas, in the very midst of the rebellion, was in fact considered the only plan of action that could turn the tables in Spain's favour, but neither such an offensive nor an abandonment of the protectorate (a constant temptation) was carried out. The first option involved a high economic and human cost and was rejected by public opinion. The second involved a huge international loss of face and the fierce opposition of the military element, particularly the Africanist faction.

Miguel Primo de Rivera, who came to power after the coup in September 1923 with the promise of a quick and dignified solution to the Moroccan problem, proved to be more resolute than his predecessors; he first implemented the option of abandonment or semi-abandonment and, later carried out the Alhucemas landing.[14] In retrospect, one might think that, in contrast to previous leaders, he was a magnificent statesman with a perfectly designed Moroccan programme structured in phases that were carried out scrupulously according to plan. In fact, General Francisco Gómez-Jordana, the proponent along with the dictator himself of his Moroccan policy first as General Director of Morocco and the Colonies, and then as High Commissioner, states in his memoirs that Primo de Rivera had an ingenious, complex, and daring plan to put an end to Spain's oppressive

African nightmare, a 'brilliant' plan that was 'totally successful' and was carried out 'with the utmost discretion'.[15] Gómez-Jordana claims that the semi-abandonment of the area brought about by Primo de Rivera in 1924 was a conscious and premeditated manoeuvre which had as its aim a solid and permanent reoccupation with the aid of the French. Historians who have some knowledge of the matter also seem to credit the idea that the dictator's objective in carrying out the withdrawal was to push Abd el-Krim towards the neighbouring protectorate in order to force France, faced with a Rif attack against French positions, to propose military collaboration with Spain.[16]

This hypothesis is, of course, suggestive in the light of subsequent events. In fact, after the Spanish retreat in 1924, a Rif attack on the French zone did take place, and it was, of course, this attack that led France to ask for Spain's cooperation and finally produced the dictatorship's most spectacular triumph. It is also true that Primo de Rivera, with French aid, ended up returning to the previously abandoned territory and embarking on a project of conquest. However, as attractive as this hypothesis may seem, documents show that it must be rejected, both with regard to the existence of a plan to provoke the Rif attack on the French and with regard to the idea that Primo de Rivera considered military collaboration with France the key to the resolution of the Moroccan problem.[17] The dictator did not act any differently here than in other aspects of his administration; he was a pragmatic leader who improvised solutions to problems as they arose and in most cases acted impulsively, guided by instinct.

Documentary sources leave no doubt about his disposition to abandon Spanish Morocco when he came to power. In 1923 he had not modified his opposition to the Moroccan enterprise, which he publicly admitted and which had cost him his post on several occasions.[18] Obsessed by the need to resolve an oppressive problem within a territory that he was certainly not attached to, he was sincerely in favour of limiting the Spanish occupation in order to save lives and reduce costs. He showed the same reluctance to fight in Morocco as the liberal government that he had so abruptly replaced. The increasingly severe Rif attacks in the Spanish zone reinforced his idea of abandoning positions and retreating towards the coast, which would allow him to fulfil his desire to repatriate troops.[19] But the Rif learned of this plan for withdrawal, and it bolstered their fighting spirit, leading them to generalize their offensive to the point of creating an emergency that would force the dictator to take immediate action. The evacuation, between September and December 1924, of more than 300 posts in the western sector in order to form, near and parallel to the coast, what became known as the 'Primo de Rivera line' was, as Shannon Fleming has pointed out, essential if another disaster like Annual was to be avoided.[20]

However, the dictator, who had come to Africa in the role of High Commissioner, was soon disappointed to discover that the withdrawal he had just undertaken was not a stable solution. It did not even seem possible that the new line would allow for a reduction of costs and troops, because Abd el-Krim, who had exploited the Spanish retreat as a great victory, reached the summit of his power and prestige among the tribes during the following months, managing to control an expanse of territory that included not only the Rif but also the Djebala and Gomara.[21] It was in this context that the dictator began to consider a landing at Alhucemas, in the central Rif, the point of origin of the rebellion, but this in no way signified a change of policy. Nothing was farther from the mind of the dictator than the conquest and occupation of the Moroccan territory.[22] Alhucemas was projected only as a punitive operation which, if carried out successfully, would deal Abd el-Krim's prestige among the tribes a harsh blow. The decision to go to Alhucemas was not part of any definite programme but only a response to the need to confront a concrete danger, a situation that threatened to become critical in view of the growing aggressiveness of the Moroccan tribes, which in increasing numbers acted under Abd el-Krim's orders. However, at the same time as he was preparing for this operation, Primo de Rivera was also considering many other possibilities. The clear impression gained from the documentary sources is that his actions were guided by such pragmatic and circumstantial criteria that he could not tell where events would lead him or which solution would finally impose itself, but always remained alert to all the possibilities.

The attempt to negotiate a peace settlement with Abd el-Krim was one of the measures into which the dictator put the most effort. It not only continued but intensified the overtures made by the previous liberal government with the aim of convincing Abd el-Krim of the appropriateness of a peaceful negotiated solution to the Rif conflict. The dictator went so far as to offer Abd el-Krim an autonomy close to independence over an extensive area and the promise of considerable Spanish sudsidies (three million pesetas a year). In fact, the multiple attempts at negotiation not only came nowhere near the objectives they had started out with – to put an end to the war and pacify the area – but, on the contrary, contributed to the encouragement of the tribes' belligerence. Abd el-Krim saw these efforts as a sign of weakness that only made him bolder.[23] If a civilian and pacifist policy in Spanish Morocco had been difficult to carry out before Abd el-Krim assumed the leadership of the Rif, it became totally impossible after 1921. Once he had attacked the Spaniards and achieved his victories, the Moroccan leader never had any sincere intention of accepting anything less than total independence of the Rif, which Spain could not grant without contravening the international treaties to which it had committed itself, in particular the Franco-Spanish Treaty of 1912. Abd el-Krim's constant filibustering and strategies when negotiating peace had no other objective than to gain time to reorganize and to reap the harvest.

Another line of action contemplated by the dictator was persuading Britain and France to accept the revision or modification of the treaties Spain had signed with them on the subject of Morocco, which it considered unjust and detrimental to Spanish interests. If, at the turn of the century, the idea had been to 'enter Morocco so as to be in Europe', now the idea that was gaining ground was to 'be in Europe so as to get out of Morocco', that is, to attempt to find a solution to this internal problem within the framework of foreign policy by negotiating with other European powers that also had interests in the area. The yearning for revisionism, the desire for an international reconsideration of the Moroccan issue, is one of the leitmotifs of Spain's Mediterranean policy during the 1920s. While the temptation to get rid of a troublesome and unproductive territory existed, the idea that Spain should free itself of this heavy burden honourably, that is, by negotiation, was also present. Any other course of action – for example, simply abandoning the area – would further damage its prestige in Europe and could only be interpreted as a breach of its international commitments and, consequently, a new and humiliating declaration of impotence. The leaders were searching for a dignified solution to the Moroccan problem that would save their 'patriotic honour', and to this end they constantly toyed with the idea of a swap, an exchange of territories.[24] Primo de Rivera cherished the hope of renouncing all or part of Spain's Moroccan territory in exchange for some other territory that could be of interest to Spain. Here the priorities were clear: Gibraltar or Tangier, in that order. The recovery of Gibraltar and the inclusion of Tangier in the Spanish protectorate were permanent demands of Spain's foreign policy. The Spaniards had always argued that these two claims did not represent any desire for expansion or domination but rather were essential to their existence; both territories had been unfairly amputated from the nation's territory.[25] The exchange with Britain of Ceuta for Gibraltar would mean abandoning Morocco for good, while the option of negotiating with France, with the blessing of the British, the cession of the interior of the protectorate in exchange for Tangier would mean keeping a strip of coastal territory in Morocco. Primo de Rivera and his colleagues thought it possible – though improbable – that both powers, whose concern over the repercussions of a Spanish withdrawal was evident, would accept one or the other of these exchanges. They were of course prepared to be satisfied with Britain and France's acceptance, as compensation for the Spanish renunciation of the interior of its zone, of the extension of the boundaries of the sovereign cities of Ceuta and Melilla, which were being strangled by too narrow limits.

The dictator was certainly naive in thinking a negotiated territorial redistribution of the area of the Strait possible, but the truth is that certain precedents gave plausibility to this otherwise wild idea. These possible exchanges had been considered and discussed during the European war both in Britain and in France.[26] In any case, in 1924, the idea of resolving the Moroccan conflict by means of negotiations with the other powers was more a persistent desire on the part of the Spanish leaders than a project that showed any sign of becoming a reality. Britain had not changed its mind regarding the Ceuta–Gibraltar exchange, and France no longer harboured any interest in annexing the interior of the Spanish zone, even less so in exchange for Tangier, where it enjoyed a predominant position.[27] Leaving aside other considerations,[28] the Spanish zone had lost the importance it had had at the turn of the century, when the power established south of the Strait would have been able to block the Mediterranean in the event of war. Since the appearance of submarines and aeroplanes and the internationalization of Tangier, no power was in a position to close the Strait. Spain, in any case, would always retain its command over its strongholds, the towns of Ceuta, Melilla, and Alhucemas, which were not part of the protectorate; apart from these cities and Tangier, the coast was too rugged to permit the construction of more ports except at a very high cost. As for the interior, it was an intricate tangle of mountains and valleys inappropriate for the construction of aerodromes. In addition to these considerations, France could not act without taking Britain's attitude into account, and, although Britain was no longer very interested in who was in possession of northern Morocco, it was in no way prepared to accept unilateral French intervention in the Rif.

Nevertheless, the principal reason for the lack of French and English receptiveness to the attempts of the dictator and his collaborators at negotiating an exchange or at least a revision of the treaties that would permit Spain a graceful exit from Morocco[29] was that both powers were interested in maintaining a *status quo* that was extremely favourable to them and, above all, wanted to hear nothing of changes that might lead other powers (that is, Italy) to call them to account and demand compensation. More than Spain, it was Italy, whose new fascist government showed clear signs of a bellicose and interventionist spirit, that was feared.

THE RESOLUTION OF THE CONFLICT IN THE RIF: FRANCO-SPANISH COLLABORATION

In any case, circumstances were to dictate a very different course from the one Primo de Rivera so desired. Indeed, the Spanish army, together with the French, ended up embarking on a policy of conquest and occupation of the territory abandoned two years before, something that the dictator had not foreseen when he decided to withdraw and developed the plan for military action at Alhucemas.

Abd el-Krim, euphoric after the Spanish retreat in 1924, attacked the French protectorate in the spring of 1925.[30] France then decided to ask for Spanish cooperation – a radical change in French policy with regard to the protectorate. It is not surprising that the Spaniards took advantage of the uncomfortable hours that France went through in Morocco in 1925 to achieve some sort of revenge. They could not conceal the deep satisfaction produced by the fact that a great military power, in a territory incomparably superior to the Spanish zone, should have been spectacularly defeated by some of the same tribes that they had fought alone for so long without a trace of solidarity from France. Quite the contrary, the French had always commented on the Spanish army's setbacks in a mocking and disdainful tone. The constant contempt with which the Spaniards were treated by their neighbours hurt their pride and self-esteem. Politicians, army officers, diplomats, journalists, even the King himself had all bitterly complained about the lack of courtesy, the rudeness, and the sarcasm of their French colleagues. The French press frequently published cutting commentaries on Spain's colonial incompetence, on its insufficient respect for native feelings and traditions, and on the cruelty of its methods. In addition, Lyautey described Spanish actions in Morocco as a model of what a colonialist nation should not do, and he claimed to be convinced that the violence of the Rif movement was due more to Spain's incompetence than to Abd el-Krim's character. Undoubtedly, objective facts existed to spark off the disparaging judgements expressed by the French. The Spanish authorities generally admitted their faults, but they considered the French criticism, which appeared not to take into account the inferiority of the Spanish zone, terribly unfair. Now that the French were themselves suffering the crushing Rif attack that had led them to the brink of disaster, they were in a position to judge for themselves the true value of the unrewarding task carried out for years by the Spaniards in their zone. This was also the time to remind France that it should have cooperated with Spain in the matter of the pacification of Morocco instead of applying the famous 'benevolent neutrality' towards the population of the Rif, which had finally turned against it.

With the aim of developing a common strategy, a Franco-Spanish conference was held in Madrid in June–July 1925. This conference took place in the midst of many difficulties and disruptions that on more than one occasion nearly destroyed the joint effort. Obviously, Franco-Spanish collaboration was no bed of roses. Primo de Rivera was still not interested in armed cooperation with France. For months he did not even want to count on the French for the action at Alhucemas – the only military action he had projected – among other reasons because he was wary of the expansionist aims France might have in mind. Once it became clear that conducting the operation alone would be rash because of the tremendous increase in means and morale of the Rif as a result of their victories in the French zone, he insisted on limiting any military commitment to the French to the Alhucemas landing, which finally took place successfully at the beginning of September 1925. Although critics of the dictatorship considered it a miracle, the truth is that it had been carefully prepared, with the participation of well equipped troops, and achieved its objective of misleading Abd el-Krim about the exact site of the landing.

Throughout the rest of 1925, the dictator remained indecisive regarding an advance into the interior of the area, despite the insistence of Marshal Pétain – in charge of directing the operations – who had pinned all his hopes of ending the conflict in the Rif on a Spanish offensive into the heart of the territory. Pétain would end up persuading Primo de Rivera, who was compelled to modify his opinion on Moroccan policy not, as has been repeatedly asserted, because of pressure from Africanist military officials[31] but because of the aggressiveness of the tribes led by Abd el-Krim, who left him no option other than to continue the fight. Abd el-Krim's intransigence was revealed once more during the Uxda peace negotiations in 1926,[32] in spite of his weakness at that point. Taking into account that the Rif leader continued to be combative, it was only logical that Primo de Rivera, under pressure from Pétain, agreed to make a new military effort in the spring of 1926. Spontaneous, pragmatic, and opportunistic, the dictator was willing to consider the new developments and take advantage of the opportunity of the moment.

The joint military campaign fulfilled the objective it had been aiming for: in May 1926 Abd el-Krim surrendered and was exiled. In order to carry out the subsequent task of subjugation and disarmament of the tribes, which was accomplished surprisingly quickly, it was necessary to penetrate farther into the interior of the territory, reconquer positions, and return to the area that had been abandoned in 1924, all of which brought Primo de Rivera face to face with the fact that he had to remain in Morocco – which, in turn, meant a continuing huge deployment of men and money. Circumstances – the driving force of the dictator's actions in Morocco – had finally led him down the road to conquest, which was something that had not at all been forseen during the first years of his leadership. By 1930, 300 million pesetas were still being spent, nearly three times as much as the limit he had set himself. The war had ended, but his objective of putting an end to the drain on public funds caused by the protectorate had not been attained.

CONCLUSION

Although Primo de Rivera finally managed to resolve the oppressive Moroccan problem that Spain had had to bear for so long, it was not because he had any clear and well-defined notion of what action to take in Morocco or any original plan different from those of the governments that had preceded him. In fact, the policy that he developed in Morocco once he was in power was identical to the one followed by the previous liberal government, specifically by the reviled ex-Minister of State, Santiago Alba. It was a policy of limitation of the Spanish occupation of the area and of attempts at negotiation that were not and never could have been the solution to the problem. The opinion of the historians who have most seriously studied the Moroccan problem during these years is that the military solution was the only one that could keep Morocco from being such a nightmare. Neither semi-abandonment nor peace negotiations with the rebels could fulfil the aim of pacifying the Rif.[33] But Primo de Rivera took much longer than is usually assumed in admitting this. Despite the strong opposition from the Africanists, he was firm and perseverant in his search for a negotiated solution to the conflict and not a military one and minimizing the occupation of the Spanish zone in Morocco. Fortunately for him, a completely unexpected event took place during his dictatorship that was crucial for the resolution of the conflict: Abd el-Krim decided to attack France as well, and this led to a radical change in the traditional French policy of non-collaboration with the Spaniards. France, for the first time since the establishment of the protectorate, proposed a joining of forces with Spain in order to achieve the pacification of Morocco. Marshal Pétain developed a very precise Franco-Spanish military plan that would definitively crush the Rif rebellion, but of course entailed the Spanish conquest and occupation of the Rif. Primo de Rivera, despite being determined to reduce Spanish action in Morocco 'to a minimum effort and a minimum commitment and cost', could not squander the opportunity offered to him by the new circumstances.

Translated by Jessica Brown

NOTES

1. Spain claimed historical rights in Morocco based on its having possessed territories along the African coast of the Strait of Gibraltar for centuries. However, it managed to participate in the distribution of the sultanate mainly because, in accordance with the policy of balance and neutralization of forces designed by Britain, it served as a counterweight to France's expansionist aspirations.
2. In addition to the fundamental motive of international prestige that encouraged Spain's presence in Morocco, an effort was made to avoid at all costs being 'walled in' by France. Some historians claim that, had its neighbouring country not had such an imperialist attitude, Spain would never have seriously intervened in Morocco. See S. Payne, *Politics and the Military in Modern Spain* (Stanford, 1967).
3. See A. Bachoud, *Los españoles ante las campañas de Marruecos, 1909–1914* (Madrid, 1989).

4. Payne, *Politics and the Military in Modern Spain;* C. Seco Serrano, *Militarismo y civilismo en la España contemporánea* (Madrid, 1984); Carolyn P. Boyd, *Praetorian Politics in Liberal Spain* (Chapel Hill, NC, 1979); R. Nuñez Florencio, 'Ejército y política bajo la Restauración', *Bulletin d'Histoire Contemporaine de l'Espagne*, 6 (1992), pp.29–73; see also, idem, *Militarismo y antimilitarismo en España, 1808–1906* (Madrid, 1990); S. Sueiro Seoane, 'Política exterior y opinión militar durante el reinado de Alfonso XIII', in *Estudios dedicados al profesor Antonio Ma. Calero* (Córdoba, 1998).
5. On the Annual disaster see S.E. Fleming, 'Primo de Rivera and Abd el-Krim: The Struggle in Spanish Morocco, 1923–1927' (Ph.D. diss., University of Wisconsin, 1974). Payne, *Politics and the Military in Modern Spain*; D.S. Woolman, *Rebels in the Riff: Abd el-Krim and the Riff Rebelion* (Stanford, 1969). All these works are, in turn, based on contemporary chronicles such as F. Hernández Mir's *Del desastre a la victoria 1921–1926* (Madrid, 1926), F. Gómez Hidalgo's *Marruecos: La tragedia prevista* (Madrid, 1921), and, of course, the *Expediente Picasso* (Madrid, 1931). More recently, see M. Leguineche, *Annual: El desastre de España en el Rif* (Madrid, 1996).
6. The Abd el-Krim family had worked for the Spanish administration. As did other tribal leaders, Abd el-Krim el-Jatabi and his two sons believed that European help was essential to get Morocco out of its backward ways and on the road towards progress and modernization. This led them to collaborate with Spain, a decision that earned them much antipathy among the Rif tribes, which accused them of treason. Mohamed ben Abd el-Krim, the eldest son and future leader of the Rif, had been in Melilla, where he was a journalist for the Spanish newspaper *El Telegrama del Riff* and later held an important post in the Office of Indigenous Affairs, earning various decorations and promotions. The turning point in his relations with Spain came about during World War I. The fact that Turkey entered the war on the German side proved decisive; the family chose to support an Islamic country in the fight against France, the biggest colonial power in Morocco. But Abd el-Krim did not limit himself to fighting against France; he also declared that Spain should be satisfied with the territory it already occupied and not attempt any further advances. This was considered a defiance by the Spanish authorities, who decided to arrest him and send him to prison for a time. Deception and rancour towards Spain and a desire to return to his own people were probably the reasons that impelled Abd el-Krim to return to the Rif in 1919, after the end of the World War, and never to go back to Melilla. From that moment onward, his objective was to become the leader of a movement of colonial resistance that would be capable of overcoming the traditional tribal quarrels.

   For further information about Abd el-Krim, his cooperation with Spain, his activities during World War I and his decision to fight against the Spaniards, see Germain Ayache, *Les origines de la guerre du Rif* (Paris and Rabat, 1981). María Rosa de Madariaga, 'L'Espagne et le Rif: Penetration coloniale et resistances locales, 1909–1926' (Ph.D. diss., Université de Paris I, 1987); idem, 'Mohammed ben Abdelkrim el Jatabi and the Ambivalences of "progress"', *Fundamentos de antropología*, 4 and 5 (1996), pp.14–32; Henry Munson Jr., *Religion and Power in Morocco* (New Haven, 1993).

   For more information on the reforms introduced by Abd el-Krim in the political, social and economic organization of the Rif, see the collective works *Abd el-Krim et la République de Rif: Actes de Colloque International d'Etudes Historiques et Sociologiques, 18–20 janvier 1973* (Paris, 1976); C. Richard Pennell, *A Country with a Government and a Flag: The Riff War in Morocco, 1912–1926* (Wisbech, Cambridgeshire, 1986); David M. Hart, *The Aith Waryaghar of the Moroccan Rif: An Ethnography and History* (Tucson, 1976). Also of interest for learning about various aspects of the organization of the Rif Republic are the chronicles of Western adventurers and journalists who were travelling through the Rif during that period and contacted the Rif leader. See, for example, Vincent Sheean, *Adventures among the Riff* (London, 1926).
7. The first treaties vaguely referred to the 'special character' that the city and port of Tangier should maintain because it was the headquarters of the diplomatic corps. However, it was gradually made clear that it would be granted international status; see G.H. Stuart, *The International City of Tangier* (Stanford, 1955).
8. When in November 1912 the agreement establishing the Franco-Spanish protectorate of

Morocco was signed, this created a reality that was to condition Spain's presence in that country throughout the twentieth century: France had assured itself a dominant position with regard to both its relations with other European powers and its equally privileged relations with the sultan. As the sultan's protector and the guarantor of the empire's integrity, it exercised its influence over a 'sole and indivisible' Morocco and ceded the northern area of the territory to Spain so that the latter might administer it as a 'sublessee'. It was clear that the Spaniards found it difficult to accept this subordinate and dependent role that the French insisted on reminding them of whenever the occasion arose, while Spain, in turn, strove to defend the principles of the legal equality of both countries and the total autonomy of one from the other with regard to their respective areas of Morocco.

9. See Bachoud, *Los españoles ante las campañas de Marruecos,* p.43. Other historians who have studied this period share this opinion. J.U. Martínez Carreras assures us that the Spanish governments were pleased to be participating in international negotiations, to be making their presence felt in North and West Africa, and to be initiating a policy of rapprochement with France and, through it, with the Western allied system. See 'La política exterior española durante el reinado de Alfonso XIII: España y la revolución alemana', *Revista de la Universidad Complutense*, 116 (1980), p.320. Regarding the 1912 agreement, Albert Mousset, a famous French Hispanist of the time, wrote in a very popular work on Spain's foreign policy that, although the Spanish position turned out to be unfavourable, 'the disappointment created by the treaty could not have been so deep or so unanimous considering that there was much hope of an alliance with France as a result of its conclusion'. See *L'Espagne dans la politique mondiale* (Paris, 1923).
10. See the reports for 1923 made by Ambassador Defrance to Poincaré, the Minister of Foreign Affairs. ADMAE (Paris), Europe, 1918–29: Espagne.
11 Lyautey, the head of the French protectorate, installed and protected by the powerful colonial party, cherished the aim of doing away with Britain's insistence that Spain occupy the northern coast of Morocco in order to avoid French domination of the area. He and the French colonialists had long aspired to the incorporation of the whole of Morocco, as was clearly revealed during the peace conference that brought an end to World War I.
12. According to Lyautey and the French authorities, the Spaniards' greatest error had been to confer sovereignty on the caliph of Tetuán, as this had humiliated and betrayed the sultan. It is true that Spain, in its eagerness to free itself from the dependency on France derived from the dogma of the sultan's sovereignty over all of Morocco (an illusion since the sultan was completely in the hands of the French), had decided to increase the prestige of the figure of the caliph who, although the sultan's delegate, was considered sovereign in his area. However, it is also true that Lyautey considered this not only a grave error but also an unacceptable show of independence on the part of the Spaniards. France, which had attained a position of superiority in Morocco that it was unwilling to surrender, systematically refused to accept the Spanish thesis that each country had total freedom of action in its own area. On the contrary, it insisted on emphasizing the difference in legal status by assigning the name 'zone of influence' to the Spanish area and maintaining that of 'protectorate' for its own. See Ayache, *Les origines de la guerre du Rif,* pp.81–2.
13. On the question of gunrunning, see S. Sueiro Seoane, 'Contrabando en las costas del Rif: Armas europeas para Abd el-Krim', in *Actas del II Congreso Internacional 'El Estrecho de Gibraltar'*, Vol.5, *Historia contemporánea* (Madrid, 1995), pp.261–9. The presence of adventurers of various nationalities who helped the Rif has been proven, but there is no proof whatsoever that any government was involved in material aid for Abd el-Krim. Doubtless there was gunrunning, but its importance was much less than the Spaniards believed (or wanted to believe).
14. It must be pointed out that he had the advantage of a dictatorial regime that had no parliament or political parties but did have rigid censorship regarding Moroccan affairs that made it much easier to take inevitably unpopular measures.
15. Francisco Gómez-Jordana, *La tramoya de nuestra actuación en Marruecos* (Madrid, 1976).
16. See Ma. T. González Calbet, *La dictadura de Primo de Rivera: El Directorio Militar* (Madrid, 1987), pp.198 and 278; idem, 'La defensa del Estrecho y la "pacificación" del protectorado marroquí en la política del General Primo de Rivera', in *Actas del Congreso*

Internacional 'El Estrecho de Gibraltar' (Madrid, 1995), pp.296–7. C. Seco Serrano, 'Prologue', in Bachoud, *Los españoles ante las campañas de Marruecos*. Abd el-Krim himself declared in an interview in 1927 that, with his policy of withdrawal, Primo de Rivera had laid a trap for him that had finally sent him into exile (see *Abd el-Krim: Memoires recuillis par J.R. Mathieu* [Paris, 1927]); F.P. de Cambra, *Cuando Abd el-Krim quiso negociar con Franco* (Barcelona, 1981), p.42.

17. See S. Sueiro Seoane, *España en el Mediterráneo: Primo de Rivera y la 'cuestión marroquí', 1923–1930* (Madrid, 1993). It must be pointed out that the large amounts of correspondence from Gómez-Jordana to the then president of the Directorate are totally contradictory to the declarations he later made in his memoirs, written during the Second Republic and not published until much later, the obvious purpose of which was to deny Primo de Rivera's support for abandonment of Morocco.
18. His proposal of abandoning Morocco and exchanging Ceuta for Gibraltar had been the cause of his removal as Military Governor of Cadiz in 1917 and as Captain General of Madrid in 1921. See *Discurso leído ante la Real Academia Hispano-Americana el 25 de marzo de 1917* (Cadiz, 1917). In effect, his attitude, while not unique, was unusual within the armed forces. See J. Tusell, *Radiografía de un golpe de estado: El ascenso al poder del general Primo de Rivera* (Madrid, 1987).
19. Spain had, by then, 120,000 soldiers in Morocco.
20. Despite the large number of casualties due to the severe Rif harassment of the Spaniards during their retreat in the midst of a torrential downpour, the truth is that, had it not taken place, the disaster would have been of tragic proportions. See Fleming, *Primo de Rivera and Abd el-Krim,* pp.172–202.
21. After eliminating the leader of Djebala, Raisuli, in January 1925, Abd el-Krim had emerged as the sole and undisputed leader of northern Morocco and the possessor of large quantities of military supplies seized from the Spaniards during their retreat and from Raisuli when his palace at Tazarut stormed and he was captured. By skilful manipulation of propaganda, the Rif leader had by that time persuaded the other tribes that the Spaniards had already been defeated.
22. There is nothing to support the theory advanced by many writers that the decision to go to Alhucemas meant a drastic alteration of the anti-occupation policy followed until then or the adoption of the opposite policy of fighting the Rif rebellion until it was completely quelled. On the contrary, Primo de Rivera explicitly rejected any advance beyond the coast and claimed that he conceived the operation as the only way of becoming able to reduce the number of troops in Morocco, which was still the main objective of his Moroccan policy. See Sueiro Seoane, *España en el Mediterráneo,* pp.187–93.
23. For more information about the repeated efforts at negotiation with Abd el-Krim, see Sueiro Seoane, *España en el Mediterráneo,* pp.140–45, 193–5, 222–5, 241–7; idem, 'El mito del estratega: Primo de Rivera y la resolución del problema de Marruecos', *Cuadernos de Historia Contemporánea*, 16 (1994), pp.113–29.
24. See, Sueiro Seoane, *España en el Mediterráneo,* pp.146, 152–6, 192.
25. According to the theories of the Spanish political classes, the aggressive imperialism of the European powers (especially of France) vividly contrasted with the anti-imperialism exemplified by Spain, for which its modest Mediterranean aspirations represented not a spirit of conquest but a vital necessity. This anti-imperialism is a leitmotif of the official discourse. Without Tangier – it was claimed – Spain's presence in its own Moroccan area made no sense; Tangier was essential to the mission of pacification of the protectorate that the European powers had laid at its door. Primo de Rivera claimed that 'there is no precedent of any protectorate's being interfered with, as is Spanish Morocco, precisely at its most vital and important point: Tangier'.
26. During the war years, a Gibraltar–Ceuta Commission had been created in Britain to study the pros and cons of this long-discussed swap in detail. See C. Ibáñez de Ibero, *Política mediterránea de España, 1704–1951* (Madrid, 1952); G. Hills, *El peñón de la discordia: Historia de Gibraltar* (Madrid, 1974). Britain finally rejected the idea after much discussion. See G. Armangue-Rius, *Gibraltar y los españoles* (Madrid, 1964); B. Lowry, 'El

indefendible peñón: Inglaterra y la permuta de Gibraltar por Ceuta, 1917–1919', *Revista de Política Internacional*, 153 (1977); J.T. Arribas Martín, 'El Estrecho de Gibraltar, los archipiélagos españoles y los intereses británicos, 1898–1918', in *II Aula Canarias y el Noroeste de Africa* (Gran Canaria, 1988); Juan Carlos Pereira, 'La cuestión de Gibraltar: Cambios, ofensivas y proyectos de búsqueda de un acuerdo hispano-británico en el primer tercio del siglo XX', in Juan Bautista Vilar (ed.), *Las relaciones internacionales en la España contemporánea* (Murcia, 1989), pp.245–66.

During that same period, France also deliberated on the possibility of handing Tangier over to Spain in exchange for a large part of Spanish Morocco. See C.M. Andrew and A.S. Kanya-Forstner, 'The French Colonial Party and French Colonial War Aims, 1914–1918', *Historical Journal*, 4 (1974), pp.79–106. To date it has been impossible to confirm the rumours about Franco-Spanish negotiations in 1919, just after the war, to sell the Spanish zone to France for a thousand million francs. In any case, the Directorate bore Marshal Lyautey's tendency to expand French Morocco to the detriment of the Spanish area very much in mind.

27. France was unwilling to relinquish the principle of the sovereignty in Tangier of the sultan, who, as we know, was under its direct influence. The French theory was that there was a single Morocco and a single sovereign, the sultan – sovereign of the French zone, sovereign of the Spanish zone, in which he had merely delegated administrative authority to the caliph, and sovereign in Tangier, where he had delegated nothing at all.
28. Factors such as the promise made by the left-wing government established in Paris to follow a pacifist and purely defensive policy in Morocco that, moreover, the serious financial crisis made obligatory and Lyautey's own strategy, dictating the avoidance of any evidently hostile action towards Abd el-Krim, were enough to discourage French intervention in the Rif.
29. The Spanish leaders also repeatedly considered the possibility of denouncing the 1912 Franco-Spanish treaty and proposing the internationalization of the Spanish zone so that all the countries with interests in the area would assume part of the responsibility. See Javier Tusell, 'La solución al embrollo marroquí, 1923–1925', in *Historia de España Ramón Ménendez Pidal*, Vol.38, No.2 (Madrid, 1997), p.271.
30. Much has been written about the reasons Abd el-Krim took this dangerous step. Moroccan historiography insists on the idea that the Rif leader did not attack but 'counterattacked', that is, that he saw himself forced to respond to a previous French offensive that, in 1924, had occupied the fertile Uarga Valley, thus depriving the Rif population of the 'granary' from which it obtained its supplies. However, the importance of the spirit of exultation that had seized Abd el-Krim by that time should not be undersetimated. He felt surer than ever of his strength and, at the same time, was still convinced that Spain and France, whose history of rivalry in Morocco he was well aware of, would never manage to come to an agreement and act jointly.
31. The impression that is usually given of the dictatorship's Moroccan policy is that of an initial stage of abandonment sharply rectified by a radically conflicting stage of conquest dictated by the Africanist military, to whom Primo de Rivera was indebted for help during the coup. However, there is evidence that the pressure from the Africanists did not influence the dictator as much as is said and that he was determined to impose his criteria over any type of resistance, no matter how strong. It is also absurd to talk of a radical turnabout. In fact, Primo de Rivera never made any clear and definitive decision regarding the future of the Spanish zone.
32. For more information about the peace proposals put forward jointly by Spain and France to the Rif rebels, see Sueiro Seoane, *España en el Mediterráneo*. pp.313–22.
33. Should any government have opted for an out-and-out military policy, it is very probable that the Rif leader would have been defeated. In any case, war was the only real guarantee of pacification. This is the opinion of historians who share a theory defended at that time not only by the Africanist military but also by anyone who had firsthand knowledge of the Moroccan problem. For example, General Weyler was sent to Morocco by the last constitutional government in 1923 to prepare a withdrawal to safer lines and returned to the Peninsula convinced that the only way to stop Abd el-Krim's aggressive escalation was

military action. It is significant that he had the absolute support of the high commissioner, Luis Silvela, the first civilian to occupy this post in all the history of the protectorate, who had come to the same conclusion as his military predecessors ('la acción militar primero'). The journalists and correspondents in Morocco who were most familiar with the details of the Moroccan problem held the same opinion.

The Mediterranean in the Foreign Policy of the Second Spanish Republic

NURIA TABANERA GARCÍA

The principal reference points for the foreign policy of the Second Republic were the League of Nations and the Anglo-French axis. In both areas of policy making, the conditioning factor was Spain's position geographically and strategically and its interest in the security of the western Mediterranean. Its participation in the successive plans to draw up a Mediterranean pact and in the Mediterranean conflicts of the period was characterized by its role as a secondary figure within that axis and by its policy of adaptation as a neutral country to the crisis of the system of collective security.

Fortunately, it is no longer necessary to begin a work on the foreign policy of the Second Republic by referring to the historiographical vacuum which characterized this period until a few years ago, a vacuum due to ignorance of the foreign policies of the Republic and biased sources, both the result of the outbreak of the Civil War. Now that it has been demonstrated that the Second Republic actually did have a foreign policy,[1] it seems high time to dismantle the idea of failure with which some have imbued it. This is possible if we examine all the different areas of Republican policy making rather than just the ones which took precedence, such as the League of Nations or the European powers, and if we are careful to avoid overgeneralization and take into account the various phases of the process.[2]

It is not the intention here to consider these matters in any great detail, but an analysis of the Mediterranean policy of the Republic may help to reconstruct the complex image of the Spanish foreign policy of the period, a foreign policy which had been envisaged from the outset as an integral part of the new regime's plan to make major changes on the domestic front. As Manuel Azaña often said,[3] while the Republic would undertake to defend the legacies and stances which had been handed down over the years due to Spain's geographic position or history, its foreign policy would be based upon the values of democracy and pacifism in accordance with the principles of the League of Nations.

The League was the main focus of the Republic's activities abroad, as it represented a peaceful and democratic conception of international relations and best guaranteed the security of a lesser power such as Spain.[4] This desire for multilateral relations did not affect Spain's traditional role as a supporter of the Anglo-French axis, which was fundamental, among many other things, to the achievement of one of the vital objectives of Spanish foreign policy: maintaining the *status quo* in the Mediterranean. This objective, along with the desire to foster good relations with Portugal and Latin America, could be traced back to the monarchy. After the Disaster of 1898 and the subsequent loss of its last colonies, Spain became a lesser Euro-African power and centred the whole of its foreign policy, always with the same interests in mind, on relations with the other Mediterranean powers: Morocco, Tangier, and the Strait of Gibraltar. It was in the western Mediterranean that its foreign and defence policies and the international aspect of its colonial policy converged.[5] The bases for these policies were established through a series of agreements and treaties signed between 1900 and 1912, creating a situation in which France assumed the role of a hegemonic power in North Africa while Britain was assured of the control of Gibraltar, the status of 'international city' for Tangier and the absence of a powerful country on the southern coast of the strait.[6]

THE REPUBLIC'S ORIGINAL STANCE

The change of regime in Spain on 14 April 1931 was received with surprise and caution by the two aforementioned European powers, although feeling ran deeper in Britain than in France. The recognition of the Republic by both was essential for the new regime not only to gain international legitimacy but also to guarantee control of its territories. As J.F. Pertierra points out, the security of the Spanish nation depended solely upon guarantees originally enforced by Britain via the 1904 agreements over Morocco between France and Spain and France and Britain and the Cartagena agreements of 1907.[7]

Once again, Spain's strategic importance within the Mediterranean led to the recognition of the Spanish Republic by Mussolini's Italy, reflecting the Italians' belief that a Spanish republic would more easily fall under French influence and thus endanger Italian interests in the Mediterranean. In the words of the Italian Foreign Minister, Dino Grandi: 'For Italy the Spanish Republic means losing a war in the Mediterranean without a fight. It may mean that France continues to retain its empire in Africa.What will London say? The new situation in Spain may alter the balance of the Mediterranean to our detriment and to that of England. Today, even more than before, it is in Rome and London's interests to collaborate with each other.'[8]

Just as they had responded to other fears in the international arena due to developments in Spain,[9] the provisional government quickly set about dispelling some of these doubts. The speed with which it quelled once and for all the violent demonstrations of Moroccan nationalists in Tetuán (which in fact began on 14 April itself) proved to a sector of British and French public opinion that the change in regime had not brought with it any new weakness or sign of Spain's wishing to renounce the responsibilities it had taken on in Morocco.[10]

Alejandro Lerroux, the Republic's first Foreign Minister, on his inaugural appearance as Spain's representative at the 63rd regular meeting of the Council of the League of Nations held in mid-May, also played a tranquillizing role. Lerroux's first visit to Geneva was characterized by a sense of haste and improvisation, partly dispelled by the incalculable aid of the Spanish diplomat Julio López Oliván.[11] During his speech to the Council, Lerroux stated that Morocco must necessarily play a part in Spain's future, because rather than a colony it was a bridge between Europe and Africa. With this statement he confirmed that the Republic would continue the monarchy's policy in the Mediterranean.[12]

Through these early declarations, the Republican leaders confirmed something that was obvious: that the new regime depended on maintaining the *status quo* in the western Mediterranean as much as its predecessor. Likewise, Spain's role in the Mediterranean, with its protectorate in Morocco and position as joint governor of Tangier, involved the fulfilment of previously acquired international obligations, and, in the words of Manuel Azaña, the objective of these obligations was not to satisfy any expansionist whim or ambition on the part of Spain but to 'prevent others from being there [in Morocco] in order to maintain stability'.[13]

For this reason the bilateral and multilateral relations which the Republic maintained with the leading European nations were also conditioned by interests in security and defence relating to its role in the Mediterranean. The close links between this area of Spanish foreign policy making and Spain's activities at the League of Nations will become apparent. While, on the one hand, the former affected the perception and evaluation of mechanisms regulating the nations' collective security – guaranteeing national interests – these same mechanisms also influenced the Republic's concept of security and stability in the western Mediterrenean.[14] At a time when regional agreements on stability proliferated, the Republic's diplomats were always receptive to and, on one occasion, at the forefront of a possible new Mediterranean pact. It was a recurrent subject of conversation because of the changes in regional stability caused by Italian revisionism.

The first test of tension in the Mediterranean that the Republic had to face occurred in July 1931, when statements by the Socialist Minister Indalecio Prieto in Bilbao gave rise to the possibility of ceding control of the Spanish protectorate in Morocco to the League of Nations. The opposition of Britain to an increase in the French presence in Morocco and of France, which feared British and Italian reactions, and the expectant attitude of the Italians forced the Republic's leaders to respond firmly.[15] The Spanish refusal to consider abandoning Morocco was the result of political consensus among the members of the coalition government. Its leaders, with Azaña at their head, were aware of the need to maintain a Spanish presence in Morocco for reasons of national security and consistency with the international role Spain aimed to play.

Azaña said as much to the Cortes in March 1932 when he linked the idea of a Spanish presence in Morocco not only with the fulfilment of international agreements but also with Spain's civilizing role and its aim of implementing the same policy of modern reforms there as on the mainland:[16]

> Our role in Morocco, while fulfilling a series of international obligations that it is not in our interests to abandon, is to 'civilize' the country, showing our European partners that we are loyally and efficiently carrying out our obligations as a leading nation, showing the Spanish a small area where we are expanding our territory commercially, industrially, and showing the Arabs and the natives that Spain can still civilize those under its guidance and protection.

It should not be forgotten that the proposal of the then President and Minister of War to lend a 'civilizing' role to Spain's intervention in Morocco was not completely new.[17] What was new, however, was the implementation of an extensive plan to reduce and rationalize military spending in order to demilitarize the colonial image of the protectorate, and this was done by making the military hierarchy subordinate to a civilian High Commissioner in addition to reducing the bureaucracy of an inefficient, obsolete administrative body.

The changes made as part of Azaña's army reforms, especially during the first two-year period, affected the military presence in the protectorate. The reforms of June 1931 and May 1932 reduced the number of troops and officers posted in Morocco, resulting in savings in the budget, and called for those posted there from the mainland to be volunteers. The opposition of officers posted in Africa to the measures adopted by the Republic is well known, as is the participation of many of them in the various military uprisings which the Republic had to deal with. It is for this reason that some writers repeatedly point to the connection between the 'civilizing' reforms imposed by the Republic in Morocco and latent disloyalty towards the Republic on the part of influential members of the army in Africa, such as José Sanjurjo and Gonzalo Queipo de Llano.[18]

At the same time as it was implementing these reforms in the protectorate, the Republican government was trying – at that point with little success – to deal with some of the disputes that it maintained with France in the Spanish zone. The disputes were over the continuing presence of French troops in *cabilas* (local tribal groups) located in territory governed by Spain and the suppression of Moroccan nationalism, following the hard-line policy that France imposed in its zone, where nationalist feeling was much greater.[19] In spite of all this, it was not the colonial administration of the protectorate which dominated bilateral relations between France and Spain in the Mediterranean but the possibility that all the powers involved might sign a new Mediterranean pact.

In fact, from 1930 onward several proposals of this nature were made. The first draft pact, drawn up during the period prior to the Naval Conference in London, was part of an effort to regulate French security after Locarno, aimed at controlling the increasing Italian political and naval presence in the western Mediterranean and in North Africa.[20] British unwillingness to assume new commitments on stability at the time prevented the agreement (in which Spain was not initially involved other than as a secondary nation) from going any farther.

THE REPUBLIC AND THE MEDITERRANEAN PACT

As 1931 came to a close and preparations were being made for the disarmament conference in Paris and London, the improvement in relations between France and Spain (which Italy had predicted with the advent of the Second Republic) had not produced any great results. On the contrary, Azaña and government minister Luis de Zulueta often complained how cold the French were, and this was taken as proof of French mistrust of Spain's new autonomy at the League of Nations.[21]

At that point, fearing that once again the conference would fail to guarantee the nations' collective security, Paris took new interest in Spain, and the latter's view of international politics and relations with France began to change. F. Quintana[22] sees greater pragmatism in Spanish diplomacy, with the defence of national interests predominating over the principles of republican fraternity. France now considered it appropriate to improve relations with Spain in order to strengthen its own troubled diplomatic relations in Europe, weakened by rifts with Britain, competition with Italy, and the gradual rise of the Nazis in Germany. The *rapprochement* between France and Spain also suited the Spanish government as a means of improving its position within Europe and resolving commercial problems with its main trading partner. In the spring of 1932, Luis de Zulueta and the French Ambassador to Madrid, Jean Herbette, openly discussed the possibility of collaboration either through an agreement on the Mediterranean which would guarantee the *status quo* or through Spain's clear support of the French stance at the disarmament conference. Both the proposed treaty guaranteeing mutual aid and the alternative non-aggression pact (drawn up by the staff of the French navy in December 1931) confirm that for France the disarmament conference and its hopes of a Mediterranean pact were closely linked. London even considered the hypothetical discussion of the terms of a pact at the conference, displaying its traditional reluctance to accept new commitments.[23] Spanish diplomats also made cautious approaches in search of the information needed to prepare a suitable response in the event of the subject's being discussed during the conference.

The evolution of the conference was disheartening for the French, despite its attempt to attract the intermediate powers to which Spain belonged to the Group of Eight. The French proposal, known as the Plan Constructif, was presented just two days before the arrival of President Edouard Herriot in Madrid on 31 October 1932, the sign of the new *rapprochement* between the French and the Spanish. Initially the visit aroused suspicion among the public and in some European political circles, especially in Italy, where it was feared that it meant secret agreements on the possible movement of French colonial troops across Spanish soil in the event of war. In reality it seems that, in spite of the confusion created many years later by Salvador de Madariaga, at no point did either of the parties involved mention this eventuality.[24]

However, in discussing the positive results of the improvement in relations between France and Spain we should mention Zulueta's open support of the Plan Constructif in Geneva in February 1933. This support had several sources: the plan combined security with disarmament, democratized decisions made by the Council of the League of Nations, and contemplated the drawing up of regional agreements as a way of guaranteeing peace in the Mediterranean.

Spain applauded the French initiative of the 'Mediterranean Locarno' as a means of reducing tensions between France and Italy and removing the danger of war from an area vital to its national security, although it was not very well protected despite the show of force in the Balearic Islands. The Foreign Office was unwilling to take on new commitments, arguing that the agreements of 1907 were still in force, alongside the pact of the League of Nations or Covenant, and (correctly) that Italy would oppose any kind of regional agreement regulating the area. Indeed, Italy considered that an agreement made at that time would favour France because of its excellent relations with Spain.[25]

The Plan Constructif failed because of the steadfast opposition of Italy and Germany, the cooling off of relations with Britain, and its tepid reception by the promoter's own allies. With its abandonment, the regional agreements also contemplated lost importance. Nevertheless, Spanish diplomats in Geneva continued to promote new attempts to strengthen security measures already in force in the Mediterranean basin, measures that were increasingly challenged by the Italian and German revisionists.

The importance of this particular objective for the Republic's foreign policy became clear in the summer of 1933, when the Socialist Fernando de los Ríos became Foreign Minister. During those months a series of factors converged that led, in the opinion of Ismael Saz, among others,[26] to the emergence of what ought to be considered an authentic foreign policy, displaying the requisite innovation, coherence, adaptability, independence, and preparation. Wide-ranging plans to reorganize and modernize the administration of the ministry were decided upon, in line with Zulueta's earlier ideas. Political and cultural plans of action were drawn up for Latin America (the other traditional area of interest for Spain's foreign policy), and a new Mediterranean pact was promoted.

The Spanish initiative came about as a result of its fear (shared by other lesser European powers) of the Italian proposal that the four major powers draw up an agreement outside the framework of the League of Nations to put an end to tensions in Europe. The Four-Power Pact (Italy, Britain, France, and Germany) was agreed upon in June 1933 but was never ratified. The terms of the agreement were so timorous and so unclear as regards the original Italian proposals that it was impossible to implement. Nevertheless, it was an important gesture showing an improvement in relations between France and Italy.[27]

Because of the upheaval in Europe during the months prior to the signing of the Four-Power Pact, Spanish diplomats chose to modify their approach, gradually distancing themselves from French proposals and falling more and more in line with London and Rome. In fact, the signing of the Four-Power Pact was good for Spanish security in the long run, as it eased tensions among the leading powers in the Mediterranean and for Spain the ideal was to keep conflicts as far away from this area as possible.

Conversations took place with Italy to improve relations with the aim of renewing the friendship and conciliation treaty in force since 1926. The two countries even came to contemplate the possibility of a Mediterranean non-aggression pact.[28] At the same time, Spanish fears regarding the effect of German revisionism on security in the Mediterranean and the weakening of Anglo-French relations (made clear at the disarmament conference) spurred Fernando de los Ríos to action. His strategy was to try to get the democracies in Geneva to agree upon an *entente* and a new Mediterranean agreement to maintain the *status quo* involving Spain, France, Britain, and Italy in line with articles 10 and 16 of the Covenant.

Manuel Azaña's farsightedness and his in-depth knowledge of international affairs again became apparent when Fernando de los Ríos informed the cabinet of his plan on 18 August. In his diary Azaña mentions the meeting and anticipates the problems that negotiators would have to overcome: [29]

> Fernando spoke to us of a huge fantasy that he has dreamt up, I don't know on whose suggestion. He wants to be at the forefront of diplomatic negotiations to draw up a 'Mediterranean Pact'. We have authorized him to sound things out in official circles in London; Fernando told us that the French ambassador is in favour of the idea. What about the Italians, though? Rather tricky ... Fernando has built up his hopes on carrying out this *glorious* project, but it seems to me that before this little marvel is actually set up, we will have been carried away by events.

In fact, French reactions to the idea were positive, consistent with their desire to come to some kind of agreement given Germany's increasing strength, although contacts never went beyond timid approval by Ambassador Herbette and by Paul Boncour.[30] The fall of Azaña's government interrrupted negotiations in London before anything more than a few comments could be made in Rome regarding the possibility of converting the non-aggression pact which Spain was trying to expand into another four-power pact.

As Quintana indicates, the initiative was abandoned partly because the powers involved considered it better not to complicate things with new projects, given the delicacy of conversations on disarmament. However, in spite of its failure, the Spanish initiative was still important. First, it confirmed that, despite internal conflicts, the Republic had developed a definite foreign policy with firm objectives. It was characterized, at the very least, by a certain sense of initiative and foresight and took advantage of the opportunities offered by the traditional subordination of Spanish foreign policy to the Anglo-French axis. Secondly, it showed the increasing importance of the Mediterranean in Spanish foreign policy for reasons of national security, and action was taken to strengthen security when the destabilizing force of Germany reached its peak.[31]

The governments of the second biennial period put a stop to some of the previous attempts to modernize the Spanish administration, and as a result foreign policy lost some of its prestige and freedom of action. This was not only because of the increasing conflict in Europe but also because the Foreign Ministry decided to deal with certain matters by freezing them.[32] From the autumn of 1933 onward, Spanish diplomacy, like that of lesser powers, was once again characterized by its neutrality in the face of the enormous cracks which were appearing in the nations' collective security.[33]

From then on, the Spanish stance as regards the Mediterranean would be influenced by French measures (led by Louis Barthou) to isolate Germany through a series of agreements regulating regional security in Europe and by an improvement in relations between France and Italy as an attempt to overcome their rivalry in the western Mediterranean.[34] The change in direction of these nations and their relative lack of concern regarding affairs in the western Mediterranean and in Spain explain the abandonment of all previous plans to draw up a Mediterranean pact and Spain's secondary role during the conversations that took place throughout 1934 outside the framework of the League of Nations.

OPPORTUNISM OR REVISIONISM?

The priority of the eastern Mediterranean in French affairs from this time on seems evident from the evolution of the new conception of a Mediterranean pact suggested by Barthou in June 1934 to complement the 'Eastern Locarno' that they hoped to achieve. It is understandable that the latter occupied second place in order of importance for French diplomacy, since the non-aggression pact between Germany and Poland of January 1934 had made dialogue with the Soviet Union a priority. Although the eastern pact never came to fruition, the *rapprochement* with the Soviet Union paved the way for the Franco-Soviet pact of May 1935.

The French proposal for a Mediterrranean pact in the summer of 1934 took the form for Spanish diplomacy of a trial balloon from the Quai d'Orsay.[35] In Spain, those responsible for the country's foreign policy were aware that many earlier obstacles could still block the project. Both the British refusal to assume new commitments and Italian lack of interest in a French initiative seemed to indicate that the objective of the French was to improve relations with Italy, distancing itself from Germany and paving the way for the approval of closer relations with the Soviet Union, rather than to conclude a multilateral agreement on the Mediterranean.[36]

As Neila points out, during the summer months of 1934 the Spanish Home Office proceeded as it usually had when the question of the Mediterranean pact was raised: information was sought, and the leading nations were asked to confirm that Spain would not be excluded from the conversations.[37] It is important, however, that at that point the attentions of the sectors of Spanish diplomacy concerned with Mediterranean affairs began to focus upon something far more specific than the Mediterranean pact: Tangier. The subject of Tangier's status as an international city came to the forefront once again when in the spring of 1934 the Tangier

Association pointed to the necessity of revising the statute regulating Tangier's status in response to the escalation of tensions in Europe.[38]

A few days before, in April 1934, the French army had concluded the unification of its part of Morocco and Spanish troops had occupied Ifni, putting an end to the former border dispute between France and Spain in West Africa.[39] This intervention, which caused joy in Spanish colonial circles supporting the Confederación Española de Derechas Autónomas (CEDA) and Alejandro Lerroux's government, should not be seen as a means of reaffirming Spain's role as a colonial power. Instead, it was really the result of French pressure to force the Spanish to bring peace to Morocco once and for all. Peace was essential, because of the risk of war in Europe, to reduce the number of troops in Africa and facilitate their removal to France while, at the same time, implementing the former French imperial plan to connect Morocco and Algeria to Mauretania and the French colonies of West Africa.[40]

This reference to the occupation of Ifni illustrates the atmosphere at that moment, characterized not so much by colonialist demands as by French political affairs, among which the question of Tangier would come under study once again. During the first biennial period Spain's limited capacity to act in North Africa beyond the stipulations of its agreement with France were obvious and were reconfirmed throughout 1934, when the French managed to block conversations on Tangier for a time.

As the deadline (November 1935) for proposing possible modification or renewal of the 1923 Tangier Statute approached, taking advantage of the convergence of various factors, the Spanish Foreign Minister suddenly became intensely active. According to J.L. Neila, this was the result of a policy of moderate revisionism regarding the Strait and Morocco.[41] Reports drawn up by the commission appointed by the Spanish cabinet in August 1934 to study the question of Tangier spoke of the need to avoid open confrontation with France and to assert any claims with prudence and moderation. In government circles, radical proposals such as that of the Falange that Tangier never be given up were rejected, although appeals were made for Spain to make the most of the situation with a view to improving its position within the local government and police force in Tangier.[42]

A further change in relations between the Mediterranean powers caused upheaval in Spanish diplomatic circles and concern on the part of the Spanish public. The Laval–Mussolini agreements of January 1935 revived fears that the eastern Mediterranean had been discussed without Spanish knowledge. A few days after the agreement was made, the Foreign Minister, Juan José Rocha, told the Cortes that the government had guarantees from Paris that these subjects had not been on the agenda of the agreement between France and Italy. However, the Spanish right-wing press clearly linked the government's wish to take part in any agreement affecting the Mediterranean with the approaching deadline for the renewal of the Tangier Statute. As the question of Tangier became every day more important, the scene seemed to be set for Spain to increase its control over the city. In fact, together with the proof of the *rapprochement* between Italy and France in January, the conclusion of the Stresa alliance between Italy, France, and Britain demonstrated a climate of goodwill among the nations with interests in the Mediterranean which could only be to Spain's benefit.

The lessening of tensions between the French and the British and recognition by both nations of the increasing importance of the role of the Italians coincided with the desires of the coalition government, composed of Lerroux's Radicals with a clear preferance for London, and the anti-French CEDA.[43] As a result of the new European alliances and the inclinations of the Spanish government, during the first half of 1935 Spain's relations with Britain and Italy improved, raising the clear possibility of coming to an agreement over Tangier. This was because the Spanish aim to modify some points of the statute coincided with British discontent with regard to its implementation (demonstrated in the spring of 1935 when proposals were made).[44]

Spain was able to defend its position to the French with relative assurance because France needed Spain's consent to modify customs procedures in Morocco and Spain was threatening to denounce the Tangier Statute. By skilfully using these two manoeuvres, although it did not actually wish to carry out the threats, Spain hoped to achieve a diplomatic success in Tangier.[45]

It did not necessarily want the statute revised. Instead it wanted some of its articles modified to allow religious jurisdiction to remain in Spanish hands and, among other things, to increase the proportion of native delegates appointed to the legislative assembly by the Spanish consul. This was to be achieved via a policy that was 'sympathetic to the other powers'.[46]

Spanish diplomacy was characterized by this conciliatory, moderate attitude both before and after achieving the support of the British in order to begin bilateral negotiations with France. This spirit of conciliation, totally contrary to the idea of putting all of Spain's cards on the table and then having to exert pressure, increased in intensity once the conflict in Ethiopia commenced. After a long, tense period of preparation, the invasion of Ethiopia in October by Italian troops put an end to the former atmosphere of goodwill and made large-scale warfare in the Mediterranean a possibility again.

For the Spanish government, the ending of good relations between London and Paris over Ethiopia and the British refusal to recognize any change in the *status quo* in the Mediterranean in favour of Italy brought prewar tensions dangerously near their safety zone. As Gil Pecharromán indicates, this possibility – albeit distant – led to dual action on the part of the Republic's diplomats, who reaffirmed their wish to remain neutral within the Mediterranean, while supporting (although with certain limitations) the League of Nations's policy of imposing sanctions.[47]

The first approach (characterized by a clear intention on the part of the Spanish to avoid any situation which might increase tensions) would affect conversations on Tangier, blocked because French diplomats had given priority to resolving the Ethiopian conflict. Coping with French delaying tactics while seeking British approval, the Foreign Ministry proposed that certain minimum objectives be considered essential: religious jurisdiction, a joint head of customs, and a Spanish administrator.[48]

Eventually, simply by exchanging notes, on 13 November an agreement between France and Spain was drawn up by which France agreed to support the Spanish candidate for the position of Administrator while increasing to two the number of representatives to the legislative assembly appointed by the Spanish Consul. The post of joint Spanish Head of Customs was to be created, and Spain was assured of having religious jurisdiction in the international zone in the person of the Moroccan apostolic vicar.[49]

As negotiations on Tangier progressed, Spanish diplomats in Geneva tried to combine their theoretical commitment to the League's principles with their anxiety to ensure the nation's security in the hypothetical event of the Ethiopian conflict's becoming a threat to Spanish neutrality. Spain's government ministers agreed on the need to defend the nation's neutrality and distance it from the centre of any conflict, although they were also divided by the crisis with the Radicals supporting the British and members of the CEDA supporting the Italians.[50] The Spanish government and its diplomats were under intense pressure from London to support its call for sanctions against the Italians. In October London combined these tactics with its ability to influence Paris with regard to an agreement on Tangier that would suit the Spanish.[51]

Spanish unwillingness to take a firm stand regarding the conflict, even once sanctions against Italy had been approved in Geneva and applied very gently by Spain, did not cause too many problems for the other countries involved in the conflict. In fact, when, in the first days of December, the British Foreign Office unofficially sounded out the Spanish Foreign Ministry regarding a possible agreement to supply mutual aid in the event of a conflict between the Italians and the British which might affect the Balearic Islands, the British understood that they should not push the rather reluctant Spanish too far for an answer, given Spain's delicate internal affairs.[52]

When Spain finally gave an answer at the end of January, it was in Geneva, and it was characterized by the usual ambiguity and pragmatism resulting from the desire to remain equidistant from the Italians, the British, and the French and to keep its interests in the Mediterranean in line with its commitments at the League of Nations. The lack of change in this aspect of Spanish foreign policy after the victory of the Frente Popular demonstrates the influence of geopolitical factors on that policy. Both Azaña and government minister Augusto Barcia were convinced that their objective should be to remove tensions from the Mediterranean, and both supported the agreement among France, Britain, and Italy against Germany without considering that it might be dangerous for Spain if Italy increased its strength in the Mediterranean basin.[53] Regardless of the ideological preferences of the members of the Frente Popular, in the months preceding the Civil War, as the system of collective security gradually broke down, the leaders responsible for Spain's foreign policy decided to preserve their neutrality and gradually adapt to the increasingly warlike European climate.

Spain reacted to the remilitarization of the Rhineland with caution, once again somewhere between London's conciliatory role and Paris's call for sanctions of Hitler's manoeuvres. In Geneva, Minister Barcia expressed Spain's condemnation but opposed the application of sanctions.[54] This opposition to sanctions was consistent with its stance in Geneva when a possible end to sanctions against Italy was proposed. At that time, Spain's priority was to avoid an increase in Anglo-Italian tensions in the Mediterranean, which could be complicated by an escalation of tensions between France and Germany in central Europe. On 13 July, less than a week before General Franco's uprising, the Assembly of the League of Nations lifted the sanctions imposed upon Italy as a result of a proposal by Britain. Thus the Spanish wish for better Anglo-French relations – with Italy as partner – seemed to have been granted.

The conflict in Ethiopia was ended without Spanish intervention, in spite of the concern among the public and in government circles that the conflict might spread to the western Mediterranean. Spain's secondary role became clear once again when new proposals for a Mediterranean pact were discussed by Paris and London in the early months of 1936 in an effort to distance Italy from Germany in the midst of the Rhineland conflict.[55]

Just as in times of severe crisis with the Ethiopian conflict, the pact's possible promoters did not consider Spanish participation important, perhaps because Britain gave priority to the eastern Mediterranean or because of Spain's defence limitations.

All of this is simply confirmation that, within the framework of events in the Mediterranean (an area of fundamental importance for Spanish foreign policy because of its implications for national security), Spain's stance was conditioned by legacies inherited by one regime and passed on to the next with their associated international commitments, links with the

Anglo-French axis, and its economic situation and position with regard to defence. This stance was very much characterized by the need to maintain the *status quo*. The evolution of the international situation in the Mediterranean, an inseparable part of the increasing failure of the nations' collective security, was greatly responsible for pushing Spain progressively towards neutrality and away from war.

NOTES

1. A long list of sources could be given, but I will only mention, as examples, M.A. Egido, *La concepción de la política exterior española durante la 2e República* (Madrid, 1987); F. Quintana, *España en Europa, 1931–1936: Del compromiso por la paz a la huida de la guerra* (Madrid, 1993); N. Tabanera, *Ilusiones y desencuentros: La acción diplomática republicana en Hispanoamerica (1931–1936)* (Madrid, 1996); and I. Saz, 'The Second Republic in the International Arena', in P. Preston and S. Balfour (eds.), *Spain and the Great Powers* (London, n.d.).
2. I. Saz and N. Tabanera, 'La República en entredicho. A propósito del reformismo republicano en la politica exterior española', in J. Tusell *et al.* (eds.), *La política exterior de España en el s. XX* (Madrid, 1997), p.104.
3. M. Azaña, 'Discurso en el campo de Comillas (20-X-1935)', in *Obras completas*, Vol.3 (Mexico City, 1966), p.277.
4. Quintana, *España en Europa,* p.24.
5. J.L. Neila Hernández, 'España, república mediterránea: Seguridad colectiva y defensa nacional (1931–1936)' (Ph. D. diss. Madrid, 1993), p.73.
6. V. García Franco, 'El Norte de Africa y la política exterior de España (1900–1927)', *Proserpina*, 1 (1984), pp.85–6; S. Sueiro, *España en el Mediterráneo. Primo de Rivera y la 'cuestión marroquí'* (Madrid, 1993), p.7.
7. J.F. Pertierra, *Las relaciones hispano-británicas durante la Segunda República española (1931–1936)* (Madrid, 1984), p.7.
8. Cf. I. Saz, *Mussolini contra la Segunda República: Hostilidad, conspiraciones, intervención* (Valencia, 1986), pp.32–3.
9. See J.W. Cortada, *Two Nations over Time: Spain and United States, 1776–1977* (Westport, CT, and London, 1978), p.176; D. Little, *Malevolent Neutrality* (London, 1985), pp.66–7 for examples of the fear of political radicalization and the ascent of communism that initially conditioned North America's attitude to the Republic.
10. M. Martín, *El colonialismo español en Marruecos* (Madrid, 1973), pp.105–7.
11. A. Lerroux, *La pequeña historia de España* (Barcelona, 1985), p.77.
12. J.L. Neila Hernández, 'Las responsabilidades internacionales de la II República en Marruecos: El problema del abandonismo', *Estudios Africanos*, 5, 8–9 (1990), pp.49–50.
13. M. Azaña, 'Discurso en el Ayuntamiento de Valencia' (21-I-1937), in *Obras completas*, p.334.
14. Neila, *España: República mediterránea*, p.76.
15. Neila, 'Las reponsabilidades', pp.57–69; Saz, *Mussolini*, pp.36–7; F. Paez-Camino, 'La significación de Francia en el contexto internacional de la Segunda República española (1931–1936)' (Ph.D. diss. Madrid, 1990), pp.506–7.
16. M. Azaña, 'Marruecos: Orientación de la política del Gobierno en la Zona del Protectorado', *Obras completas*, 2, (1966), p.238.
17. V. Morales Lezcano, 'El protectorado español en Marruecos bajo la IIe República (Las reformas administrativas)', *Actas de las Jornadas de cultura árabe e Islámica* (Madrid, 1981), p.463.
18. V. Morales Lezcano, *España y el Norte de Africa: El protectorado en Marruecos (1912–1956)* (Madrid, 1986), pp.120–22; Páez-Camino, 'La significación de Francia', p.508.

19. Martín, *El colonialismo español*, pp.118–24; Egido, *La concepción de la política*, pp.161–5.
20. P. Brundu Olla, *L'equilibrio difficile: Gran Bretagna, Italia e Francia nel Mediterraneo (1930–1937)* (Milan, 1980), pp.3–7.
21. Páez-Camino, 'La significacion de Francia', p.657.
22. Quintana, *España en Europa*, p.130.
23. Neila, *España: República mediterránea*, pp.441–4.
24. I. Saz, 'La política exterior de la II República en el Primer Bienio (1931–1933): una valoración', *Revista de Estudios Internacionales*, 4 (1985), pp.849–54; Quintana, *España en Europa*, pp.133–43.
25. Neila, *España: República mediterránea*, p.503.
26. Saz, 'La política exterior', p.858.
27. C. Zorgbibe, *Historia de la relaciones internacionales.* Vol.1, *De la Europa de Bismarck hasta el final de la Segunda Guerra Mundial* (Madrid, 1997), p.543; J.B. Duroselle, *Politique etrangere de la France, 1871–1969*: *La decadence, 1932–1939* (Paris, 1979), p.74; A. Adamthwaite, *Grandeur and Misery. France's Bid for Power in Europe 1914–1940* (London, 1995), p.194.
28. Saz, *Mussolini contra la II República,* p.44.
29. M. Azaña, 'Diarios, 1932–1933', in *Los cuadernos robados* (Barcelona, 1997), p.417.
30. Páez-Camino, 'La significacion de Francia', pp.841–2.
31. Quintana, *España en Europa*, p.174; Saz, 'La política exterior', p.858.
32. Saz and Tabanera, 'La república en entredicho', p.109.
33. Saz, 'The Second Republic in the International Arena'.
34. Brundu, *L'equilibrio difficile*, p.50.
35. Cf. Neila, *España: República mediterránea*, p.809.
36. Brundu, *L'equilibrio difficile*, pp.53–5; Duroselle, *La decadence, 1932–1939*, p.112.
37. Neila, *España: República mediterránea,* p.809.
38. J.L. Neila, 'Revisionismo y reajustes en el Mediterráneo: Tanger en las expectativas de la II República española (1924–1936)', *Hispania*, 52, 181 (1992), p.661.
39. F. Quintana, 'La ocupación de Ifni (1934): Acotaciones a un capítulo de la política africanista de la Segunda República', in *II Aula Canarias y el N.O. de Africa* (Las Palmas, 1986), pp.95–124.
40. Egido, *La concepción*, p.276; Quintana, 'La ocupación de Ifni', p.124.
41. Neila, 'Revisionismo y reajustes', p.663; J.L. Neila,'Marruecos, piedra angular del revisionismo moderado de la II Republica, 1935–1936', *Portugal, España y Africa en los ultimos cien años,* IV Jornadas de Estudios Luso-Españoles (Mérida, 1992), p.200.
42. M.A. Egido, 'Las reivindicaciones españolas sobre Tánger durante la II República: Cuestiones políticas y debate ideológico', in *Actas. Congreso Internacional el Estrecho de Gibraltar* (Madrid, 1988), p.487.
43. Saz, 'The Second Republic'.
44. Pertierra, *Las relaciones hispano-británicas*, p.27.
45. Páez-Camino, 'La significación de Francia', pp.990–91.
46. Neila, 'Revisionismo y reajustes', p.675.
47. J. Gil Pecharroman, 'España y el estrecho en la crisis de Abisinia', in *Actas. Congreso Internacional el Estrecho de Gibraltar* (Madrid, 1988), pp.494–5.
48. Neila, 'Revisionismo y reajustes', p.683.
49. J.M. de Areilza and F. Castiella, *Reivindicaciones de España* (Madrid, 1941), pp.483–4.
50. I. Saz, 'Acerca de la política exterior de la 2 República: La opinión pública y los gobiernos españoles ante la guerra de Etiopia', *Itálica*, 17 (1982), p.275; Quintana, *España en Europa*, p.271.
51. Quintana, *España en Europa*, p.289.
52. Neila, *España: República mediterránea*, pp.1059–68.
53. Saz, 'Acerca de la política exterior', p.282.
54. Quintana, *España en Europa*, p.326.
55. Neila, *España: República mediterránea*, p.1182.

Spanish Morocco and the Second Republic: Consistency in Colonial Policy?

SHANNON E. FLEMING

This article discusses the evolution of the Second Republic's colonial policies in Spanish Morocco from April 1931 to July 1936. It traces these through the administrations of three high commissioners: Luciano López Ferrer, Juan Moles Ormello, and Manuel Rico Avello. It argues that despite the frequency of administrative and personnel changes in the protectorate during this period, the Second Republic's colonial policies remained fairly consistent. These included a commitment to the colonial ethos, the installation of a civil in place of a military administration, the introduction of administrative efficiencies and cost-cutting measures, especially the reduction of military personnel and expenditures, the funding of concrete developmental programs and public works, and on going efforts to seal the protectorate off from the political and social issues that prevailed in the Peninsula.

Given the difficulties that Spain experienced in establishing its Moroccan protectorate, it is not surprising that the period from its official pacification in July 1927 to the proclamation of the Second Republic in April 1931 witnessed a number of significant efforts to implement a strict law and order regime and to ease concerns that the protectorate would continue to be a major drain on Peninsular human and material resources. The most important of these efforts was the disarming and monitoring of the rural tribes. In the aftermath of Abd el-Krim's surrender to the French in 1926 and the suppression of the remaining pockets of indigenous resistance in 1927, the Spanish army either captured or recaptured a considerable store of heavy artillery, machine-guns, and ammunition. Further, as it occupied tribal areas, it systematically disarmed a heavily armed rural society, confiscating, by June 1930, some 66,269 rifles.[1]

At the same time, a system of combined military and administrative control, modelled on the French colonial system, was implemented for both rural and urban areas. Under the authority of the Delegation for Indigenous Affairs, which reported to the Spanish High Commissioner in Tetuán, the *interventores* were primarily Spanish military officers organized into a hierarchical team that supervised and controlled the local population through contingents of 'native' police and an indigenous counterpart, the tribal *caid* and the urban *pasha*. In particular, the *caids* were paid officials who had broad discretionary powers over the tribes. Generally distrusted by their countrymen, they were hand-picked by the army for their loyalty to Spain, their ability to provide administrative management and control, which included the replacement of Berber custom with Koranic law and, where applicable, Spanish law, and the competence to gather useful intelligence on their fellow Moroccans.[2]

Of secondary importance was the 'civilizing and modernizing' mission implicit in the protectorate concept. After 1927, with pacification an accomplished fact, the Spanish were seriously confronted with this aspect of their mandate. The primary problem for a southern European country as poor as Spain was finding the resources to support such an effort.[3] Even during the comparatively prosperous latter years of the dictatorship, Primo de Rivera himself repeatedly called for the reduction of protectorate expenditures and indeed accomplished this to some degree in 1927 and 1928, mostly through military cutbacks. At the same time, while budget outlays for public works, education, and other socioeconomic programs were increased, they still constituted a small part of the entire protectorate budget. In 1928, for instance, only ten per cent of expenditure went to these areas, while military spending still accounted for 70 per cent of the total.[4] In addition, the public works plans that were credited for 54 million pesetas in May 1925 and 80 million pesetas in May 1928 defined specific projects such as railroad and road construction that chiefly supported military and security needs.[5]

SANJURJO AND LÓPEZ FERRER, APRIL 1931–JANUARY 1933

For the approximately 566,000 indigenous Moroccans, the protectorate regime combined aspects of a mild police state and very limited state paternalism, the former being more apparent than the latter. From the Spanish perspective the protectorate entailed an administrative apparatus whose primary purpose was order and control and only secondarily the 'civilizing and modernizing' of an essentially rural and agricultural population. It was the maintenance of order that faced the most serious challenge when the Second Republic replaced the monarchy. On 14 April 1931, Spanish Republican enthusiasts organized a demonstration in Tetuán, the protectorate's capital, against the incumbent monarchist administration. When this got out of hand, the khalifian guards were called out and in the ensuing mêlée fired on the crowd, killing two and wounding 12. Despite the efforts of the delegate for indigenous affairs, Colonel Osvaldo Capaz, to control the situation, the demonstration continued, and the High Commissioner, General Francisco Gómez-Jordana, with the help of the local Republican leadership, judged it prudent to abandon his post. On 15 April 1931 he fled to Ceuta and then on to Spain.[6]

Despite their years of opposition to colonial involvement, many members of the new republic's provisional government found it impractical to consider abandoning the protectorate given the foreign and domestic pressures to maintain what Manuel Azaña would later describe as 'a very complicated and difficult' mandate. Consequently, the government moved with haste to reconfirm Spain's commitment to the protectorate and to reestablish order in the zone, fearing that the Tetuán disturbances would spread to the indigenous populations of other cities and, more dangerously, to the countryside. Francisco Ramírez Montesinos, the High Commissioner's General Secretary, was named acting High Commissioner, and military reserves were moved from Ceuta into the protectorate. Of even more significance, on 22 April 1931 the government appointed General José Sanjurjo, the former High Commissioner who had overseen the conclusion of the Rif war and the pacification efforts of 1927, as both High Commissioner and chief of the protectorate's military forces. The message this selection sent was one that Alejandro Lerroux, the Republic's Minister of Foreign Affairs, reemphasized to a general European audience on 26 April 1931 when he bluntly told the press: 'We will not abandon Morocco.'[7] Sanjurjo was basically given *carte blanche* to restore order in the protectorate. Faced with a series of mixed European and indigenous strikes and mob actions supporting various socioeconomic and political demands, Sanjurjo imposed martial law, and, on 4 May 1931, undertook the military occupation of Tetuán.[8] 'Morocco is not Spain', Sanjurjo remarked in justification of his actions. 'We cannot have, like Spain, the spectacle of political battles ... our policy should be: authority and justice on the part of the protector, submission and order on the part of the protected.'[9]

Sanjurjo's forceful measures had the intended impact, calming the zone and giving the provisional government time to plan and institute what they publicly characterized as a cost-conscious 'civil regime' whose primary objectives were law and order and public works. The first step in this process was the appointment on 5 June 1931 of Luciano López Ferrer as High Commissioner. The first civilian to hold this post since Luis Silvela in 1923, López Ferrer was a career diplomat serving as Spanish Consul in Gibraltar, and had a long history of service in the protectorate, having been Spanish Consul in Tetuán prior to and during its occupation in 1913 and for a number of years in the 1920s the General Secretary, or second in command, to the High Commissioner. In addition to these Africanist credentials, the new High Commissioner, according to Indalecio Prieto, was also a partisan of Lerroux's Partido Radical. In short, López Ferrer seemed to personify the felicitous combination of seasoned civil colonial bureaucrat and committed Republican. Not as apparent were his less positive attributes, which included problematic working relationships with peers and subordinates, a lack of partisan savvy, and a tendency to talk too much to the press. At the same time, the provisional government appointed General Miguel Cabanellas Ferrer supreme commander of the protectorate's military forces. From the Republican perspective, this too was a fortuitous choice, as Cabanellas had Africanist credentials dating back to the 1909 campaign and at the same time a history of opposition to the Primo de Rivera dictatorship and support for the Republic.

Even before this team was in place, Niceto Alcalá Zamora's provisional government initiated a number of significant policy changes in Ceuta and Melilla and the protectorate which confirmed the Republic's desire to give its North African possessions civil rather than military administrations. On 21 May 1931, the Republic replaced Ceuta's and Melilla's centrally appointed *juntas municipales* with popularly elected city governments. This was followed on 16 June 1931 by a fundamental decree which separated the authorities and functions of the High Commissioner and the supreme commander of the protectorate's military forces. In so doing, it gave preeminence to civil leadership, specifying that 'the supreme commander of all land forces will be exercised by an army general under the authority of the high commissioner'.[10] This was the second time in the protectorate's history that this had been done, the other being the short-lived attempt in 1923 to subordinate military to civilian authority. The third significant change was an 18 June 1931 decree which reorganized the *Dirección General de Marruecos y Colonias,* the central colonial bureaucracy established by Primo de Rivera, putting it under the direct authority of the President of the Council of Ministers and reconstituting it into seven sections that dealt with specific administrative areas (that is, intervention, finance, public works, and so on).[11] Simultaneously, in early June 1931, Manual Azaña, the provisional government's Minister of War, undertook the reorganization of the Army of Africa, simplifying its command structure and reducing staffing in most of its units. This would ultimately save 27 million pesetas in the coming year and decrease total on-duty staffing by over 20 per cent from 57,285 men in 1930 to 44,423 men in 1932.[12]

In keeping with the Republican pledge to civilianize the protectorate, these initial measures were only preliminary to the major restructuring plan implemented by the Azaña ministry on 29 December 1931. This decree elaborated the responsibilities of the High Commissioner, who was charged with two essential duties: the maintenance of order in the protectorate and the 'provision of assistance' to the Makhzan or khalif's government. Further, the supervisory nature of the High Commissioner's relationship with the chief of the protectorate's military forces was spelled out in more detail. All general organizational issues, military operations, and other contingencies would be handled through the High Commissioner, while appointments and other personnel issues would continue to be the Ministry of War's responsibilities. The decree also reconstituted the High Commissioner's immediate staff, reconfirming the Secretary General position and denoting four other broad administrative areas: Indigenous Affairs, Development, Finance and Budget, and the Intervention and Khalifian Forces. The decree's most significant provision, however, was the creation of six 'civil and military regions' for the purpose of intervention designation. In so doing, it established a civilian cadre of *interventores* who reported directly to the Delegation for Indigenous Affairs and were charged with improving 'the moral and material condition' of the tribes located in the pacified areas proximate to Ceuta, Melilla, and Tetuán. On the basis of data published in 1932, this civilian corps of *interventores* was responsible for indigenous populations in some 39 per cent of the protectorate's territory or about 38 per cent of its total indigenous population. Military *interventores* administered the remaining tribal territories, which were concentrated in the Jbalan highlands, the Ghmara, and the Central Rif. While these latter individuals remained in the military chain of command, they also worked administratively through the Inspector of Intervention and Khalifian Forces, which ultimately gave the High Commissioner control over their activities and those of their indigenous counterparts.[13]

These changes were intended, as López Ferrer pointed out, to 'inculcate ... the ideas of the new government' into the protectorate's administrative infrastructure while ensuring that 'undesirable elements' and ideas were kept from infiltrating a non-European society.[14] What is notable about the Second Republic's initial protectorate policies, despite the civilian emphasis, however, was how similar they were to those of the dictatorship and the interregnum governments of 1930–31. The unquestioning colonial commitment, the concern for internal control and order, the emphasis on administrative economies and military staff reductions, and the pledge to fund necessary public works and other initiatives were all policies that had been firmly in place since 1927. Moreover, the presence of civilian *interventores* was hardly a new concept, and even those individuals who were initially selected for civil positions were mainly ex-military officers who had experienced a period of protectorate service.

Another notable commonality that Republican administrators had with previous regimes was their suspicious attitude towards an indigenous nationalism which had started to develop in Morocco's cities in the late

1920s. Moroccan nationalist efforts on 6 June 1931 to present Alcalá Zamora with a series of 'just and equitable reforms' for the protectorate's indigenous population proved futile. In fact, the Republicans' attitude towards the Moroccan nationalists, which one would have expected to be fairly sympathetic given their progressive credentials, proved quite the opposite.[15] They were regarded as a potential political threat. During one press conference, López Ferrer referred to them contemptuously as 'a score of young madcaps' whom the urban police had entirely under control. Moreover, while López Ferrer stated that his indigenous policy was one 'of order, of *rapprochement*, and above all of assuagement', the emphasis was clearly on order. By 1932, for instance, all Moroccan males 14 years and older were required to have and carry photo identification papers, and protectorate authorities did the best they could to ensure that the strikes and demonstrations that seemed endemic to the Peninsula and Ceuta and Melilla during this period did not infect the protectorate.[16]

At the same time, the Republic's indigenous policy was in many ways more pragmatic than that of the French. Despite some enthusiasm in the late 1920s for a 'Berber policy', the Spanish never instituted the controversial *Berber Dahir* in their protectorate, and their attitude towards nationalist activities in general and the distribution of pan-Arabist literature and even some Moroccan nationalist publications was much less restrictive than that of the French. In the countryside, where most of the protectorate's population lived, Spanish *interventores* developed, if not cordial, at least respectful relationships with the tribes which ensured a certain level of tranquillity and cooperation, as protectorate officials frequently pointed out to the press.[17]

This is not to say that events outside Spanish Morocco did not have a critical impact on conditions and attitudes there. The worldwide depression certainly had negative consequences for the protectorate's economy, and the military reductions adversely affected those local merchants and businessmen who had come to rely on army contracts and business. Unemployment or underemployment became a notable social issue in the cities. For Europeans alone, the estimated unemployment rate in Tetuan in 1932 probably approached 15 per cent.[18] According to the British Consul in Tetuán, this stimulated a notable exodus of Spanish nationals either to the French zone or back to Spain and gave new impetus to the seasonal Rif migrations to find work on French Algerian farms and vineyards.[19] The protectorate's chronic trade imbalances showed an even more conspicuous disparity between 1930 and 1933. Exports dropped from 30.6 million pesetas in 1930 to 18.3 million pesetas in 1931 and 11 million pesetas in 1933. Hardest hit were iron ore exports, which fell from 50 per cent of the protectorate's total exports in 1931 to only 18 per cent in 1932.[20] The contraction of this market in particular had an immediate impact on the economies of Melilla and the cities of the eastern protectorate. In July 1931, layoffs led to the first strike in the history of the protectorate's largest iron ore company, the Minas del Rif, and forced the protectorate authorities to work with the government, the unions, and the company to arbitrate a settlement.[21] At the same time, the value of the official protectorate currency, the peseta hassaní, continued to fall against the Spanish peseta, dropping by 15 per cent between 1930 and 1934.[22] In short, the British Consul probably summarized it best when he wrote in July 1931 that 'economic conditions have during the past year taken a turn for the worst. It is clear that the general situation cannot be viewed with optimism'.[23]

Indeed, by early 1932 the protectorate did seem adrift. The economy showed few signs of improvement. Most public works projects, with the exception of major road construction, which was deemed essential to the protectorate's security, had been put on hold as a result of an August 1931 government investigation into fiscal irregularities in this area.[24] The army's Africanist elements and the monarchist right were becoming increasingly critical of the Republic's civilianization of the protectorate, particularly as it applied to the *interventor* corps. Elements of the Republican left criticized what they felt was a colonial bureaucracy rife with waste and corruption and questioned whether López Ferrer, who had served as a career bureaucrat under the monarchy, was the right man to lead the protectorate towards a more enlightened and Republican future. López Ferrer himself was proving problematic. His relationship with General Cabanellas, for instance, had turned personally contentious and led to the latter's reassignment and replacement by General Augustín Gómez Morato in February 1932. Further, López Ferrer managed to displease indigenous elites by appointing a number of non-Tetuanis to important positions in the protectorate's indigenous bureaucracy.[25]

It was in this context, during a 29 March 1932 Cortes debate, that Manuel Azaña defended his ministry's protectorate policies against criticism that the zone was in disarray and that millions of pesetas were being wasted on a 'quaint' and 'comic' colonial administration. While acknowledging past and current difficulties and a 'mismanaged' bureaucracy, Azaña felt that, given the situation the Republic had inherited in April 1931, it would take time to 'put things in order'. In this process, he indicated that his government had complete confidence in the López Ferrer administration. He then defined three fundamental policies that his ministry supported in the protectorate. These included the continued implementation of a civilian 'structure and organization' to sustain the zone's civilian orientation, the reduction of protectorate expenses by cutting 'unnecessary services' and overstaffed bureaucracies and the further reduction of the Army of Africa and its eventual replacement by an all-volunteer force.[26]

While the Azaña government refused to consider the extensive restructuring that the Socialists called for both in the Cortes and during their October 1932 party congress, the measures that it did put in place followed the dictates of Azaña's March policy statement.[27] López Ferrer's administration moved forward to fill the civilian *interventor* positions that represented the cornerstone of the civil protectorate. The overall protectorate budget of 1932 was reduced by 40 million pesetas (from that of 1930), representing a decrease of non-military administrative expenditures by 20 per cent between 1930 and 1933 and of military expenditures by 32 per cent during the same period. Military reductions also continued, with total Army of Africa staffing falling below 44,000 by the end of 1932. Further, Azaña's plan to create an all-volunteer force was approved by the Cortes in July 1932. It offered single Spanish males between the ages of 18 and 40 monetary incentives, early retirement opportunities, and colonization assistance to volunteer for service in Morocco.[28]

By mid-1932, the Republican agenda of civilianization, restrictive budgets, military reductions, and a strict law and order regime had basically been put in place. It would be difficult not to see consistency in policy implementation in Morocco in 1931 and 1932, but this was not the perception of informed opinion. The Madrid press, particularly that of the moderate left, judged the protectorate to be mired in a general 'malaise', with a 'defective' bureaucracy and a 'failure' of leadership. This judgement was hardly altered by the assassination of Colonel Juan Mateo, the legion commander, in March 1932, and the violent worker demonstrations in Ceuta in April 1932. However, the most troubling event was the so-called Bab Taza incident of December 1932, which for the Spanish brought back the traumatic memories of Anwal 11 years earlier. It involved the mutiny of a detachment of indigenous *regulares* against their Spanish officers at the Ghmaran army encampment of Bab Taza. While the origins of this abortive plot were never completely established, López Ferrer proved clearly out of step with the government, which saw it as a monarchist conspiracy, when he blamed 'communist propaganda and Arab nationalism'.[29]

In fact, for the Azaña Ministry, López Ferrer's continued incumbency was an obvious political liability. At the same time he had antagonized the Africanist military with his strong support of civilianization, collided with the left in his efforts to seal off the protectorate from Peninsular social issues, and annoyed indigenous elites with what they considered inappropriate appointments. In Spain, the campaign against him, particularly from the political left, moved inexorably ahead. *El Sol* accused him of getting rid of protectorate personnel because they were either leftists or Freemasons, of tolerating the circulation of monarchist newspapers and other subversive, reactionary journals, and even of supporting Sanjurjo's

August 1932 conspiracy against the Republic. On a more personal level, he was charged with using his office for personal profit, of too freely expressing his conservative viewpoints, and of displaying a contentiousness that brooked no opposition from either peers or subordinates.[30] 'As a weak man', Azaña later pointed out in his memoirs, 'he had explosions of authoritarianism.'[31] The controversy surrounding the Bab Taza incident was apparently the last straw for the Azaña government. On 20 January 1933, López Ferrer was replaced by Juan Moles Ormella, the civil Governor of Barcelona and a man whom the Prime Minister described as 'able and quiet'. In turn, the former High Commissioner was sent off to a less controversial post as Ambassador to Cuba.[32]

MOLES, JANUARY 1933–JANUARY 1934

A lawyer and a member of the Esquerra Republicana de Catalunya with a long history of involvement in both Barcelona city politics and national affairs, the 61 year old Moles had served in the Cortes as a deputy and later senator from the province of Lérida during the late Restoration period. Since January 1932, as Barcelona's civil Governor, he had done a creditable job of keeping that city's complex and volatile political and social situation under control. The Moles profile was that of a low-key, practical, and effective political insider who, unlike López Ferrer, had no Moroccan experience but, as one commentator noted, looked at Moroccan affairs 'from a spirit free of preconceived prejudices'.[33] An important adjunct to the Moles appointment was the selection of Manuel de la Plaza Navarro as his Secretary General. A highly respected legal expert on protectorate jurisprudence and Muslim law, de la Plaza had been President of the Tetuán Audiencia or Court of Appeals, the protectorate's highest court. Despite later Francoist critique, at the time many in the protectorate felt that in Moles and de la Plaza they had the perfect combination at the top: a savvy national political insider complemented by a savvy protectorate insider.

Moles's initial press interview proved short both on content and substance, which is precisely what the Azaña ministry preferred after López Ferrer's public relations *faux pas*. He frankly stated that he had no background in Moroccan affairs and indicated that his policies would be the continued 'republicanization' of the zone, the establishment of 'excellence and good order' in protectorate services, and the implementation of 'public works according to a concrete plan'.[34] His first order of business was an extensive trip around the zone. He paid perfunctory visits to the significant public works projects in progress and to the army encampments. However, as a politician he focused special attention on business organizations, community groups, and agricultural cooperatives. He lent a particularly sympathetic ear to the small groups of Spanish agriculturalist *colóns* in the central and eastern Rif. They petitioned him to augment agricultural credits and services, to speed up public works projects such as the damming and canalization of the Muluya River, to expand the protection of the zone's agricultural products, and to pressurize the Army of Africa into purchasing protectorate agricultural products rather than those from outside the zone.[35]

Although Moles informed the editor of the Melillan daily, *El Telegrama del Rif*, on 24 April 1933 that he would be presenting the government with 'a project of reforms and plans to follow in the future', much of what his administration accomplished in its remaining ten months had an *ad hoc,* unplanned character about it.[36] Upon his return to Tetuán, for instance, he initiated a number of activities that responded to the requests made of him during his trip around the protectorate. These included the establishment of three additional agricultural stations, the implementation of a policy that required the Army of Africa to give preference to the purchase of local agricultural products, and a 19 June 1933 announcement concerning the availability of 400,000 pesetas in agricultural credits (at five per cent interest) for individual *colóns* and agricultural cooperatives and federations.[37]

Nonetheless, Moles's insider credentials did indeed prove of practical value. In August 1933 he persuaded the government to annul the 1928 public works plan, which had proved somewhat structured and restrictive. This action gave him the flexibility to apply the plan's remaining credits not only to railway and road construction but to a variety of other public works and economic projects. In late September he presented the new Lerroux ministry with a list of seven proposed projects including a major sanitarium at Llano Amarillo, a permanent exhibition hall in Tetuán, an indigenous penitentiary, eight new dispensaries, various reforestation projects, additional indigenous schools, and a study of potential protectorate industries. At the same time, his administration moved ahead with the construction of the 360-mile Ceuta–Melilla road, which promised to facilitate the efficient movement of security forces into potential trouble spots, thus providing the rationale for further army reductions. This important project was finally completed in October 1933 and inaugurated by Alcalá Zamora on 2 November 1933.[38]

In the administrative area, 1933 proved less eventful than the previous two years. The Republic's basic political initiatives – at least those of the centre/left Azaña ministry of 1931–33 – had been put in place, and it was Moles's job to sustain and expand the direction that had been initiated by López Ferrer. The political issues that Moles encountered in 1933 were therefore much more basic. In September 1933 he told the press that his primary preoccupation was the maintenance of 'the best possible harmony' among the protectorate's three ethnic groups: Muslims, Jews, and Spanish Christians. This was proving difficult, since many of the High Commissioner's recent economic, and social initiatives clearly favoured the Spanish minority (about six per cent of the protectorate's approximately 600,000 inhabitants) over the Muslim majority. At the same time, the protectorate's Jewish community, which constituted about two per cent of the population, also seemed the beneficiary of Republican support and largesse, particularly in the areas of educational subsidies and government contracts. The reaction to such conditions, coupled with a wave of Peninsular social unrest, produced what *L'Afrique française* described as a 'veritable epidemic' of strikes and protests, including a number of anti-Jewish incidents, in the protectorate's cities. The reaction of the Moles administration was not unlike that of its predecessors. The indigenous police quickly responded to such situations, and on one occasion Moles cancelled a speaking engagement by three Socialist deputies at the Centro Cultural Obrero de Tetuán, fearing that it would create a public disturbance. The Foreign Ministry archives for this period contain lists of publications that were now prohibited in the protectorate, including the Communist and anarchist press, far-right publications, and some Moroccan and Arab nationalist newspapers such as *El Pueblo* and *al Falastin*.[39]

As a result of the national elections of November 1933, which ensured a right-centre majority in the Cortes, Moles's incumbency proved precarious. While both the Lerroux and Martínez Barrio ministries left Moles in office for continuity's sake and in order to focus on more pressing domestic issues, Moles basically found himself unable to initiate anything new in the protectorate. Budget allocations for the last quarter of the year were drastically cut, forcing the administration into deficit spending and curtailing the projects that Moles had submitted to the government in September 1933. Moreover, an anti-Moles *camarilla* led by Plácido Alvarez Buylla, a former Tangier Consul General and the Director of the Dirección General de Marruecos y Colonias, persuaded the government to implement a 5 November 1933 decree which expanded the Prime Minister's appointment authority in the protectorate – thus denigrating that of the High Commissioner's – and removed the Tangier Consul General from the High Commissioner's direct control. Frustrated by the budget *impasse* and the political machinations, Moles submitted his resignation at the end of December 1933, with an official departure date of 23 January 1934 to give the government time to name a replacement. In a parting partisan shot at the Lerroux ministry, Moles noted in an *El Sol* interview on 27 January 1934 that 'Republicanization' in the protectorate context had now become synonymous with the placement of political cronies in administrative positions. An article in the colonialist periodical *Africa* made an equally telling observation about Moles' departure, noting that 'when a high functionary has no other reason to be in a position but his political situation, then it is natural that his permanence in that position should be subject to political fluctuations'.[40]

RICO AVELLO, JANUARY 1934–JANUARY 1936

Moles's replacement was indeed another 'high functionary', the 47-year-old Asturian lawyer and right-centre independent Manuel Rico Avello. In 1931 Rico Avello had been associated with José Ortega y Gasset's Agrupación al Servicio de la República movement and had subsequently served as Subsecretary of the Navy in the provisional government. By 1933 he had aligned himself with Lerroux's Partido Radical and in late 1933 was given the Interior portfolio in the Martínez Barrio cabinet. His tenancy as Interior Minister proved quite traumatic because of the development of anarchist insurrections in many parts of Spain in December 1933. Accordingly, it has been suggested that he was pressurized into accepting the protectorate's high commissionership as a means of removing him from a post in which his performance had been judged less than satisfactory.[41]

To furnish a degree of continuity with the previous regime, the competent Secretary General, de la Plaza, and the chief of the protectorate's military forces, Gómez Morato, were left in place, and the experienced Capaz was brought back as delegate for indigenous affairs. Rico Avello himself sent a message of continuity by consulting with Juan Moles before journeying to Morocco to assume his new post. Moreover, Rico Avello's initial press pronouncements gave no indication that either he or the government planned any notable break with policies that had been instituted over the past two and a half years. He stated that his 'principal directions' would be in three areas: the promotion of 'indigenous confidence' through a 'policy of justice and plain dealing'; the continuance of prior public works initiatives especially in the areas of communications, public health, and education; and the encouragement of Spanish colonization by ameliorating two conditions that previous administrations had frequently defined as barriers, 'a good definition of property' and agricultural credits. His statements concerning three other key issues – the civil-military governor dichotomy, military staffing, and Moroccan nationalism – were moderate and balanced. Concerning the latter issue, he actually sounded more liberal than his predecessors, indicating that some of the Moroccan nationalists' demands were reasonable and noting that, compared with those of the French protectorate, who seemed to be in constant 'opposition and protest', the nationalists of Spanish Morocco appeared to be 'channelled to service'.[42]

One of the first issues that the Rico Avello administration faced had very little to do with protectorate policy or administration, but involved one of the last instances of Spanish imperial expansion: the occupation of Ifni, a small enclave of 2,000 square kilometres and some 20,000 inhabitants on Morocco's south Atlantic coast. It is a historical curiosity that the Second Republic should have been the agent for fulfilling one of the articles of the 1860 Spanish–Moroccan peace treaty, which obliged Morocco to cede an Atlantic fishing station to Spain. However, acquiescing to pressures from the French to collaborate in the definitive pacification of Morocco and from elements in the Spanish army and the political right to pursue a more activist policy in North Africa, the Lerroux Ministry sanctioned Capaz's 6 April 1934 occupation of Ifni. In the ensuing Cortes debate, Lerroux argued that Ifni served Spanish interests not only as a fishing station but as a refuelling stop for air travel between Spain and its Saharan possessions and as a safe harbour for the Spanish navy's defence of the Canary Islands. The opposition parties pointed out that the occupation cost eight lives and some four million pesetas and, more significant, that it added even more costs to a protectorate budget that the Republic had supposedly vowed to reduce. One Communist deputy even went so far as to compare its occupation to the recent Japanese invasion of Manchuria, implying that it was a threat to international peace.[43]

Rico Avello's second priority, after the seemingly requisite tour of the protectorate, was the development and submission in May 1934 of a public works plan. It covered six primary initiatives, a few of which dovetailed with Moles's plan of the previous summer. These included the expansion of agricultural extension services, a variety of water projects (for example, irrigation canals and harbour improvements), road construction, a panoply of civil construction projects (for example, public buildings, markets, and sewers), the construction of nine significant urban schools and a variety of small rural schools, and an anti-malaria campaign. The eventual implementation of these projects was aided by the adoption of a slightly increased budget in June 1934, by the employment of the remaining credits from the 1928 public works allocation, and by surpluses from the Makhzan budget. This healthier administrative picture was complemented by relative improvements in the economy. By 1935 general revenues had increased by 20 per cent (over those of 1933), allowing direct Spanish subsidies to be reduced to less than half of the total budget as opposed to about two-thirds in 1930–31. Further, the peseta value of the protectorate's exports, while still less than half the value of its imports, had more than doubled over that of 1932–33. More significant were the savings realized from further military reductions. While such eminent military Africanists as Francisco Franco and Manuel Goded publicly excoriated this policy as short-sighted and dangerous, Lerroux's Minister of War, Diego Hidalgo, continued to reduce Army of Africa staffing to 37,481 men in 1934 and cut military spending in Morocco from 144.5 million pesetas in 1933 to 114 million in 1934.[44]

Significantly, the political changes implemented by the Samper and Lerroux ministries in 1934 and 1935 seemed both to validate the civilianization of the Azaña years and smooth over the military–civil dichotomy issue and enhance the authorities and prerogatives of the High Commissioner and his immediate staff. On 26 June 1934, for instance, a decree fused the civil and military *interventores* into one corps and centralized them under the Delegation of Indigenous Affairs. The following month, the Samper ministry completely eliminated the Dirección General de Marruecos y Colonias, which it judged more of a hindrance than a support to efficient administration and policy making, and replaced it with the smaller Secretaría Técnica de Marruecos, which reported directly to the Prime Minister and ultimately allowed the High Commissioner more discretionary authority. This was complemented by a second decree which again brought Ceuta and Melilla under the High Commissioner's civil governorship. A third decree in August 1934 centralized the Ifni and the Spanish Sahara administration under the authority of the High Commissioner. However, the capstone of these changes was the 15 February 1935 decree reorganizing the protectorate's administrative structure without really challenging any of the underlying civil assumptions of prior Republican legislation. The protectorate was divided into five geographical regions – Oriental, Rif, Ghmara, Occidental, and Jbala – to replace the six administrative areas that since December 1931 had been based on disproportionately sized civil and military regions. Further, the High Commissioner's immediate staff was reorganized into five administrative departments: a Secretariat General, a Delegation of Budget, a Delegation of Public Works, a Controller of Marine Services, and a Delegation of Indigenous Affairs and Inspection of Mehallas and Khalifian Guards. The latter unified all indigenous services under one authority and reflected, as did the protectorate's new regional structure, an effort to deemphasize the civil–military dichotomy within the *interventor* ranks. At the same time, it kept the preeminence of civil authority intact.[45]

In a February 1935 commentary assessing the preceding year, the editors of the colonialist journal *Africa* highlighted what they felt were a number of 'beneficial activities' undertaken by the Rico Avello administration. These included the recent administrative reorganizations, the redirection of Makhzan rents into useful services for the indigenous population, the establishment of additional urban services, the payment of pensions to the widows of indigenous policemen killed in service, and the timely approval and distribution of municipal and local budgets. They might also have added the work that the authorities had initiated to sort out the tangle of property titles, the sponsorship of the first protectorate trade and design fair in Tetuán in September 1934, and the outreach to the Moroccan nationalists, which resulted in the addition of one of its leaders, Abdel Khalaq Torres, to the Makhzan as Director of *habus* (Muslim religious and charitable organizations) in November 1934. Furthermore, the dahir of 18 July 1935 defining the protectorate's educational structure and curricula and the 29 September 1935 decree reforming and reorganizing its customs services provided fundamental starting points for all future efforts in these areas. In short, despite budget constraints and ongoing political and social turmoil in the Peninsula, which periodically spilled over into Ceuta and Melilla, if not the protectorate, Rico Avello's administration demonstrated, admittedly in a colonial context, solid political, economic, and social achievements. Further, notwithstanding the administrative changes and the renewed emphasis on law and order that first Francisco Franco and later Emilio Mola emphasized as commanders of the protectorate's military forces in 1935, the hegemony of civil authority was never questioned.[46]

Ironically, it was the continued political and social turbulence in Spain that negatively affected the perception that the protectorate was a thoroughly civil and 'republicanized' entity. Specifically, the use of indigenous *regulares* and legionnaires to suppress the insurrections in Asturias in October 1934 generated particularly negative impressions, this being the first time that indigenous troops had been aggressively deployed against Spanish nationals in the Peninsula. As an Asturian, Rico Avello was personally shocked by the events in Oviedo and intended to submit his resignation, but was persuaded not to by Lerroux. What eventually did bring an end to the Rico Avello administration was, as with the Moles administration, political change in Madrid. The dénouement of Radical hegemony in December 1935 and the pending elections, which Rico Avello hoped to stand for, prompted his resignation on 11 January 1936. The Secretary General, Manuel de la Plaza, was named interim High Commissioner, and Rico Avello accepted the Finance portfolio in the Portela Valladares government.[47]

1936 AND CONCLUSIONS

The six months from the end of Rico Avello's administration to the start of the Civil War constituted what can best be described as a holding period. The interim High Commissioner, Manuel de la Plaza, and the chief of the Army of Africa, Emilio Mola, remained in place until Azaña's Popular Front government had been firmly established. At that point, on 28 February 1936, Mola was reassigned to Pamplona and replaced by the faithful

Republican Gómez Morato, and on 11 March 1936 Juan Moles returned as High Commissioner. A second Moles administration was not unwelcome. He was a known quantity, a moderate, and had the complete support of the government, and a reputation for listening to the 'producing classes' and the powerbrokers. Moreover, his initial pronouncements to the press were considerably more moderate than the partisan rhetoric that now constituted political debate in the Peninsula. He basically endorsed the continuance of Rico Avello's programmes in education and health care and supported, as had his predecessors, a policy of keeping the protectorate free of the political and social movements prevalent in the Peninsula.[48]

Moles's second administration, however, was simply too brief to have any impact on policies or programmes. On 13 May 1936 he was appointed Interior Minister in the Casares Quiroga Ministry and replaced on a interim basis by his ill-fated Secretary General, Captain Arturo Alvarez Buylla. Within in a matter of 15 hours after units of the Army of Africa rose in rebellion against the Second Republic in a Melillan suburb on 17 July 1936, the Republic's authority simply ceased to exist in the protectorate. This fact might lead one to question what impact almost four and a half years of Republican policies and programmes had on Spanish Morocco. It would seem on the surface very little, given the apparent speed with which the nationalists turned the protectorate into an armed camp and recruiting ground for their cause.[49] Was this because, as those on the left maintained, the Republicans made no fundamental changes to programmes or policies but expediently bowed to foreign pressures, to a still potent Army of Africa and entrenched colonial bureaucracy, and to their own fears that the recently subdued rural Moroccans might yet constitute, as they did in 1921, a potential embarrassment or even a threat to Spain's political system?[50] Or was it the case, as the Nationalists' supporters argued, that the Republic's administrators and policy makers lacked the colonial experience, goodwill, and policy-making consistency to have any positive, long-term impact in the protectorate?[51]

While it may be, as has been argued, that the protectorate's administrations during the period 1931 to 1936 were 'prey to the many upheavals which shook the Republic's short life',[52] the Republic did implement and sustain a number of specific and consistent protectorate policies. Despite changes in political orientation and ministries, these policies remained in place for the duration of the Republic and were in fact little changed or influenced by these upheavals. These included the staunch commitment to the idea of protectorate, that is, to the colonial ethos and everything that this implied in the context of the 1930s; the endorsement of the concept that a pacified protectorate should be governed by a civil rather than a military administration; the idea that everything should be done to make the protectorate's administration as efficient and cost-effective as possible and, in particular, to reduce military personnel and expenditures; the notion that it was the protecting power's duty to implement concrete developmental programmes that would better the socioeconomic situation of the protectorate's inhabitants; and the sentiment that the protectorate should be sealed off as much as possible from the political and social issues that prevailed in the Peninsula. In sum, the Republic's speedy demise in Spanish Morocco in 1936 was not the result of 'hesitant and wavering' policies or programmes. It was the consequence of a well-organized military rebellion that brought Peninsular divisions and tensions to the North African colony.

NOTES

1. Francisco Gómez-Jordana Souza, *La tramoya de nuestra actuación en Marruecos* (Madrid, 1976), pp.217–22; D.M. Hart, *The Aith Waryaghar of the Moroccan Rif: An Ethnography and History* (Tucson, AZ, 1976), pp.401–3.
2. María Rosa de Madariaga, 'The Intervention of Moroccan Troops in the Spanish Civil War: A Reconsideration', *European History Quarterly*, 22 (1992), pp.70–71. See also D.M. Hart, *Emilio Blanco Izaga: Coronel en el Rif* (Melilla, 1995), pp.37–52.
3. Ramón Salas Larrazábal, *El Protectorado de España en Marruecos* (Madrid, 1992), p.172.
4. Ministerio de Trabajo y Previsión, Servicio General de Estadística, *Anuario estadístico de España*, 14, 1928 (Madrid, 1928), p.381.
5. Gómez-Jordana, *La tramoya*, pp.223–46.
6. 'La République espagnole et le Maroc,' *Bulletin du Comité de l'Afrique française* (hereafter *L'Afrique française*), 41 (July 1931), p.475.
7. Ibid., p.474.
8. The events of 3 and 4 May 1931 are covered in some detail in Emilio Esteban-Infantes, *General Sanjurjo* (Barcelona, 1957), pp.154–9.
9. Quoted in Salas Larrazábal, *El Protectorado*, p.182.
10. This decree is reprinted in 'La République espagnole et le Maroc', *L'Afrique française*, 41 (Aug. 1931), p.569.
11. Ibid., pp.568–9.
12. 'Ecos', *Africa*, 78 (June 1931), p.120. See the staffing numbers in Víctor Morales Lezcano, 'L'exercit d'Africa I, Les reformes militars: 1931–1936', *L'Avenç*, 41 (June 1980), p.424.
13. This decree can be found in 'Possessions espagnoles', *L'Afrique française*, 42 (March 1932), pp.201–3. A summary was provided in 'Ecos', *Africa*, 84 (Dec. 1931), pp.247–8. For data on *interventor* administrative breakdowns, see Alta Comisaría de España en Marruecos, *Memoria relativa al régimen y actuación de los servicios del Protectorado* (Ceuta, 1932), p.20.
14. 'La République espagnole et le Maroc', *L'Afrique française*, 41 (July 1931), pp.479–80.
15. The rather low-key civil rights and developmental issues that were included in this petition are reproduced in Miguel Martín, *El colonialismo español en Marruecos (1860–1956)* (Paris, 1973), pp.108–10. For a summary of the Moroccan nationalist attitude towards the Second Republic's protectorate policies, see Mohammad Ibn Azzuz Hakim, *La actitud de los moros ante el Alzamiento, Marruecos 1936* (Malaga, 1997), pp.19–24.
16. For López Ferrer's comments, see 'La République espagnole et le Maroc', *L'Afrique française*, 41 (July 1931), p.480, and 'L'Espagne en Afrique', *L'Afrique française*, 42 (April 1932), pp.242–3.
17. See, for instance, Cándido Lobera, 'La política bereber del Protectorado', *Africa: Revista de Tropas Coloniales*, 18 (June 1926), p.126. Madariaga, 'The Intervention of Moroccan Troops', pp.73–4.

18. This estimate is based on data in Alta Comisaría de España en Marruecos, *Memoria relativa*, pp.97–100.
19. Department of Overseas Trade, *Economic Conditions in Morocco, 1930–1931* (London, 1932), pp.50–51.
20. V. Tomás Pérez, *La economía marroquí* (Barcelona, 1943), pp.149, 273–6.
21. This had been preceded in early July 1931 by the creation of a bipartisan committee (owners/workers) in Melilla to work out agreements in construction, furniture making, clothing manufacture, printing, transportation, hotel, and health industries. When efforts were made to take this concept to Tetuán and Larache it was rejected by protectorate authorities. For this issue and the Minas del Rif strike see 'La République espagnole et le Maroc', *L'Afrique française*, 41 (Sept. 1931), pp.591–2.
22. Pérez, *La economía*, p.285.
23. Department of Overseas Trade, *Economic Conditions*, p.51; see also A.E. Sayous, 'Le Maroc espagnol', *Revue Economique Internationale*, 3 (July 1931), pp.7–50.
24. Ibid., p.53; 'Le République espagnole et le Maroc', *L'Afrique française*, 41 (Sep 1931), p.590.
25. See, for instance, Francisco Franco, 'Ruud ... Balek!' *Africa*, 98 (Feb. 1933), pp.24–5; 'L'Espagne et l'Afrique', *L'Afrique française*, 42 (July 1932), pp.408–9; Tomás García Figueras, *Marruecos*, 3rd edn. (Madrid, 1944), pp.250–53.
26. Azaña's comments are reprinted in Manuel Azaña, *Una política (1930–1932)* (Madrid, 1932), pp.379–92.
27. For the Socialist recommendations see 'L'Espagne et l'Afrique', *L'Afrique française*, 42 (Nov. 1932), p.664.
28. For military budget data and military staffing, see Víctor Morales Lezcano, *España y el Norte de Africa: El Protectorado en Marruecos (1912–1956)* (Madrid, 1986), pp.116, 118. For non-military budget data, see Pérez, *La economía*, pp.290–91. For the all-volunteer force issue, see 'L'Espagne et l'Afrique', *L'Afrique française*, 42 (July 1932), p.409.
29. 'Possessions espagnoles', *L'Afrique française*, 43 (Jan. 1933), pp.61–3; García Figueras, *Marruecos*, p.253.
30. Ma. A. Egido León, *La concepción de la política exterior durante la II República (1931–1936)* (Madrid, 1987), pp.157–8; 'L'Afrique et l'Espagne', *L'Afrique française*, 43 (Jan 1933), pp.38–9.
31. Quoted in Egido León, *La concepción,* p.157.
32. Ibid., p.158.
33. For Moles's and de la Plaza's backgrounds, see 'Los altos cargos en Marruecos', *Africa*, 97 (Jan. 1933), p.13; 'L'Afrique et l'Espagne', *L'Afrique française*, 43 (Nov 1933), p.655.
34. 'Possessions espagnoles', *L'Afrique française*, 43 (March 1933), pp.181–2.
35. 'Viaje del Alto Comisario de la Zona Española a la Región Oriental', *Africa*, 100 (April 1933), pp.67–9.
36. Ibid., p.69.
37. 'Ecos', *Africa,* 102 (June 1933), p.117.
38. 'L'Afrique et l'Espagne', *L'Afrique française*, 43 (Nov. 1933), pp.653–7. For a description of this important road, see Naval Intelligence Division, *Geographical Handbook: Morocco*, Vol.2 (London, 1942), pp.268–70.
39. 'L'Afrique et l'Espagne', *L'Afrique française*, 43 (Nov. 1933), p.654; 'L'Afrique et l'Espagne', *L'Afrique française*, 43 (July 1933), p.415; 'Crónica mensual de Tetuán', *Africa*, 103 (July 1933), p.127; Egido León, *La concepción*, pp.159, 166n., 216.
40. 'L'Afrique et l'Espagne', *L'Afrique française*, 44 (Jan. 1934), pp.37–41. 'L'Afrique et l'Espagne', *L'Afrique française*, 44 (Feb. 1934), pp.108–9; 'Ecos', *Africa*, 109 (Jan. 1934), p.20.
41. 'Ecos', *Africa*, 110 (Feb. 1934), p.26; Paul Preston, *Franco* (New York, 1994), p.95. In August 1936 Rico Avello would be murdered in the Cárcel Modelo in Madrid by leftist *milicianos.*
42. 'L'Afrique et l'Espagne', *L'Afrique française*, 44 (Feb. 1934), pp.109–11. 'L'Afrique et l'Espagne', *L'Afrique française*, 44 (April 1934), pp.243–4. 'L'Afrique et l'Espagne', *L'Afrique française,* 44 (Sept. 1934), pp.559–60.
43. 'L'Afrique et l'Espagne', *L'Afrique française*, 44 (May 1934), pp.298–301; see also Salas Larrazábal, *El Protectorado*, pp.193–6.

44. 'L'Afrique et l'Espagne', *L'Afrique française*, 44 (June 1934), pp.354–5; Pérez, *La economía*, pp.290–91. Morales Lezcano, *España y el Norte de Africa*, pp.116, 118.
45. 'L'Afrique et l'Espagne', *L'Afrique française*, 44 (July 1934), pp.420–21; V. Morales Lezcano, 'El Protectorado español en Marruecos bajo la II República (Las reformas administrativas)', *Actas de las jornadas de cultura árabe e islámica* (Madrid, 1981), pp.467–70; 'L'Afrique et l'Espagne', *L'Afrique française*, 45 (April 1935), pp.246–8.
46. 'Crónica mensual de Tetuán', *Africa*, 122 (Feb. 1935), p.28; 'L'Afrique et l'Espagne', *L'Afrique française*, 44 (Sept. 1934), pp.559–60. Abdelmajid Benjelloun, *Le patriotisme Marocain face au Protectorat espagnol* (Rabat, 1993), pp.74–6; F. Valderrama Martínez, *Historia de la acción cultural de España en Marruecos (1912–1956)* (Tetuan, 1956), pp.186–90; 'L'Afrique et l'Espagne', *L'Afrique française*, 45 (Nov. 1935), p.680.
47. 'L'Afrique et l'Espagne', *L'Afrique française*, 44 (Oct. 1934), p.604; 'L'Afrique et l'Espagne', *L'Afrique française*, 45 (Dec. 1935), p.760.
48. 'L'Afrique et l'Espagne', *L'Afrique française*, 46 (March 1936), p.168; 'L'Afrique et l'Espagne', *L'Afrique française*, 46 (April 1936), pp.232–4.
49. See in particular, J.M. Gárate Córdoba, 'Las tropas de Africa en la guerra civil española', *Revista de Historia Militar*, 70 (1991), pp.9–66, and Michael Alpert, 'The Spanish Zone of the Moroccan Protectorate during the Spanish Civil War, 1936–1939', *The Maghreb Review*, 18 (1993), pp.34–44.
50. See, for instance, Martín, *El colonialismo*, pp.133–43.
51. See, for instance, García Figueras, *Marruecos*, pp.259–73.
52. Madariaga, 'The Intervention of Moroccan Troops', p.72.

Fascist Italy and Spain, 1922–45

STANLEY G. PAYNE

A long and complex relationship developed between Fascist Italy and Spain. The first phase, from 1923 to 1930, produced friendly relations between two dictators, Mussolini and Primo de Rivera, but no decisive changes. The second phase, from 1930 to 1936, largely coincided with the years of the Second Republic. During this period the relationship was adversarial, but Mussolini was unable to intervene or significantly influence Spanish affairs, which had a comparatively low priority for Italian diplomacy. The third phase was that of the Spanish Civil War, from 1939 to 1939, in which Mussolini intervened, providing more support to the Spanish Nationalists, both absolutely and proportionately, than did Hitler. During the fourth phase, involving most of World War II, from 1939 to 1943, relations remained both close and very friendly and yet dwindled in importance compared with those between Spain and Nazi Germany. After the fall of Fascism, similarly close relations were not reestablished with the Italian Social Republic, and the Spanish regime then initiated its own slow process of 'defascization'.

The close relations between Spain and the Italian principalities which had characterized the early modern period did not continue into the nineteenth century. Early Spanish liberalism did, however, serve as a clear inspiration for Italian liberals, and when the Spanish throne became vacant after 1868, D. Amedeo, a younger son of the Italian house of Savoy, was eventually selected to become Spain's first 'democratic' monarch. His complete political frustration and abdication in 1873 were perhaps more accurately symbolic of the relations between the two countries. Because of its separation of church and state and occupation of papal territory, the Italian state formed in 1860 was generally viewed negatively by the more conservative constitutional monarchy which largely governed Spain until 1931.

Spain essentially withdrew from the main currents of European diplomacy during the nineteenth century. If France was perceived as the main rival, this did not have the effect of aligning Spain very directly with the opposing Triple Alliance of which Italy was a part. During World War I

Spain became the most important neutral state. Though the war did bring increasingly close economic involvement with France, greatly benefiting the Spanish economy, relations with Italy remained secondary.

The point of inflexion in the rather distant Italian–Spanish relationship was the March on Rome in October 1922. Like Italy, Spain was undergoing considerable internal social and political conflict, and the formation of a strong government under Mussolini in Rome was hailed by Alfonso XIII, the Spanish Foreign Minister, and a number of other figures in Madrid. This had no immediate consequences, however, for Mussolini gave little priority to foreign affairs during his first months in office, and some months later the Liberals returned to power in Madrid. Mussolini nonetheless had at least one eye on Spain from the beginning. He knew full well that tensions remained between Spain and France and early indicated to the Spanish Ambassador that he sought closer relations between Rome and Madrid as the real leaders of the Latin world (including Portugal and Latin America) in opposition to France.

Within Spain, the immediate impact of Fascism was far greater in Barcelona than anywhere else, for the Catalan capital was the peninsula's most sophisticated city and the one with the highest level of political consciousness. Some of the more radical sectors of Catalan nationalism were fascinated by Fascism, though they made little effort to imitate it.[1] Their chief opponents, the *españolista* minority in Barcelona, in some cases sought to embrace Fascism more directly. In December 1922, two months after the March on Rome, a publication called *La Camisa Negra* appeared in Barcelona in direct imitation of Fascism, but it was unable to print a second number. Subsequently, during the spring of 1923 a few offficers in the local garrison formed a small circle called *La Traza* (The Project). They adopted a blue shirt as their uniform and hoped to extend their tiny group throughout Spain. Though it would be an exaggeration to call La Traza a Fascist organization, it was clearly inspired by Italian Fascism and was the first radical new nationalist group to be formed in Spain through such inspiration.[2]

The *pronunciamiento* of Miguel Primo de Rivera in September 1923, creating the first formal dictatorship in Spanish history,[3] drastically changed the political equation and offered the possibility of a new political convergence between Rome and Madrid.[4] At the time of the takeover, Primo de Rivera emphatically denied that he had been inspired by Mussolini, more discreetly invoking the authors of liberal military *pronunciamientos* in nineteenth-century Spain,[5] but in fact he was greatly impressed by Fascism. Within two months, Alfonso XIII and the new dictator made a formal visit to Rome, marking the first offficial visit abroad by any Spanish chief of state in the twentieth century (and, aside from Franco's meetings with Mussolini and Salazar, the last until the reign of Juan Carlos). Don Alfonso is supposed to have remarked to King Vittorio Emanuele of Primo, 'This is my Mussolini'. Mussolini hailed his Spanish counterpart as 'the chief of Spanish Fascism', while Primo called Mussolini his inspiration and teacher.[6] He was even more fulsome in an interview with the Fascist journal *Impero*, expressing his desire that 'Spain would follow in the footsteps of Italian Fascism', and that 'Spanish Fascism' (which he otherwise failed to identify or define) would help to 'liberate the country from harmful elements'. 'Fascism is a universal phenomenon that ought to conquer all nations ... Fascism is a living gospel.'[7] Primo de Rivera extolled Mussolini in Rome as a 'world figure' and an 'apostle of the campaign against revolution and anarchy' who had achieved 'order, work, and justice'.[8]

Every indication at that time pointed towards very close relations and a special *entente* between the two regimes. A new economic agreement was signed by which Spain and Italy would grant each other most-favoured-nation status, but no further treaty resulted. The two regimes shared the themes of nationalism and authoritarianism, but had little in common in concrete terms, given the lack of new political development and institutionalization in Madrid. Nor was it so easy to join forces against France. Though Primo de Rivera sought to improve the status of Spain in Tangier and Mussolini also had further ambitions in the area, neither was in a position at that time to force any major alteration in the *status quo*, while Primo de Rivera came to realize that it was undesirable to permit too much Italian influence on Spanish policy. During 1925, in fact, the two regimes tended to drift apart, and when a broader agreement was made in August 1926 it took the form not of a grand treaty but simply of a pact of conciliation and arbitration.

As the Italian Fascist Party expanded its network of party groups abroad, the Fasci all'Estero,[9] these became especially numerous in the United States, but also included sections of Italians resident in Madrid, Barcelona, and at least four other Spanish cities.[10] Though the goal of the Fasci all'Estero was not primarily to create Fascist political movements in other countries, the sections in Spain maintained contacts with supporters of Primo de Rivera and did diffuse some degree of knowledge and enthusiasm about Fascism.

More important from the viewpoint of the Italian regime, however, was the general extension of Italian cultural influence, particularly in Barcelona but also in Madrid and several other larger cities.[11] It subsidized the publication of Italian works in Spain, and the Istituto Cristoforo Colombo, a new agency designed to expand Italian influence in Latin America, also sought to make use of Spanish facilities.[12]

Though there was never any plan in Madrid merely to copy Italian practice, given the differences between the two countries, the Fascist regime always remained the nearest thing to a model for Primo de Rivera. His Labour Minister, Eduardo Aunós, was charged with developing a new labour arbitration system and thus made a personal visit to Italy in April 1926 to learn about the Fascist system, being personally received by Mussolini and also by Giuseppe Bottai, the Italian Minister of Corporations.[13] Mussolini was, of course, interested in seeing the Primo de Rivera regime develop into a permanent system, whether or not it directly copied Italian Fascism, and through Aunós urged the Spanish dictator to create some sort of political forum or parliament with which to legitimate his regime.[14]

If Mussolini had been slow to move towards an institutionalized authoritarian system, Primo de Rivera was slower yet and much more confused. The National Assembly which he eventually created in 1928 was too little and too late and failed to develop a viable new blueprint; by this point the political and economic situation was rapidly degenerating. Particularly noticeable was the lack of support for the dictatorship among Spanish youth, contrasting, as Bottai's journal *Critica Fascista* pointed out, with Italian Fascism's notable dimension as a youth movement. Italian diplomatic correspondence from Madrid in the last days of 1929 reported that Primo de Rivera was finally indicating that he would soon begin a fundamental reorganization of his amorphous Unión Patriótica more along the lines of the Italian Fascist Party, but this reorganization, like other plans of the dictator, was never initiated. Javier Tusell and Ismael Saz have concluded:[15]

> What the Spanish dictator felt for Mussolini was considerably more than platonic admiration. He was pathetically incapable of transferring Italian institutions to Spain and often childish in his effusive expressions of admiration for Mussolini. But, at the same time, the degree of political and ideological enthusiasm for the neighbouring peninsula produced actions which frequently have not been sufficiently taken into account, such as creation of the Assembly partly as a consequence of Mussolini's recommendation, the request for the latter's advice about the new Spanish constitution project of 1929, the close collaboration in the persecution of their respective oppositions, and the final telegram of farewell to Mussolini. In the last phase of the regime there existed the real historical possibility of the 'fascistization' of Primorriverism, even if always much more in the personal wishes of the dictator than in the actual Spanish context.

Though it would be a considerable exaggeration to blame the first Spanish dictatorship on Italian Fascism, the latter served as one source of inspiration for an authoritarian assault which destroyed the traditional terms of political coexistence in Spain, opening the door for the collapse of the monarchy and the drastic new polarization of the Second Republic. Nor was the example of the downfall of the Spanish dictatorship lost on Mussolini. Italian commentary had always pointed out the differences between the two regimes and the weak political and cultural development of the new Spanish state compared with Italy, but it had been the south European system most similar to Fascism and most congenial to the Duce. Seeing the Spanish King and much of the possessing class turn against the dictatorship seems to have strengthened Mussolini's growing conviction that his own regime could not rest foreover on the existing semipluralist compromise, but must become more totalitarian and revolutionary. To that extent, the Spanish experience was at least a minor factor in the Duce's turn towards a more radical policy in 1932.[16]

The advent of the Second Republic was a blow to Mussolini's policy, for if Fascist Italy had been something of a model for Primo de Rivera, the French Third Republic – which the Duce considered perhaps his number-one enemy – was clearly the model for the Spanish Republicans. Spanish diplomacy eventually became more active under the Republic than in previous years, but it was oriented towards the League of Nations (where the Spanish representative, Salvador de Madariaga, played a leading role) and towards a close relationship with France, while Italy was regarded with disfavour.

For three years, Italian policy towards the new Republic was essentially correct, even though the new regime in Madrid was seen as tipping the balance of power in the Mediterranean away from Italy. This came to an end at the close of March 1934, when Italo Balbo, a leading Fascist Party *gerarca* and also Italian Air Force Minister, received in Rome a small delegation from the two Spanish monarchist parties, the Alfonsian *Renovación Española* and the Carlist *Comunión Tradicionalista*.The next day, on behalf of the Italian government, Balbo signed a secret agreement with the monarchists pledging Italian arms, financial support, and training facilities for a monarchist-engineered military overthrow of the Republican government. Nonetheless, only a limited amount of this assistance was ever provided, and a year later, in March 1935, the agreement was cancelled by Mussolini, partly because the Spanish monarchists had shown scant initiative, but primarily because the Duce preferred not to complicate his now accelerating plans for the invasion of Ethiopia, which gave preference to a quiet and neutral Spain.[17]

Fascist propaganda remained active in Spain, and Italian representatives regularly surveyed the country's political landscape for signs of an emerging Spanish Fascist movement. The first clear-cut Spanish Fascist intellectual was Ernesto Giménez Caballero, editor of the country's leading avant-garde literary journal, *La Gaceta Literaria*, who was married to an Italian woman and came out vigorously on behalf of Fascism for Spain in 1928. Giménez Caballero, however, was an aesthete rather than an activist, a half-D'Annunzio minus the physical heroics. As a pro-Fascist organ, the *Gaceta* soon collapsed, and after a while the political identity of Giménez Caballero also began to blur.[18] A tiny organization formed separately in 1930, the Partido Nacionalista Español (PNE) adopted certain trappings of Fascism, its new militia, the Legionarios de España, becoming the first of the many Fascist/Communist-type shirt movements to be created in Spain. Yet the PNE was small and basically monarchist and right-wing.

The first genuine Fascist organization to appear was made up of the dozen followers of the young intellectual and philosophical essayist Ramiro Ledesma Ramos, who began to publish a small paper in Madrid in March 1931. Its title, *La Conquista del Estado*, was obviously derived from the well-known Italian Fascist weekly of the same name, *La Conquista dello Stato*, edited by the Fascist writer Curzio Malaparte. Its doctrine, that of revolutionary 'national syndicalism', also reflected the terminology of the left wing of the Italian Fascist Party. In October 1931 Ledesma joined forces with another small Fascistic group in Valladolid to create a movement called the Juntas de Ofensiva Nacional-Sindicalista (JONS) – again a sort of verbal analogue, in this case of 'Fasci Italiani di Combattimento', the original name of the movement in Italy in 1919. There was, however, no direct Italian support for any of these initiatives, and the JONS stagnated.

The most significant initiative to build a Spanish Fascist movement was undertaken two years later by José Antonio Primo de Rivera, eldest son of the late dictator (who had died only three months after losing power). José Antonio, as he later became known to friend or foe alike (the only figure in twentieth-century Spanish politics prior to Felipe González to be known by his first name), had only entered politics in a limited manner after his father's downfall. A very successful attorney, elegant and attractive in personal manner, and a *grande de España* after the inheritance of his father's title, José Antonio was not cut out to be a Mussolini- or Hitler-type figure. By 1933, however, he had become obsessed by the need to vindicate his father's name and complete the latter's work by helping to build a new nationalist and authoritarian political force that could save Spain from chaos and revolution by constructing a powerful new nationalist state.[19] The formula, he believed, had largely been provided by Italian Fascism, and a genuine revolutionary nationalist movement on the Italian model would generate the strength and support and the clear-cut doctrine and programme that his father's regime had lacked. José Antonio was not an intellectual like the grim and taciturn Ledesma, and it is not clear exactly how much he knew about Italian Fascism in mid-1933; certainly his own ideas were much less fully developed than those of the latter, even though Ledesma was two years younger.

However that may be, José Antonio declared in a newspaper interview that it was a matter of adapting 'the magnificent Italian effort' to the needs of Spain.[20] Only two weeks before the founding of the new movement, he felt the need for a personal meeting with his new role model and asked the Italian Embassy to facilitate a quick trip to Rome in order to obtain 'advice about the organization of an analogous movement in Spain'.[21] The interview with Mussolini took place on 19 October 1933 and lasted about 30 minutes, though he also met briefly with the Vice Secretary of the party, Arturo Marpicati, and was given a brief tour of several Fascist organizations.[22] The new movement was founded in Madrid on 29 October, and its leaders were determined to use the initials 'FE' for it; originally to be called 'Fascismo Español,' to avoid excessive imitation it was introduced on 2 November as 'Falange Española' (Spanish Phalanx).

In February 1934 the new movement was merged with the exiguous JONS, resulting in the bizarre official title of Falange Española de las Juntas de Ofensiva Nacional Sindicalista (FE de las JONS). During the first months of the Falange José Antonio often referred to his new movement as Fascism, but the politically more experienced and intellectually more sophisticated Ledesma warned vehemently of the political danger involved in appearing merely to be copying a foreign movement. In March José Antonio publicly warned his followers not to try merely to imitate the Italian formula of the corporate state and by the latter part of the year he began publicly to deny that the Falange was a Fascist movement. There was increasing criticism of the semipluralism of the Italian regime as merely too conservative or rightist, and Falangist National Syndicalism adopted the formula of 'el sindicato vertical', in which capital and labour were to be combined in a single union.

The Italian Embassy provided the Falangist leaders with propaganda literature and occasional advice, but no financial or other direct support. In 1928 Mussolini had publicly renounced earlier plans for the political expansion of Fascism into other countries, but this began to change when Italian foreign policy grew more aggressive. By 1930 the Italian regime was providing modest support to a number of Fascist or proto-Fascist movements in other lands, and the political export of Fascism became official policy once more in 1932. In the following year the regime organized the Comitati d'Azione per l'Universalità di Roma (Action Committees for the Universality of Rome – CAUR) to serve as the network for a sort of 'Fascist international'. One of the main problems encountered by its director, Eugenio Coselschi, and other leaders concerned the criteria by which to identify Fascist-type movements in other countries. There was no complete and official codification of Italian Fascist doctrine to serve as a touchstone, so the proponents of the new 'universal Fascism' made up their own, however vaguely, and by April 1934 had identified 'Fascist' movements in 39 countries (including every European country except Yugoslavia, as well as the United States, Canada, Australia, South Africa, five countries in Asia, and six in Latin America). All manner of problems then ensued as many different groups tried to cadge subsidies and extreme disagreements developed on issues such as racism, anti-Semitism, corporatism, and state structure.[23]

When a representative of the CAUR came to Madrid in May 1934, José Antonio signed a membership form and received a carnet (or membership card), but the eventual committee formed in Spain was headed by Giménez Caballero, by that time a member of the Falange. The latter was the Spanish representative to the first international meeting of the CAUR in Montreux, Switzerland, on 16–17 December, for which José Antonio declared his 'support'.[24] Nonetheless, the Falangist chief issued a press release in Madrid declaring that the Falange as an organization had refused to participate because it was not a 'Fascist movement'.[25]

In the months that followed, the financial situation of the Falange (now abandoned by the Spanish right) grew desperate, and José Antonio therefore made his second and last visit to Rome in April 1935. He met with Coselschi, and, though on this occasion Mussolini refused to receive him, the Duce personally approved his request for financial support. Beginning in June, the Falange was promised 50,000 lire (about $3,500) a month, to be paid through the press attaché of the Italian Embassy in Paris. This sum may be compared with the more modest subsidy of 10,000 lire per month being paid to the Francistes, then the only categorically Fascist movement in France. José Antonio personally travelled to Paris each month for the next eight months to obtain payment, the last of which was made at a reduced rate in January 1936.[26]

There does not appear to have been a regular Falangist delegate to the second and last 'Fascist international' conference at Montreux in September 1935, but José Antonio himself made a brief appearance and delivered remarks which have been quoted as follows:[27]

> I feel moved by your reception and transmit very sincere greetings from Falange Española and myself. For the moment I am under the obligation of not participating in the labors of your conference. The reasons have already been explained by the president. Spain is not yet prepared to join, through my mediation, a movement whose character is not only international but supranational, universal. And that is not just because the Spanish character is too individualistic but also

> because Spain has suffered a great deal from the leftist Internationals. We are in the hands of at least three Internationals: one Masonic, another capitalist and perhaps of other powers, of an extranational character, who intervene in Spanish affairs. If we appeared before Spanish opinion joined with another movement, and without slow, careful and profound preparation, the public conscience – and also the democratic conscience – of Spain would protest. Thus it is necessary to prepare public consciousness for these supranational labours.

This was a recognition of the Falange's identity with generic Fascism and of the reasons José Antonio pretended inside Spain that the movement was not generically Fascist. He had been more frank in a special report prepared in the preceding month for the Italian Embassy, in which he had affirmed decisively that 'Falange Española de las JONS has succeeded in becoming the sole Fascist movement of Spain, though this has been difficult, in view of the individualistic character of the Spanish people'.[28]

The Falange had indeed become the 'sole Fascist movement of Spain', but it remained a weak and largely insignificant one, failing to elect a single deputy in the final Republican elections of February 1936 and then being outlawed as a political organization by the government a month later. By that point the Italian Embassy saw no way of influencing the political situation in Spain, though the latter's steady deterioration was cause for mounting concern. Later, during the Civil War that broke out in mid-July, Republicans would charge with increasing vehemence that the military revolt had in fact been engineered by German Nazis and Italian Fascists, though there was in fact no basis for such allegations.[29] Hitler and Mussolini were more surprised by the outbreak of the Spanish conflict than were Manuel Azaña and Casares Quiroga, the Republican leaders, though within little more than a week they had quickly decided – independently of each other – to provide the rebels with a limited amount of military assistance. Parallel intervention on the same side in the Spanish Civil War was a significant factor in facilitating the formation of the Rome–Berlin Axis in October 1936, the first major agreement between the two dictators. From that point their intervention escalated, more on the part of Italy than of Germany. Faithful to the scheme first outlined in *Mein Kampf*, Hitler reiterated that he regarded the Mediterranean as primarily an Italian sphere and later declared to his generals that the Spanish struggle was of primary use to Germany not as a decisive strategic contest but as a diversion of attention from German rearmament and expansion in central Europe.

Mussolini, in contrast, soon became fully committed to the Spanish conflict, primarily for geostrategic reasons. The spectacle of a leftist revolutionary Spanish Republic, oriented towards France and the Soviet

Union, would constitute an intolerable challenge to the Fascist concept of 'Mare Nostrum'. Compared with this fundamental concern, any interest in directly influencing political developments within the nationalist zone to create a Fascist Spain in imitation of Italy was altogether secondary. Thus it would be Italy more than Germany which would provide the greater quantitative bulk of *materiel* for Franco's army, together with a sizeable commitment of Italian military manpower, which, briefly, early in 1937, would total nearly 70,000 men. Moreover, the duration of the Spanish war and the slow, unimaginative strategy of Franco would anger Mussolini and occasionally drive him to momentary despair, though ultimately the entire enterprise would be crowned with total victory.[30]

From 1 October 1936 onward the political destinies of nationalist Spain were controlled by the personal dictatorship of Francisco Franco. He was determined that his regime should not be a repetition of the amorphous, unstructured, 'hollow dictatorship' of Primo de Rivera, and thus it would require formal political organization and a coherent new programme. In his public statements he immediately identified his regime with the new nationalist dictatorships, specifying those of Italy, Germany, and Portugal, the three regimes which were providing varying degrees of military support. Of these, the one which came closest to providing a sort of political model was Italy, for it was more important than Portugal and politically more structured, while its Latin and Catholic identity made it much more congenial than Nazi Germany. This orientation was strongly reinforced by Franco's brother-in-law, Ramón Serrano Suñer, who arrived in the nationalist zone in February 1937 and quickly became the Generalissimo's chief political adviser. He had briefly studied law in Bologna at the beginning of Mussolini's government and had a very high opinion of the Fascist model.

In April 1937 Franco seized direct control of the Falange and of the Carlist Comunión Tradicionalista to create the official *partido único* of his regime, to be called Falange Española Tradicionalista y de las JONS (FET). In the months before the unification, Falangist leaders had publicly affirmed their solidarity with Italian Fascism and German Nazism, though insisting that they were developing a specifically Spanish form of movement. For his part, Franco had formally denied that the Falange was Fascist, though admitting that there were possibly Fascists among its members. Nonetheless, the official Fascistic programme of the original Falange, now called the Twenty-Six Points, was retained as the formal doctrine of the FET. At the same time, Franco announced that all other political forces were invited to join the new party and that its programme was not necessarily final but simply a beginning.[31]

Though the Italian and German representatives had urged Franco and the Falangists to join forces and create a unified state party, they figured very little in the process. Neither Axis partner harboured any grand design to control the nascent Franco regime; both governments informed their diplomats that the basic policy would be to avoid political interference in internal nationalist affairs. The Falange had received propaganda and other materials from the Fascist and Nazi parties, but the leadership of the independent party prior to unification had made little effort to maximize contacts with Rome and Berlin. Italian and German officials, whether regular diplomats or occasional visiting party officials, were virtually unanimous in their low estimate of the Falangist leaders and usually of the party itself. While recognizing the essentially Fascist character of the party, German and Italian officials referred pointedly to the amorphous nature of a formerly tiny organization which had suddenly swelled enormously under conditions of civil war and lacked leadership and a firm direction. Similarly, Franco usually made a poor impression physically, personally, and politically. Throughout the Civil War Italian and German officials persistently made disparaging comments in their reports to Rome and Berlin about the 'clerical' and 'reactionary' atmosphere found in the nationalist zone, so different from the 'revolutionary' ethos of Fascism and Nazism. Nor were such remarks misleading, since a strong emphasis on neotraditionalist Catholicism constituted the other, essentially contradictory, ideological polarity on which the new Spanish regime was based.

Javier Tusell has argued that during the last year and a half of the Civil War, as his military forces grew more dominant and his government better established, the Fascist tonalities of Franco's public language, as well as his internal policies steadily increased.[32] To some extent, at least, this seems correct and reflected a tendency to evolve more and more along a course parallel to the Italian regime's, while not imbibing the sinister peculiarities of German National Socialism. Thus the regime's only major institutional step so long as the war lasted was the development in March 1938 of the Spanish labour charter, to a considerable degree inspired by the Italian Carta del Lavoro of a decade earlier. In its final redaction, the charter adopted much of the language of social Catholicism, though – true to the peculiarly bipolar spirit of the Spanish regime – it retained the basic ideas and principles of the Italian model.[33]

Italian and German assistance was fundamental in enabling Franco to win complete military victory, and, as already noted, total aid from Italy was quantitatively greater than that from Germany. Later, as Italian arms met disaster in World War II, Mussolini and other Italian leaders would lament the great cost of helping Franco to victory, which allegedly depleted Italian strength for the larger contest. In fact, there seems little validity to such an interpretation. The real sources of Italian weakness in World War II were deficient leadership and organization, an inadequate industrial base, and the failure to develop advanced weaponry equivalent to that of the Allies. The arms sent to Spain would have been obsolete in the battles of World War II, while Italian combat dead in Spain did not exceed 3,000. The Italian military budget actually declined temporarily during 1937–38.[34] Exertions in Spain did not in themselves significantly handicap the Italian effort in World War II.

By the close of the Civil War the Spanish regime was fully identified with the Axis New Order, but its relationships with the two Axis partners differed. By mid-1940 relations with Berlin had become more important than those with Rome, and from the latter part of the Civil War onward the minority of genuine Fascist radicals in the FET looked more towards Nazism than towards Italian Fascism for inspiration, but nonetheless both diplomatic and personal relations of regime leaders with the Italians remained much more cordial than those with the Germans. It is true that by this point Mussolini hoped to make of Franco a junior ally or high-level Italian satellite, but his general policy towards Spain, compared with that of Germany, was always relatively generous and non-exploitive. Whereas Berlin badgered Franco for major economic concessions and early repayment of the entire war debt owed to Germany, Mussolini forgave approximately one-third of the amount owed Italy and offered lenient terms of repayment. Thus the Spanish government in 1941 initiated a 20-year repayment programme to Italy that was completed punctually, as Franco faithfully followed the payment schedule with the postwar democratic Republic in Italy until the remaining amount was paid in full. By contrast, all payments to Germany were cancelled with the downfall of the Third Reich.

It was nonetheless inevitable that with the fall of France in 1940 relations with Nazi Germany become the Spanish government's uppermost concern. Even then, the change in Spanish policy from neutrality to non-belligerence in June 1940 was made at the behest of Rome, not Berlin, and adopted the same line that had been followed by Mussolini from the outbreak of the conflict until his attack on France that same month.[35] During the next three years, the Spanish leaders generally looked to Rome for understanding and support in their increasingly difficult relations with Germany. By the winter of 1941, with negotiations between Madrid and Berlin at an *impasse* over the exact terms of Spanish entry into the war, Hitler momentarily turned the task over to Mussolini, and this led to the only direct personal encounter between the Spanish and Italian dictators, which took place at Bordighera in February 1941. The issue was awkward for the Duce in two respects. On the one hand lay a latent rivalry between Madrid and Rome for the potential succession to French imperial territory in North Africa, since parts of Algeria were coveted by both. On the other was the unavoidable fact that the war was going very badly for Italy and demoralization had begun to spread even within the Duce's personal entourage. Though he made an effort to persuade Franco to join the Axis partners, his heart was not entirely in this endeavour, and he did not place very heavy pressure on the Generalissimo.[36]

There were occasional notes of humour in the increasingly sombre relations between the two Latin dictatorships. In April 1941, for example, Franco's Foreign Minister and brother-in-law, Serrano Suñer, received a personal telephone call from his Italian counterpart, Mussolini's Foreign Minister and son-in-law, Count Galeazzo Ciano, demanding the immediate recall of the First Secretary of the Spanish Embassy in Rome, the Falangist writer and noted wit Agustín de Foxá, on charges of being a subversive and a spy. Foxá's mordant sarcasm, already legendary in Madrid, had found easy targets in the pretensions, pomposity, and failures of Italian Fascism, which he liked to refer to in private conversation as 'comparsa de los nazis' (a masquerade of the Nazis). Mussolini, routinely hailed as 'Fondatore dell'Impero' (Founder of the Empire), was termed by Foxá 'Affondatore dell'Impero' (Sinker of the Empire). The Spanish government withdrew Foxá for his wicked tongue but rejected the insinuation of sabotage.[37]

Much more than was the case either with Nazi Germany or the Estado Novo of Salazar in neighbouring Portugal, Franco and his collaborators continued to view Fascist Italy as their principal kindred regime. When Franco belatedly followed the advice which Mussolini had first given Primo de Rivera in 1926 and took the step in February 1943 of introducing a corporative-style Cortes to add a screen of pseudo-representative legitimacy to his regime, the new parliament was modelled not on institutions in Lisbon or Berlin but to a considerable measure on the Chamber of Fasces and Corporations in Rome.

Though a partial distancing from political Fascism began at certain levels of the Spanish regime in mid-1942, this was limited and far from categorical. As late as July 1943, Franco continued to endorse the Falange without qualification, and the Spanish press expressed its customary identity with the Axis position in foreign affairs. The overthrow of Mussolini on 25 July therefore came as a shock. Many Falangists were stunned, and the impact in Madrid was compounded by a lengthy letter from the personal secretary of Raimundo Fernández Cuesta, past Secretary General of the FET, who was currently Ambassador in Rome, to friends in Spain describing scenes of disorder in the Italian capital, including attacks on Fascists and on party headquarters, and concluding with an analogy to potentially similar consequences in Madrid. This missive was widely copied and circulated throughout the capital among Falangists and government personnel. The reaction was summarized by a police report of 17 August to Franco: [38]

> This produced great disillusionment in the party, and in the first moments there was no energetic response but an impulse to avoid the problem. In the general secretariat of the Movement some were frankly frightened; some did not want to leave their papers there, while others wanted to destroy them. Others lamented the impossibility of finding refuge in neutral countries, and so on, all this in an atmosphere of fear and alarm as though something similar might happen in Spain ...
>
> After the first moments passed, in order to be prepared for any contingency it was agreed to prepare a sort of special guard of groups of twenty men each of Falangists in every district of the capital organized as neighbourhood blocs under the political leaders of the district organization in each area, with all ready for action at the appropriate signal.

The covert neutralist, General Francisco Gómez Jordana, who had succeeded Serrano Suñer as Foreign Minister in September 1942, was convinced that the moment was propitious for the Spanish regime to abandon altogether its pro-Axis orientation and was at first exasperated to find Falangist leaders still publicly voicing their support for the fallen Mussolini.[39] Franco was, as usual, slow to respond, but did draw the logical conclusion. The following month of August 1943 was the time in which he and some of the top FET leaders decided that they must initiate a basic redefinition to differentiate the regime and the party from general Fascism. The formal defascistization of the FET began, on orders from the top, though it was a manoeuvre which would require considerable time to make relatively effective.

Once policy changed, some aspects were altered drastically. When Mussolini's post-Fascist successors under Marshal Pietro Badoglio sought to make use of Spain's good offices and diplomatic contacts to expedite negotiations with the Allies, Franco and Gómez-Jordana largely refused assistance, fearing to have Spain involved in any way in the Italian debacle. Mussolini's subsequent Italian Social Republic (ISR), organized as a German puppet in occupied northern Italy, was denied official recognition. Franco only dispatched a personal representative similar in status to the one attached to De Gaulle's Free French government in London, and major Italian Fascist figures who sought Spanish passports and the opportunity to flee to Spain were almost always denied assistance.

Diehards in the FET organization nonetheless held out as long as they could, and as late as the winter of 1944 some Falangist leaders were still publicly expressing support for Mussolini's neo-Fascist regime. They participated in minor ISR propaganda ceremonies and permitted ISR propaganda to be printed on FET presses. The Falangist journalist Ismael Herraiz enjoyed great success with his account of Mussolini's original downfall, *Italia fuera de combate*, published in Madrid in 1944. He praised the Duce but criticized his regime for having been insufficiently Fascist and forceful, holding up revolutionary and totalitarian Germany as the superior model. At least a few Falangists managed to find their way to northern Italy to fight for the dying Fascist regime in its final year.

The political metamorphosis of the Spanish regime, from a semi-Fascist pro-Axis dictatorship into a corporative, Catholic monarchist state, was carried out between 1945 and 1947. Though never fully convincing, it achieved its basic goal of helping the regime to survive. One characteristic, however, which some of the regime leaders did not relinquish was their personal regard for the fallen Duce, who would still be praised from time to time in the Spanish press.

There is no doubt of the importance of Fascist Italy to the rise of the Franco regime, even though that importance was never quite so great as some enemies of the regime would insist. The Spanish government came close to succumbing fully to the Fascist temptation in 1940–41 but was saved by geographical distance, Spanish weakness, and the stubborn, demanding diplomacy of Franco and his colleagues. The return to official neutrality in November 1943 made it possible for the regime to develop the political possibilities of its other ideological polarity, Catholic neotraditionalism, to create a surrogate post-Fascist identity for itself. In the process, the political sequencing and periodization of the Spanish dictatorship tended to reverse those of its Italian counterpart. The second half of the Mussolini regime was a time of increasing Fascistization and bellicosity, while the later phases of the Franco regime were analogous to the semipluralism of Mussolini's early years. Franco learned a good deal from Mussolini's example, including how to avoid the fatal mistakes of the latter's last years.

NOTES

1. This has been little studied. The best approach is through the work of E. Ucelay da Cal, 'Vanguardia, fascismo y la interacción entre nacionalismo español y catalán', in J. Beramendi and R. Maiz (eds.), *Los nacionalismos en la España de la II República* (Madrid, 1991), pp.39–95, and his unpublished 'Estat Català: The Strategies of Separation and Revolution of Catalan Radical Nationalism' (Ph.D. diss., Columbia University, 1979), pp.1–473. See also V. Panyella, *J. V. Foix: 1918 i la idea catalana* (Barcelona, 1989), pp.108–9.
2. See S. Bengoechea and F. del Rey Reguillo, 'En vísperas de un golpe de estado: Radicalización patronal e imagen del fascismo en España', in J. Tusell *et al.* (eds.), *Estudios*

sobre la derecha espanola contemporánea (Madrid, 1993), pp.301–26, and J. del Castillo and S. Alvarez, *Barcelona: Objetivo cubierto* (Barcelona, 1958), pp.115–22.

3. The best general account of the first Spanish dictatorship is S. Ben Ami, *Fascism from Above: The Dictatorship of Primo de Rivera in Spain* (Oxford, 1983), while the most detailed political narrative is J. Tusell, 'La dictadura regeneracionista', in J.M. Jover (ed.), *Historia de España* (Madrid, 1995), 38, 2, pp.131–623. J.L. Gómez Navarro, *El regimen de Primo de Rivera* (Madrid, 1991), presents a useful political, institutional, and comparative analysis.
4. The most detailed account of the relations between the two is G. Palomares Lerma, *Mussolini y Primo de Rivera: Política exterior de dos dictadores* (Madrid, 1989), though J. Tusell and I. Saz, 'Mussolini y Primo de Rivera: Las relaciones políticas y diplomáticas de dos dictaduras mediterráneas', *Boletín de la Real Academia de la Historia*, 179 (1982), pp.413–83, is a carefully focused briefer treatment.
5. Quoted in Marquis de Cáceres (ed.), *Dos años de directorio militar* (Madrid, 1926), pp.2–5.
6. G. Maura Gamazo, *Bosquejo histórico de la Dictadura* (Madrid, 1930), pp.51–2.
7. Quoted in F. Duarte, *España: Miguel Primo de Rivera* (Madrid, 1923), pp.197–8, in Ben Ami, *Fascism from Above*, p.132.
8. Quoted in J. Capella, *La verdad de Primo de Rivera* (Madrid, 1933), p.19.
9. The fullest treatment of the founding of the Fasci all'Estero will be found in Luca de Caprariis, 'Fascism and Italian Foreign Policy, 1924–1928' (Ph.D. diss., University of Wisconsin-Madison, 1998).
10. Palomares Lerma, *Mussolini y Primo de Rivera,* pp.251–53.
11. See V. Peña Sanchez, *Intelectuales y fascismo: La cultura italiana del 'Ventennio Fascista' y su repercusión en España* (Granada, 1995).
12. Palomares Lerma, *Mussolini v Primo de Rivera,* pp.262–78.
13. E. Aunós, *La política social de la Dictadura (*Madrid, 1944), pp.58–9.
14. J. Calvo Sotelo, *Mis servicios al Estado* (Madrid, 1932), p.336.
15. Tusell and Saz, 'Mussolini y Primo de Rivera', pp.482–3. The differences between the two regimes are apparent in the only near-contemporary study that I have found, Wolfgang Scholz's *Die Lage des spanischen Staates vor der Revolution (unter Berücksichtigung ihres Verhaltnisses zum italienischen Fascismus* (Dresden, 1932). Scholz correctly noted that although both countries were underdeveloped, Spain was distinctly more so and had a specific tradition of military praetorianism to which Primo de Rivera could be related. He further observed that the 'idea world' of Fascism was lacking in Spain. Italy had a much broader Fascist culture that enjoyed considerable support from the intelligentsia. In Spain, most of the intelligentsia had turned against the dictatorship by the late 1920s. Probably the only sophisticated commentary on Italian Fascism written in Spain under the dictatorship is in two works by the Catalan statesman Francesc Cambó: *Entorn del feixisme italià* (Barcelona, 1925), originally a series of newspaper articles published in *La Veu de Catalunya* in mid-1924, and the broader and more comparative book-length essay *Las dictaduras* (Barcelona, 1929).
16. Cf. R. de Felice, *Mussolini il Duce* (Turin, 1974), Vol.1, p.131
17. The best account is Ismael Saz, *Mussolini contra la II República* (Valencia, 1986), pp.66–85.
18. See D.W. Foard, *The Revolt of the Aesthetes: Ernesto Giménez Caballero and the Origins of Spanish Fascism* (New York, 1989).
19. A mountain of literature, most of it superficial and hagiographic, has appeared about José Antonio Primo de Rivera, and new titles by his dwindling circle of admirers continue to appear. The only scholarly and objective biography is J. Gil Pecharromán, *José Antonio Primo de Rivera: Retrato de un visionario* (Madrid, 1996), which is highly recommended.
20. *La Nación* (Madrid), 26 Aug. 1933.
21. Quoted in Saz, *Mussolini contra la II República,* p.115.
22. The visit has best been reconstructed in ibid., pp.114–16.
23. The principal study is M.A. Ledeen, *Universal Fascism: The Theory and Practice of the Fascist International. 1928–1936* (New York, 1972).
24. Saz, *Mussolini contra la II República*, pp.127–31.
25. A. del Río Cisneros (ed.), *Obras completas de José Antonio Primo de Rivera* (Madrid, 1956),

pp.391–2.
26. Saz, *Mussolini contra la II República*, pp.138–43.
27. Quoted in ibid., p.137.
28. The full text may be found in A. Viñas, 'José Antonio analiza las fuerzas políticas', *Actualidad Economica*, 23 Nov. 1974, pp.69–73, and in Viñas, *La Alemania nazi v el 18 de Julio* (Madrid, 1977), pp.420–25.
29. See Saz, *Mussolini contra la II República*, pp.147–93, and, concerning German policy, Viñas, *La Alemania nazi*.
30. The basic study is J.F. Coverdale, *Italian Intervention in the Spanish Civil War* (Princeton, 1975). See also the collective volume *Italia y la Guerra Civil española* (Madrid, 1986); I. Saz and J. Tusell (eds.), *Fascistas en Espana* (Madrid, 1981); and J.L. de Mesa, *El regreso de las legiones (La ayuda militar italiana a la España nacional 1936–1939)* (Granada, 1994).
31. For the details of this process, see J. Tusell, *Franco en la guerra civil* (Madrid, 1992), pp.79–171; P. Preston, *Franco* (London, 1993), pp.248–74; and my *The Franco Regime 1936–1975* (Madison, 1987), pp.163–78.
32. In *Franco en la guerra civil*.
33. The contest between social Catholic, rightist, and secular Fascist principles in the drafting of the charter is revealed in ibid., pp.257–61; D. Ridruejo, *Casi unas memorias* (Barcelona, 1976), p.195; R. Fernández Cuesta, *Testimonio. recuerdos y reflexiones* (Madrid, 1985), pp.194–95; L. Suárez Fernández, *Francisco Franco y su tiempo* (Madrid, 1984), Vol.2, pp.288–9; and, to some extent, J.J. Azpiazu, *Orientaciones cristianas del Fuero del Trabajo* (Burgos, 1939).
34. V. Zamagni, *The Economic History of History 1860–1990* (Oxford, 1993), p.246.
35. *I Documento Diplomatici Italiani*, 9 serie (Rome, 1960), Vol.4, pp.620–30.
36. The chief study of Italo-Spanish relations during these years is J. Tusell and G. García Queipo de Llano, *Franco y Mussolini* (Barcelona, 1985). For a comparison of Franco's relations with the two dictators, see R. García Pérez, 'España en el Eje: La beligerancia y la opinión de los historiadores', and G. García Queipo de Llano, 'Franco y Mussolini entrevistados: La política exterior hispanoitaliana durante la guerra mundial', in S. Payne and D. Contreras (eds.), *España y la Segunda Guerra Mundial* (Madrid, 1997), pp.11–35, 89–102.
37. This is according to the recollections of Serrano Suñer as recounted in I. Merino, *Serrano Suñer: Historia de una conducta* (Barcelona, 1996), pp.267–8.
38. Fundación Nacional Francisco Franco, *Documentos inéditos para la historia del Generalisimo Franco* (Madrid, 1994), Vol.4, pp.366–70.
39. Ibid., p.41.

Fascism and Empire: Fascist Italy against Republican Spain

ISMAEL SAZ

From 1931 onward, Fascist Italy tried to influence Spanish politics through a combination of formal diplomatic action and clandestine support for monarchist conspirators. Spain did not, however, become an axis of Italy's foreign affairs until the outbreak of the Civil War in 1936. Supporting Franco was a way of helping to destroy international Communism and the democratic challenge and also served Mussolini's claims to Italian hegemony in the Mediterranean. From the point of view of domestic politics, helping Fascism in Spain would help to maintain the mobilization of the Italian people. In Italy's participation in the Spanish Civil War imperial Fascism, defined as foreign aggression, ideological imperialism, and domestic revolution, found its best expression.

The proclamation of the Second Republic in Spain in April 1931 constituted a serious setback for Fascist Italy from nearly every point of view. On the ideological side, it cut short an almost unstoppable process of retrocession in parliamentary democracy, and at precisely the moment that Mussolini was indulging himself in announcing to the four winds the inescapable Fascist or Fascistized future which awaited Europe.[1] It is therefore not surprising that the Duce should have expressed his disgust in this regard with the aphorism 'The Spanish Republic is not a revolution: it is a plagiarism – a plagiarism with a 150 year delay'.[2] In addition to the ideological offence were the possible repercussions at the level of Italian domestic policy; the events in Spain might constitute some encouragement for the Italian anti-Fascists. If the regime had been able to use the existence of a dictatorship in the neighbouring peninsula in terms of prestige, it is clear that this line of discourse could now be inverted. Although the Fascist Party and the church read the fall of the dictatorship and the monarchy in Spain in opposite ways, they seemed to concur in considering the Republic the worst of results.[3]

The repercussions at the level of foreign policy seemed more direct and verifiable. The relations with the dictatorship of Miguel Primo de Rivera had turned out to be fundamentally positive. It is true that the treaty of friendship, arbitration, and conciliation signed by the two countries in 1926 had been limited and had lacked any clause of military scope, but their much-publicized friendship gave both dictatorships somewhat greater negotiating capacity regarding France and the United Kingdom. Concerning Morocco, it had by then become clear that Fascist Italy's support of Spain's aspirations had sought at least to halt the process of consolidation of French hegemony in the zone and at most to employ the Spanish hopes as a pretext for raising the matter of the reopening of the entire western Mediterranean.[4] After the fall of the Spanish dictator, Italian fears multiplied, especially when, with the visit to Spain by the French Minister of War, André Maginot, at the end of 1930, the inevitable rumours about a possible agreement that would allow the passage of the French colonial troops through Spanish territory began to surface. Similar rumours circulated with regard to a supposed pact signed by the Spanish revolutionary committee with the French authorities.[5] Whatever the scope and verisimilitude conceded to these rumours, the proclamation of the Republic seemed to imply a leap backward. As the then Foreign Minister, Dino Grandi, wrote, 'The republic in Spain probably supposes an alliance with France ... for Italy it means losing a war in the Mediterranean without a fight'.[6]

Thus there was more than sufficient reason for the Italian government to receive the Spanish Republic with hostility. As the Republic consolidated, however, it became a matter of fact in the face of which it was necessary to establish a line of official policy. The Italian government recognized the new regime, although certainly not warmly, and before the end of April Grandi made some notes in his diary which were in notable contrast with earlier ones. He wrote that, since the Republic was consolidating, it would be best that it did so 'as soon as possible and with force'. Republican or not, a strong Spain – capable of resisting French pressures – was in Italy's interest.[7]

Can it be deduced from this that, once the initial impact was overcome, Rome placed its stakes on the consolidation of the Republic?[8] Later events do not at all favour this interpretation. However, as will be seen, the idea that Mussolini's hostility towards the Spanish Republic translated into a firm resolution to do everything possible to encourage the downfall of Spanish democracy does not fit the facts either. This is partly because, at least until 1936, neither Spain nor the western Mediterranean was the fundamental point of reference of Fascist foreign policy. Instead, this point of reference was the Balkan–Danubian basin and, at the colonial level, the eastern Mediterranean and the Middle East.[9]

At this relatively secondary level, the Italian attitude towards the Spanish Republic could follow two different but complementary lines depending on the circumstances. The first of these – secret, subterranean, and imperialist – was based on ideological hostility and a policy of maximums in the foreign-policy area. A Spain that was a dictatorship and allied with or at least favourably disposed towards Italy was the most attractive hypothesis, and to this end Mussolini was willing to collaborate with any conspiracy against the Republic. The second line – which we could call official, open, and realistic – tended to relegate the political and ideological differences to the background and advocate a good-neighbour policy aimed at neutralizing as far as possible the Spanish government's Francophile inclinations. As we shall see, the greater preeminence of one or the other of these lines was almost always dictated by the evolution of Spanish domestic policy as well as by the international situation.

FROM HOSTILITY TO COEXISTENCE

The same cadence which we have seen in the first weeks of existence of the Republic would be repeated and amplified in the following two years. The relative normalization of relations was frequently affected by the activities of Italian exiles in Spain. The Spanish press was largely hostile to Fascism. Gestures of friendship towards France multiplied, and the Republic's support of the League of Nations was not exactly the orientation which most coincided with the assumptions underlying the Italian positions.[10] Above all, signs of instability of the Republic increased. In this context, the monarchist right began to plot, and – as it would do from then on – it immediately looked to Rome for support. As early as the spring of 1932, some conspirators travelled to the Italian capital and obtained a promise from Italo Balbo of significant quantities of arms and munitions. Although they were in effect issued, the speedy collapse of General José Sanjurjo's *coup d'état* in August of that year prevented the collection of those arms.[11]

The failure of the attempted coup proved that the Republic was less fragile than had been supposed. Moreover, the efficiency and energy shown by Manuel Azaña notably enlarged his figure in the eyes of Mussolini, to the point that – coincidentally or not – the Duce never again supported a plot while Azaña was in power. From the weakness of some and the strength of others the Italian government concluded that it had to improve its official relations with Spain. The emergence of so efficient and experienced a diplomat as Raffaele Guariglia was probably in great part attributable to this, and although among the instructions he received was to maintain contact with the enemies of the regime, the emphasis clearly shifted towards the improvement of official relations.[12]

Of course, France still constituted the centre of Mussolini's policy regarding Spain. In fact, the decision to improve bilateral relations was made with the express objective of preventing the Spanish government from being drawn even closer to Paris out of a sense of international isolation. That same summer, Italian naval manoeuvres were conceived from the supposition that in a Franco-Italian war the Balearic Islands would have been occupied by France with the approval of Spain.[13] The visit to Madrid by the French Prime Minister, Edouard Herriot, a few months later once again stirred the inevitable rumours about the signing of a secret pact. There was none of this, and, thanks to Guariglia's well-balanced reports, the Italian authorities were soon able to reassure themselves on this matter.[14]

Paradoxically, Herriot's visit to Spain turned out to benefit bilateral relations, thus completing the effects of Sanjurjo's failed coup attempt. If the latter had indeed shown the relative strength of the Spanish government, the former manifested the will to independence of that same government.[15] Thus, without abandoning the principle of privileged friendship with France, the Republican diplomatic corps began to show evidence of its autonomy regarding Paris, manifesting a clear openness towards London and a better disposition towards Rome.[16]

All of these signs were noticed by Italian diplomacy, which judged the situation favourable enough to propose an early renewal of the 1926 treaty of friendship. By that renewal they sought, as an indirect effect, to clear up old speculations about the scope of the said agreement and, directly, to favour an improvement in bilateral relations. The initiative was well received by the Spanish Foreign Minister, Fernando de los Ríos, who in addition took advantage of these circumstances to table an initiative long cherished by Republican diplomats: the negotiation of a Mediterranean pact between the principal powers with interests in the area. That proposal was difficult to bring to fruition, because although it enjoyed French approval it had to confront the foreseeable resistance in London to the adoption of new agreements. It was, however, favourably received, at least in principle, by Italian diplomacy.

The fall of the Spanish government prevented the negotiations from going farther, but the fact that they had been proposed demonstrated that in the summer of 1933 Spanish–Italian relations had entered an era of relative *rapprochement* and mutual respect. In this sense, it is not without significance that the fall of the Republican-Socialist government at the beginning of September was seen in Rome as a sign that the Spanish Republic was entering a new phase of instability and therefore it was advisable to freeze the aforementioned conversations.[17]

THE AGREEMENTS OF MARCH 1934

Contrary to what might be expected, the victory of the right in the elections of November 1933 did not translate into an improvement of bilateral relations. It was, of course, welcomed in Italian journalistic and diplomatic circles, but this response soon changed to disappointment when it was ascertained that the defeat of the left had not meant the fall of the Republic or at least of its parliamentary character, and disappointment soon became coldness if not open hostility. According to the Spanish Ambassador in Rome, this unfavourable disposition was displayed with the same intensity in the highest circles, including Mussolini. Nor did Guariglia in Madrid seem especially benevolent towards the Spanish government. In March 1934, for example, he felt that the political confusion in Spain made it inadvisable to raise the question of the renewal of the 1926 treaty. In short, the Fascist authorities considered the Republic less consolidated than ever.[18]

It was in this context that the agreements with Rome were signed in March 1934. At the end of that month, a delegation of Alfonsian monarchists and Carlists travelled to the Italian capital for talks with Balbo and Mussolini. As a result of these, the Fascist authorities agreed to deliver a significant quantity of arms and 1.5 million pesetas to the Spanish conspirators, as well as provide military training to selected troops. In compensation, in a 'secret pact' signed by Balbo and the Spanish conspirators, both parties agreed to sign a treaty of neutrality and friendship which would guarantee the *status quo* in the western Mediterranean as far as Spanish interests there were concerned; the new Spanish government would denounce any type of secret treaty which might exist with France, and the two governments would enter into a commercial agreement that would ensure a 'close economic relation' between them.[19]

As has been observed, the treaty did not contemplate any territorial cessions by Spain to Italy,[20] But this does not mean that it was not the result of an imperialist strategy. In fact, it mentions guaranteeing the *status quo* in the western Mediterranean *only* in reference to the Spanish territories there. Furthermore, the fact that Italy appeared as a guarantor of the integrity of Spanish territory carried the implicit recognition of Italy's hegemony in that area of the Mediterranean.[21] At the same time, it does not seem probable that the Italian authorities conceded credibility to the information regarding the existence of some type of Spanish–French pact. Indeed, in the Italian diplomatic correspondence either there is no reference to this or the reference is precisely to deny its existence.[22] Thus it may be that the mention of such a pact was intended to suggest a possibility or to allow the denunciation of other treaties of less secrecy and scope that contributed to linking Spain to the sphere of French influence. The combination of the reference to the nonexistent secret pacts and the signing of the treaty of neutrality is the key to the objective of the agreements, which was none other than to make Spain a friendly nation strongly linked to – and dependent on – Italy.

Nor does it make much sense to divorce these agreements from ideology.[23] The fact is that Mussolini made a pact with the sector of the

Spanish opposition which was – apparently – in a position to overthrow the Republic and did so for precisely this reason. It was unnecessary that they be Fascists in the strict sense of the term. On one hand, the squalid formations of Spanish Fascists hardly constituted a political force of even minimal significance. On the other, it was clear that the monarchist conspirators sought the destruction of the parliamentary democracy and the establishment of some type of dictatorship. The fact that the Spanish right had won the election some months earlier did not constitute any type of obstacle to what was now being promoted. On the contrary, the elections had demonstrated that the Republic was fragile, and the right had not known how – or not wanted – to take full advantage of that fragility.

WITH ETHIOPIA IN THE BACKGROUND

In all of the above, the opportunity factor had, as always, carried fundamental weight, sufficiently so for the Italian authorities to place the promised means at the disposal of the Spanish conspirators.[24] But it was also sufficient for Mussolini to answer these same conspirators, seeking to put the project into effect a year later, with a resounding no. In fact, many things had changed by March 1935. The very fact that the conspirators had hesitated so long contributed to reducing their credibility in the eyes of Mussolini, and now in a nearly definitive manner. At the same time, the conservative Republic had largely overcome the so-called October revolution, and its evolution towards the right seemed clearer than ever. The Catholic conservatives of the Confederación Española de Derechas Autonómas (CEDA) shared the government with the radicals, and both the anti-parliamentary vocation and their pro-Italian attitudes in foreign policy were perfectly well known in Rome.[25]

But the fundamental change had occurred on the international scene. Italy's foreign policy had decidedly shifted towards pursuing its ambitions in Ethiopia, and, as the Mussolini–Laval agreements of January 1935 in Rome clearly demonstrated, France's good disposition in this regard was fundamental. It is clear that in these circumstances what the Duce would least desire would be the appearance of a focal point of tension in an area of traditional Franco-Italian rivalry such as Spain. Complementarily, the diplomatic preparation for the attack on Ethiopia advised attempting to obtain a favourable attitude from the Spanish government.

Indeed, Republican foreign policy had for some time been shifting back to a line of relative distancing from Paris and closer approximation to London and Rome. In normal conditions this might have been considered highly favourable to Italy, but to the degree that the Ethiopian conflict would mean substituting British–Italian tension for the traditional Franco-

Italian, the situation appeared more complex and problematic. Whereas the President of the Republic and the radical party were tendentiously pro-British, the CEDA clearly leaned in favour of Italy. As tension heightened and the problem of League of Nations sanctions of Italian aggression in Ethiopia arose, the contradictions at the heart of the Spanish government became apparent. Some supported compliance with the League obligations, while others were willing to do anything possible to evade them. The result was a relative neutralization of Spanish foreign policy. As long as it was possible, the Spanish government took a position equidistant from the two alternatives or simply sought refuge in vagueness or silence. When there was no alternative it voted in favour of the sanctions, although it did so in absolute silence and then proceeded to apply them in the manner most favourable to Italy.[26]

The Italian government was fully cognizant – as were the League of Nations observers – of the friendly attitude adopted by Spain. Of course, this had something to do with the actions, overt or covert, of the Italian diplomatic corps. At one level, relations with the Spanish government and its diplomats were cultivated, and special attention was given to the CEDA, even resorting to the good offices of Vatican diplomacy. On another level, every available means was employed to shape the evolution of Spanish public opinion and of the government itself. Hence, the beneficiaries of the aid – now only economic – granted in March 1934 did everything in their power to defend the Italian cause in the press and the parliament. Specifically, Antonio Goicoechea made repeated speeches in the Cortes proposing anything and everything that was suggested to him by the Italian Embassy, and the Falangists did likewise, as beneficiaries of the financial aid that their leader, José Antonio Primo de Rivera, received monthly from the Italian Embassy in Paris.[27]

All of these circumstances contributed to situating Italy's relations with Spain on the same level of normality as those it maintained with other western European states. It was no longer a matter of encouraging a coup to bring down the Republic, but instead one of using every available means to influence its policy and evolution. Relations with the monarchist conspirators themselves shifted to having them act as spokespersons – almost propagandists – for the interests of Italy. The subvention which was granted to Primo de Rivera was not fundamentally different from those given to other European Fascist leaders such as Marcel Buccard in France. Although the Spanish Fascist leader was pleased to draft insurrectionary plans, of which he punctually informed the Italians, it does not seem that they gave these plans much credence.[28]

IGNORING CONSPIRACY

Apparently, the triumph of the Frente Popular in the February 1936 election was for Italy the worst of all possible news. Not in vain had the Spanish left wing once more given signs of a militant anti-Fascism in relation to Ethiopia. The Italian Ambassador, Orazio Pedrazzi, was aware of this, although he had not ceased to warn that the scope of Spanish foreign policy was narrow. What was most to be feared, he said, was its passage from a position of passive adherence to the League of Nations to a more active, pro-League stance but without ever doing anything which could bring the country nearer to armed conflict. At the same time, Azaña had appeared to be quite understanding towards Italy in relation to the Ethiopian conflict. After the inauguration of the new government, according to Pedrazzi, he had reiterated his feelings of friendship and even expressed his admiration for the work of the Duce.[29] The truth is that Azaña was still the staunch democrat he had always been, and his manifestations of understanding towards Italy in the Ethiopian conflict were due to a well-considered concept of what the Republican foreign policy should be.

In the Republican leader's opinion, the relations between the various states should be based on broader criteria than the strictly circumstantial not allowing differences with regard to the latter to endanger the future. He felt, however, that the principal risk to European peace came not so much from Italy but from Germany, and that, from a strictly Spanish point of view, anything that would remove the main centre of tension from the Mediterranean would be positive. Consequently, the Spanish government opposed the stiffening of sanctions on Italy from the beginning, and as soon as Addis Ababa had been conquered it advocated that the sanctions be lifted. After all, they had been adopted in order to obtain certain objectives, and once the attempt had failed it made little sense to prolong the tension.

It is possible that behind Azaña's attitude there was a calculation of domestic policy in the sense of causing an Italian withdrawal from the intrigues of the Spanish extreme right. If this was so, it was a complete success, since Fascist Italy displayed a more benevolent attitude than might have been expected regarding the convulsions which shook the Spain of the Frente Popular. If Pedrazzi is to be believed, both Azaña and his Foreign Minister, Augusto Barcia, had expressed their satisfaction at the tone with which the Italian press dealt with the events in Spain.[30]

Obviously, the Italian Fascists were not sympathizers of the governing left in Spain, and, indeed, Pedrazzi constantly reported the deterioration of the situation to his superiors. Nevertheless, the Italian Ambassador seemed to feel either that there was no solution whatever for the deterioration or that a solution would have to come from a governmental initiative. Both the extreme right and the extreme left were ill-equipped to empower a radical turnover – the latter because for the moment it seemed to prefer announcing the social revolution instead of carrying it out and the former because it was still suffering the consequences of the electoral defeat. Only the Falangists showed some capacity to react, but their leadership was imprisoned, and although they resorted to violence they seemed unable to win the battle in the street. Nor could even a successful military coup be expected, for the majority of the military chiefs sympathized with the left.[31]

The good bilateral relations and the absence of counter-revolutionary perspectives help to explain the fact that, after supporting all the proposed insurrections presented to them until 1934 and financing the various groups of the Spanish extreme right until 1936, the Italian authorities denied both forms of aid to precisely the conspiracy that would prove to be definitive. Between March and July 1936, all of these groups sought aid for the conspiracy under way. The first to attempt it was the Fascist leader José Antonio Primo de Rivera, who arranged from prison a meeting between Mussolini and his brother Miguel, but this initiative was blocked by Pedrazzi. Then in June it was Goicoechea, one of the participants in the 1934 agreements, who approached the Italians. In an extensive report in which he described the preparations for and expectations of the coup in detail, he solicited the concession of one million pesetas and the rapid acknowledgement of the new government. Mussolini's answer to both requests was again a resounding no. And an attempt led by another participant in the March 1934 meeting, the traditionalist Rafael Olazábal, scarcely three days before the *pronunciamento* obtained no better results.[32]

THE CAUTIOUS STEPS TOWARDS INTERVENTION

The failure of the coup of 18 July 1936 created an extremely unfavourable situation for the rebels. Practically all of the major cities were controlled by forces loyal to the government, as were the majority of the industrial areas of the country. Among the several zones controlled by the insurgents, the most important were the north of Madrid and the area under General Gonzalo Queipo de Llano in Seville. The fundamental part – in quantity and quality – of the troops that had mutinied belonged to the African army, but the failure of the uprising in the navy prevented their transport from Morocco to the peninsula. Hence, the situation was dramatic, and its outcome was foreseeable unless the Republican navy's blockade of the Strait of Gibraltar could be broken.[33]

As this situation started to take shape, the rebels began to arrange for foreign aid; General Franco, through two different channels, and General

Emilio Mola through another, took the initiative. Already on 19 July, Franco commissioned a monarchist journalist, Luís Bolín, to negotiate the purchase of aeroplanes from 'England, Germany, or Italy'. Bolín went to Rome, where, after an apparently positive initial conversation with Galeazzo Ciano, he received a definite rejection from Mussolini.[34] Two days later, on 25 July, a delegation sent independently by Mola arrived in Rome and met with Ciano. This delegation was comprised of the monarchists Goicoechea, Pedro Saínz Rodríguez, and Luis María Zunzunegui. If a report generally attributed to the first of them is to be believed, this was the definitive negotiation.[35] According to it, Mussolini had rejected the previous petitions for aid because he did not know if they were in any way connected to the agreements of March 1934. Thus, once Goicoechea had confirmed that they were, Ciano gave the operation his approval.[36] Nonetheless, as this author has demonstrated elsewhere, everything referring to the monarchists' negotiations was constructed after the fact with the aim of politically capitalizing on an arrangement for aid in which their participation had been practically nil. The document in question is almost entirely false, and above all it ignores the approach by Goicoechea himself in June.[37]

Actually, the definitive negotiation was carried out directly by Franco through the Italian Consulate in Tangier. By 20 July he had approached the Italian military attaché in Tangier, Major Giuseppe Luccardi, regarding the possibility of acquiring planes in Italy to transport the troops. Two days later he had his first meeting with the Italian Consul in Tangier, De Rossi Del Lion Nero, who transmitted the petition to Rome, where Ciano received it favourably. However, Mussolini's negative was confirmed on the following day. Both Luccardi and De Rossi were openly partisan to Franco's cause, and they continued to defend his petitions, emphasizing the opinions that the rebels communicated to them: the situation of anguish, France's belligerent attitude in favour of the Republic, the offers of a solid and close Spanish friendship, and the risk that an Italian negative would mean an increase in German influence.[38]

After 24 July, things began to evolve more favourably for Franco. That day Ciano telegraphed De Rossi, asking him to report on the likelihood that the movement would triumph. The following day De Rossi answered, stressing Franco's statement that the sooner aid came, the more certain victory would be. Two days later, on 27 July, Ciano informed De Rossi that the planes – 12 S-81s – were ready in Sardinia. But he added some indications that the decision was not yet definite: without assuming any commitment, the Italian Consul was to report the exact situation and whether or not compliance with the dispatched petitions was still urgent. Only after receiving the pressing response from De Rossi was the definitive decision made. It was thus communicated to Tangier on 28 July, and the transport of the 12 planes – as well as a ship, the *Morandi*, and pertinent munitions – was immediately arranged.[39]

The *Morandi* arrived without mishap in Melilla on 2 June, but of the 12 planes that took off on the morning of the 30 July only nine arrived at their destination. One had crashed into the sea, and two others had attempted to land in French Morocco. For this reason, the first Italian involvement in the Spanish Civil War became worldwide headlines the following day. It is therefore not surprising that in the anti-Fascist media – and also, for a time, in historiography – the idea that there had been Italian participation in the conspiracy itself gained strength.

OPPORTUNITY AS A FACTOR

Nevertheless, as has been seen, not only there was no Italian participation in the conspiracy, but, furthermore, the process was long and complicated. Contrary to the German case, which contemplated a rapid, expedient decision on the night of 25 July by Hitler,[40] Mussolini went from a negative response to doubt, then to a conditioned acceptance, and finally to a definitive decision. It is precisely the complexity of the process which allows us to draw several conclusions. The first is that the Italians – like the Germans – made Franco a privileged interlocutor, and this was to have considerable importance in his race to absolute power.[41] Ciano's central role in the process is equally outstanding; his willingness to embark on the Spanish adventure was much clearer than that of Mussolini himself. Yet it was the Duce who had, less than a month before, placed his son-in-law at the head of the Foreign Ministry with the precise objective of dynamizing Italian foreign policy.[42] The difference should therefore not be exaggerated; the two coincided completely at the end, and Ciano himself was obsessed throughout the process with the possibility of the rebels' success. Thus, it was only when both were certain that the movement could triumph with a little Italian aid that the definitive decision was taken.

But this is only one side of the opportunity factor. The other was constituted by the international situation itself and, more concretely, by the reactions of the other powers to the events in Spain. Numerous historians have assumed that the Italian decision was made after learning of the French aid to the Republic, thus supposing a strong defensive component behind it.[43] Actually, the process followed a completely opposite path. Of course, one cannot dismiss the existence of a certain preoccupation in Rome with the possibility that a victorious Republic would shift its foreign policy to a pro-French, anti-Italian focus. And the truth is that as soon as the Spanish government asked to buy arms from the French, the latter showed their willingness to comply.

Yet, from the first moment, the French right had unleashed a violent campaign against its government's intentions. This, together with the coldness which Léon Blum had thought he observed in the British government, introduced the first elements of doubt into the cabinet. And thus, as early as 24 July, the Quai d'Orsay began to back down. The following day the Council of Ministers decided 'not to intervene in any way in the internal conflict in Spain'. Only after learning of the Italian intervention was the decision made to permit the sale of war matériel to Spain, and then in the hope that the non-intervention agreement that was simultaneously proposed would come to fruition meanwhile.[44]

Propagandistic declarations aside, Mussolini was perfectly well informed by his own diplomats and agents in France of the veracity of the withdrawal of the French government. It seems evident, therefore, that the causal relations between one intervention and the other are contrary to what has been mentioned above.[45] When the French government was willing to help the Republic, the Italian government withdrew, probably because of fear of a direct confrontation with France. When the latter began to vacillate for one reason, Mussolini began to doubt for the opposite reason. The definitive French decision not to intervene was followed by the Italian one to do so. The first French planes arrived in Spain several days after the Italian ones. In short, it was the Italian intervention which caused the French one – albeit always timid and wavering – and not the reverse.

Nor did the Soviets, the others who were supposedly responsible for the internationalization of the Spanish Civil War, show any hurry at all to assume this role. And this is a circumstance of which – it should once again be stressed – Mussolini was perfectly cognizant. Indeed, on 27 July a report from Moscow was received in Rome in which the Soviet desire to take refuge in a position of 'prudent neutrality' was reflected. In summary, according to the report, the Soviet authorities would be 'cynically' willing to make a declaration of platonic sympathy towards the Republic in the press. The historiography has widely manifested the reasons for this attitude on the part of the USSR, but what is of interest here is the importance of remembering that the Soviet intervention in the Spanish Civil War was later than the Italian one, and, to a great extent, linked to the failure of the Non-Intervention Committee.[46]

The British reaction was at least as important to Rome as the French one. Although from the beginning of 1936 the Fascist diplomatic corps had given unmistakable signs of *rapprochement* with Germany, the improvement of relations with the United Kingdom was still one of the basic objectives of Italian diplomacy.[47] This wish was shared by London. The British empire could not withstand a war on three fronts, and most of its defensive capacity had to be reserved for the most powerful, Germany and Japan. Hence, the necessity for dispelling the third potential front, in the Mediterranean, which was, in addition, vital for communications with the Far East. For the same reasons, however, the United Kingdom could not allow any farther expansion of Italian power in the Middle East. Consequently, the margin of agreement was reduced to that which Mussolini had outlined: steps towards the recognition of the new Italian empire and some type of declaration of mutual acknowledgment of the respective interests in the Mediterranean. Because of the limited area of agreement, neither of the two powers could be interested in the development of a new area of confrontation.[48]

Hence the importance of the signals that Rome might perceive in the British attitude and the even greater importance of their being fundamentally hostile towards the Republic. Such was, in the first place, the tacit disapproval of the original French decision to help the Republic. In the second place were the small but significant acts in Tangier and Gibraltar which were contrary to the activity of the Republican fleet. In the third place (in this case a passive and involuntary sign) was Franco's desire to be on friendly terms with England, Germany, and Italy. Finally, there was the ill-disguised sympathy which individuals as important as the Conservative leader of the Commons, D. Margesson, or the First Lord of the Admiralty, Samuel Hoare, held for the rebels. Of course, there were certain matters on which the United Kingdom was unwilling to compromise, such as a possible Fascist occupation of the Balearic Islands. Nevertheless, contrary to Paris, London did not give this possibility much credence, and it completely trusted its ability to avoid it by exerting diplomatic pressure. But if Mussolini was quite soon aware of the existence of these limits, he was equally aware of the fact that, as long as he did not overstep them, he would be permitted many other things.[49]

It has been suggested that the German decision to help Franco was fundamental in giving Italy the decisive boost.[50] There is no documentation whatsoever to support this suggestion and every consideration seems to indicate that the two decisions were made independently. What was indeed known in Rome was that the Spanish rebels had gone to Berlin and had even allowed themselves an attempt at minor blackmail in this regard, as discussed above. Consequently, what is most probable is that the German factor had some influence on Mussolini's decision, although certainly much less than the British or French.

No less important than the reaction from the various powers, and especially the Western ones, was the fact that, from a global viewpoint, the conservative opinion of the world leaned decidedly towards the rebels. This was clearly reflected by the overwhelming dominance in that milieu of the anti-Communist paradigm versus the anti-Fascist paradigm. The Spanish Civil War would later contribute decisively to a certain inversion of the weight of the two paradigms, but for the moment the Spanish Republic would be the first victim of that predominance. It is possible that in the Fascist or Nazi media the possible process of Bolshevization, beginning in Spain, was seen as an immediate danger. But what is certain is that both Hitler and Mussolini were well aware that they could pose as standard-bearers of Western civilization by espousing anti-Communism.

In summary, in barely ten days the situation had undergone a complete about-face, both in Spain and in the international context. Before 18 July there had seemed to be no alternative whatsoever for the government of the Frente Popular, and the conspirators no longer merited any belief at all in Rome. Any interference in the internal affairs of Spain could be considered – or it could be feared that it would be considered – a provocation which could endanger the fundamental objectives of Fascist foreign policy. Ten days later, the Spanish government seemed to be shipwrecked between the rebellion and the revolutionary violence unleashed in response, and the uprising had serious possibilities of succeeding. At the international level, Spain had surprisingly been left terribly isolated. Neither France nor the USSR came to its aid. No one seemed to be ignorant of the fact that the British neutrality scarcely concealed an underlying hostility towards the Republic. The cause of anti-Communism recovered an enormous amount of credibility in worldwide opinion.

THE EMPIRE AS THE HORIZON

The decision process which we have studied says little about the underlying objectives of the Italian intervention. At most it refers to the existence of that negative point of reference which France always was, and to certain ideological contents of an anti-Communist tone. The truth is that it was logical that this should have occurred. First, in such a process, the fundamental weight is in the conjunction of situational factors, and secondly, the decisions had to be oriented towards preexisting objectives identified with a secret imperialist policy based on ideological hostility: the overthrow of the Spanish democracy and the attainment of a friendly and anti-French Spain.

It was not, as we have seen, a matter of conquering or acquiring any part of the Spanish territory or its colonies. Nor was there any aspiration regarding the Balearic Islands other than their possible strategic use by agreement with the Spanish government.[51] If there was an economic objective, it was secondary and not immediate, more in the nature of favouring Italian investments in Spain or the existence of commercial policies rather than of any possible scavenging of Spanish raw materials. What was sought was something much less and, at the same time, much more than all this: to make Spain an ally that would contribute to cementing Italian hegemony in the Mediterranean. Anti-French, at minimum, and anti-British if the circumstances finally allowed, Spanish friendship was basic to the liberation of Italy from the sense of a bottleneck in the Mediterranean. As Mussolini would later say, with the victory in Spain, Italy gained free access to the ocean.[52]

The mere posing of this issue reveals the magnitude of the change that took place in Italian foreign policy. The opportunity factor had been essential to the decision to intervene: the aid granted was small and at the same time presumed to be decisive. The risks were slim, and the foreseeable results were ample. But once it was adopted and the hypothesis of a quick and easy triumph was discarded, Italian foreign policy remained trapped in the Spanish scenario. This was not, however, an almost involuntary slip into a kind of quicksand.[53] The Italian empire had been proclaimed in Ethiopia, thus fulfilling one of the fundamental aspirations of Italian foreign policy on its eastern side. But this would contribute to the introduction of an imperial logic in confronting the problems of the whole Mediterranean. As we have seen, in July 1936 Mussolini had not planned to start the game in the extreme west, but once it had started and participation in it had been decided, there was no turning back. From being a relatively secondary element in the framework of Fascist foreign policy, Spain had come to place itself at the centre of it.

The destruction of the Spanish democracy was another of the elements of Mussolini's policy towards Spain. This avenue had seemed to be blocked at the end of 1934, but when events evolved in a direction which made it possible, it could be retaken with strength. In a way, the situation reverted to the one of five years earlier, when Mussolini had written his maxim regarding the proclamation of the Republic, or when, at a more general level, he had begun to prophesy about the inevitably Fascist – or Fascistized – future of Europe. From this perspective, whether Mussolini aspired to the construction of a new Fascist state in Spain is largely a false problem.[54] The Duce may well have aspired to it, but his sense of reality made him content himself with much less; it was enough for him that a vaguely corporate dictatorship, generically inspired by Fascism, was established. Before 1936 he had supported the reactionary monarchists while they seemed able to overthrow the Republic. After July 1936, there could well have been a complete and absolute triumph of the Falange, but if this proved an obstacle to victory it was better to support Franco, who was, after all, a Fascistized conservative.[55]

The defeat of the Spanish democracy was also important from the point of view of Italian domestic policy, in part because of the open anti-Fascist sentiment that the Spanish Republicans brought to their fight. But it was also because the Spanish conflict would function as a point of reference for the various sectors which converged in support of Mussolini's regime. Outside the Fascist Party, the intervention in Spain was supported by the Catholics, who had been won over by the religious and law-and-order character of the struggle. Within the party, it was supported by moderates who wished to give the intervention a sense closer to that of earlier ones and thought that this stance might also influence the internal dynamics of the regime. But the more radical and less compromising sector of the party supported the intervention as well, although for the opposite reason – to reinforce the importance of the party itself in regard to other conservative sectors. Similarly, the militia supported an intervention that would be, for it, a 'Fascist war', in revenge for the greater role played by the army in the war in Ethiopia.[56]

Mussolini himself could not have been unaware of all this. Not in vain did the Spanish war coincide with the beginnings of what would in time become the *svolta totalitaria* of the regime, a shift characterized precisely by a strong movement against the conservative sectors, against the 'bourgeoisie', and in favour of the Fascist ideologization of Italian life, in which warmongering was central.[57] The Italian intervention in Spain was therefore, from this point of view, seemingly perfectly interwoven with the domestic dynamics of the regime and its political-ideological evolution.

In summary, there were no contradictions between the strategic, ideological, and domestic policy objectives of the Italian intervention in the Spanish Civil War. Gaining hegemony in the Mediterranean, empowering the existence of a new Fascist or Fascistized dictatorship, and dynamizing domestic policy, far from being contradictory or mutually exclusive, harmoniously corresponded to the very nature of the regime. The ten days from 18 to 28 July were in this regard crucial on the international scene as well as the Spanish one, in the area of bilateral relations as well as in the regime's internal dynamics. It was probably Giuseppe Bottai who best captured the specificity of the moment and everything involved in it. For him, the Italian intervention in the Spanish war was in fact a problem of imperial and revolutionary coherence. Other types of imperialism, such as the British, might be trapped by the contradiction between their imperial objectives and their democratic politics, but not so the Fascist one.[58] In fact, imperial Fascism, defined as foreign aggression, ideological imperialism, and domestic revolution, found its best expression in Italy's participation in the Spanish Civil War.

Translated by Susan E. Núñez

NOTES

1. R. De Felice, *Mussolini il duce. Gli anni del consenso, 1929–1936* (Torino, 1974), p.308.
2. B. Mussolini, 'Aforismi', Archivio Centrale dello Stato (ACS), Segretaria particolare del Duce (1929–1943), Autografi del Duce (1931), b.6.
3. See De Felice, *Mussolini il duce*, pp.129–31; I. Saz, *Mussolini contra la II República* (Valencia, 1986), pp.30–32; J. Tusell and I. Saz, 'Mussolini y Primo de Rivera: Las relaciones políticas y diplomáticas de dos dictaduras mediterráneas', *Boletín de la Real Academia de la Historia*, 179, 3, pp.471–80.
4. I. Saz, 'The Dictatorship of Primo de Rivera: Halfhearted Revisionism', in P. Preston and S. Balfour (eds.), *Spain and the Great Powers* (London, 1999) Cf. S. Sueiro, *España en el Mediterráneo: Primo de Rivera y la 'Cuestión Marroquí', 1923–1930* (Madrid, 1992); and G. Palomares, *Mussolini y Primo de Rivera: Política exterior de dos dictaduras* (Madrid, 1989).
5. Cf. M. Mazzetti, 'I contatti del governo italiano con i cospiratori militari spagnoli prima del luglio 1936', *Storia Contemporanea* (1979), pp.1181–93.
6. Quoted in De Felice, *Mussolini il duce* (Torino, 1981), pp.360–61.
7. Ibid.
8. Ibid.
9. Cf. R. Quartararo, *Roma tra Londra e Berlino. La política estera fascista dal 1930 al 1940* (Rome, 1980), p.305.
10. At the same time, no great importance should be attributed to the existence of a report by Italo Balbo explaining the military importance for Italy of the possession of Melilla. It was in fact a report drafted in response to declarations made by a Spanish minister, the socialist Indalecio Prieto, in favour of abandoning Morocco. These declarations caused a certain stir in Europe and gave rise to an Italian study of what claims could be asserted in the case of such a Spanish abandonment. The Spanish government's rapid disavowal of Prieto's declarations immediately resolved the matter. Saz, *Mussolini contra la II República*, p.36.
11. J.A. Ansaldo, *¿Para qué...? (De Alfonso XIII a Juan III)* (Buenos Aires, 1951), pp.31–5; R. Guariglia, *Ricordi 1922–1946* (Napoli, 1949), pp.188–9; Saz, *Mussolini contra la II República*, pp.35–40.
12. Guariglia, *Ricordi*, pp.193–9; idem *Primi passi in diplomazia e rapporti dall'ambasciata di Madrid (1932–1934), a cura di Ruggero Moscati* (Napoli, 1972), p.187.
13. Guariglia, *Ricordi*, pp.185–7.
14. Guariglia, *Primi passi in diplomazia*, pp.196–204
15. Ibid., pp.261–3; also P. Brundu Olla, *L'equilibrio difficile: Gran Bretagna, Italia e Francia nel Mediterraneo (1930–1937)* (Milan, 1980), pp.39–41.
16. I. Saz, 'The Second Republic in the International Arena', in Preston and Balfour, *Spain and the Great Powers*.
17. Ibid.
18. Saz, *Mussolini contra la II República*, pp.76–82.
19. J.F. Coverdale, *La intervención fascista en la Guerra Civil española* (Madrid, 1979), pp.61–4; Saz, *Mussolini contra la II República*, pp.66–74.
20. Mazzetti, 'I contatti del governo italiano con i cospiratori militari spagnoli', p.1185.
21. R. Quartararo, 'Política fascista nelle Baleari (1936–1939)', *Quaderni FIAP* (1977), p.1011.
22. Saz, *Mussolini contra la II República*, p.78.
23. See Coverdale, *La intervención fascista*, p.63.
24. Specifically, 250 machine-guns, almost three million cartridges, 9,540 hand grenades and 9,984 rifles. Approximately 45 men were trained at the Furbara airport. Mazzetti, 'I contatti del governo italiano con i cospiratori militari spagnoli', pp.1190–91; Saz, *Mussolini contra la II República*, pp.73–4.
25. On the foreign policy inclinations of the CEDA, see, M.A. Egido León, *La concepción de la política exterior española durante la 2a República* (Madrid, 1987), pp.217–70.
26. I. Saz, 'Acerca de la política exterior de la 2a República: La opinión pública y los gobiernos españoles ante la guerra de Etiopía', *Itálica*, 17 (1982), pp.265–82; F. Quintana Navarro, *España en Europa, 1931–1936. Del compromiso por la paz a la huida de la guerra* (Madrid, 1993), pp.251–31.

27. Saz, 'Acerca de la política exterior de la 2a República', pp.271–4.
28. The subvention, set at 50,000 lira per month, was received by Primo de Rivera between June 1935 and January 1936. After that time it was reduced to half, as was the aid received by Buccard. Primo de Rivera's detention later prevented the reception of this aid, although this amount was still allotted until November 1936. A. Viñas, *La Alemania nazi y el 18 de julio* (Madrid, 1977), pp.299 ff. and 420–25; Saz, *Mussolini contra la II República*, pp.138–45 and 242–3.
29. Saz, *Mussolini contra la II República*, pp.151–6.
30. Ibid.
31. Coverdale, *La intervención fascista*, pp.70–71; Saz, *Mussolini contra la II República*, pp.156–63.
32. Saz, *Mussolini contra la II República*, pp.163–74.
33. P. Preston, *Franco: A Biography* (London, 1993), pp.144–56.
34. L. Bolín, *Spain. The Vital Years* (Philadelphia, 1967), pp.159–68; Coverdale, *La intervención fascista*, pp.79–80; P. Preston, 'Mussolini's Spanish Adventure. From Limited Risk to War', in P. Preston and A.L. Mackenzie (eds.), *The Republic Besieged: Civil War in Spain 1936–1939* (Edinburgh, 1996), pp.25–95; Saz, *Mussolini contra la II República*, pp.179–81.
35. See that text in Viñas, *La Alemania nazi*, pp.308–10; also in J. Gutiérrez Ravé, *Antonio Goicoechea* (Madrid, 1965), pp.34–6.
36. The decisiveness of Goicoechea's negotiations is assumed by, among others, Coverdale, *La intervención fascista*, pp.81–2; De Felice, *Mussolini il duce,* p.365; Viñas, *La Alemania nazi*, pp.305–11; A. Rovighi and F. Stefani, *La participazione italiana alla guerra civile spagnola (1936–1939)* (Rome, 1992), Vol.1, *Testo,* pp.77–8; and F. Pedriali, *Guerra di Spagna e aviazione italiana* (Rome, 1992), p.33.
37. Saz, *Mussolini contra la II República*, pp.187–91; similarly, Preston, 'Mussolini's Spanish Adventure', pp.24 and 32–5.
38. Saz, *Mussolini contra la II República*, pp.181–6 and 247–51; Preston, 'Mussolini's Spanish Adventure', pp.29–42.
39. Ibid.
40. Viñas, *La Alemania nazi*, pp.337 ff.
41. Preston, *Franco*, pp.158–60
42. J. Petersen, *Hitler e Mussolini: La difficile alleanza* (Rome and Bari, 1975), pp.407–34.
43. J. Salas Larrazabal, *Intervención extranjera en la guerra de España* (Madrid, 1974), p.31; F. Swartz, *La internacionalización de la guerra civil española, julio de 1936–marzo de 1937* (Barcelona, 1972), p.76; Coverdale, *La intervención fascista*, pp.83 ff; De Felice, *Mussolini el duce*, pp.366–8
44. D.W. Pike, *Les Francais et la guerre d'Espagne* (Paris, 1975), pp.79–93; P. Renouvin, 'La politique exterieure du primer gouvernement Léon Blum', in *Léon Blum chef du gouvernement 1936–1937* (Paris, 1967), pp.329–34; J.-B. Duroselle, *La décadence 1932–1939* (Paris, 1979), pp.301–5; Preston, 'Mussolini's Spanish Adventure', pp.36–9.
45. Saz, *Mussolini contra la II República*, pp.197–202.
46. Ibid., pp.205–7; Preston, 'Mussolini's Spanish Adventure', pp.39–40; J. Haslam, *The Soviet Union and the Struggle for Collective Security in Europe, 1933–1939* (London, 1984), pp.107ff.
47. Petersen, *Hitler e Mussolini*, pp.407–10; R. Quartararo, *Roma tra Londra e Berlino*, pp.271–2.
48. E. Moradiellos, *Neutralidad benévola* (Oviedo, 1990), p.129; I. Saz, 'El fracaso del éxito: Italia en la guerra de España', *Espacio, Tiempo y Forma*, 5, 5 (1992), pp.109–10.
49. J. Edwards, *The British Government and the Spanish Civil War, 1936–1939* (London, 1979), pp.16–20; Moradiellos, *Neutralidad benevola*, pp.147–69; Preston, 'Mussolini's Spanish Adventure', pp.37–9; Saz, 'El fracaso del exito', pp.107–8.
50. D.M. Smith, *Mussolini's Roman Empire* (London, 1976), p.99.
51. Coverdale, *La intervencion fascista*, p.84.
52. MacGregor Knox, 'Il fascismo e la política estera italiana', in *La política estera italiana (1860–1985): A cura di R. J.B. Bosworth e S. Romano* (Bologna, 1991), p.326; Saz, *Mussolini contra la II República*, p.235.

53. Cf. De Felice, *Mussolini il duce*, pp.364 ff.
54. Cf. Coverdale, *La intervención fascista*, pp.89–91 and 119–24.
55. Saz, *Mussolini contra la II República*, pp.219–24; idem, 'Salamanca, 1937: Los fundamentos de un régimen', *Revista de Extremadura*, 21 (1996), pp.91ff.
56. A. Aquarone, 'La guerra di Spagna e l'opinione pubblica italiana', *Il Cannocchiale*, 4–6 (1966), pp.3–36; A. Albonico, 'Accenti critici di parte fascista e cattolica alla "Cruzada"', in *Italia y la guerra civil española* (Madrid, 1986), pp.1–8; De Felice, *Mussolini il duce*, pp.375–81.
57. Cf. De Felice, *Mussolini il duce*, pp.3–155.
58. G. Bottai, 'Sul piano imperiale', *Critica Fascista*, 21 (1 Sept. 1936), pp.321–2.

The International Policy of the Second Republic during the Spanish Civil War

RICARDO MIRALLES

The Spanish Civil War, lasting from 1936 to 1939, awakened passions in its time as have few other conflicts. Concerned that events in Spain might drag France and Britain into an international war, successive French and British governments used what was known as 'non-intervention' to try to isolate their countries from the hostilities. The policy of non-intervention in Spanish affairs proved detrimental to the Republican regime. This article analyses the diplomatic moves made by the Spanish government to counteract its effect.

Consideration of the international dimension of the Spanish Civil War is clearly essential to a proper understanding of the conflict, if only because the war itself would never have taken on the proportions it eventually did without the intervention of a number of European powers. Although the international repercussions of the Spanish Civil War have been widely studied, historiography has tended to concentrate either on the impact of the conflict on the major powers of the time or on the repercussions of the foreign policies of those powers in Spain. Such approaches do not, however, give a complete view of the international dimension of the Spanish Civil War, as they tend not to consider the effects of the foreign policy followed by Spain itself. Having accepted the international ramifications of the conflict, it hardly seems appropriate to ignore the diplomatic activity of the Republic.

International relations involving Spain during the Civil War were overshadowed by the non-intervention pact, despite the obvious tendency of different powers to ignore the pact as and when it suited them.[1] The main consequence was that the Second Republic, the legitimate regime in Spain in 1936, was subjected from the beginning to a highly damaging policy of embargo which deprived it of its legal right to buy arms in friendly countries or on the international markets. The arms problem favoured General Franco's rebel faction, which managed to procure all kinds of materials and military aid from Germany and Italy. Non-intervention also blocked the diplomatic initiatives of the Republic, as it was forced to go through the committee set up in London to supervise the observance of the non-intervention policy. Not being a member of the committee, it was unable to make direct diplomatic moves.

Far from being able to ignore these circumstances, the Second Republic clearly had to adapt to them in devising its foreign policy. The policy itself was based on four principles. First, the Republic accepted non-intervention on the condition that it be effective. In second place, and at the same time, efforts were made either to end non-intervention by accusing Germany and Italy of not observing it, or, if this were not possible, at least to persuade France to relax its border controls to allow the traffic of arms. Third, the Republic worked to achieve the diplomatic support of France and Britain (and, in the case of France, military aid) by trying to involve both powers in an active pursuit of a solution to the conflict. Fourth, it sought to use offers of international mediation as a diplomatic trump card, although this option produced serious divisions within the Republic.

ENFORCING NON-INTERVENTION

The government in Madrid had no alternative but to accept non-intervention and fully understood that its opposition to the initiative would only forestall budding diplomatic activity. Therefore, it concentrated on trying to ensure that the policy was rigorously and impartially enforced while at the same time criticizing it as a failure that merely camouflaged aid to Franco.[2] This was in fact the Republic's most consistent diplomatic line of action throughout the war. Continual violations of the arms embargo led to the adoption of two projects designed to ensure that the agreement was effectively carried out. The first monitoring plan was approved by the London committee on 12 November 1936 and proposed to the two sides on 1 January 1937. It provided for a system whereby impartial observers stationed on borders and in Spanish ports would supervise the entry by land or sea of arms and equipment into Spain. On 16 January 1937, following a proposal made by Foreign Secretary Anthony Eden on 9 January, the committee decided to extend the non-intervention agreement to the recruitment and transport to Spain of non-Spanish nationals to take part in the war.

The issue of foreign 'volunteers', not dealt with in the initial August 1936 agreement, was a new factor with a potential that the Republic was quick to take advantage of by attempting to have it applied to the foreigners already fighting in Spain. As the balance of military personnel was so clearly tipped in favour of Franco's rebel faction, the withdrawal of foreign soldiers would at least restore equilibrium and might even benefit the Republic. This explains why the Republic's continued diplomatic attempts to make non-intervention effective involved successive proposals for an international agreement that would make it possible to expel all foreign combatants from Spain. The idea that all non-Spanish combatants should be withdrawn might help to bring about foreign intervention designed to enforce such a proposal that would bring the two sides even, making a hypothetical negotiation with Franco's faction more feasible; if not, it was still possible for a refusal by Franco to accept the withdrawal of the 'volunteers' to blow the lid off non-intervention, which would bring about the end of the embargo imposed on the Republic. This was a constant concern of Spanish foreign policy, particularly where France and Britain were concerned, although the Republic had nothing to show for it in the end.

A number of the Republic's diplomatic initiatives were in fact designed to involve Britain and France in the issue directly. The most important of these was undoubtedly the memorandum presented to both powers on 9 February 1937, according to which, in return for certain territorial sacrifices by Spain and a renunciation of its neutrality, the French and British governments were asked to take measures to block the supply of arms and men to the rebels and, especially, to promote the withdrawal of the combatants already engaged in the war.

The idea of foreign combatants being withdrawn was immediately taken up by the Western democracies. From that moment on, the efforts of the London committee entrusted with supervising the non-intervention pact, and of its main promoters – France and, in particular, Britain – concentrated on the issue of such a withdrawal.

Although the British proposed an agreement for the withdrawal of foreigners on 1 March, the second monitoring plan, approved on 8 March and implemented from 20 April, did not take this possibility into account. The new plan, which created a council to preside over its application, together with controls at external frontiers and naval patrols, immediately caused serious problems, and the whole thing fell apart in May 1937. After several incidents at sea, Germany and Italy decided to withdraw from the naval patrols, and it seemed that non-intervention was headed for failure, apparently bringing the tantalizing possibility of the Republic recovering its international freedom that much closer. It was not to be, however. Quite the contrary, in fact: Franco-British policy now concentrated on finding a means of making the two Axis powers return to the monitoring system, with Britain offering a halfway-house proposal on 14 July 1937 that provided for the withdrawal of foreigners, the concession of limited belligerents' rights to both sides once the withdrawal was well under way, and the replacement of the naval patrol by observers located in Spanish ports, along with monitoring of the borders.

Franco's rejection of the new proposal, together with the pirate campaign carried out by the Italian submarine fleet in the western

Mediterranean in August, was a matter of grave concern in diplomatic and French government circles and led to the Nyon conference held 10–14 September that same year. With regard to Spain, the diplomatic involvement of France and Britain in the issue resulted in the presentation, on 2 October 1937, of a joint note to Italy with a proposal for tripartite conversations on the withdrawal of combatants.[3] However, Italy flatly refused any talks that did not involve Germany, and forced Britain once again to accept the ineffective London committee as the framework for dealing with the problem. This development signalled the abrupt end of the admittedly dim Spanish hopes of seeing non-intervention either properly enforced or done away with altogether.[4]

Further, the agreement in principle on the withdrawal of combatants was not reached until 4 November, on the basis of the three-point proposal of 14 July regarding limited belligerence, departure of foreigners, and sea and frontier controls. The Spanish Republicans, who were forced into accepting the proposal to avoid being accused of boycotting it, rightly feared that its application would lead to the closure of the frontier. On 26 May 1938, a British transactional proposal was approved by the Non-Intervention Committee, enabling the reestablishment of land and sea controls, the scaled withdrawal of foreign combatants, and the limited concession of belligerent rights. London reckoned that this was sufficient to clear the way for an armistice that both sides would be forced to accept, although closing the frontier was considered essential. The plan for controlling the withdrawal of the 'volunteers' did not in fact take shape until a British proposal was accepted by the London committee on 5 July,[5] by which time, as the Spanish government had feared, the frontier had been closed for nearly a month.

In short, the Spanish Republic reaped no particular benefit from the diplomatic formula founded on the agreement to withdraw foreign combatants. On the contrary, in practice it proved highly damaging, particularly when, in the last phase of the proposal's existence, Britain linked the withdrawal plan to the need to seal the French border hermetically, a step taken on 13 June 1938. The London proposal eventually came to nothing anyway when, on 15 August, Franco raised a series of major objections to the plan.[6] After this, the Republic naturally abandoned the proposal for an agreement to withdraw combatants. Perhaps the only positive thing about the agreement, which never actually materialized, was that it prevented Franco from being given belligerent's rights, something he was never to receive.

FRENCH AID: 'ATTENUATED NON-INTERVENTION'

The Spanish Republic's second, simultaneous, line of foreign policy action concentrated on trying to bring about the end of non-intervention by accusing Germany and Italy of not observing it. Although the chances of achieving this aim were always slim, it was thought that France might at least be persuaded to relent and allow its frontier to be used for the transfer of arms. Indeed, French collaboration took the form of what the French Prime Minister, the Socialist Léon Blum, referred to as 'attenuated non-intervention' – in other words, a kind of official contraband that permitted the passage of Soviet armaments through its territory. This was about the extent of French aid: no sales of arms, much less military intervention. Even so, despite the paucity of the help provided, it is true that if Soviet equipment had not been allowed to cross French territory the war would certainly have ended much sooner with the defeat of the Spanish Republic. The Republic's diplomats had to work very hard to keep the passage open, as the threat of closure, which eventually occurred in June 1938, hung over it from the very first day. Besides, the Pyrenean border became vitally important to Spain from the summer of 1937 onward, when supplies from the USSR were prevented by Italian submarines from arriving via the Mediterranean and were subsequently diverted to ports on France's Atlantic coast, from where they were either sent on to Marseilles *en route* to other destinations or, as occurred more frequently, crossed directly into Spain by land over the Catalonian border.

The potential of this second path lay in the continual violations of the non-intervention pact by the two Fascist powers, Germany and Italy, and their intervention on behalf of the Franco faction, which gave the Republic the opportunity to criticize the pact itself and to call for the border to be completely opened up. This two-pronged line of attack seemed especially productive in the second half of 1937, and from July to October in particular, when the French government decided it could not tolerate further infringements of non-intervention or, at least, the lack of any effective response to such infringements. So, in July, the French government suspended the monitoring activities of the international observers on the border, which became much easier to cross. At a meeting of the League of Nations in September, the new head of the Republican government, Juan Negrín, took advantage of this development to ask Eden and Delbos to open up the border completely, as well as asking the latter to send French officers and non-commissioned officers to reinforce the Republican army.

The international situation became even more favourable for Republican interests in the last quarter of 1937, when France toyed with the idea of opening up the border completely to the traffic of arms. It was in fact French concern about this that led to the presentation of the abovementioned Franco-British note to Italy on 2 October of that year. As a result of the subsequent Italian refusal, France provided all sorts of facilities at its Spanish border. Renewed Spanish diplomatic efforts during the second half of 1937 and the first quarter of 1938 facilitated the supply of arms to the Republic via the French border. As long as it remained impossible to bring non-intervention to an end, it was clear that the Republic's diplomats needed to do their utmost to ensure that the door was kept open. The French authorization for the passage of equipment over the border into Catalonia helped to compensate for both the difficulties the Republic encountered on the international scene and the times when Nazi-Fascist intervention in Spain intensified.

RELATIONS WITH THE DEMOCRATIC POWERS

The third ingredient of the Spanish Republic's foreign policy was the attempt to win French and British diplomatic support for its cause by forcing both powers to become actively involved in the search for a solution to the conflict rather than just standing by. This was the reason behind the support for the monitoring plans and the withdrawal of foreign combatants proposed by France and Britain; the Republic wanted to be seen to be willing to collaborate with Franco-British diplomatic initiatives in the London committee. But not all the Republic's efforts were concentrated on the committee. It also made number of other diplomatic moves designed to convert the democratic powers.

The most ambitious of these initiatives during the early part of the war was the presentation to both countries on 9 February 1937 of a memorandum in which the Republic declared itself willing to contribute to a 'general European settlement'. To this end, the Republic proposed an international policy 'in the form of an active collaboration with France and the United Kingdom' and an agreement with both countries which would involve Spain abandoning its neutrality. The Republic's 'contribution' was to be its area of the protectorate of Morocco, provided that any such modification to the situation of its possessions in North Africa did not benefit powers other than France or the United Kingdom. The Republic hoped that 'the mobilization of the Spanish possessions' would, through more extensive territorial agreements, facilitate 'solutions to problems at the very heart of the present difficulties'. According to the Spanish Ambassador in London, Pablo de Azcárate, the reason for this project was that 'it would then be possible to satisfy some major claims made by National Socialist Germany and would also open the door to a possible revision of its policy in Spain'. But for this to happen France and Britain would themselves have to be willing, in exchange, to make certain territorial 'mobilizations' in their colonies favourable to Germany. Unfortunately for Spain, Britain was not willing. Further, the condition set by Spain for its territorial sacrifices and for abandoning its neutrality was that the French and British governments should take measures to block the supply of arms and men to the rebels and, above all, to promote the 're-embarkation on a specific date ... of all foreign persons, without exception and whatever their mission, currently taking part in the domestic Spanish conflict'. Minister Delbos and members of the staff at the Quai d'Orsay like René Massigli and Pierre Vienot received the idea with a good deal of caution, although Blum was rather more taken with it. However, the rejection by the British meant that this specifically Spanish-promoted formula for appeasing Germany came to nothing.[7]

On this occasion, as always when it came to dealing with the Spanish problem, France preferred not to do anything that might lead to its isolation, particularly from Britain. Spain was aware of this from the beginning and fought to break the link that bound France to Britain and deprived the former of its freedom of action with regard to the Spanish Civil War. This French dependence on British policy at the time has now been demonstrated beyond doubt, and, bearing in mind the widespread animosity towards the Madrid government in British government circles and the early British preference for a victory for Franco (provided it did not imply his future alignment with the Axis powers), it is not hard to guess at the consequences for Spain of France slavishly following British foreign policy. But it is also clear that any deviation from the policy dictated from London would have resulted in the absolute isolation of Paris. Even so, non-intervention became a powerful restraint on French governments while they fretfully watched Germans and Italians 'intervene' with impunity just a few kilometres from their border.

In these conditions, the Republic aimed above all to reorient French diplomacy with regard to the Spanish Civil War. The main thrust of Spanish diplomacy was that the war in Spain was an issue closely involving French national security. Over and over again, the Republic's diplomats insisted that it was not so much a question of helping Spain as of avoiding the danger for France represented by a hostile regime, supported by the Axis powers, installed just over the border. In this period, the Republic unfailingly kept up this line of argument, occasionally causing a certain amount of discomfort on the French side. The collaboration of the Axis powers with Franco tended to consolidate a situation that put its own security in danger, and France needed to treat the facilities granted to the Republic as vital.[8] However, the pressure on France only gave rise to the understandable belief that the Spanish Republic was trying to extend the conflict as a means of saving itself. This policy was only going to be successful, in the Republic's view, if France could be freed from the dictates of British foreign policy. Undoing the very solid knot that united France and Britain but strengthening rather than weakening France's position in the process was therefore a priority for Republican diplomacy. The Republic reckoned that France was weakened every time it made a concession in line with the British policy of appeasement of Europe's dictators. However, the objective proved impossible to achieve. Any reactivation of French diplomacy regarding Spain, such as the ones that occurred between August and November 1937 and in March 1938, was smartly stifled by Britain. And from April 1938 on, with the formation of the Daladier government and, above all, the new diplomatic orientation of French foreign policy with Georges Bonnet at the helm, things clearly took a turn for the worse for the Spanish Republic.

The French policy under Bonnet of alliance with England at any price was highly detrimental to Spain's interests, to those of other countries, and to France itself. Appeasement meant *rapprochement* with Italy and Germany and the relegation of its commitments to eastern European countries. Altogether, French diplomatic potential disappeared from view, and Spain was left to count the cost of its neighbour's growing weakness.

Rapprochement with Italy was one of the conditions of the British policy of appeasement, with Bonnet providing the French version. London was anxious that nothing should disturb understanding between Mediterranean countries, and much less a minor country like Spain. But it must be said that, while France gained nothing from its approaches to Italy, Spain felt the consequences.

The French approximation to the British view of things, which had adverse consequences for Spain, began with the Franco-British conversations held in London on 28 and 29 April 1938. The pressure brought to bear by the British on the French government was intensified with a view to getting the Spanish border closed. As we have seen, on 26 May the Non-Intervention Committee approved a British transactional proposal which backed restoring the land and sea controls, the beginning of a scaled withdrawal of foreign combatants, and the concession of limited belligerents' rights. London felt that, on this basis, the way should be opened to imposing some kind of armistice. The closure of the border, however, was considered essential and occurred on 13 June 1938.

The Republic could only lament a measure which caused it serious harm without offering any clear advantage in return. Azcárate, for whom the only result of 12 months of 'wrangling and discussions' was the closure of the French border, the main, if not the only, channel available for supplying the Republican army with equipment, described the French and British governments as 'accomplices' of Hitler and Mussolini.[9] The closure of the

French border was extremely serious for the Republic; although it was reopened at the end of the year to allow the passage of refugees fleeing from Franco's offensive in Catalonia, the slow strangulation of the line of supply was to prove fatal to the legal Spanish regime. The closure was opposed by leading French politicians of all hues and tendencies, including León Blum, Edouard Herriot, Paul Reynaud, and Georges Mandel, who protested at such a move being made without real compensation. But the protests went no farther.

The solution adopted by France can only be explained in the light of the new policy guidelines introduced under Bonnet. While policy before Munich, led by Britain, tended towards a *rapprochement* with Italy with the aim of linking it to the Western powers, the turn taken in European affairs at Munich led Bonnet to attempt *rapprochement* with Hitler's Germany. As René Girault has pointed out, between September 1938 and March 1939 French foreign policy under Bonnet took an original line designed to exploit the results of Munich rather than just meekly accepting them.

The Munich crisis revived Republican hopes of a favourable change in the general European situation or at least a strengthening of France's position through a firm commitment to the cause of the Spanish Republic. In both cases, this proved to be wishful thinking.

The Czechoslovak crisis of September 1938 furnished the Republic's diplomats with an apparently irrefutable argument in support of the basic Spanish case linking the mutual security of the two republics. Attempts to provoke a reaction in the French were, however, doomed to failure.[10] Not only did the argument prove ineffective; it is in fact fair to say that the solution to the Czech crisis marked the end of Spanish Republican hopes of a change in French policy. From then on, the general impression was that it was pointless to expect anything of France. Republican disillusionment at the Munich arrangement was clear. The French Ambassador, Eirik Labonne, informed his own government of the profound disenchantment that Munich had caused in the Republican government in Barcelona, despite its official line of relief that peace at least had been preserved.[11]

The government of the Spanish Republic attempted to respond to the new situation through a diplomatic manoeuvre involving the presentation to the governments in London and Paris on 30 December 1938 of a memorandum entitled 'Position of the Spanish Government Concerning the Problem of the Mediterranean'. It was to be one of the last diplomatic cards the government of the Spanish Republic was to play and was an attempt to become involved in a four-sided Mediterranean agreement that included Italy and the two Western democratic powers. The memorandum stated that the first step of the policy the Republic was willing to agree to would consist in 'persuading Italy that the triumph of the Republic in Spain would not exclude normality in political and economic relations between the two countries'. Spain offered a 'solemn commitment', which could be guaranteed by the French and British governments, to respect such interests. In our view, the memorandum was the Spanish version of the policy of appeasement of Italy. However that may be, it came to nothing, as Bonnet's approach was already oriented exclusively towards seeking mediation that would make an end to the conflict possible, even while it was throwing out feelers towards the faction that looked well set to win the war.[12]

MEDIATION ATTEMPTS

The fourth and final governing principle of the Spanish Republic's foreign policy action consisted in using the offers of international mediation as an extra diplomatic trump card. Not that this approach was ever tried with much conviction; on the contrary, it caused some very serious divisions within the Republic itself.

To a certain extent, it is true to say that none of the Republican governments of the period followed a policy of mediation with any degree of determination, among other reasons because such a course might easily be interpreted by the enemy as a sign of weakness. But the possibility of mediation was seen not just as *non-negotiable* but also as *unacceptable*, particularly after Munich, when 'mediation mania' took hold in France and Britain. The government of Barcelona simply interpreted it as the announcement of a Spanish replay of the Czechoslovak drama.

Manuel Azaña, President of the Republic, had always believed that this was the only way to end the war. He thought that in military terms the Republic was beaten but diplomacy could still save it. From the very beginning, he insisted that the outcome of the war should be prepared politically and did everything he could to ensure that the political groups that might have some influence on the situation would work on the Republic's behalf. His plan involved the withdrawal of combatants through agreements between the powers that the Spanish government would not need to subscribe to formally. When Negrín formed his government in May 1937 he did not oppose these ideas, but he always felt that they would be very hard to put into practice if the Republic was unable to continue fighting the war. This was why, for Negrín, continuing the war was a prerequisite for any attempt at mediation or pacification.

The Western democracies also attempted mediation. On 5 December 1936, the first proposal was made simultaneously by France and Britain to the governments of the powers involved in the war in Spain. According to this proposal, Germany, Italy, Portugal, and the USSR would associate themselves with a Franco-British plan for mediation designed to 'place the country as a whole in a situation whereby the national will could be expressed'. However, the idea came to nothing, largely because it was rejected by Germany and Italy. It was also rejected by the government of the Spanish Republic, whose biggest problem lay in appearing to be willing to follow the initiatives of other governments while avoiding suggesting mediation itself, which might easily be construed as an acknowledgement of defeat and deprive the Republic of any support it might otherwise have achieved. The Republic could consider the withdrawal of combatants and a cease-fire as formulas for arriving at mediation, but it could not make such a proposal, however much it might be disposed to cooperate with a move of that kind. On 1 March 1937, Azcárate met René Massigli, Assistant Director at the Quai d'Orsay, in Paris to tell him that his government agreed that the withdrawal of combatants, followed by a cease-fire, could well favour mediation if the fighting did not flare up again. But, for reasons already explained, he warned against any use of the word 'mediation'. A little later, at the beginning of May, Azaña entrusted Julián Besteiro, a moderate Socialist leader who was travelling to London for the coronation of George VI, with the task of asking the British government to take the initiative towards mediation. During the interview, Eden assured him that he was determined to take the measures necessary to bring the non-intervention powers to agreement on a plan for withdrawing combatants and a cease-fire. However, his plan, of which the powers involved and the Vatican representative, Monsignor Pizzardo, were informed, met with no success. Neither Italy or Germany accepted it, and Franco refused to discuss a peace involving mediation, which, according to him, would be equivalent to a defeat. Nothing but unconditional surrender would satisfy him.[13]

During the second half of 1937, diplomatic discussions centred on the plan for the withdrawal of foreign combatants, a prerequisite for any mediation, and it was not until March 1938 that the proposal resurfaced, at a time of military difficulties for the Republic. During Franco's major offensive on the Aragón front, José Giral, the Spanish Minister for Foreign Affairs, told the French Ambassador, Labonne, how critical the situation was, and that Azaña, Indalecio Prieto, and all the other ministers except for the Communists agreed that things were desperate. Six of them (Prieto included) were in favour of mediation, while five were against. However, when it met officially with Negrín as leader, the government rejected any attempts at mediation. Negrín let the Ambassador know that he was willing to wait for a more favourable international situation and that any agreement by that means was impossible: neither the Spanish people nor Franco himself would accept it.[14] At their 25 March meeting Negrín explained the situation in the following terms: 'At this time, given the present state of mind of the Spanish people, any government that accepted talks on conciliation, that acknowledged defeat in any form, would simply be swept away. It would immediately be replaced by another, infinitely more violent one with a view to carrying on the fight.'[15]

Labonne's report to the Quai d'Orsay declared that the Spanish government rejected mediation for fear that, once news of such a move had spread, resistance would crumble. Azaña felt that a good opportunity had been lost and met Labonne on 31 March. According to what he told him, before the defeat in Aragón (in April 1938) Azaña had thought that the solution was for the Republic to 'declare' the armistice and request – and undoubtedly secure – the involvement of the Western powers in the safeguarding of a regime of transition. Now, however, after the defeat, he thought that political mediation of any kind was impossible and asked Labonne to see that his government was ready, when the situation became 'desperate', for mediation of a humanitarian kind, which would guarantee a reasonably honourable presentation of the defeat and prevent the victors from following a policy of revenge. Labonne had in fact expressed a similar point of view to his government a few days earlier, on 24 March: 'The end of hostilities, the armistice, [should] not [be] "requested" but "declared" and be more or less incorporated into the ambiguity of the international talks on conciliation.' All Labonne's proposals, however, were blocked by France's impotence. The Ambassador was aware that, at that particularly difficult time for the Republic, there was little difference between 'coercive mediation' and 'intervention', but he recommended it all the same. Perhaps that was why first Léger, the Secretary General at the Quai d'Orsay, and then Massigli made it clear to him that France could only 'favour' the aid of others but could do little or nothing on its own.[16]

From April 1938 on, the situation within the Spanish Republic tended to strengthen the position of those in favour of resistance to the bitter end. The French Ambassador described the cabinet formed at the time as a 'ministry of war' that was 'extremely hostile to mediation'. 'In some respects', he told his minister, 'the ministerial change is simply the epilogue to the great debate on mediation that so deeply divided the previous government'.[17] The sector in favour of continuing the war had seen its position consolidated. Negrín, the head of the government, differed from the supporters of mediation on the best way of finding a solution for the Republic. He thought the war could not be given up for lost, as that way the only negotiable thing was defeat itself. So the reaction of Negrín's government to the closure of the border in June 1938 was to reject 'compromises': the word in Barcelona was 'resist or surrender, that is the only alternative'.[18] At its meeting of 27 June, the cabinet agreed to reject mediation or a cease-fire as long as the unfavourable military situation brought about by the closure of the border was not redressed. That was the kind of mediation that Negrín wanted.[19]

According to London, a negotiated settlement was almost impossible while Germany and Italy did not consider it of interest. This view of things clearly meant that any diplomatic initiative would depend on the will of the Axis powers, which made it equally clear just how impotent Britain and France were to 'impose' a settlement. This had already been demonstrated, as we have seen, by the Quai d'Orsay's refusal to consider the proposals of Ambassador Labonne made in March.

The solution found for the Czech crisis in September 1938 destroyed any hope of mediation acceptable to the Republic. And yet support for mediation continued to be serious and widespread after the Munich conclave. This was particularly true in France, where Blum, Herriot, Vincent Auriol, Reynaud, Mandel, and other friends of the Republic advised acceptance of the formula. But for the Spanish government, after Munich a negotiated settlement would be equivalent to surrender pure and simple: 'after the experience of Munich, the only attitude, the only line of conduct to take' was resistance, according to Negrín. On 21 November, the Spanish government publicly rejected any eventual 'solution' arising from the Franco-British talks that were shortly to be held in Paris. The document in question states that 'the Spanish Government could not accept external attempts to solve ... the issue without its collaboration'.[20] In December, Bonnet returned to the attack, telling Pascua once again that mediation was the only solution for peace, but that nothing would be done so long as the Spanish government refused to accept the feasibility of the idea.[21] To the Spanish government the idea of mediation, in the new international situation, would only lead to defeat with a certain number of guarantees, something that it was still not willing to accept. However, when Franco's offensive against Catalonia began on 23 December, things began to move definitively in that direction. It now became difficult to think of any other solution. Azaña at least thought so, especially after 28 January, when General Vicente Rojo, the man in charge of the Republican defences, said in Negrín's presence that further resistance was impossible. The President of the Republic said that the only thing the government could do was to request mediation as a last resort by Britain and France that would ensure expatriation for the Republican political leaders and prevent repression by the victors. Azaña was not willing to accept the policy of his head of government,[22] and on 4 February, with Barcelona lost, he forced a meeting with the British and French representatives, Skrine Stevenson and Jules Henry, at the border. 'We have lost the war', he said to Ambassador Henry, 'not just in Catalonia but in the rest of Spain too.' Azaña added an anguished plea: 'Please do something.'[23] Henry saw Negrín four days later. The French Ambassador realized that the end was near and that Negrín would also now accept help from France. But it was all useless. Franco's refusal to accept anything other than unconditional surrender made it impossible to palliate the final trauma.

The Second Republic did not profit from any of its diplomatic options. It was unable to force a denunciation of non-intervention, despite Germany and Italy's clear violations of the terms of the agreement. It was also unable to separate France from Britain's policy of appeasement. It was scarcely able to prevent Franco from being given belligerents' rights and gained nothing from the offers of mediation that were debated throughout the war. But it did manage one very important thing: keeping the French border largely open. Without that, it could not have carried on the war.

NOTES

1. For the genesis and chronology of the non-intervention pact, see Angel Viñas, 'Los condicionantes internacionales', in M. Tuñón de Lara and others, *La guerra civil española, 50 años después* (Barcelona, 1996), pp.123–97.
2. This was how Alvaro de Albornoz, first Ambassador of the Republic in Paris during the war, put it in a note dated 10 August 1936, addressed to the French Minister for Foreign Affairs: 'The Spanish Government is willing to acknowledge the advantages that such an agreement would have, principally as a means of preventing general international complications ... My Government would be willing to collaborate faithfully in the application of an agreement of this kind ... but it believes it should draw the French Government's attention to the decisive importance of both the time in which the agreement could come into force and the effectiveness of the guarantees for its strict application.'
3. The joint note stated categorically that 'the governments of France and the United Kingdom, however great their desire to uphold the obligations they have accepted under the international agreements on the supply of arms and men to Spain, cannot close their eyes to the difficulty of upholding those obligations unless measures are taken to make the policy of non-intervention real and effective'. At the time, Anthony Eden and Yvon Delbos, the respective heads of British and French diplomacy, certainly did not dismiss the possibility of reopening the frontier if an agreement on the withdrawal of combatants was not speedily reached.
4. The French Foreign Minister, Yvon Delbos, confessed to Eric Phipps, British Ambassador in Paris, that should no such agreement be forthcoming in the committee, either they would have to move towards a joint Franco-British authorization for the free passage of arms to the Spanish Republic or France would be reduced to the status of a second-class power. *Documents Diplomatiques Français* [*DDF*], 2e série, 1936–39, Vol.2, doc.138, and Juan Avilés, *Pasión y farsa: Franceses y británicos ante la guerra civil española* (Madrid, 1994), p.112.
5. The plan of 5 July 1938 was a new, improved version of the 14 July and 4 November agreements of the previous year. It was unfavourable to the Republic, as it linked the concession of belligerent status to the simple constitution of international commissions to monitor and count the combatants, but the legal Spanish regime had to accept the agreement in order not to antagonize the democracies. By July 1938 the British proposal was of course completely useless, except for helping to maintain the fiction of non-intervention, the real objective of British diplomacy.
6. According to Oliver Harvey, private secretary to Lord Halifax, head of the Foreign Office, Edouard Daladier, the head of the French government, and Edouard Herriot, President of the National Assembly, were in favour of denouncing non-intervention now that the border had been closed and Franco was still receiving reinforcements. However, Georges Bonnet, the

French diplomatic chief, gave way to England, for whose support he looked against his own colleagues. See John Harvey (ed.), *The Diplomatic Diaries of Oliver Harvey (1937–1940)* (London, 1970), p.238.

7. Pablo de Azcárate, *Mi embajada en Londres durante la guerra civil* (Barcelona, 1976), p.266.
8. A communique from the government of the Spanish Republic of 18 March 1938 addressed directly to the President of the French cabinet, Edouard Daladier, provides a good example of this approach: 'In the light of the seriousness of the present situation [in reference to Germany's annexation of Austria and Franco's offensive on the Aragon front], the government of the Spanish Republic is obliged to ask the government of the French Republic if it may expect urgent and decisive help. The government of the Spanish Republic considers this request fully justified considering that, by defending the integrity of its own territory, it is also defending the security of France. France cannot remain indifferent to the installation of Germans and Italians in the Pyrenees and on the Mediterranean coast, and less still to Spain's incorporation into the alliance of totalitarian countries. If Europe hopes for a victory, which would be the first that France and Great Britain need to ward off the risk of a general conflagration, we must be given aid in a resolute, determined manner. There is no need to exaggerate the scope that the final outcome of the war in Spain might have to comprehend that France's fate is linked to that outcome.' Archivo Marcelino Pascua (AMP), in the Archivo Historico Nacional, Madrid, box 2, file 1, 18 March 1938.
9. Azcárate, *Mi embajada en Londres*, p.238.
10. This was the main thrust of the argument put by Marcelino Pascua, Spanish Ambassador in Paris, to Bonnet during an interview held on 22 September. Pascua asked the minister 'if the French Government would deem the moment opportune to reconsider, discreetly and with all due caution, its policy of support with regard to the Government of the Republic, in the sense of a direct but prudent supply of a certain kind of armament, of staff officers and other economic facilities', with the object of 'preventing a new Fascism, heavily influenced by Germany, on its Pyrenean border'. Telegram from Pascua to Vayo, 22 Sept. 1938, in AMP, box 1, file 21.
11. *DDF*, Vol.12, p.28.
12. Memorandum, in AMP, box 1, file 22.
13. Azcárate, *Mi embajada en Londres*, p.66, n.1.
14. *DDF*, Vol.8, p.435.
15. *DDF*, Vol.9, p.56.
16. Archives du Ministere des Affaires Etrangeres (Paris), serie 'Papiers d'Agents', Papiers René Massigli, 217, Vols.1 and 14.
17. *DDF*, Vol.9, p.117.
18. Letter from Vayo to Pascua, 15 June 1938, in AMP, box 1, file 21.
19. AMP, box 2, file 1.
20. AMP, box 9, file 2.
21. Conversation between Pascua and Bonnet, 10 Dec. 1938, in AMP, box 1, file 22.
22. Negrín's idea of 'going to the end' was clearly reflected in a telegram he sent to Pascua on 14 January 1939 'Daladier, Reynaud, Mandel must understand resistance continues while we hold inch of land. Firm decision Government and people. Events Catalonia due to absolute lack of most elementary *materiel*. With advance equipment can guarantee all of border that remains in our hands. ... Insist that effort by Spain also benefits France and England. Every day that passes will make result more indecisive and weaken position western powers against Germany and Italy.' AMP, box 2, file 19.
23. Cf. *DDF*, Vol.14, p.38.

The Spanish Civil War and the Mediterranean

MICHAEL ALPERT

The Spanish Civil War occurred at a time when the British navy considered itself insufficiently strong to fight Italy in the Mediterranean while defending Britain's widespread empire. Italy was rearming and resented Britain's refusal to consider Italian rights in the Mediterranean or to recognize its conquest of Abyssinia. The Spanish Civil War gave Italy the chance to support a right-wing regime which would comply with the Italian interests in the Mediterranean, to challenge the security of British and French sea routes, and to inflict damage on British power and prestige. Though Britain in the end did not permit the Italian navy to dominate the entire Mediterranean, it could not prevent the risk of dominance in the western part. The sea route to Republican Spain became increasingly hazardous and by 1938 the Spanish Republic was effectively blocked, which was an important factor in its defeat.

The Spanish Civil War came at a critical moment for the Italian challenge to British domination in the Mediterranean, Britain's route to the east at a time when the empire and the British sphere of influence were at their most extended. Traditionally, that sea had been controlled by the Royal Navy. From 1935 onward, however, Britain's Mediterranean preeminence was challenged by Fascist Italy, which saw the Spanish Civil War of 1936–39 as a vehicle for contesting French and British hegemony. The Italian leader, Mussolini, was creating a powerful navy which, allied with a modern air force, was intended to establish Italy's status as a great power.[1] Italy did not lack sympathy for its aspirations.[2] Although Britain had rejected Italian demands for colonies, the Italian regime was widely admired in Britain. However, the Italian invasion and conquest of Ethiopia in 1935–39, Italian intrigue in the Middle East, and specifically Italian intervention in the Spanish Civil War would bring Italy into conflict with Britain, fundamentally over hegemony in the Mediterranean.

Italy claimed that Britain refused to discuss matters which concerned Italian interests in the Mediterranean and the Middle East.[3] Yet any British concessions to Italy might mean having to accept Italian dominance in the eastern Mediterranean and, if the rebel, or Nationalist, Spanish leader, General Francisco Franco, were victorious, in the western Mediterranean also. The Spanish war would allow Italy to stand in the centre of the European stage and offered it a strong card in its demands for Anglo-French respect and recognition of its Ethiopian empire. Such a changed perception might go some way towards alleviating Italy's view of its difficult position, dependent as it was for vital raw materials on passage through a sea whose entrances it could not command. [4]

For Britain, the Italian challenge came at a time of economic stringency and pervasive pacifism whose consequence was that since 1919 defence estimates had been based on the assumption that it would not be engaged in a major war during the following ten years.[5] Britain's difficulties were compounded by its world-wide responsibilities. A British fleet could not be sent to the Far East in an emergency without jeopardizing security in the Mediterranean. Between 1935 and 1939 the Royal Navy was faced with two crises, Ethiopia and Spain, with insufficient resources to back up a strong response to Italy,[6] which had created the former and turned the latter into a challenge to Britain.

ETHIOPIA

The menace had become manifest when in July 1935 Italy quadrupled its naval construction programme.[7] Italy had more modern and technologically advanced ships than Britain and more tonnage in cruisers and submarines. In August 1935 the British chiefs of staff had told the Prime Minister, Stanley Baldwin, that if Italy invaded Ethiopia and if League of Nations sanctions against it led to war the navy would require far more resources as well as French cooperation, especially since the Italian navy was mobilized and in control of the eastern Mediterranean and the Red Sea.[8] It might be true that Italy, with its lack of fuel resources and its long coastline, could easily be strangled by the British and French navies in the Mediterranean, but in the short term it had quick access by warships and bombers to all British Mediterranean bases.

It was the Ethiopian crisis of October 1935 to June 1936 which would condition British and French attitudes to Italy over the Spanish Civil War. The British armed services adopted the criterion that action would be taken only in response to a direct threat to British interests. Admiral Sir Ernle Chatfield, the Chief of Naval Staff, told his French colleagues that he saw no objection to the Italian conquest of Ethiopia.[9] This view combined the unwillingness of leading figures in Britain to take on the role of a policeman and to fight friendly powers for the sake of internationalist principles, with a sneaking sympathy for the Fascist regime and profound doubts about the ability of the Royal Navy to defend the Far Eastern empire unless it was not diverted by unnecessary wars in the Mediterranean. It was not that the Italian navy was considered particularly efficient, despite its technological lead. Indeed, many observers considered its equipment poor, its training faulty, and its officers second-rate,[10] but the fears of Britain's leaders were reflected in a letter sent on 9 August 1935 by Sir Robert Vansittart, Permanent Under-Secretary, to the Foreign Secretary, Sir Samuel Hoare, and Admiral Chatfield: 'This country has been so weakened of recent years that we are in no position to take a strong line in the Mediterranean ... we should be very cautious as to how far and in what manner we force the pace in Paris, with an unreliable France and an unready England.'[11] The situation had not changed a year later, at the end of the Ethiopian crisis. Britain had not used military sanctions against Italy and had not closed the Suez Canal to its vital supplies of oil. All sanctions had been removed by mid-1936. Despite fierce public condemnation of Italy, Britain was paralysed and unable to act the part of a great naval power.[12]

Britain's inability to face up to Italy in the Mediterranean over Ethiopia led its government to accept that collective security against an aggressor was an unrealistic ideal, at least for the time being. Consequently, Italian naval and air superiority in the Mediterranean would be a significant factor during the Spanish Civil War. The importance of the Spanish war in the Mediterranean was that Italian intervention and British reactions reflected a major struggle for power. Were Britain and France's position in the western Mediterranean and their communications with North Africa, Gibraltar, and Malta going to remain secure? The constraints on British action were, however, firm. Britain must not attack Italy, which was a potential ally against the growing German threat, and should not dissipate or diminish its naval strength. The services chiefs insisted that no further commitments could be made in the Mediterranean.[13]

WAR IN SPAIN: JULY 1936

This was the atmosphere in which, at the beginning of the Spanish Civil War, the Foreign Office strongly dissuaded the newly elected French Prime Minister, Léon Blum, from sending aircraft to help the Spanish Republic against its rebellious armed forces. The Spanish war began at a low moment in Anglo-French relations.[14] France had been slow to support the Royal Navy over Ethiopia.[15] Now, however, the French government was of the Popular Front. Its new political complexion and French ratification at the end of February of the recent mutual assistance agreement with the USSR alarmed Britain, whose fundamental policy was to reassure Nazi Germany and Fascist Italy that the West was not seeking to surround them with hostile left-wing alliances.[16] France, however, saw itself seriously threatened by possible Italian dominance in the western Mediterranean, which would menace its vital routes from North Africa. The new feature in the area was the presence, at first in the Strait of Gibraltar only, of what the British Admiralty saw as a mutinous Spanish fleet. The crews of most of the Spanish navy had deposed their officers over the weekend of 18–20 July 1936 and within a month would murder many of them, but the mutiny was not, as so many British observers thought, similar to the classic twentieth-century mutinies on the battleship *Potemkin,* at Kronstadt, and at Kiel. The Spanish sailors had mutinied in favour of their government against insurgent officers and had asked for orders. Nevertheless, a combination of doubt and understandable Royal Navy prejudice led the British authorities in Gibraltar and London to refuse to sell fuel to the ships and to expel them. Similar fears led to the expulsion of Spanish government ships from the international harbour of Tangier. Since the insurgents had control of all the other harbours in the strait, the relatively powerful but officerless government navy found itself in difficulties over water and fuel.[17]

While the Spanish government kept its base at Port Mahon on Minorca, its importance was eclipsed by Palma on the island of Majorca. This harbour and the seaplane base at Pollensa were lost by the government, which failed to support a landing to recapture Majorca in August 1936. This would turn out to be a major strategic error, as Palma became the principal base from which the insurgent Nationalists and the German and Italian aircraft which flew for them during the war would increasingly harass Spanish Republican shipping.

The attitude in London from the beginning of the Spanish war emphasized that it was an internal Spanish conflict which must not be allowed, through international intervention, to develop into a major European war. Consequently, though General Franco's Nationalists were rebelling against an internationally recognized government, London and Paris established the policy known as non-intervention, which meant that, in theory at least, they supported and sold arms to neither combatant and hoped that other countries would do the same.[18]

From the naval perspective, non-intervention meant refusal to grant belligerent rights to the Republic or to Franco, whose exiguous navy was extremely energetic and would soon be significantly strengthened by the entry into service of two new cruisers superior in fire power and speed to any of its enemy's ships. Consequently, neither side could, under international law, establish a blockade or interfere with the merchant traffic of other countries making for an enemy port. The Republic's blockade, declared on 13 August 1936, was rejected by Britain. General Franco's declarations of blockades were never accepted as legal. While the Republican navy did hamper the movements of some merchant vessels in the first month of the war, forcing German ships in particular, which were carrying supplies to Franco, to leave the Spanish coast and discharge their cargoes in Lisbon,[19] the Royal Navy protected British shipping in the Strait of Gibraltar. The effect was to neutralize the potential naval power of the Spanish Republic, as its government was unwilling to prejudice its international standing or to provoke Germany and Italy by trying to enforce a blockade of rebel ports.

German and Italian presence in the strait was a matter of concern to Britain. Some warships were there to protect foreign lives and property, but it soon became evident that this task did not require the presence of the pocket battleships *Deutschland*, *Admiral Scheer*, and *Admiral Graf Spee*, and the cruisers *Leipzig* and *Köln.*[20] Their real role was to cooperate with the insurgents by passing them information about enemy movements and to act as liaison with the German and Italian aircraft which had been flying in the same area since the beginning of August in response to Franco's urgent requests for aid. As Admiral Rolf Carls, the German naval commander in the area, wrote in his diary: 'Now we are going to start the hidden but active participation of the German naval forces in favour of White Spain.'[21] For a brief period German submarines patrolled the Spanish coast; the *U-34* sank the Republican submarine *C-3* off Malaga.[22]

Once the new Nationalist cruiser, the *Canarias*, put to sea from El Ferrol and entered the Mediterranean in the early morning of 29 September 1936, it ensured Nationalist dominance at sea. It immediately sank the Republican destroyer *Ferrándiz* and put another, the *Gravina*, to flight.[23] This made it easy for Franco to ship his forces from Morocco to the Peninsula while the *Canarias* cruised at its ease bombarding the coast.

Most of the Spanish government fleet was deployed in the Mediterranean, but its passivity for most of the war arose partly from its lack of clear policy, partly from shortage of fuel, shells, torpedoes, and spare parts, and largely from a decision, probably imposed by the Soviet naval attaché, Captain Nikolai Kuznetsov, that the fleet should be 'kept in being' according to current naval doctrine and used to escort ships arriving in the western Mediterranean with war *materiel* shipped mostly from Black Sea ports.[24]

The geographical position of Spain meant that all supplies to the Nationalists came by sea, as did a considerable proportion of the *materiel* which the Republican government received. Though German supplies did not use the Mediterranean for most of the war, Italian traffic was escorted by Italian warships as far as Palma and was then protected by Spanish warships as far as a Moroccan or southern Spanish port. Spanish government warships never attacked or even stopped merchant ships flying foreign flags and suspected of supplying Franco's forces. Over 73,000 men, 3,427 cannon and mortars, 3,436 machine-guns, 157 tanks, 6,797 other vehicles, 320 million cartridges and 7.7 million shells, as well as 759 aircraft that Italy contributed to General Franco, used the western Mediterranean as their route.[25]

MAJORCA: THE CTV

What particularly concerned Britain and France, however, was the growing military and, it was feared, political presence of Italy on Majorca. The British chiefs of staff had reported on the potential danger of a hostile Spain or the occupation of Spanish territory by a hostile power. Such a situation would imperil British communications in the western Mediterranean. While the militarily undeveloped Balearics 'would not vitally affect British strategical interests', wrote the British chiefs of staff, 'the menace to our control of the Straits and to Gibraltar itself would be increased.' This ambiguous conclusion led them to write that, since Britain could not risk war with Italy and it was undesirable to antagonize it, the non-intervention scheme was the best chance. Mussolini, however, had to be made aware of the consequences of overstepping the mark. A British ship should be present in every Spanish port where there was an Italian vessel, and the British commanding officer should be senior to his Italian opposite number.[26] Italian aircraft and an Italian cruiser protected Majorca against any attempt to recapture it by the Spanish Republic. A dynamic and brutal young Fascist, Arconovaldi Bonaccorsi, known as Count Rossi, sent at the request of the Majorcan Fascist authorities, dominated the island with a mixture of swagger and terror. In particular, he made violently anti-British speeches and was reported to have proclaimed that Italy would occupy the island in perpetuity. Aware of Bonaccorsi's youth and intemperance, the British government worried nevertheless that he was accurately reflecting Italian policy.[27]

Italy sent a naval and military mission to Spain and stationed warships to watch traffic passing through the channel between Sicily and North Africa towards Spanish Republican ports. Since the Nationalists possessed no submarines, four Italian boats under nominal Spanish command began operations in November 1936. One of them seriously damaged the Republican cruiser *Cervantes* outside the naval base of Cartagena. Though it was known that no Spanish submarines were serving in Franco's navy, nothing was done about the torpedoing by the Non-Intervention Committee in London, even though Italy had agreed not to send arms to Spain and took a prominent part in the committee's debates. Once the USSR began to send massive supplies of arms to Spain in mid-October 1936, Italy dispatched 24 more submarines to Spanish waters.

By early December, Mussolini had decided to send major infantry forces to Spain. If, for fear of British reaction, Italy did not sink significant numbers of merchant ships carrying arms to the Republicans over the winter of 1936–37, its navy successfully escorted the Italian Expeditionary Force (the Corpo di Truppe Volontarie or CTV) to Spain without incident and hindered the movements of enemy warships by its presence near Republican cruisers and destroyers, which felt constantly watched and insecure.[28]

ARMS TRAFFIC: THE 'GENTLEMAN'S AGREEMENT'

The Franco authorities constantly complained that British merchant ships were carrying war *materiel* to the other side and threatened to blockade Republican ports.[29] The British way of dealing with this was not to give belligerent rights to Franco, which would have allowed him to stop and search neutral ships on the high seas. The British parliament passed the Merchant Shipping (Carrying of Munitions to Spain) Act of early December 1936, forbidding British-registered ships to carry arms to Spain from anywhere and insisting that Franco abstain from attacking British arms smugglers and instead inform the Royal Navy, which would take the necessary steps.[30] In general, with several ups and downs, the pattern followed by the Nationalists was to respect the British flag, but, as it became obvious that the British reaction, for political reasons, to Nationalist interference and even the sinking of British ships was to do no more than protest, such attacks became commonplace.

In the meantime, the USSR had begun its major programme of shipments of war *materiel* through the Mediterranean to the Spanish Republic. Most of this came in ships heavily escorted by the Spanish government navy, though one ship, the *Komsomol*, which had brought the first Russian tanks to Cartagena on 16 October 1936, was sunk on its third journey to Spain by the *Canarias,*[31] and numerous other Russian ships, usually found not to be carrying arms, were stopped and searched by Nationalist armed merchantmen. Events such as these underlined Soviet naval weakness.

Meanwhile, the Italian presence on Majorca was worrying Britain and even more so France. The French admirals sent by Blum on 5 August 1936 to London to try to persuade Admiral Chatfield of the dangers of the Spanish war to their common strategic interests, now that Italy and Germany were manifestly helping Franco, had failed to convince the Admiralty that Franco would concede permament bases to Mussolini.[32] However, by November, the activities of Bonaccorsi and, most important,

Mussolini's Milan speech of 1 November, in which he announced the 'Axis' between Italy and Germany, worried London so much that the Foreign Office reacted favourably but guardedly to Mussolini's offer to discuss a 'gentleman's agreement' on Mediterranean matters.[33] Mussolini had said at Milan that the Mediterranean was 'life' for Italy but merely a 'road' for others. A 'gentleman's agreement', as suggested by Mussolini, might be, in the Italian view, the beginning of general discussions on an overall accord about Italian rights in the Mediterranean and the Middle East.

The 'Gentleman's Agreement' of 2 January 1937[34] stated that neither side wanted to change the territorial *status quo* of any State in the Mediterranean. Italy specifically refused to include mention of Spain in the text but in a later note assured Britain that Spanish territorial integrity was to remain unchanged.[35] All in all, the talks appeared to be successful, considering the fears expressed by the British chiefs of staff, who had concluded that Britain would be ill-advised to try to oust Italy forcibly from Majorca unless the 'territorial integrity' of Spain were compromised. Anthony Eden, however, doubted Italian good faith and feared increased Italian power in the western Mediterranean and the consequent loss of British prestige.[36]

Unfortunately for Britain, Italy interpreted the terms of the gentleman's agreement narrowly, in the sense that, since it had no intention of remaining on Majorca, its intervention in the Spanish war did not come under the definition of altering the territorial *status quo*.[37] Eden immediately condemned Italian bad faith in signing the gentleman's agreement at the same time as Italian infantry was disembarking in Spain. This was probably an example of the different kinds of language employed by the two sides. For Italy it seemed that, by helping Franco defeat the 'Reds', it was doing no more than what was in Britain's interest also.

THE NAVAL PATROL

The Mediterranean situation therefore became very tense in the early months of 1937. Mussolini had reinforced Libya, the Dodecanese, and Pantelleria. The defeat of the Corpo di Truppe Volontarie at Guadalajara in early March had reinforced Mussolini's determination to stay in Spain until Franco won with Italian support. Even the British right wing, long admirers of Mussolini, now saw him as a threat and his grievances as contrived.[38] It was therefore a great relief for Britain that the Non-Intervention Committee, after weeks of discussion, agreed on a plan for a naval patrol by the British, French, Italian, and German navies around the coasts of Spain, to operate from 20/21 April 1937 onward. Italy would patrol the northern half of the Mediterranean coast. The point was not to capture arms smugglers. If it had been, Germany and Italy, major suppliers to Franco, would not have agreed to it. The naval patrol gave Italy and Germany the status of equal partners with the prestigious British Royal Navy. The naval patrol, together with the frontier inspection plan which accompanied it, brought all the signatories of the non-intervention agreement into a common undertaking to stop war *materiel* from entering Spain.

Just over a month later, on 28 May 1937, Neville Chamberlain became Prime Minister of Britain. Since he had been the leader in the campaign to end sanctions against Italy in mid-1936, his appointment was received optimistically in Italy. Soon afterwards, however, an incident occurred to exacerbate the always latent crisis in the western Mediterranean.

Given the presence of two inexperienced Spanish fleets and air forces in the Strait of Gibraltar and the western Mediterranean, as well as the heavy merchant traffic around Spain and the increase in the number of foreign warships in the area, accidental attacks were to be expected. The British battleship *Royal Oak* had been attacked on 3 February 1937 by Spanish aircraft off Europa Point. The same ship was hit by a spent anti-aircraft shell while in harbour at Valencia on 23 February. On 13 February two British destroyers were bombed by a Junkers aircraft in Franco's service. On 13 May the destroyer *Hunter* hit a mine off Almería, killing eight of its crew. The gravest incident occurred on 29 May 1937, when two newly arrived Russian aircraft bombed the German pocket battleship *Deutschland*, which was lying at anchor in Ibiza, killing 31 sailors and wounding 70. At the time it was impossible for the Spanish government to admit the reason for the bombing, which was the inexperience of the Soviet crews, who thought they were bombing one of the Nationalist cruisers.[39] However, the German battleship was in an enemy harbour and had not advised the Republican government of its presence there. The air crew insisted that the ship had fired first. The British view was that such unfortunate incidents would always happen if neutral ships anchored in war zones.

Hitler demanded revenge. The German navy bombarded Almería on 31 May 1937, leaving 19 dead and 55 injured. Had it not been for the opposition of the Communist ministers of the Republic, meeting later that morning, Republican ships and aircraft might have launched a concerted attack on German ships in the area and provoked a general European war. Moscow, however, urged caution. Germany and Italy, infuriated by what they considered 'Red pirates', threatened to leave the Non-Intervention Committee, which was the linchpin of Anglo-French policy over Spain. They were, with difficulty, pacified, but after episodes in June when the cruiser *Leipzig* insisted that it had been attacked by a Spanish submarine while the Spanish government denied the accusation and the Admiralty also doubted its truth, Germany and Italy withdrew from the naval patrol, which came to an end in September 1937.[40]

The naval patrol was regarded as a great success for Britain's Mediterranean policy. It had led Germany and Italy to cooperate with Britain and France to limit the Spanish war. It was thought to have inhibited Germany and Italy from sending arms to Franco, which may have been a reason for those two countries to abandon it when they realized that it was only cosmetic in any case. Shipping registered in countries which were signatories to the non-intervention agreement had been required to take on inspectors before sailing to Spain and to fly the flag of the non-intervention patrol scheme. In other words, whether or not the naval patrol had any real effect, it created and reinforced the view that the European nations as a group wanted the Spanish war to be strictly limited to Spain.

ITALY AND FRANCO ATTACK SHIPPING: NYON

Fearing that the collapse of the naval control system would permit the arrival of large amounts of war *materiel* in Republican ports on the Mediterranean coast, the Francoist authorities urgently requested help from Italy to stop these arms either in the Sicilian channel or as they neared Spain.[41] The Italian naval staff agreed to cover not only the Sicilian channel but also the Aegean Sea and the coasts of North Africa. Submarines would sink any ship trying to use the hours of darkness to slip into Barcelona, Tarragona, Valencia, Alicante, or Cartagena. Italy stationed flotillas at the exit from the Dardanelles and in the Sicilian channel, while destroyers and submarines patrolled the Algerian coast and six submarines kept watch over the Spanish ports.

From 6 August 1937 onward, merchant ships began to report attacks by unidentified submarines. Up to 2 September, at least 30 ships were attacked and eight of them sunk, mostly by submarine torpedo, though a few were the victims of aircraft and destroyer attacks. Twelve of the victims were British, including the destroyer *Havock*, which an Italian submarine attempted to torpedo on 31 August. Three Russian transports were sunk. The rest were French-registered or Spanish Republican ships. The attacks took place all over the Mediterranean, from the Dardanelles and the Aegean to the Algerian coast, the Gulf of Valencia, and Cartagena.[42]

The situation was clearly intolerable. Even when Franco's armed merchant ships had sunk a foreign ship in the past, they had saved the crew and, at least in theory, agreed to pay compensation according to international law as if they had been granted belligerent rights. The present situation was one of unrestricted warfare by submarines which, though the Admiralty knew they were Italian through British Intelligence services ably directed on Majorca by Commander Alan Hillgarth, did not identify themselves and, indeed, did not even assure themselves that the ships they attacked were bound for Spain.

A few days later, therefore, orders were given to the Royal Navy to sink any submarine which attacked a British ship without warning. Given the delicate diplomatic situation, Italy was not officially accused, for fear it might leave the Non-Intervention Committee altogether. Therefore the most that *The Times* of London could say, on 25 August 1937, was that the sinkings were by ships operating on Franco's side. The official Italian claim was that the submarines were Spanish Republican. After all, the Republic had kept its 12 boats, though most of these were inoperative.[43] Perhaps sickened by the limits to which British diplomacy had been forced by its decision not to challenge Italy in the Mediterranean, one British official minuted on the Italian press cutting which blamed the Republic, 'What a monument of lies and hypocrisy!' It was an accurate observation, for when Mr Ingram, the British chargé d'affaires in Rome, approached Count Galeazzo Ciano, Mussolini's son-in-law and Foreign Minister, about the attacks, the latter answered him, as he writes, 'quite brazenly':[44]

> The difficulty was that the British government could not reveal that its naval intelligence had broken the Italian naval codes for fear that Italy would change the cyphers. At the end of August, therefore, Eden and the Admiralty decided that the only thing to do was to send destroyers to the Mediterranean to sink 'unknown' submarines. This had the desired effect, and the attacks ceased.[45]

Eden and the French government decided to profit by this apparent though not officially declared Italian retreat. They called a conference of Mediterranean powers to be held at Nyon near Geneva. Eden wanted a joint agreement to sink all unidentified and submerged submarines. 'Spanish' boats (that is, the Italian submarines under nominal Spanish Nationalist command) were to restrict their activity to Spanish territorial waters. Eden hoped that such an agreement would restrict the war to the Spanish coastline. The point was to do all this without naming Italy as the guilty party, which was why, when the Soviet Union accused Italian ships of torpedoing its merchants, Italy had an excuse to boycott the conference. By now, in any case, the British authorities were fully informed that Italian ships had ceased their attacks.[46]

The Nyon agreements were, therefore, largely cosmetic. British and French destroyers would patrol the Mediterranean attacking unidentified 'pirate' submarines. The Italian and German aircraft operating against shipping from Majorca bore Spanish markings, and as long as they attacked ships only inside territorial waters the British reaction need be no more than a protest. The other Mediterranean naval powers, such as Greece and Turkey, were satisfied, especially since the Russians, who never showed any great wish to send their warships into the Mediterranean, were not going to participate in the patrol.[47]

Negotiations to include Italy in the pact continued. Finally it was granted the Tyrrhenian Sea as a patrol zone. Since Italy had ceased its attacks in any case, this was a mere diplomatic measure, but Eden saw it as a triumph. The Spanish war had once more been prevented from spreading all over the Mediterranean. Italy was content. Ciano wrote, 'It is a fine victory. From suspected pirates to policemen of the Mediterranean – and the Russians, whose ships we are sinking, excluded!'[48] The comment shows Ciano's limited view. He was right up to a point, but Italy's piratical behaviour had been checked. The USSR was probably sending little to Spain by then and had not been barred from the Mediterranean, only from participating in the patrols, which it probably did not want to do in any case. Everyone knew that the pirate submarines had been Italian and that they had had to stop. Franco was forced to limit his blockade to territorial waters and to attack largely from the air.

Very typically, the Nationalist commanders went as far as they could in their attacks on neutral shipping. Prudence often counselled moderation. As Admiral Francisco Moreno cabled Franco's Foreign Ministry on 6 November 1937, 'repeated energetic protests by the British and French admirals mean we have to be very prudent with their flags and attack only ships carrying contraband within territorial waters'.[49]

Friction over attacks on British ships would occur for the rest of the war. Britain would protest. The Spanish Nationalist authorities would claim that the attacked vessel was inside the territorial limit or blame the bombing on the lack of skill of the plane's observer. Sometimes the Nationalists would insist that they had information to say that the ship was carrying war *materiel*. The British would say that the ship had a non-intervention observer on board and that interference would not be tolerated. At other times the Nationalists could say nothing because their pilot or bomb-aimer was Italian or German. They considered any ship bringing anything at all to their enemies as a fair target. They saw the denial of belligerent rights – which would have allowed them to capture neutral ships on the high seas – as unfair, while Britain had agreed to grant those rights only after a substantial reduction of 'volunteers' – that is, Italian troops – on Franco's side, a reduction which never happened. The war against merchant naval traffic was becoming a matter of diplomatic fencing. It did not matter very much provided the conflict did not spread any further.

Nevertheless, Nationalist pressure became more and more intense, and British merchant ships knew that they could not expect protection from the Royal Navy once they were in Spanish territorial waters. More submarines sent by Italy were withdrawn in February 1938 when it became evident that they could not be safely used to sink British merchant ships after the fierce anger created when they sank the Dutch ship *Hannah* and the British *Endymion* in January 1938.[50] The Nationalists were testing the limits of British tolerance. From now on they relied on aerial bombing of ships in ports or close to shore. While in absolute terms only a minority of the large number of ships of all flags (though mostly British) sailing to Spain was affected, the danger was sufficient for the skippers of 12 merchants lying at anchor in Valencia to send a telegram of protest to the British government.[51] The Nationalists came to realize that British concession of belligerent rights depended on withdrawal of the Italians and that official recognition of their regime would not be given until they won the war. Belligerent rights, however, became a mere matter of prestige once the Nationalists saw that all they had to fear was protests and, as *The Times* rather weakly warned on 2 June 1938, 'more energetic protests'. As the Foreign Office admitted, little could be done except warn the Nationalists of the effect on international opinion of the bombing of neutral ships.[52] By mid-1938, British ships in Mediterranean ports were being bombed almost daily.[53]

While British public opinion was outraged, the Admiralty view was that many of the merchant ships had been placed on the British register only for the advantages of protection while their owners made large profits by shipping desperately needed goods to Republican Spain. Any potential measures against the Nationalists were seen as counter-productive. Chamberlain wrote in his diary: 'I have been through every possible form of retaliation, and it is absolutely clear that none of them can be effective unless we are prepared to go to war with Franco, which might quite possibly lead to war with Italy and Germany, and in any case would cut right across my policy of general appeasement.'[54] The last part of the statement was true, but there was no reason to think that an effective Royal Navy blockade of Spanish Nationalist ports would have brought about war with Franco, or that Italy and Germany would have risked war for the sake of the Spanish general. More importantly, by the spring of 1938 it did look as if the Republic was about to collapse.

FRANCO REACHES THE MEDITERRANEAN

In spring 1938 Franco's armies had driven right across eastern Spain, reaching the Mediterranean at Vinaroz, north of Valencia, on 15 April. The only setback to his triumph had been the loss of his new cruiser, the *Baleares*, which was sunk on 6 March 1938 off Cape Palos by torpedoes launched by Republican destroyers. This loss might have had serious consequences for the Nationalists, for the Republic still had most of its fast destroyers. These, however, were often desperately short of spares, shells, and torpedoes, as well as being kept back for escort duties.

Franco's forces reached the Mediterranean the day before Britain and Italy came to an agreement. The Anglo-Italian agreement had been reached only after the resignation in February 1938 of Anthony Eden, who had insisted on an Italian withdrawal from Spain before holding any talks.[55] Italy reaffirmed the Gentleman's Agreement of January 1937 and agreed to desist from intrigue and propaganda in Palestine and Egypt, while Britain agreed to try to persuade the League of Nations to recognize the Italian empire. Britain accepted that Italian forces would stay in Spain until Franco's final victory. Even though Italy assured Britain that Italian troops would eventually leave and that Italy had no territorial ambitions in Spain, British suspicions remained and led to London's facilitating the surrender of the Republican-held island of Minorca on the condition that no Italian troops would land there.

MINORCA

Minorca had been isolated by the war, though it had a sizeable garrison. In early February 1939 the British Consul on Majorca, Commander Alan Hillgarth, suspecting that a Nationalist landing in Minorca was imminent, asked London to allow a British warship to carry a senior Nationalist officer to the island to negotiate a surrender and evacuation in exchange for excluding Italian forces from Minorca. By this time, the Spanish Republican government was leaving Spain after Franco's armies had reached the French frontier. The Republican Commander of Minorca accepted the good terms of surrender and evacuation that he was offered. Spanish Nationalist forces landed in Minorca while the Foreign Office congratulated itself that Italian troops would not be stationed there.[56]

After Britain recognized the Franco government on 27 February 1939, it decided that it was unwise to evacuate large numbers of politically compromised Republicans, though a few merchant ships took refugees off. The Royal Navy, however, rescued Colonel Segismundo Casado, who had led an internal rebellion against the Republican government and negotiated the surrender to Franco. In the meantime, the Spanish Republican fleet left its base at Cartagena and sailed into temporary internment at Bizerta.

CONCLUSIONS

Control of the Mediterranean was a vital issue in the Spanish Civil War. Helped by the reaction of Britain, the Nationalists and their Italian and German allies managed to dominate the Spanish coast, while the French were paralysed by their dependence on Britain and the Russians by their weakness. The Spanish Republican navy, in principle more powerful than its opponents, was hampered by indiscipline, lack of officers, indecisive political leadership, and equipment shortages.

In the event, Italy did not gain a base in the Balearics. France was defeated in 1940 by its internal contradictions, not by Italian control over its routes from North Africa. Gibraltar was not threatened because the Royal Navy maintained a stranglehold over Spain's vital imports.

The Spanish war seemed to have led to nothing more than shadow-boxing in the Mediterranean. Even today it is difficult to understand whether the British chiefs of staff were or were not alarmed by the Italian presence on Majorca. On 11 January 1937, they said 'Italian occupation of Majorca ... would not affect British strategical interests vitally'. As Sir Robert Vansittart commented, 'It all depends on what is meant by "vitally"'.[57] Surely Italian presence on Majorca would have been a major threat to both British and French communications in case of war. However, Britain's attitude to France was hesitant. France wanted a Mediterranean pact, but Britain saw in such an agreement a threat of limitation to its own naval superiority in the Mediterranean.[58] As has been seen, as early as 5 August 1936, the British admirals and the First Lord of the Admiralty, Sir Samuel Hoare, rejected a suggestion that Britain and France should act together to forestall a Francoist concession to Italy in the Balearics. How far this hesitation in tackling Italy was due to political prejudice against the Spanish Republic[59] and the French Popular Front, how far to perceptions of British weakness in the Mediterranean, and how far to a view that the situation was better left alone because more important British interests in the Middle East were at stake remains a matter of debate.

Post-World War II historiography tends to think in terms of its own epoch, one in which the United States obtained heavily fortified bases from which bombers could be launched rather than mere harbours and aerodromes for refuelling and minor repairs. The frequently found statements in the British records that 'proud' Spaniards, especially the ultra-nationalist Francoists, would not concede territory to Italy begs the question, for no nation had bases on another's territory rather than in its own colonial possessions. The British chiefs of staff were probably right; there was no grave strategic threat from the Italian presence on Majorca. What they did not see was the real danger: allowing foreign countries to intervene openly to overthrow freely elected and unthreatening, if unfavoured, regimes.

NOTES

1. J.J. Sadkovich, 'The Indispensable Navy: Italy as a Great Power 1911–1943', in N.A.M. Rodger (ed.), *Naval Power in the Twentieth Century* (Basingstoke, 1996), pp.67–8; see also Steven Morewood, 'Anglo-Italian Rivalry in the Mediterranean and the Middle East', in R. Boyce and E. Robertson (eds.), *Paths to War: New Essays on the Origins of the Second World War* (Basingstoke, 1989).
2. Morewood 'Anglo-Italian Rivalry', p.170; see also Jill Edwards, *The British Government and the Spanish Civil War 1936–1939* (Basingstoke, 1979), pp.153–7.
3. R. Quartararo, *Roma tra Londra e Berlino: La politica estera italiana dal 1930 al 1940* (Rome, 1980), p.278.
4. On 19 August 1936 the British Foreign Office wrote a memorandum for the Cabinet Foreign Policy Committee summarizing its views on Italian policy in the Spanish Civil War (see *Documents on British Foreign Policy 1919–1938*, 2nd series, Vol.17, London, 1979 [hereafter *DBFP*] No.115). The memorandum admitted that Italy was unlikely to consent to remaining 'in a military sense, at our mercy'. For Mussolini's views on Italy's needs, see MacGregor Knox, 'Il fascismo e la politica estera italiana', in R. Bosworth and S. Romano (eds.), *La politica estera italiana 1860–1985* (Bologna, 1991), pp.287–330, particularly 297–8. Foreign Secretary Anthony Eden's view was that the British government needed to clarify to Rome the limits of acceptable Italian action.
5. For a luminous exposition of this issue see P. Kennedy, *The Realities behind Diplomacy: Background Influences on British External Policy 1865–1980* (London, 1981), and his *The Rise of British Naval Mastery* (London, 1976).
6. *DBFP*, No.115. The Foreign Office admitted that it could suggest nothing more than a public statement of British views over the Mediterranean balance of power.
7. See Reynolds M. Salerno, 'Multilateral Strategy and Diplomacy: The Anglo-German Naval Agreement and the Mediterranean Crisis, 1935–1936', *Journal of Strategic Studies*, 17 (June 1994), pp.39–78. See also the old but useful K. Edwards, *Uneasy Oceans* (London, 1939), especially ch. 8 for its description of the Italian fleet in 1939.
8. Ibid.
9. R.A.C. Parker, *Chamberlain and Appeasement: British Policy and the Coming of the Second World War* (Basingstoke, 1993), p.48.
10. Sadkovich, 'The Indispensable Navy'.
11. Quoted in A.J. Marder, 'The Royal Navy and the Ethiopian Crisis of 1935–36', *American Historical Review*, 75 (June 1970), pp.1327–56.
12. These issues are well described by Marder, 'The Royal Navy', and Kennedy, *The Rise of British Naval Mastery*, p.290. The fullest account is by Stephen Roskill, *Naval Policy between the Wars*, Vol.2, *The Period of Reluctant Armament 1930–1939* (London, 1976).
13. L. Pratt, *East of Malta, West of Suez: Britain's Mediterranean Crisis 1936–1939* (Cambridge, 1975), p.37.
14. For an analysis of the international situation in July 1936 see Michael Alpert, *A New International History of the Spanish Civil War* (Basingstoke 1994), Ch.1.
15. Marder, 'The Royal Navy'.
16. See the illuminating Foreign Office minute in *DBFP*, No.84, of 12 August 1936, arguing that to avoid a split into ideological blocs British policy should be to encourage the French Popular Front government to free itself from communism and to remove Italian and German fears of isolation.
17. On all matters having to do with the Spanish Civil War at sea, the following contain the primary source material: Michael Alpert, *La guerra civil española en el mar* (Madrid, 1987); Ricardo Cerezo, *Armada española siglo XX* (Madrid, 1983); Willard Frank, 'Seapower, Politics and the Onset of the Spanish Civil War' (Ph.D. thesis, University of Pittsburgh, 1969); 'Naval Operations in the Spanish Civil War', *Naval College War Review*, 37, 1 (Jan.–Feb. 1984), pp.24–55; and Admiral Sir Peter Gretton, *El factor olvidado: La marina británica y la guerra civil española* (Madrid, 1984). Many references can be found also in Hugh Thomas, *The Spanish Civil War* (Harmondsworth, 1977).
18. On the establishment of non-intervention, see Michael Alpert, *New International History,*

Ch. 4, and Dante A. Puzzo, *Spain and the Great Powers 1936–1942* (New York, 1962), Chs.4 and 5.

19. *DGFP*, Series D, Vol.3 (London, 1951), No.52, 22 Aug. 1936.
20. On the German navy in the Spanish Civil War, see S. Tanner, 'German Naval Intervention in the Spanish Civil War as Reflected in the German Records' (Ph.D. thesis, The American University, Washington, DC, 1976).
21. Quoted by Tanner, 'German Naval Intervention', p.134.
22. See Frank, 'Seapower', p.342 and 'Naval Operations'. See Alpert, *Guerra civil española en el mar*, pp.149 and 160 for comment.
23. Alpert, *Guerra civil española en el mar*, pp.142–3; British report in Public Record Office, Admiralty files PRO ADM 116/3052.
24. Alpert, *Guerra civil española en el mar*, p.187: see Kuznetsov's two memoirs, *Nakanune* (Moscow, 1966) and, *Na dalyokom meridiane* (Moscow, n.d.).
25. On Italian participation in the Spanish war, see in particular J. Coverdale, *La intervención fascista en la guerra civil española* (Madrid, 1979) [first published as *Italian Intervention in the Spanish Civil War*, Princeton, 1975], who gives these figures on p.347, and, more recently, Paul Preston, 'Mussolini's Spanish Adventure: From Limited Risk to War', in P. Preston and A. Mackenzie (eds.), *The Republic Besieged: Civil War in Spain 1936–1939* (Edinburgh, 1996), pp.21–51.
26. *DBFP*, No.151, 24 Aug. 1936.
27. *DBFP*, No.355, 6 Nov. 1936
28. J.L. Alcófar Nassaes, *La Marina italiana en la guerra de España* (Barcelona, 1975), p.134; see also N. Kuznetsov, 'Con los marinos españoles en su guerra nacional-revolucionaria', in *Bajo la bandera de la España republicana* (Moscow n.d.), pp.131–217, a shorter and probably earlier version of Kuznetsov's book cited above.
29. *DBFP*, Nos.381 and 382, 17 Nov. 1936.
30. Franco was informed of the proposed British legislation on 23 November 1936 (*DBFP*, No.402).
31. See Research Program on the USSR, *Soviet Shipping in the Spanish Civil War* (New York, 1954), for interesting details of the organization of Soviet arms shipments to Spain.
32. *DBFP*, No.46, 5 Aug. 1936.
33. In an interview on 5 Nov. 1936 with Ward Price of the London *Daily Mail*, Mussolini had categorically denied any designs on Majorca.
34. *DBFP*, No.530.
35. See Quartararo, *Roma tra Londra e Berline*, pp.305–24, insisting that Britain agreed to talk to Italy only because the Italian military and naval presence on Majorca threatened to neutralize Gibraltar and menaced French communications. It is doubtful whether this author is correct to say that Italy would be able to use Palma permanently. Certainly this was not British opinion. The view of Anthony Eden was that Franco was unlikely to grant any foreign power facilities which would attract a British attack in the event of a general war but there was no certainty in the matter; Mussolini might well extract concessions from Franco (A. Eden, *Facing the Dictators* [London, 1962], pp.422–3). Quartararo's highly scholarly work illustrates the Italian view largely from British sources to show how obstinately Britain refused to discuss general questions of Italian legitimate interests in the Mediterranean. At the same time, however, this author rarely mentions, except in asides, the volume of Italian intervention in Spain or Italian piracy in the Mediterranean, calling them 'incidents' (p.346).
36. Eden's comments in *DBFP*, No.471, 14 Dec. 1936. The negotiations for the agreement are well described by the outstanding recent work on British policy in the Spanish war: E. Moradiellos, *La perfidia de Albión* (Madrid, 1996) pp.123–31.
37. Eden, *Facing the Dictators*, p.429, emphasizes the British refusal to discuss anything with Italy except Spain. The secret treaty of 28 Nov. 1936 between Italy and Franco Spain promised neutrality in case of war with a third party but underlined the territorial integrity of Spain. See G. Ciano, *Ciano's Diplomatic Papers*, ed. M. Muggeridge (London, 1948), pp.76–7.
38. Pratt, *East of Malta*, pp.70–71.
39. Kuznetsov, *Na dalyokom meridiane*, pp.205–9.

40. The episode of the *Deutschland* is described and analyzed in Alpert, *Guerra civil española en el mar*, pp.273–84.
41. See *DGFP*, No.407, 4 Aug. 1937. The German authorities did not believe that such large amounts were arriving.
42. See list of attacks in PRO ADM 116/3522; Gretton, *El factor olvidado*, pp.307–18; Alcófar, *Marina italiana*, p.202; Alpert, *Guerra civil española en el mar*, pp.288–9; see also Admiral Peter Gretton's detailed study, 'The Nyon Conference: The Naval Aspect', *English Historical Review*, 90, 354 (Jan. 1975), pp.103–12. PRO ADM 116/3534 gives the details of the attack by the submarine *Iride* on the destroyer *Havock.*
43. G. Rodríguez Martín-Granizo and J. González-Aller, *Submarinos republicanos en la guerra civil* (Madrid, 1982), studies the histories of the 12 boats.
44. Galeazzo Ciano, *Ciano's Hidden Diary 1937–1938* (New York, 1953), p.3.
45. Ciano, *Hidden Diary*, p.9.
46. PRO ADM 116/3523.
47. Eden, *Facing the Dictators*, p.467. See PRO ADM 116/3522 for the official minutes of the meetings.
48. Ciano, *Hidden Diary*, p.15.
49. *Servicio Histórico del Estado Mayor de la Marina* (Madrid), pp.99–100.
50. Cerezo, *Armada española*, Vol.4, p.185.
51. *The Times*, 9 May 1938.
52. PRO FO 371 W7267/6755/41 of 1 June 1938.
53. Alpert, *Guerra civil española en el mar*, p.331, lists 15 British and French merchant ships bombed between 4 and 27 June 1938.
54. Keith Feiling, *The Life of Neville Chamberlain* (London, 1946), p.352.
55. For details of Eden's resignation and the Anglo-Italian agreement, see Alpert, *New International History*, pp.152–6. See also D.C. Watt, 'Gli accordi mediterranei anglo-italiani del 16 aprile 1938', *Rivista di Studi Politici internazionali*, 26, 1 (1959), pp.41–57.
56. On this episode, see Alpert, *La guerra civil española en el mar*, pp.348–51, based on correspondence with the later Captain Hillgarth, PRO ADM 116/3896 and *Servicio Histórico Militar* (Madrid) DR. L. 383, C6.
57. PRO FO 371, Vol.21391, document W16978.
58. See *DBFP*, No.224, 23 Sept. 1936.
59. How much importance should be attributed to attempts by the Italian Ministry of Marine to persuade the Admiralty by means of unofficial contacts that the Italian navy wanted at all costs to avoid conflict with the Royal Navy? (Renzo de Felice, *Mussolini il Duce: Lo stato totalitario* (Turin, 1981), Vol.2, pp.334–5, n.5.

Franco's Bid for Empire: Spain, Germany, and the Western Mediterranean in World War II

NORMAN J.W. GODA

Using German and Spanish records, this article argues that Spanish foreign policy during World War II must be understood within the context of Madrid's aims in the western Mediterranean, particularly in French Morrocco. Unwilling to enter the European war when it erupted in 1939, the Franco government changed its policy with the impending French defeat in June 1940. Franco's first attempts to gain French colonial territory were made without consulting the Germans or Italians. Only after attempts to negotiate with the new Vichy regime had failed did Madrid offer to enter the war on the Axis side. Confluent aims in Northwest Africa, however, combined with the German need to support the temporary sanctity of the French empire, would keep Spain out of the war.

Shortly after the conclusion of World War II, the diplomatically isolated Spanish government of Francisco Franco argued to the world that Spain had never seriously considered entering the conflict on the side of Adolf Hitler's Germany. True, Spain had supplied the Germans with vital war *materiel*, a Spanish division had fought against the Soviets, the government-controlled Spanish press had openly favoured the Axis, and German agents had remained on Spanish territory through the end of the war.[1] But Spain, so the official story went, had to comply with Hitler to a certain degree, lest the German army, which stood at the Pyrenees by June 1940, overrun the country at a moment of weakness caused by the recently concluded Civil War. Franco, in other words, had shielded his nation from invasion by providing Germany with a meaningless brew of minimal aid and friendly rhetoric.[2] These arguments influenced the historiography of the war until the 1970s,[3] when Franco's death, key revelations by subordinates, and the opening of some Spanish records began to change it.[4] In so far as consensus exists today, scholars argue that at the very least Franco seriously entertained the idea of belligerence at the moment of Germany's victory in the west; at most, they see the Caudillo as completely enthralled with

Hitler's victories and Germany's miracle weaponry through the end of the conflict.[5]

The truth of Spain's policy towards Germany, still inscrutable to a degree, may lie somewhere in between. That the government-controlled press remained pro-German and anti-Allied to the end of the war may be disturbing, but it is not surprising. Given the regime's nature, origins, and military participation in the USSR, it could hardly have been expected to applaud the extension of Soviet power into central Europe. Nor could it bring itself to abandon – at any rate rhetorically – the German government which had provided open aid to the military revolt in Spain nearly a decade before. During World War II German agents had also provided intelligence concerning the regime's internal enemies, and many Germans in Spain were still well connected to top Spanish officials.[6] Answers to the puzzle of Spain's policy towards Hitler's war are perhaps best discovered in an investigation of Madrid's territorial aims during the period of German ascendancy, which would have formulated the *casus belli* for the Franco regime. Of course, as have all Spanish governments since 1714, the Franco government wanted the return of Gibraltar. More important, Spanish aims across the strait in Northwest Africa must be taken into account as a barometer for Spanish policy. The staggering German victories of 1940 and the tremendous power shift which they brought seemed to open a window not only for the return of the Rock but for an extension across the strait into Northwest Africa and particularly into French Morocco. Spain's policy would seem to have been determined more by these factors than by any inherent avoidance of or subservience to the Axis powers.

The conviction that the British presence at Gibraltar was a thorn in the side of Spain linked Spaniards regardless of politics – even Anglophiles – and was no novelty of the Franco regime. Attendant humiliations could come at any time, such as during the war with the United States in 1898, when Madrid, under British pressure, agreed not to fortify Algeciras because of the threat that heavy weapons there might pose to Gibraltar's usability. A possible way out of this maze lay in a trade for Spain's Mediterranean Moroccan enclave at Ceuta. Some British observers in the 1920s and 1930s argued that Gibraltar's geographic vulnerability combined with the increasing size of battleships and the importance of air power would limit its use while Ceuta, if properly equipped, could serve as the Royal Navy's western Mediterranean base for years to come. The Spanish dictator, General Miguel Primo de Rivera, who was opposed to Spain's entire venture in Morocco, favoured such a trade as well. Yet though he went so far as to broach the idea with Ramsay MacDonald, a trade was not in the offing. Neither parliament nor the British population would be persuaded to part with something as seemingly solid as the Rock of

Gibraltar, or to assume the costs of creating a modern base at Ceuta. In the meantime, Spain's military operations in Morocco in 1926 made Ceuta a key base. All the same, the Spanish Republican government, whatever its feelings on the traditional roles of army and church, maintained the traditional stance on Gibraltar's return.[7]

Spain's disappointments in Morocco were more recent, and here the object of Spanish anger was France. In 1902, during the beginnings of Morocco's partition, French Foreign Minister Théophile Delcassé had promised Madrid a sizeable zone of influence there, which was to have included northern Morocco down to the Sebu and Mulaya Rivers, and a large piece of territory south of Agadir. Yet after France's Entente Cordiale with Britain in 1904, the French shrank much of the proposed Spanish zone, and the final division of 1912 retracted the zone to what King Victor Emmanuel III of Italy called the bone of the Moroccan cutlet – a mountainous coastal strip of 20,000 square kilometers, nearly impossible to conquer and barely worth improving.[8] Spanish Morocco would not include the port city of Tangier either, for it had been placed under international administration in 1923.[9] In 1925, the French further occupied the rich and populous Beni Zerual and two smaller tribal areas on the Spanish side of the border as part of their needed contribution to the effort against the Moroccan revolt under Abd el-Krim. A French–Spanish border agreement of 1925 had obliged the French to leave these areas, but, as of 1940, the French remained.[10]

It is in this context that the policy of Franco's government towards the entire western Mediterranean region must be understood. Franco's military career had made him a hero of the Spanish right even before Spain degenerated into civil war in 1936, and he came to view himself as a national saviour because of the numerous plaudits which he had received.[11] As a soldier he had no use for abstract political thought – his single meeting with José Antonio Primo de Rivera, the founder of the Spanish Falange, left the latter unimpressed.[12] In April 1937, after José Antonio's execution, Franco united the various Spanish rightist elements into a more malleable conglomeration (Falange Española Tradicionalista y de las Juntas de Ofensiva Nacional Sindicalista – FET y de las JONS) under his own command.[13] He was the authoritarian career army officer once described by his military aide and cousin, Francisco Franco Salgado-Araujo, as 'Francoist above everything ... one hundred per cent Francoist'.[14] Yet Franco and his fellow Africanists in the army shared certain aims with the political right, namely, the eradication at home of the degenerate republicanism which had brought Communism, anarchism, and atheism in its wake and the reconstruction of Spain's ancient empire, or at least the parts of it that were within reach. Gibraltar was certainly an obvious focus for redemption. To

José Antonio, it was a constant reminder of Spanish servitude and debility, and the Franco government's official historical study on Spanish claims in 1941 viewed it as a symptom of a 'mutilated' nation while arguing that Britain's continued presence there was an 'unending source of hatred ... rising from the very heart of our people'.[15] Franco shared all of this but concentrated more specifically on Morocco – the focus of Spain's most recent imperial gains and disappointments – partly because he had built his military career fighting a revolt in the Spanish zone. In 1924, when Miguel Primo de Rivera had argued for a military withdrawal from the Spanish protectorate, Lieutenant Colonel Franco had countered that 'Morocco is Spanish earth because it has been acquired at the highest price and paid for with the dearest coin – Spanish blood'.[16] On the eve of his victory in Spain in 1939, General Franco commented that Spain's greatness, its future, and the 'revival of Spain's historic mission' lay in Morocco.[17] Franco, wrote his brother-in-law and Interior Minister, Ramón Serrano Suñer, after his death, 'was a man of Africa. In Morocco he had brilliantly made his entire career, and in Morocco his destiny seemed to lie'.[18] Britain's wartime Ambassador to Madrid, Sir Samuel Hoare, summed it up best in a letter to his government in July 1940: 'You cannot imagine what Morocco means to the new Spanish generation and particularly to the present Spanish leaders. Franco, Beigbeder and many others made their careers in Morocco and they are much more interested in Morocco than they are in Europe.'[19]

Franco's government had tried to weaken France's position in Morocco even before the outbreak of war in Europe. The most active figure was Colonel Juan Beigbeder y Atienza, an expert on Morocco who had served as the Spanish High Commissioner in Tetuán from April 1937 to August 1939.[20] During the Civil War, Beigbeder kept the tribal leaders behind Franco and supplied him with 70,000 Moroccan troops by granting them an autonomy hitherto unseen in either zone while hinting that such freedoms could even flower into independence. Beigbeder's interests spread into the cultural arena as well, with a new Institute for Moroccan Studies and the rebuilding of mosques and Arabic schools. He also allowed the Moroccan nationalist press in the Spanish zone to blast the neighbouring French administration. After the Civil War, the Caliph, the sultan's representative in the Spanish zone, told Beigbeder that Franco had won the heart not only of Morocco but of all of Islam.[21] None of this sat well with the French, who had enough problems without the addition of nationalist agitation in Morocco. There was even an invasion scare in the Spanish zone in May 1938, and in February 1939 the French asked Foreign Minister Count Jordana to counter the Pan-Islamic movement, the centre of which, they stated, was in Tetuán.[22] The German government helped Spain exacerbate French headaches in Morocco whenever possible, and relations between the

High Commissioner and the German Consulate in Tetuán, under Herbert Georg Richter, were quite friendly. Beigbeder set up German contacts with the Moroccan nationalist leaders in the French zone, and after war erupted between Germany and France, Richter funnelled cash to nationalist groups in French Morocco while promoting German propaganda in both zones.[23] Beigbeder surely hoped that Spain would be the beneficiary of this sort of activity, especially in the event of an eventual French defeat, and Richter understood this. While praising Beigbeder to the German Foreign Ministry upon the Colonel's promotion to the office of Foreign Minister in August 1939, Richter commented that 'Beigbeder's personal wish is to incorporate Tangier into the Spanish zone and also to advance the frontiers against French Morocco; nonetheless he openly admits that this [would only be] possible in the event of a general conflict'.[24] The new Spanish administration in Tetuán after Beigbeder's promotion was also headed by Africanists friendly to the German Consulate. General Carlos Asensio, a divisional commander during the Civil War, was the new High Commissioner. Tomás García Figueras, an expert on Morocco who had written a polemical book on the Spanish protectorate, became his Secretary General.[25]

Still, Franco hoped to stay clear of the general war when it began in September. In June he told Italy's Foreign Minister, Count Galeazzo Ciano, that Spain needed five years' recovery time, and on 4 September Madrid proclaimed strict neutrality. Yet France's military disasters of May and June 1940 opened new possibilities. 'We believed then certainly in a German victory', wrote Serrano Suñer, 'and we had to ... forsee the accommodation of Spain in the European order.'[26] Air Minister Juan Yagüe was serious when he told the Germans in May 1940 that 'the Spanish air force rejoices in this victory as if it were our own'.[27] Franco especially was fully convinced of a German victory,[28] and in the first week of June Beigbeder informed the German Ambassador to Madrid, Baron Eberhard von Stohrer, that Spain's national aspirations would include Gibraltar, French Morocco, and an enlargement of Spanish Guinea. The Foreign Minister added that he would regret it if the Italians desired to occupy Morocco.[29] On 12 June the Spanish government switched its official stance from neutrality to non-belligerency,[30] and, during a speech on 17 June, Franco announced that it was necessary 'to make a nation, to forge an empire. To do that our first task must be to strengthen the unity of Spain. There remains a duty and mission, the command of Gibraltar, African expansion, and the permanence of a policy of unity'.[31] Two million soldiers stood ready, he said, to fulfil the mandate of Queen Isabella. Though the British government paid little heed to this particular speech, the prospects for the Royal Navy's continued presence at Gibraltar did not look good. On his arrival in Madrid, the new

Ambassador, Sir Samuel Hoare, feared for his own safety and thought that the chances of continued Spanish abstinence were remote. Street demonstrations proclaiming 'Gibraltar Español' accompanied by polemics in the Spanish press seemed to confirm his pessimism. Yet despite his predisposition towards opening a dialogue with Madrid over the Rock's future, Prime Minister Winston Churchill held firm. 'The Spaniards', he argued on 21 June, 'know that if we lose they will get [Gibraltar] anyhow, and they would be great fools to believe that if we win we shall mark our admiration for their conduct by giving it to them.' Madrid surely understood this as well. Whatever the content of subsequent discussions over Gibraltar and despite the openly friendly relationship which developed between Hoare and Beigbeder, London promised Madrid nothing concerning the Rock's future beyond a certain degree of sensitivity.[32] Madrid for its part took only tentative steps concerning Gibraltar, such as Franco's insistence that the 29 June 1940 protocol to the Spanish–Portuguese friendship treaty of March 1939 tacitly acknowledge the possibility of a Spanish attack despite Lisbon's 'ancient alliance' with London.[33]

Spanish military activity in fact centred far more on Morocco than on Gibraltar, and it is significant that Madrid did not consult Berlin, Rome, or London in any substantial way. The preferred course was to act alone without help from Germany, whose tendencies during the Civil War had been to keep what they could of Spanish mining concerns, or from Italy, which had had more than a passing interest in the isle of Majorca.[34] After the proclamation of non-belligerency on 12 June, a united Morocco under Spanish protection became the overriding aim, and Tangier was the immediate objective. Despite the city's international character, France enjoyed primacy there; the chief of the International Control Commission had always been French. This practice had always piqued the Spaniards in general and Beigbeder in particular,[35] but recent events gave Beigbeder a chance to act. In April the French government had proposed a joint French–Spanish military occupation to guarantee Tangier's neutrality against possible Italian encroachments. Neither Beigbeder nor the rest of the Spanish government cared to act jointly with a belligerent power in Tangier, especially a rival on the brink of defeat. Beigbeder had the French informed in June that Spain wished to proceed alone with a temporary occupation.[36] From Rabat, General Charles Noguès, the French resident general in Morocco, vehemently opposed any concession to Spain in Tangier, but the French Foreign Ministry registered no objections.[37] An agreement emerged on the evening of 13 June on the condition that Spain's occupation remain provisional.[38] Still, the French were not expecting the swift Spanish action that followed, for they had not informed any of their representatives in Morocco on the agreement with Madrid. On the same evening of 13 June,

Beigbeder ordered Asensio to mobilize two troop detachments for entrance into the city at seven the next morning. At the moment of the occupation the chief of the Control Commission and the mendub (the sultan's representative in Tangier) were to be informed that Spain was temporarily assuming security functions 'in the name of the sultan' and that Spain would respect all international rights. Noguès was to be informed of the occupation 15 minutes earlier with the comment that it had come with the agreement of the French government.[39] The following morning the operation proceeded as smoothly as Beigbeder had described it, to the surprise of all but the Spanish authorities there.[40] It was a fine victory for the Foreign Minister, who for several days was visibly pleased with the proceedings.[41] He even convinced Stohrer and Hitler himself that there had been no contact with France,[42] and, though Beigbeder publicly characterized the occupation as temporary, the truth was different. His notes to Berlin and Rome studiously omitted the proviso given to all other capitals that the occupation was a provisional measure in the sultan's name.[43]

Would Madrid be as daring with French Morocco? Here Spanish intentions are less clear because of the continued secrecy on the matter of Spain's military archive, the Servicio Histórico Militar, but from the available evidence, mostly from German records, it appears that Madrid seriously considered an invasion in the days preceding the French surrender. On 15 June, the day after the Tangier occupation, Stohrer visited Beigbeder and found the latter fully occupied with maps of French Morocco. The Ambassador quickly cabled Berlin that Spain was prepared to take action in the French zone soon, though he remained unsure when.[44] On the same day in Tetuán, Asensio told Richter that a Spanish action was forthcoming.[45] Meanwhile, in France, Franco's chief of staff, Jorge Vigón, met Hitler and Ribbentrop on 16 June, delivered a congratulatory letter from Franco, and made several exploratory remarks.[46] Vigón announced Spain's expectation of a united Morocco under its protection and said that Spain was counting on material help should the Americans land there. Vigón offered Hitler no promises of any kind from Franco, apparently wishing only to divine the level of German support for Spanish aims.[47] Hitler's remarks, however, could not have pleased Madrid. Though the Führer supported a devolution of Gibraltar to Spain and promised to fight an American landing in Morocco, he balked on the issue of Morocco's ultimate protector, stating that Germany and possibly Italy had interests there. Ribbentrop quickly interjected that a solution satisfactory to all sides was necessary. Madrid could only have concluded from this meeting that it would have to make its own rules in Morocco. Richter meanwhile reported considerable Spanish troop movement at the French Moroccan frontier during the entire week, and Asensio predicted that there would be a large advance into the French zone. Reliable sources told Richter that the marching order was to have come from Madrid on 16 or 17 June 1940 but had been postponed. Meanwhile, a nervous Asensio hourly awaited orders to invade.[48]

If Franco had intended to invade the French zone during the final week of the Franco-German war, then why did Spanish troops not march? One explanation could lie in the shrewd request of French Foreign Minister Paul Baudouin in the small hours of 17 June for Spain to mediate a Franco-German cease-fire.[49] The request surprised the Spaniards, who had expected that the French would ask the Swiss for this favour, but, as Ambassador José Félix de Lequerica in France noted, the request was an appeal to the moral stature of Spain and of Franco himself.[50] Could Franco have invaded French territory under such circumstances? Even if he could have forsaken honour and marched into the French zone, military considerations might well have persuaded him not to do so. Noguès kept his troops moving along the northern frontier of the French zone to bluff the Spaniards into overestimating his strength, and in fact the Spaniards, as García Figueras told Richter on 19 June, estimated that the French forces were still quite strong. Richter agreed that the invasion would not have been as easy as the Spaniards had originally expected, and he was relieved when the Spaniards called it off because, as he said, 'one cannot describe the Spanish military organization here in bad enough terms'.[51] The pre-armistice movement of French aircraft to North Africa cooled Spain's ardour even more. On 23 June Beigbeder admitted that Spain could pursue no operations in the area because of French air power.[52] He would lose no opportunity, however, in the following months to complain to the Germans and Italians that French forces in Morocco were not disarming quickly enough, particularly after General Charles de Gaulle's *coup* in French Equatorial Africa in August.[53]

While the Spaniards were weighing mixed signals from Hitler, intelligence reports from Africa, and the French request for mediation, Beigbeder attempted on 17 June – the very day of Baudouin's mediation request – to wring whatever concessions he could from the French before the expected European peace settlement. Yet, despite his argument that France would be better off losing parts of its empire to Spain than to Germany, he met with no success. Neither Noguès nor the French Foreign Ministry had any intention of allowing another Tangier, especially with the peace terms from Germany and Italy still unclear. Beigbeder's proposal included the Beni Zerual, which according to the 1925 border agreement was to have gone to Spain anyway, and the Beni Snassen area on the Algerian border. The French Foreign Ministry stalled Beigbeder and was willing to 'concede' nothing more than the Beni Zerual. Yet shrill objections from Noguès killed even this concession, and when Baudouin finally received a proposal for negotiation in August it included a truncated version of the Beni Zerual which Noguès himself designed on the basis of security. In short, Spain could expect nothing from France.[54]

Thus the Spaniards, with the road to imperial expansion closed in Morocco and in France, had to make a diplomatic detour via Germany. Madrid was too late to take advantage of Germany's victory over France, yet perhaps there was still time to capitalize on Germany's impending victory over Britain. On 19 June Beigbeder informed Stohrer that Spain would enter the war against Britain in exchange for a united Morocco under its protection, the Oran district of Algeria, an extension of Río de Oro to the 20th parallel, and an extension of Spanish Guinea. Spain also demanded the materials for an attack on Gibraltar, German submarine help in defending the Canary Islands, and food.[55] Why did it make this offer now? It would seem that this was its last hope for an empire in French Northwest Africa. With the exception of Gibraltar, all Spanish claims were on French territory. Spain had made no official suggestion up to this time that it wanted a war with Britain and, as the Germans would soon discover, had no military plans for an attack on Gibraltar.[56] Spain's actions of 19 June were symptomatic of desperation. Its aspirations combined with its military weakness and France's stubbornness had forced it farther into Germany's camp than when Vigón had met Hitler only three days earlier.

Yet, as Hitler had hinted to Vigón, Berlin was interested in Northwest Africa too. Morocco offered strategic base sites which the Germans could develop for future conflicts, most likely against the United States. Already German naval and aircraft firms had received official contracts for the construction of six 56,000-ton battleships (*Bismarck* and *Tirpitz* were a mere 48,000 tons) and for the Messerschmitt 264 – a four- engine long-distance bomber which would be able to bomb targets across the Atlantic.[57] With this in mind, Hitler would demand bases near Casablanca on 15 July 1940 as a *quid pro quo* for Axis disarmament concessions following the British raid of 3 July at Mers el-Kebir.[58] When Marshal Henri Philippe Pétain's government rejected Hitler's demand as beyond the scope of the Franco-German armistice treaty, Berlin began to view Spain and the Gibraltar Strait as a route by which it could place troops in Northwest Africa and perhaps take coastal bases on its own. Hitler and the German navy also coveted a base in Spain's own Canary Islands. The Germans began serious talks with the Spaniards in August 1940, and on 16 September Ramón Serrano Suñer, now Franco's Interior Minister, arrived in Berlin for talks with Hitler and Foreign Minister Joachim von Ribbentrop. The Germans had yet to reveal to the Spaniards the true nature of their aims, and even as they spoke with Serrano Suñer in Berlin a secret German Luftwaffe mission was in Casablanca reconnoitring base sites.[59]

Though unaware of the German agents in Casablanca, Serrano Suñer knew of Berlin's earlier demand for air bases there thanks to a deliberate French Foreign Ministry leak.[60] Thus, though the Germans tried to rattle him by prohibiting the new Spanish Ambassador, Eugenio Espinosa de los Monteros, from assisting during his discussions,[61] Serrano still opened his first audience with Ribbentrop with a lengthy, rather pugnacious discourse on Spain's entitlement to Morocco and Oran; the former was the 'natural and historical objective of Spanish expansion', and the latter had a Spanish population. He further based Spain's earlier demand for 56,000 tons of fuel on the possibility that French troops in North Africa would return to action and expressed indignation that Berlin had yet to respond to the Spanish *démarche* of 19 June.[62] Ribbentrop accepted in principle the idea of a united Morocco under Spanish rule but then insisted on 'the Führer's wish' that Spain cede to Germany two bases there (Agadir and Mogador), as well as one of the Canary Islands. Serrano, who had hardly expected to discuss *new* Gibraltars, was visibly upset, and when Hitler raised the issue of islands the next day the Spaniard insisted that the defence of the Euro-African hemisphere should be settled in the context of a general alliance rather than in the cession of Spanish territory to Germany.[63] The Germans, clearly disappointed, quickly added meetings to Serrano's agenda in Berlin. But when Ribbentrop commented on 17 September that the islands had to be equipped as soon as possible with technology that the Spaniards were 'perhaps not in a position to provide' and added that Spain would not receive Morocco at all without Germany's victory, Serrano testily noted that Spain would gladly conquer Morocco with its own blood. He waved off new German demands for Spanish Guinea and Fernando Po with the comment that the entire issue would have to be taken up with Franco.[64] His angry subsequent comments to the Italian dictator, Benito Mussolini, were damning enough that they had to be deleted from the discussion record handed to the Germans.[65]

Franco was indignant about the German demands too, commenting privately that 'the world is big enough that Spain need not suffer any mortgage on its territories'.[66] Still, he remained hopeful that he could find an arrangement with Berlin over Morocco and for the future. His letters from Madrid to Serrano Suñer and Hitler – letters which followed Council of State discussions – reveal that Franco accepted even the possibility of a long war and was banking on a long-term alliance in which Spain would replace Britain as the gatekeeper of the western Mediterranean region. He wrote to Serrano on 21 September:[67]

> Our presence in the Axis offers … the security of and domination of the western Mediterranean and the possibility of defense of our continent including North Africa, making it invulnerable to Anglo-

> American attacks. … In this it is necessary to open a channel to the idea of what an alliance is; in the order of war, the bases of one become the bases of the other. If we are able to defend a European front, we will prepare our bases with one accord.

Franco echoed these thoughts, albeit in more diplomatic language, in a letter to Hitler on 22 September, commenting that once Spain was at war he would mass troops in Spanish Morocco to counter the danger of a Gaullist revolt in French North Africa.[68] These arguments were beyond the Germans, who were simply irritated that they could not get the Spaniards to agree to the cession of bases. Ribbentrop had complained to Mussolini on 20 September:[69]

> The Führer had had this wish presented to the Spaniards in order to counteract through a series of naval bases dangers which could arise for the European and African continents far in the future … from the western hemisphere under American leadership. The Spaniards are surely loyal friends. … But on certain points like the one just mentioned … they were somewhat difficult.

Adding to the complexity of the issue was the British–Gaullist attack and coup attempt at Dakar in the early hours of 23 September. Operation Menace was a dismal failure because of a vigorous French defence.[70] But for Germany it raised the spectre of African bases falling to the British or even the Americans. Concerned about an Anglo-American presence in French Northwest Africa and impressed with Vichy's display of loyalty, Hitler for a time would place some faith in collaboration with Vichy in Africa, at least to the point where Pétain's forces would continue to defend French bases, possibly reconquer Equatorial Africa, and perhaps even allow Germany to use bases in West Africa. Collaboration with Vichy did not mean full trust – Gibraltar would still have to be taken as a bridge to North Africa to guard against defection, and thus Spain would remain part of the equation. But, as Hitler explained to Mussolini on 4 October, Spain would have to accept lesser rewards in Africa, lest Vichy not defend its holdings there. At most, Spain would receive an extension of Spanish Morocco, and it would not receive Oran at all. Perhaps Vichy could be compensated at Britain's expense in Nigeria. In any event, neither the Pétain government (which sought legitimacy partly through the retention of empire) nor the Franco government (which sought legitimacy partly through the conquest of empire) would learn the full truth until the peace. Germany, meanwhile, would get its bases in Morocco one way or another. Sharing with the Spaniards was out of the question, for, as Hitler said, 'Germany is not interested in Spanish harbours … but rather needs bases of its own, already developed and equipped … in peacetime'.[71] It is in this context that Hitler and Ribbentrop's famous western rail journey in late October to meet with the French at Montoire and the Spaniards at Hendaye must be seen.

Franco's only meeting with Hitler on 23 October 1940 is usually portrayed as a disappointment to the latter thanks to Hitler's oft-quoted comment about preferring dental surgery to another meeting with the Caudillo.[72] But the Spaniards came away far more disappointed than the Germans because of expectations in Madrid which included no awareness of recent German thinking.[73] Two weeks before the Hendaye meeting Serrano Suñer had written to Ribbentrop that Madrid was continuing work on a late-September proposal for a ten-year alliance with the Axis states,[74] and Spain seems to have been preparing for action of one form or another. Franco had recently ordered measures for the storage of drinking water in the Canaries, and German intelligence reported in early October that the Spaniards had raised their troop contingent in the islands to 40,000 men. German observers also noticed – and Serrano confirmed this – that two Spanish divisions had moved to Morocco, thus bringing the troop strength there to over seven infantry divisions.[75] The Spanish build-up in Morocco was enough to bring significant responses from the French, who after Serrano's mission to Berlin had attempted to woo the Spaniards with a peaceful arrangement over Morocco. On 30 September Foreign Minister Baudouin had his Ambassador in Madrid, Robert de la Baume, present to Beigbeder his proposal to settle the Moroccan border issue by implementing the border agreement of 1925. Baudouin also gave formal recognition to the Spanish *fait accompli* in Tangier. He had sensed correctly that Serrano's visit to Berlin had dealt extensively with Morocco and was determined, as he told Lequerica, that the Germans should never have a hand in Moroccan affairs.[76] For good measure, on 5 October Baudouin appointed the Hispanophile François Piétri as the new Ambassador to Madrid.[77] Yet the Spaniards made no response to Baudouin's overtures until mid-October, and even then Beigbeder rejected the French offer.[78] Franco seems to have been equally unimpressed with Ambassador Hoare's confidential statement on 15 October that Britain recognized Spanish claims in Morocco and would welcome a Spanish occupation of the entire area.[79] Beigbeder, who had established a relationship with Hoare strong and candid enough to have brought about such a statement, was fired the very next day, and his replacement as Foreign Minister was Serrano Suñer, who was openly unfriendly to Vichy and London.[80] The French used the only option still available – they complained to Berlin on several occasions about the Spanish build-up in Morocco, claiming that a Spanish advance into the French zone would be difficult to stop given French disorganization and that it would have incalculable effects elsewhere in the French empire.[81] Though the French asked Berlin to use its influence with Madrid to bring to a halt whatever it was that the Spaniards were planning, the Germans did nothing here to ease Vichy's concerns. Hitler thought that his own deceptive formula would work.

Thus the idea pushed at Hendaye by the Germans – that for France's sake Spain would have to accept smaller and unspecified rewards – stunned both Franco and Serrano, as did the so-called Hendaye Protocol, which the Germans presented during the meeting as a regulative document for Spain's entry into the war. Article 5 of the protocol, though promising Gibraltar to the Spaniards, contained only the vaguest provisions concerning Spain's future in Africa.[82] As Hitler explained:[83]

> there would arise a considerable danger if America and England established themselves on the islands lying off Africa in the Atlantic Ocean. The danger was all the greater because it was not certain whether the French troops stationed in the colonies would under all circumstances remain loyal to Pétain. *The greatest threat existing at the moment* was that a part of the colonial empire would, with abundant material and military resources, desert France and go over to de Gaulle, England, or the United States. ... *The great problem to be solved at the moment* consisted in hindering the de Gaulle movement in French Africa from further extending itself and thereby establishing in this way bases for England and America on the African coast.

It was thus essential to strengthen the position of the Pétain government in the French colonies, and this would have to be done at the expense of Spain's ambitions. The Spaniards were fully alive to the Gaullist threat but had assumed from the start that Spain would fight it rather than sacrifice its territorial future to it. They argued that Spain's troops could neutralize a Gaullist movement in North Africa, spoke at length on Spain's historic claim to Morocco and Oran, and insisted on a formal agreement concerning rewards before Spain's entry into the war.[84] Hitler, visibly irritated and yawning, noted privately that 'nothing can be done with these people'.[85] But the Spaniards were irritated as well. 'Apparently', said a surprised and angry Serrano Suñer, Berlin was viewing the African issue in a new way.[86] Franco privately noted to Serrano Suñer after the meetings that 'this new sacrifice of ours ... would only be justified with the counterbalance of that which is to be the basis of our imperium. After the victory they would give us nothing if it is not agreed to now, despite what they are saying'.[87] Still, the Germans rejected a transparent supplementary protocol presented by the Spaniards the following morning. This economic protocol ostensibly dealt with mineral concessions but contained the phrasing 'in the French zone of Morocco, which is later to belong to Spain'.[88] Predictably, the Germans rejected the wording, which brought the following response from Serrano Suñer: 'I would not like to pass up this opportunity of expressing the bitter feeling produced in the Caudillo and myself by the fact that regardless of our friendship, the entirely trivial changes which we had suggested and which gave us a somewhat greater measure of security without encroaching at all on the crux of the issue...were rejected.'[89]

Franco, who could have allowed the entire matter to drop after Hendaye, did not give up. In a letter to Hitler of 30 October he argued that the French lands in question were in fact not French at all but natural *Spanish* territory which France had stolen at the time of the Entente Cordiale. 'It is not French territory that we want', claimed Franco, 'nor do we claim to profit from French blood. We want only that which a clever liberal diplomacy ... wrested from us in complete injustice. ... I thus repeat the Spanish aspiration ... to the part of Morocco which is in French hands.'[90] This intriguing attempt to prove that French Morocco was not French failed. In fact Hitler believed, thanks to the letter's opening statement of solidarity with the Axis, that the document simply confirmed Franco's intention to enter the war. On 4 November, the day after he received Franco's letter,[91] Hitler told his military staff that Spain would join the conflict; Germany would soon conclude political negotiations with Madrid and capture Gibraltar.[92] Hitler's War Directive 18, which contained orders for the high command to prepare for the overland capture of Gibraltar (code-named Operation Felix), was prepared within three days of these comments.[93] Hitler would also insist on the movement of a substantial force to Spanish Morocco immediately after the Rock's capture.[94]

All that remained was the conclusion of a political settlement with Madrid. In the first week of November Serrano Suñer, at Ribbentrop's request, affixed his signature to the Hendaye Protocol,[95] but since that document left the timing of Spain's entry to the joint decision of Germany, Italy, *and Spain*, further talks with the Spaniards were essential. On 11 November Ribbentrop summoned Serrano to Hitler's retreat at Berchtesgaden for what was to be a final meeting to iron out the political details of Spanish belligerence. Madrid's continued eagerness for an arrangement is reflected in Serrano's immediate acceptance of the invitation without even consulting with Franco, despite Ribbentrop's comment that Hitler could only meet on 18 November because of a full schedule. A Spanish rejection of the German request would have been easy, but Serrano probably viewed the invitation as Germany's reply to Franco's letter of 30 October, which had yet to receive a written answer.[96] Serrano's postwar claim that the invitation had to be accepted for fear of what the Germans might do otherwise should probably be seen in light of his selective amnesia concerning his own signing of the Hendaye Protocol.[97] In any event, the

Berchtesgaden meeting was a disaster for both parties. Hitler's hope to start the Gibraltar operation within six to eight weeks was stymied by Serrano's irritation that Germany was sacrificing Spanish aims for the sake of Vichy and his insistence that Germany grant Spain clear guarantees concerning its aims in North Africa. An angry and impatient Hitler then showed all of his cards. Germany, he said, could not risk the defection of French Morocco from Vichy by promising it to the Spaniards, especially since the latter had repeatedly expressed the intention to use such a promise as a public justification for belligerence. Besides, any agreement with the French was only to last until the German capture of Gibraltar, for after the Rock was taken German troops would travel across the strait to French Morocco to guard against such a defection. As for the future delineation of territory in North Africa, Franco would simply have to trust Hitler. Spain would receive just rewards in Morocco, and Germany would have a base there. But no closer discussion concerning Morocco could take place now, he said, nor could the previous discussions become public knowledge. Otherwise, said Hitler, 'Morocco would immediately defect and the conquest of Gibraltar would have *no sense any more*. ... He [Hitler] would then prefer that Gibraltar remain in English hands and Africa with Pétain'.[98] These statements, in retrospect, seem to have been pivotal. Hitler had not only refused to take any cognizance of Franco's arguments of 30 October but also revealed to a Spanish official for the first time that Germany would use Spanish belligerence to place its *own* troops in French Morocco – the prime objective of Spanish belligerence. Hitler's revelation that he would prefer the continued British control of Gibraltar to the defection of Morocco at the very least would have struck any listener as odd.

The story of Franco's refusal on 7 December 1940 of the German request that Spain enter the war by 10 January is well known.[99] Franco said that his nation was unready, blamed the economy, and refused to say when Spain might *become* ready for belligerence. Yet economic issues, though surely important and growing more severe, were hardly new. The Spanish economy was wretched throughout the autumn of 1940,[100] and the Spaniards remained willing to enter a long war and assume a long-term alliance throughout that time. Madrid's reluctance in December may well have stemmed more from German aims in Africa, which Spain could not have prevented had it entered the war and permitted German passage through the Iberian Peninsula. Much evidence supports this contention. Germany's stance on territorial rewards drew loud and frequent complaints from Franco and Serrano Suñer, particularly at Bordighera, where on 12 February 1941 the two Spaniards met Mussolini for some frank talk about Berlin's recent heavy pressure on Spain to enter the war.[101] Franco here insisted on enough grain to last the duration and enough equipment to fight effectively, but the Spaniards also complained profusely about the Hendaye meeting, which they said had been a great disappointment because of Germany's lack of understanding and its desire to work with Vichy to Madrid's detriment. The Hendaye Protocol, they said, would have to be rewritten so that Spain would receive French Morocco. Franco also made the surprise announcement that he preferred to take Gibraltar without German aid, thus obviating the need for German troops in Spain or in Morocco. How he thought this last announcement would play in Berlin is a mystery, but Berlin read it – together with the long list of material demands – as a *de facto* Spanish refusal to enter the war.[102] In any case, heavy German pressure on Madrid to enter the war faded after Bordighera because of the timetable for the German campaign in the east.

More telling than Franco's comments on the Italian Riviera was the precipitous decline of Spanish–German cooperation in Spanish Morocco – which Richter had lauded before the war – after Serrano's Berchtesgaden meeting with Hitler in mid-November. Madrid's possessiveness towards Morocco had increased in early November when Spain incorporated the Tangier zone into Spanish Morocco. On 3 November Spain formally dissolved Tangier's international institutions – the International Control Commission, the Legislative Assembly, and the Mixed Information Bureau. Spanish officers filled these positions, and Colonel Antonio Yuste, commander of the June occupation, became military Governor of Tangier, replacing the French head of the Control Commission. The Spanish press announced that Tangier was now Spanish, warning the French not to protest. Extra artillery in the zone punctuated the warning. On 28 November Franco proclaimed unity of law between Tangier and Spanish Morocco.[103] The fact that these moves came a few days after the Hendaye meeting with no warning to Berlin or Rome was not lost on the Germans. Stohrer commented that it was 'due to a certain feeling which has spread [in Madrid] after Hendaye that [Spain] should act independently in order to assure itself of at least Tangier', and Serrano said nothing to dispute this theory.[104]

It was also no coincidence that Spain also began to combat the German position in Spanish Morocco in late November 1940, after Hitler's revelations at Berchtesgaden. Sources on German activity in Spanish Morocco during the war are scarce, yet the number of Nazi Party, SD, and Abwehr agents in Spanish Morocco was not insignificant, while print, radio, and film propaganda was quite lively.[105] Effective connections also existed between the German consulate in Tetuán and Moroccan nationalists.[106] Spain's attitude had begun to simmer in June 1940, when the Spaniards saw a chance to realize their aims in French Morocco. In late June Asensio told Richter that Spain was displeased both with German propaganda in Spanish

Morocco and with German contacts with the nationalist underground in the French zone. He tried unsuccessfully to reach agreement with Richter that German propaganda function under Spanish supervision.[107] Remaining cooperation between Berlin and Madrid in Morocco disintegrated after Hitler's statements at Berchtesgaden. On 30 November Ambassador Espinosa slapped an indignant Ribbentrop with blistering indictments of German propaganda in Morocco, noting that German agents were disregarding Spanish interests and had occasioned complaints from the High Commissariat for some time.[108] Spanish authorities in Morocco acted accordingly. By the end of the year Richter, who once held up the High Commissariat as a Germanophile body, complained bitterly:[109]

> The sympathies of the natives for us are well known to the Spaniards and drive them to a morbid jealousy of any German influence in the country. The Spanish effort to exclude us systematically from Morocco has been evident in the course of the year on unimportant occasions as well as in matters of principle. The greatest obstacles were placed in the way of exhibiting German war films; permission for Germans to enter Tangier, which could be occupied by Spain in June only as a result of the German victories in France, was delayed for months; the return of the former German legation property in Tangier is being postponed beyond reason.
>
> In the French zone, too, which certainly does not belong to the Spaniards, they do not want any German influence. A shipment from the Madrid Embassy to the Consulate containing Arabic propaganda material, which by reason of its text and sense could only be used in the French zone, was confiscated by the High Commissioner in a way that I consider to be contrary to international law ...The Spanish policy here in this country is a bad sign for the future, if Spain should really succeed in gaining possession of the French zone entirely or even in part. Spain would have only one aim: she would never rest until the last German had left the country – the heart's desire, openly expressed, of the secretary general [García Figueras] of the Alta Comisaría here.

Symptomatic of these problems was the question of the German legation building in Tangier. The property had been confiscated from the Germans during World War I and given to the mendub, the sultan's representative in the city.[110] Berlin requested its return soon after Spain occupied Tangier in June 1940. This was no small issue of protocol. The return of the legation would have boosted German prestige in Morocco, and the general Consulate in Tangier, once set up in 1941, would become Germany's espionage hub in the region.[111] From early September Stohrer pressed

Beigbeder for the building's return, but Beigbeder would not risk the insult to the sultan that the eviction of the mendub would have caused.[112] Spain's incorporation of Tangier in early November created a ticklish situation. Since it came on the heels of the Hendaye conference, Berlin feared that Moroccan natives would see it as the result of a Spanish–German agreement.[113] Moreover, Spain's possessive attitude seemed to bode ill for German interests. Thus the legation issue became more acute. Ribbentrop had Serrano informed that Germany still had a 'considerable interest' in Tangier and Morocco and expected a restoration of its pre-1914 status and the return of the legation.[114] At first the request presented few problems. Serrano told Stohrer before leaving for his meeting with Hitler at Berchtesgaden that Spain would see to the legation's return, and the German Embassy planned a large ceremony to celebrate it and to impress the Moroccan natives.[115] But Madrid's attitude changed after the Serrano–Hitler meeting. On 4 December Serrano told Stohrer that the legation's return would be postponed indefinitely because of anger among Spanish authorities in Morocco over subversive German activities. Berlin denied all charges and pressed for the return of the building, but when Stohrer challenged Serrano to prove the allegations the latter produced a list of German agents in Spanish Morocco and refused to give a date for the legation's return.[116] Madrid would finally bend to Berlin's wishes, but not until March 1941, after the heaviest pressure from Hitler for Spanish entry into the war had passed. The mendub was evicted on 16 March, and the next day, in a grand ceremony with thousands of spectators, the German legation was restored, with the German Consulate in Tangier opening soon after.[117] Yet the Spaniards were not to be outdone. Four days after the German celebration, Madrid staged its own parade for the caliph's entry into the city. Tangier's streets were adorned with Spanish and Moroccan flags, and military processions followed the caliph. In a touch of irony Spain invited a surprise guest to add an anti-French lustre – Abd el-Aziz, the boy sultan whom the French had deposed in 1908.[118]

In the end, the dream of a new empire in the western Mediterranean would not materialize. Churchill's prophecy that London would not return Gibraltar to Spain after a victory came true, and Spain gained nothing in Africa either. On their return trip from their meeting with Mussolini at Bordighera on 13 February 1941, Franco and Serrano paid a visit to Marshal Pétain and Admiral Jean-François Darlan (who had just assumed the Foreign Minister's portfolio) at Montpellier. Amidst tremendous pomp and detailed discussions about the extradition of republican refugees to Spain, Pétain and Franco agreed that close cooperation in North Africa was desirable, as was keeping the Germans out of the western Mediterranean region.[119] But Spanish pressure on Vichy for a new Moroccan border arrangement over the next year and a half met with no success.[120] For the rest, friction continued between Noguès and the Spanish High Commissariat over Spanish public statements regarding colonial claims, even when such speeches were made as far away as Barcelona.[121] Meanwhile, Spain's relationship with Germany over Morocco was not entirely normal either. The Germans would complain about Spanish propaganda with an anti-German slant, Spanish authorities would raise objections to German propaganda in the Spanish zone, and each watched the other with the utmost care.[122] The German General Consulate at Tangier would serve as a nest for German spies in the western Mediterranean until May 1944, when Allied economic pressure (together with lists of names of German spies) forced its closure amidst strong German protests. Even afterwards, German agents remained on Spanish territory through the end of the war.[123] Yet Spanish policy, though not entirely coherent and not at all successful, was surely its own. Though isolated after the war, Franco survived in part because he followed a course that was not particularly pro-German or pro-Allied. Instead, the phantasm of a new empire in the western Mediterranean, however unrealistic, was 'Francoist above everything ... one hundred percent Francoist'.

NOTES

1. For broad consideration of these arguments, see David Wingeate Pike, 'Franco and the Axis Stigma', *Journal of Contemporary History*, 17 (Jan. 1982), pp.369–480, and more recently Paul Preston, 'Franco and Hitler: The Myth of Hendaye 1940', *Contemporary European History*, 1 (March 1992), pp.1–16. On Spain's economic relations with Germany, see Christian Leitz, *Economic Relations between Nazi Germany and Franco's Spain 1936–1945* (New York, 1997), and on the Spanish Blue Division, see most recently Denis Smyth, 'The Dispatch of the Spanish Blue Division to the Russian Front: Reasons and Repercussions', *European History Quarterly*, 24 (1994), pp.537–53. On the issue of Germans in Spain, see Carlos Collado Seidel, 'Zufluchtsstätte für Nationalsozialisten? Spanien, die Alliierten und die Behandlung deutscher Agenten 1944–1947', *Vierteljahrshefte für Zeitgeschichte*, 43 (1995), pp.131–58.
2. Ramón Serrano Suñer, *Entre Hendaye y Gibraltar: Noticia y reflexión, frente a una leyenda sobre nuestra política en dos guerras* (Madrid, 1947); José Maria Doussinague, *España tenía razón, 1939–1945*, 2nd edn. (Madrid, 1950).
3. Charles B. Burdick, *Germany's Military Strategy and Spain in World War II* (Syracuse, NY, 1968), and Donald S. Detwiler, *Hitler, Franco und Gibraltar: Die Frage des spanischen Eintritts in den zweiten Weltkrieg* (Wiesbaden, 1962), present a friendlier appraisal of Spanish policy than that offered earlier by Herbert Feis, *The Spanish Story: Franco and the Nations at War* (New York, 1948).
4. See especially Ramón Serrano Suñer, *Memorias: Entre el silencio y la propaganda, la historia como fue* (Barcelona, 1977); Heleno Saña, *El franquismo sin mitos: Conversaciones con Serrano Suñer* (Barcelona, 1982).
5. Various fine interpretations can be found in Stanley G. Payne, *The Franco Regime 1936–1975* (Madison, WI, 1987); Paul Preston, *Franco: A Biography* (New York, 1994); Xavier Tusell and Genoveva García Queipo de Llano, *Franco y Mussolini: La política española durante la segunda guerra mundial* (Barcelona, 1985); Denis Smyth, *Diplomacy*

and Strategy of Survival: British Policy and Franco's Spain, 1940–41 (Cambridge, 1986).

6. On the latter two issues see especially Collado Seidel, "Zufluchtsstätte."
7. George Hills, *Rock of Contention: A History of Gibraltar* (London, 1974), pp.385–411.
8. See Christopher Andrew, *Théophile Delcassé and the Making of the Entente Cordiale: A Reappraisal of French Foreign Policy 1898–1905* (London, 1968), pp.191–3, 216–27; William A. Hoisington Jr., *The Casablanca Connection: French Colonial Policy, 1936–1943* (Chapel Hill, NC, 1984), pp.136–7. Spanish claims in Morocco (and elsewhere) are elaborated in the contemporary officially sponsored Spanish account, José María de Areilza and Fernando María Castiella, *Reivindicaciones de España*, 2nd edn. (Madrid, 1941), pp.267–501. The account is of course polemical but at least complete with excellent maps. For Spain's problems in its zone, see Víctor Morales Lezcano, *España y el Norte de Africa: El protectorado en Marruecos (1912–1956)* 2nd edn. (Madrid, 1986), pp.163–217; David S. Woolman, *Rebels in the Rif: Abd el-Krim and the Rif Rebellion* (Stanford, CA, 1968).
9. Charles R. Halstead and Carolyn J. Halstead, 'Aborted Imperialism: Spain's Occupation of Tangier 1940–1945', *Iberian Studies*, 7 (Autumn 1978), pp.53–5; Hoisington, *Casablanca*, p.150.
10. See Hoisington, *Casablanca*, p.153; Woolman, *Rebels*, pp.165–6, 208–9. Areilza and Castiella, *Reivindicaciones*, pp.420–32, contains the documentation on the 1925 border agreement.
11. Preston, *Franco*, pp.1–373.
12. Serrano Suñer, *Memorias*, pp.54–6; Payne, *Franco Regime*, p.92.
13. Payne, *Franco Regime*, pp.171–9.
14. Quoted in Smyth, *Diplomacy*, p.16.
15. Areilza and Castiella, *Reivindicaciones*, p.98.
16. Preston, *Franco*, pp.35–68.
17. Quoted in Smyth, *Diplomacy*, pp.17, 45.
18. Serrano Suñer, *Memorias*, p.285.
19. Quoted in Smyth, *Diplomacy*, p.46.
20. Charles R. Halstead, 'A "Somewhat Machiavellian" Face: Colonel Juan Beigbeder as High Commissioner in Spanish Morocco, 1937–1939', *The Historian*, 37 (November 1974), pp.46–66; idem, 'Un africain méconnu: le colonel Juan Beigbeder', *Revue d'histoire de la deuxiéme guerre mondiale*, 21 (July 1971), pp.31–60.
21. Reported by the German consul in Tetuán, Herbert Georg Richter, to the Foreign Ministry, No.707/Pol. 3, 10 May 1940, Politisches Archiv des Auswärtigen Amtes (Bonn)(hereafter AA), Deutsche Botschaft Madrid (hereafter DB Madrid), Marokko – Allgemein, Vol.5.
22. On the invasion scare, see Hoisington, *Casablanca*, p.149. On the French request of 1939, which was one of the French government's prime criteria for a normalization of relations between France and Spain, see Foreign Ministry (Berlin), to DB Madrid, Pol. 3 359g, 18 Feb. 1939, AA, DB Madrid, Frankreich und Beziehungen zu Spanien; Estado Español, SIPM, No.10/8–390, 6 May 1939, Archivo del Ministerio de Asuntos Exteriores (Madrid)(hereafter AMAE), legajo 1065, expediente 5.
23. Richter to Stohrer, unnumbered, 24 June 1940, AA, DB Madrid, Marokko – Allgemein, vol.5; Richter to Foreign Ministry, No.469/40, 15 April 1940, ibid; Richter to Foreign Ministry, No.915/Sekr., 26 June 1939, ibid.
24. Richter to Foreign Ministry No.1192/39, 11 Aug. 1939, enclosed in Foreign Ministry to DB Paris, Pol. 3 3318, 18 Aug. 1939, AA, DB Paris, Spanien: Politische Akten, Bundle 1363.
25. Richter to Foreign Ministry, No.1231/Pol. 3, 18 Aug. 1939, enclosed in Foreign Ministry to DB Paris, Pol. 3 3380, ibid; Richter to Foreign Ministry, No.626/41, 10 May 1941, AA, DB Madrid, Marokko – Allgemein, vol.5. For the book by García Figueras, see *Marruecos: La acción de España en el Norte de Africa* (Madrid, 1939).
26. Serrano Suñer, *Memorias*, p.288.
27. Stohrer to Foreign Ministry, No.1496/20, 20 May 1940, AA, DB Madrid, Entwicklung der allgemeinen Lage, Vol.1.
28. Preston, *Franco*, pp.355 ff.
29. Stohrer to Foreign Ministry, 3 June 1940, in Germany, Auswärtiges Amt, *Akten zur*

deutschen auswärtigen Politik, 1918–1945: Aus dem Archiv des deutschen Auswärtigen Amtes – Serie D: 1937–1941 (Baden-Baden, 1950–64)(hereafter *ADAP* with series, volume, and document numbers), D, Vol.9, p.380.

30. The public announcement was made on 13 June. On the legal issues surrounding this status, see Víctor Morales Lezcano, 'Las causas de la no-beligerancia española, reconsideradas', *Revista de Estudios Internacionales*, 5 (July–Sept. 1984), pp.609–31; idem, *Historia de la no-beligerancia española durante la segunda guerra mundial (VI, 1940 – X, 1943)* (Las Palmas, 1980), pp.25–6.
31. Quoted in Samuel Hoare (Viscount Templewood), *Ambassador on Special Mission* (London, 1946), p.48. See also Smyth, *Diplomacy*, pp.41–2. On Spanish press comments, see *ADAP*, D, Vol.9, p.380; Stohrer to Foreign Ministry, 7 June 1940, No.1769, AA, Büro des Staatssekretärs (hereafter StS), Marokko, Vol.1.
32. On these issues, see Smyth, *Diplomacy*, pp.29–75.
33. Charles R. Halstead, 'Consistent and Total Peril from Every Side: Portugal and its 1940 Protocol with Spain', *Iberian Studies*, 3 (Spring 1974), pp.18–19, and Smyth, *Diplomacy*, p.35, n. 65.
34. On Germany and the Spanish economy, see Leitz, *Economic Relations*, Ch. 1 and 2. On Italy and Majorca, see John F. Coverdale, *Italian Intervention in the Spanish Civil War* (Princeton, 1975), Ch.5, pp.198 ff.
35. On Tangier's administration see Halstead and Halstead, 'Aborted Imperialism', pp.54–5; Hoisington, *Casablanca*, pp.150–51. For Spanish irritation, see the newspaper articles by Beigbeder's Press Chief Enrique Arquéz, '¿Ha sido Tánger neutral alguna vez?', *España*, 8 June 1939 and the 'prize-winning' 'Cómo perdimos Tánger', ibid., 8 Jan. 1940. *España*, a Tangier newspaper under the Arquéz's editorship, was generally recognized as Beigbeder's voice. Richter still called it 'Das Blatt Beigbeders' even after Beigbeder had become Foreign Minister. Beigbeder commented to Richter in June 1939 that he aimed to keep polemic over Tangier at a steady flow so that the question would remain open. See Richter to Foreign Ministry, No.839/Pol. 3, 12 June 1939, AA, DB Madrid, Tanger Zone, Vol.3; Richter to Foreign Ministry, No.30/Pol. 7, 10 Jan. 1940, ibid. Arquéz later wrote a polemic on Morocco entitled *El momento de España en Marruecos* (Madrid, 1942).
36. Beigbeder to Lequerica, No.330, 8 June 1940, AMAE, legajo 1217, expediente 69. Beigbeder argued to the French that sole Spanish occupation would be a better guarantee of Tangier's neutrality.
37. Hoisington, *Casablanca*, pp.151–2.
38. The principles of the agreement are in Beigbeder's note to the Portuguese Embassy in Madrid, No.56, 14 June 1940, AMAE, legajo 1217, expediente 69, and in his note of the same day to the French Ambassador, Beigbeder to Robert de la Baume, No.324, 14 June 1940, ibid.
39. Beigbeder to Asensio, No.20 Cif., 13 June 1940, ibid.
40. Manuel Amieva (Spanish Consul in Tangier) to Beigbeder, No.69, 14 June 1940, ibid.
41. Stohrer to Foreign Ministry, No.1895/14, 14 June 1940, AA, DB Madrid, Tanger Zone, Vol.3; Stohrer to Foreign Ministry, No.2621/40, 17 June 1940, ibid.
42. Of all Beigbeder's announcements of the occupation to the foreign missions in Madrid, the only announcements that made no mention of a previous agreement with the French government were those to the embassies of Italy and Germany. See AMAE, legajo 1217, expediente 69. On the convincing of Berlin that no contact had been made with the French, see Woermann to DB Madrid, No.846/15, 16 June 1940, AA, DB Madrid, Tanger Zone, Vol.3; Stohrer to Foreign Ministry, No.1925/16, 16 June 1940, ibid.; *ADAP*, D, Vol.9, p.456.
43. For Beigbeder's statements to various European capitals, see AMAE, legajo 1217, expediente 69. Beigbeder explained to Stohrer that public mention of the sultan and the ephemeral nature of the occupation were purely to avoid hostile French–British reaction. See Stohrer to Foreign Ministry, No.2621/40, 17 June 1940, AA, DB Madrid, Tanger Zone, Vol.3. On the occupation regime see Hoisington, *Casablanca*, pp.150–52; Halstead and Halstead, 'Aborted Imperialism', pp.55–7; Smyth, *Diplomacy*, pp.46, 133–72; Payne, *Franco Regime*, p.268.

44. Stohrer to Foreign Ministry, Nr. 1906, 15 June 1940, AA, StS, Marokko, Vol.1. Payne, *Franco Regime*, p.270, states that there had indeed been military plans for an advance in Northwest Africa since June 1940.
45. Richter to Foreign Ministry, No.8, 15 June 1940, AA, StS, Marokko, Vol.1.
46. For the protocol see *ADAP*, D, Vol.9, p.456. For Franco's letter to Hitler, dated 3 June, see ibid., 378.
47. Asensio had told Richter on 15 June that the imminent Spanish advance into Morocco hinged on the outcome of the negotiations in Berlin with Franco's representative, which surely meant the negotiations with Vigon. See Richter to Foreign Ministry, No.8, 15 June 1940, AA, StS, Marokko, Vol.1.
48. Richter to Foreign Ministry, No.725/40, 20 June 1940, encl. In Foreign Ministry to DB Rome, Pol. 3 1734, 4 July 1940, AA, DB Rom, 'Lage an der französisch–spanischen Zonengrenze'. For Italian perspectives see Italy, Ministera degli Affari Esteri, *I documenti diplomatici italiani,* series 9, 1939–1943 (Rome, 1954–) (hereafter *DDI* with series, volume, and document number), Vol.5, p.42.
49. *ADAP*, D, Vol.9, p.459 and n.1.
50. Lequerica to Beigbeder, No.824, 18 June 1940, AMAE, legajo 2295, expediente 4; Lequerica to Beigbeder, unnumbered, 16 June 1940, ibid., legajo 1217, expediente 69.
51. Richter to Foreign Ministry, No.725/40, 20 June 1940, enclosed in Foreign Ministry to DB Rome, Pol. 3 1734g, 4 July 1940, AA, DB Rom, 'Lage an der franzosisch–spanischen Zonengrenze'; Richter to Foreign Ministry, No.732/40, 25 June 1940, enclosed in Foreign Ministry to DB Rome, Pol. 3 1765g, 4 July 1940, ibid.; Richter to Stohrer, Unnumbered, 24 June 1940, AA, DB Madrid, Marokko – Allgemein. On Noguès, see Hoisington, *Casablanca*, p.152 n.53.
52. Stohrer to Foreign Ministry, 23 June 1940, *ADAP*, D, Vol.10, p.3; Zoppi to Ciano, 22 June 1940, *DDI*, Series 9, Vol.5, p.86. On the French air force in Africa see Martin Thomas, 'Plans and Problems of the *Armee de l'air* in the Defence of French North Africa before the Fall of France', *French History*, 7 (Fall 1993), pp.472–95.
53. The Spaniards had paid close attention to the disarmament aspects of the Italian–French armistice, since the Italians were responsible for monitoring French disarmament and demobilization in French African territories bordering the Mediterranean. See the undated memorandum containing Marshal Pétain's comments to Lequerica on this issue in AMAE, legajo 2295, expediente 4. See also Vidal to Beigbeder, 31 Aug. 1940, AMAE, legajo 1083 expediente 10. Beigbeder's many complaints to the Germans and Italians from July through September regarding the slow pace of French disarmament in Morocco and the Gaullist danger there can be found in AA, StS, Marokko, Vol.1; AA, Friedensverhandlungen mit Frankreich, Vol.1; *DDI*, Series 9, Vol.5, pp.323, 394, 539, 566, 577, 591.
54. Hoisington, *Casablanca*, pp.150–55; Francois Charles-Roux, *Cinq mois tragiques aux Affaires etrangeres (21 mai–1er novembre 1940)* (Paris, 1949), pp.224–48.
55. Stohrer to Foreign Ministry, No.1971, 19 June 1940, AA, StS, Marokko, Vol.1; *ADAP*, D, Vol.9, p.488. The Spaniards gave an analogous message in Rome omitting the requests for weapons and foodstuffs. See *DDI*, Series 9, Vol.5, p.54.
56. Smyth, *Diplomacy*, pp.32–3, 42–4, 47–9; Burdick, *Germany's Military Strategy*, p.25.
57. On the naval contracts, see Jost Dulffer, *Weimar, Hitler und die Marine: Reichspolitik und Flottenbau 1920–1939* (Dusseldorf, 1973). On the Messerschmitt 264 see Jochen Thies, *Architekt der Weltherrschaft: Die "Endziele" Hitlers* (Dusseldorf, 1980).
58. See my 'Hitler's Demand for Casablanca in 1940: Incident or Policy', *International History Review,* 16 (Aug. 1994), pp.491–510.
59. For these issues see my 'The Riddle of the Rock: A Reassessment of German Motives for the Capture of Gibraltar in the Second World War', *Journal of Contemporary History*, 28 (April 1993), pp.297–314.
60. Lequerica to Beigbeder, unnumbered, 18 July 1940, MAE, legajo 1190, expediente 97; Lequerica to Beigbeder, Nos.526/27/28/29, 20 July 1940, ibid. Beigbeder had in fact hinted to Stohrer in late July that a demand for German installations in Morocco could push the French colonies into the arms of de Gaulle. See *ADAP*, D, Vol.10, p.231.

61. Espinosa de los Monteros to Beigbeder, 3 Oct. 1940, AMAE, legajo 1188, expediente 3.
62. *ADAP*, D, Vol.11, p.63. German silence was all the more puzzling to the Spaniards in light of the fact that Franco had asked for and obtained Mussolini's support for Spanish aims in principle in the third week of August on the condition that Spain enter the war. Franco received Mussolini's reply with a true show of enthusiasm. See Franco to Mussolini, 15 Aug. 1940, *ADAP*, D, Vol.10, p.346; Mussolini to Franco, 25 Aug. 1940, ibid., 392; Tusell and Queipo de Llano, *Franco y Mussolini*, pp.94–7.
63. *ADAP*, D, Vol.11, p.66.
64. Ibid., p.67. For Serrano's original itinerary, which included only one meeting with Ribbentrop and Hitler each, see AMAE, legajo 1188, expediente 3. For the full scope of the changes see Espinosa de los Monteros to Beigbeder, 3 Oct. 1940, ibid; *ADAP*, D, Vol.11, pp.97, 117.
65. Malcolm Muggeridge (ed.), *Ciano's Diary 1939–1943* (London, 1947) (hereafter *Ciano Diary*), 1, 5 Oct. 1940; idem, *Ciano's Diplomatic Papers* (London, 1948) (hereafter *Ciano Papers*), pp.393–4; Tusell and Queipo de Llano, *Franco y Mussolini*, pp.107–8.
66. Franco to Serrano Suner, 21 Sept. 1940, Serrano Suñer, *Memorias*, pp.331–40.
67. Ibid.
68. *ADAP*, D, Vol.11, p.88.
69. Ibid., p.79.
70. See most recently Martin Thomas, 'The Anglo-French Divorce over West Africa and the Limitations of Strategic Planning, June–December 1940', *Diplomacy & Statecraft*, 6 (March 1995), pp.252–78.
71. *ADAP*, D, Vol.11, p.149. See also *Ciano Papers*, pp.395–8; *Ciano Diary*, 4 Oct. 1940. On these issues in general, see my *Tomorrow the World: Hitler, Northwest Africa, and the Path towards America* (College Station, TX, 1998), Chs.5 and 6.
72. *Ciano Papers*, p.402. Hitler's comment that his meeting with Franco lasted nine hours is an exaggeration which likely included subsequent dinner discussion. Serrano Suner, *Memorias*, p.299, shows that the meeting lasted three hours though there were subsequent comments over dinner in Hitler's car.
73. For a full consideration of this meeting, its sources, and its controversies, see Preston, 'Hitler and Franco', and my *Tomorrow the World*, Ch.6. For the protocols of the Hendaye meetings between Hitler and Franco and Serrano Suñer and Ribbentrop respectively, see *ADAP*, D, Vol.11, pp.220, 221. See also Serrano Suñer, *Memorias*, pp.289–301.
74. Serrano Suñer to Ribbentrop, 10 Oct. 1940, *ADAP*, D, 11, 172. See also Serrano's memorandum of 27 Sept. 1940 in ibid., 116.
75. On Spain's preparations, see OKH/GenStdH/Abt.Fremde Heere West/IV Lageberichte West No.419, 3 Oct. 1940, AA, Handakten Hasso von Etzdorf 1940–1941; Memorandum by Stein, 14 Oct. 1940, AA, Friedensverhandlungen mit Frankreich, Vol.2, 107137–40; [OKH/GenStdH] Op. Abt. (IIb.) Vortragsnotiz, gKdos.: Sperrung der Meerenge von Gibraltar, 13 Nov. 1940, Bundesarchiv/Militärarchiv (Freiburg i.B), RH 2/444. See also Werner Rahn and Gerhard Schreiber (eds.), *Kriegstagebuch der Seekriegsleitung 1939–1945: Teil A* (Bonn, 1988–), Vol.14, 4 Oct. 1940; Serrano Suñer, *Memorias*, pp.341–2; *ADAP*, D, Vol.11, p.172.
76. Lequerica to Beigbeder, No.1137, 30 Sept. 1940, AMAE, legajo 2295, expediente 5; Charles-Roux, *Cinq mois*, pp.243–8. Petain was appropriately concerned that Hitler was using Franco to push into North Africa. The issue is covered in Ricardo de la Cierva, *Hendaye: Punto Final* (Barcelona, 1981), pp.123–4, though without source citations.
77. The importance of Piétri's appointment should not be underestimated, since the previous Ambassador, Robert de la Baume, had been Baudouin's primary contact with the British government via the British Ambassador in Madrid, Sir Samuel Hoare. In his memoirs, Hoare assumes that Piétri's replacement of de la Baume was due to Laval's Anglophobia, apparently because Piétri did not arrive in Madrid until after Laval had replaced Baudouin as Foreign Minister on 28 October. See Hoare, *Mission*, p.90. Yet Baudouin had made the appointment in early October, and Piétri's prior experience as the Director-General of Finances in Morocco (1917–24) and a delegate to the Technical Conference on Tangier (1920) and his scholarly work on Joseph Bonaparte's tenure in Spain can only lead one to

believe that Baudouin made the appointment with consideration for a possible future settlement with the Spaniards over Morocco. A lengthy evaluation of Piétri is in Lequerica to Beigbeder, No.1774, 7 Oct. 1940, AMAE, legajo 2295, expediente 5, which describes Piétri as one with the mental agility to understand Spain's new position in relation to France. Lequerica also noted that Piétri's service in Morocco would make him amenable to Spanish claims there. See also Cierva, *Hendaye*, p.124; Francois Piétri, *Mes anées d'Espagne, 1940–1948* (Paris, 1954); Matthieu Séguéla, *Pétain-Franco: Les secrets d'une alliance* (Paris, 1992), pp.199–22.

78. There is no evidence to support de la Baume's assertion in Charles-Roux, *Cinq mois*, p.247, that Beigbeder's refusal was due to German pressure.
79. Hoare's statements were made to General Agustin Muñoz Grandes. Discussions on Gibraltar, he said, would have to come later. See Memorandum by Muñoz Grandes to Franco, 15 Oct. 1940, Archivo de la Presidencia del Gobierno (Madrid), Jefatura del Estado, legajo 1, expediente 6.2.
80. On the relationship between Beigbeder and Hoare, see the excellent account in Smyth, *Diplomacy*, pp.74 ff. Though the timing of Beigbeder's dismissal is suggestive, there is no evidence to support French and British rumours that Hitler had prompted his removal. Beigbeder's ostensible Anglophilia, especially as a reason for his dismissal, is also a debatable issue. See Smyth, *Diplomacy*, pp.74–5, 95–101; Payne, *Franco Regime*, p.271; Preston, *Franco*, pp.366, 391; Cierva, *Hendaye*, p.124.
81. Memo by Grote, Pol IM, 14022g, 17 Oct. 1940, AA, StS, Friedensverhandlungen mit Frankreich, Vol.2; Memo by Grote, 18 Oct. 1940, ibid; Memo by Grote, Pol IM 14069g, 19 Oct. 1940, ibid.
82. See *ADAP,* D, Vol.11, pp.394–5 for the only surviving version of the protocol, which had been revised from the original presented at Hendaye. Tha article, which dealt with compensation to Spain, reads as follows: '5. Apart from the reunion of Gibraltar with Spain, the Axis Powers state that in principle they are ready to provide, in the course of a new general settlement in Africa, such as is to be carried out in the peace treaties after the defeat of England, that Spain be ceded certain areas in Africa in precisely the same extent to which France can be compensated by other cessions of territorial possessions in Africa of equal value. The claims to be made on France by Germany shall not be affected thereby.'
83. *ADAP*, D, Vol.11, p.220, my emphasis. Serrano Suner, *Memorias*, p.294, confirms that Hitler's preoccupations at Hendaye concerned Gibraltar, the Canary Islands, and Morocco.
84. Franco's explanation on what Spain could do militarily to minimize the Gaullist threat in North Africa is not contained in the incomplete protocol of the Franco–Hitler discussion, but Serrano mentioned that Franco had detailed contingency plans. Ribbentrop and Hitler told the Italians subsequently that the Spaniards had grossly overestimated their capabilities in North Africa and that it had been difficult to convince them that they could not handle the Gaullist threat alone. See *ADAP*, D, Vol.11, pp.221, 228, 246.
85. For Hitler's comments, see Pike, 'Axis Stigma', pp.376–8, and Payne, *Franco Regime*, p.273. The German memoir literature cited in Detwiler, *Gibraltar*, p.59 n.25 says that Hitler lost his patience and threatened to leave on one or two occasions. Serrano Suner, *Memorias*, pp.298–9, states that Hitler never made this threat but that he was reduced to yawns during Franco's monologue.
86. *ADAP*, D, Vol.11, p.221.
87. Quoted in Serrano Suñer, *Memorias*, p.299.
88. For the draft of the Spanish supplementary protocol see *ADAP*, D, Vol.11, p.222. For German comments see Memorandum by Wiehl, 5 Nov. 1940, AA, StS, Spanien, Vol.2.
89. Stohrer to Ribbentrop, 26 Oct. 1940, *ADAP*, D, Vol.11, p.235.
90. Printed in Serrano Suñer, *Memorias*, pp.301–5. Serrano Suñer's claim that the letter was written to buy time does not ring true. On 2 November he told Stohrer that the intent of the letter lay in clarification of the issues discussed at Hendaye. Stohrer to Foreign Ministry, No.3718, 2 Nov. 1940, AA, StS, Spanien, Vol.2. In fact, Franco sent a similar message to Mussolini the same day while Serrano Suñer made his own representations over Morocco with the Italian government. For Franco's letter, see *DDI*, Series 9, Vol.6, p.18. For Serrano's exchanges, see ibid., pp.16, 54, 59, 66, 68.

91. Hitler received Franco's letter of 30 October on 3 November by a special courier from Serrano Suñer's secretariat, who waited in Berlin to take back a reply from Hitler. Yet Hitler made no reply. See Stohrer to Foreign Ministry, 1 Nov. 1940, *ADAP*, D, Vol.11, p.273; Memo by Weizsäcker, 4 Nov. 1940, AA, StS, Spanien, Vol.2.
92. Percy Ernst Schramm (gen. ed.), *Kriegstagebuch des Oberkommandos der Wehrmacht (Wehrmachtführugsstab)* (Frankfurt am Main: Bernard & Graefe 1961–65), Vol.1, 4 Nov. 1940; Hans-Adolf Jacobsen (ed.), *Generaloberst Halder: Kriegstagebuch* (Stuttgart: Kohlhammer, 1963), Vol.2, 4 Nov. 1940.
93. The text of the directive, signed 12 November, is printed in Walter Hubatsch (ed.), *Weisungen fur die Kriegführung 1933–1945: Dokumente des Oberkommandos der Wehrmacht*, 2nd edn. (Frankfurt am Main, 1983), pp.67–71. For the drafting, see *KTB/OKW*, Vol.1, 4–9 Nov. 1940. For full consideration of Operation Felix, see Charles Burdick, *Germany's Military Strategy*, passim.
94. Contemplated for service in Spanish Morocco were the Third Armored Division, which had until this point been earmarked for service in the Italian North African campaign, and the Adolf Hitler SS Division. The troops were to cross the Gibraltar Strait on German ships then located in Italy. See *Halder Diary*, Vol.2, 4, 7, 8, 13, 20 Nov. 1940; *KTB/OKW*, Vol.1, 25 Nov. 1940.
95. Ribbentrop to Stohrer, 6 Nov. 1940, *ADAP*, D, Vol.11, p.294 and n.3.
96. On the invitation and its acceptance see Ribbentrop to Stohrer, 11 Nov. 1940, *ADAP*, D, Vol.11, p.312; Stohrer to Ribbentrop, No.3834, 12 Nov. 1940, AA, StS, Spanien, Vol.2.
97. Serrano Suñer, *Memorias*, pp.305–8.
98. *ADAP*, D, Vol.11, p.352, my emphasis.
99. *KTB/OKW*, 1, 8 Dec. 1940; *ADAP*, D, Vol.11, p.500.
100. Smyth, *Diplomacy*, pp.77 ff.
101. For the Bordighera meeting, see *Ciano Papers*, pp.422–6; *ADAP*, D, Vol.12, p.49; Tusell and Queipo de Llano, *Franco y Mussolini*, pp.120–22. Germany's pressure on Spain reached its height in the third week of January 1941, perhaps because of Hitler's belief that the dismissal of Pierre Laval from the vice-premiership and Foreign Ministry in Vichy signalled a duplicitous French policy in North Africa. For a full consideration, see my *Tomorrow the World*, Ch.8. Ribbentrop's ultimatum for Spain to enter the war in January 1941 included the threat that a refusal could mean 'the end of Nationalist Spain', but also foolishly included the statements that German troops would be needed elsewhere soon and the rationale that the capture of Gibraltar would open *for Spain* a route to Africa. For the exchanges see *ADAP*, D, Vol.11, pp.677, 682, 692, 695, 702, 707, 725, 728, and AA, StS, Spanien, Vol.2, frame numbers 745984–7. Though Franco meant to hold firm, the German threats were taken seriously enough for Madrid to have solicited promises of British aid for the event of a German invasion. See Smyth, *Diplomacy*, p.164.
102. The Spanish government had on 7 February presented Stohrer with a list which included one million tons of grain, 8,000 trucks, 16,000 railroad cars, 400 anti-aircraft guns, and three squadrons of aircraft. See Stohrer to Ribbentrop, 7 Feb. 1941, *ADAP*, D, Vol.12, pp.28. Franco told Mussolini at Bordighera that if Germany fulfilled the list, then Spain would indeed enter the war.
103. On the incorporation, see Halstead, 'Aborted Imperialism', passim. For the movement of the Spanish artillery, see Richter to Foreign Ministry, No.28, 4 Nov. 1940, AA, StS, Marokko, Vol.1. On the Spanish press, see Stohrer to Foreign Ministry, No.3752, 5 Nov. 1940, ibid. The Spanish proclamation of 23 Nov. 1940, signed by Franco, is printed in Britain, Foreign and Commonwealth Office, *British Foreign and State Papers*, Vol.144, *1940–1942* (London, 1952), p.539. Britain's reaction is covered thoroughly in Smyth, *Diplomacy*, Ch.7.
104. Stohrer to Foreign Ministry, 5 Nov. 1940, *ADAP*, D, Vol.11, p.286; Stohrer to Foreign Ministry, No.3757, AA, StS, Marokko, Vol.1, 58188–90.
105. A long list of German citizens in Spanish Morocco in late 1939 is in AA, DB Madrid, Marokko – Allgemein, Vol.5. Richter made specific references to Abwehr, SD, and party agents in Spanish Morocco in early 1941. See Richter to Foreign Ministry, J. No.373/41, 5 March 1941, ibid.

106. See the lengthy reports of 1 Nov. 1940 and 17 Dec. 1940 from Dr. Markus Timmler, the Foreign Ministry representative with the Reichsrundfunkgesellschaft in AA, Kulturpolitische Abteilung, Rundfunkpolitische Abteilung, Referat B, Vol.14. In the Spanish zone German broadcasts were said to have a positive reception among the native Moroccans in spite of jamming signals from Rabat. See Richter to Foreign Ministry, J. No.1416/40, 5 Nov. 1940, ibid., Vol.15; Dr. Theodor Auer (German Foreign Ministry Representative in Casablanca) to Foreign Ministry, P.57/41, 12 March 1941, ibid.; Richter to Foreign Ministry, No.31, 8 Nov. 1940, AA, StS, Marokko, Vol.1.
107. Richter to Stohrer, 24 June 1940, ibid.
108. Espinosa to Ribbentrop, No.620, 30 Nov. 1940, AA, StS, Marokko, Vol.1.
109. Richter to Foreign Ministry, 26 Dec. 1940, *ADAP*, D, Vol.11, p.573. On the entrance of Germans into Tangier, see German Embassy (Madrid), Note Verbale No.473/40, 2 July 1940, AMAE, legajo 1267, expediente 101; Beigbeder to Amieva, unnumbered, 12 July 1940, ibid.; Amieva to Beigbeder, No.76 cif., 14 July 1940, ibid. See also Woermann to Stohrer, Nr. 1095, 20 July 1940, AA, StS, Marokko, Vol.1; Stohrer to Foreign Ministry, No.2505, 25 July 1940, ibid. On the cooperation of Spanish authorities, a 25 Feb. 1941 Abwehr report stated that for 'some time' Spanish military and administrative authorities had been distancing themselves from Germany. This Abwehr officer blamed Spain's disappointment regarding its colonial aspirations and Jewish influence. The report is enclosed in Richter to Foreign Ministry, J. No.373/41, AA, DB Madrid, Marokko, Allgemein, Vol.5. An SS report of the same time states that German propaganda among the Moroccan natives in the Spanish zone was proceeding effectively with little hindrance from the Spanish authorities, so clearly the Spanish efforts against German meddling were somewhat uneven. See C.S.P. u. S.D. VI E 2 Kei/Li. AZ: VI E 502/41g, 21 Jan. 1941, AA, Inland IIg, Nordafrika, Bundle 335. Spanish–German friction over German propaganda in Morocco continued well into the war. See AMAE, legajo 2199, expediente 12 and AA, StS, Marokko, Vol.1, passim, for 1941 and 1942.
110. On the confiscation, see Richter to Foreign Ministry, 28 June 1940, AA, DB Madrid, Französisch Marokko u. Nordafrika. For the official fate of German property in Morocco, movable and immovable, following World War I, see Harold W.V. Temperley, *History of the Peace Conference at Paris*, reprint edn. (London, 1969), Vol.3, pp.183–4.
111. Collado Seidel, 'Zufluchtsstatte', passim.
112. Stohrer to Foreign Ministry, No.3018, 6 Sept. 1940, AA, StS, Marokko, Vol.1.
113. C.S.P. u. S.D. VI E 22 To/Kg AZ: VE 5889/40, 8 Nov. 1940, AA, Inland IIg, Nordafrika, Bundle 335. This problem was also a serious concern of Richter's, and he requested that German radio broadcasting to Morocco exercise the utmost reserve in the Tangier affair. See Richter to Foreign Ministry, J. No.1497, 13 Nov. 1940, AA, Kulturpolitische Abteilung, Rundfunkpolitische Abteilung, Referat B, Vol.15.
114. Weizsacker to Stohrer, Pol. 3 2751/40, 16 Nov. 1940, AA, StS, Marokko, Vol.1.
115. Stohrer to Foreign Ministry, No.3874, 14 Nov. 1940, ibid., 58193; Schroeder to Stohrer, No.2073, 22 Nov. 1940, ibid. The delegation which was to go to Tangier to accept the return of the legation building included Hans Heinrich Dieckhoff, who had been a member of the expelled legation in 1914. See Stohrer to Foreign Ministry, No.4041, 26 Nov. 1940, ibid.
116. Stohrer to Foreign Ministry, No.4157, 4 Dec. 1940, AA, StS, Marokko, Vol.1; Stohrer to Foreign Ministry, No.4266, 12 Dec. 1940, ibid.; Stohrer to Foreign Ministry, No.4343, 18 Dec. 1940, ibid.; Weizsacker to Stohrer, No.86, 14 Jan. 1941, ibid.; Stohrer to Foreign Ministry, No.362, 31 Jan. 1941; Stohrer to Foreign Ministry, No.721, 26 Feb. 1941, ibid.
117. Stohrer to Foreign Ministry, No.875, 6 March 1941, ibid.; Richter to Foreign Ministry, No.14, 17 March 1941, ibid.; Dr. Herbert Nöhring (German Consul in Tangier) to Foreign Ministry, No.5, 9 April 1941, ibid. The German Consulate in Tangier was raised to a General Consulate in May 1942, when Dr Kurt Rieth became the new German representative. See Stohrer to Foreign Ministry, No.2721, 19 May 1942, ibid. General Noguès protested in the name of sultan the eviction of the mendub. See his 'Une protestation de sa Majesté le Sultan auprès du Gouvernement Espagnol', *L'Echo du Maroc* (Rabat), 8 May 1940, No.7.136. See also Nöhring to Foreign Ministry, B. No.23, 10 May

1941, AA, StS, Marokko, Vol.1; A. Renschhausen (German Consul in Larache) to Heberlein, 10 May 1941, ibid.

118. Nohring to Foreign Ministry, B. No.1, 4 April 1941, AA, DB Madrid, Tanger Zone, Vol.3.

119. Pietri had suggested to Franco on 7 Dec. 1940 (before the latter's meeting with Admiral Wilhelm Canaris, in which Franco refused the German request for entry into the war) that Vichy considered the Moroccan border issue still open if Franco wished to discuss it. Though the French were unaware of the most recent turns of Spain's policy towards Germany, it was Pietri who was instrumental in setting up the meeting at Montpellier. While a full archival analysis awaits, the best secondary treatment of the meeting is in Seguela, *Petain–Franco*, Chs.4, 5. For German and Spanish takes on the meeting see Abetz to Ribbentrop, 15 Feb. 1941, *ADAP*, D, Vol.12, p.56; Lequerica to Serrano Suñer, No.114, 18 Feb. 1941, AMAE, legajo 2295, expediente 6.

120. José María Doussinague to Conde de Jordana y Souza (Foreign Minister since 3 Sept. 1942), 17 Sept. 1942, AMAE, legajo 1913, expediente 6; 'Conversación del Señor Doussiague con el Embajador de Francia, día 26 septiembre 1942', ibid., legajo 1686, expediente 4; Pietri, *Mes années*, pp.102 ff.

121. AMAE, legajo 1686, expediente 4, passim.

122. For Spanish complaints from 1942, see AMAE, legajo 2199, expediente 12, passim. A poignant German complaint is in Stohrer to Serrano Suñer, 13 Aug. 1941, ibid., legajo 1912, expediente 10.

123. See Hoare to Jordana, 21 March 1944, MAE, legajo 5162, expediente 3. For the issue in general see Collado Seidel, 'Zufluchtsstatte'.

In Pursuit of Votes and Economic Treaties: Francoist Spain and the Arab World, 1945–56

RAANAN REIN

During the second half of the 1940s the Franco regime found itself isolated in the international arena and confronting severe economic distress. As a strategy for ending the diplomatic boycott imposed on it by the United Nations and expanding foreign trade, Spain began to cultivate close relations with the Arab world. This article examines Francoist Spain's systematic campaign to woo the Arab countries, in the course of which even the regime's failure to establish diplomatic relations with the Jewish state founded in 1948 became a vehicle for improving its ties with the Arabs. In contrast to the diplomatic front Franco was only partially successful in his efforts to foster economic cooperation with these Muslim countries. Finally, all his hopes that hostility towards Israel and political and economic relations with the Arab countries would allow him to maintain Spain's control over northern Morocco proved illusory.

At the end of World War II, Spain found itself isolated in the international arena. General Francisco Franco's regime, although formally neutral during the war, was perceived as a Fascist collaborator with Nazi Germany and accordingly denounced on all sides. The second half of the 1940s was in any case a time of trial for the dictatorship because of the ravages of a severe drought that exacerbated Spain's already profound economic distress. As a strategy for breaking through the barriers of international isolation and ending the diplomatic boycott imposed on it by the United Nations in December 1946 – as well as expanding foreign trade – the Franco regime began to cultivate relations with two blocs of nations: Latin America and the Arab world. Invoking historical, spiritual, and blood ties, Spain strove to build a political and economic alliance that would serve its current needs.[1]

The Spanish dictatorship confronted different sets of problems in its efforts to mobilize support and sympathy in the two cases. At home, too, it had to contend with occasional contradictions between the image it sought to maintain and the achievement of its foreign policy goals. For example, it pursued its pragmatic commitment to ties with the nations of Islam even though one of the pillars of the Franco regime was the Catholic church and the Spanish authorities spoke much of the battle to protect Christian civilization from the trends of secularization, liberalization, and socialism appearing all over the Western world.

This was not the only apparent contradiction in Francoist Spain's relations with the Muslim world. At the same time that it eulogized the 'Catholic sovereigns', Isabella and Ferdinand, it tried to appropriate the achievements of the Jewish and Muslim cultures that had flourished in Spain during the Middle Ages until Isabella and Ferdinand took steps to extirpate them from Spanish soil. By manipulating the medieval history of his country, the Caudillo was able to present Spain as a bridge and a mediator, a meeting-point between east and west, between the Atlantic and the Mediterranean cultures, between the Latin race and the Arab-Semitic race, between Christianity and Islam. Of the many and lengthy struggles that the Christian rulers of Spain had pursued against the Muslims, both on the Iberian Peninsula and elsewhere, the spokespersons of the Franco regime preferred to say nothing in their contacts with Arabs. Similarly, while his country continued to hold colonial possessions in North Africa, Franco portrayed himself as a defender of Islam and an enemy of colonialism and European imperialism.

This article examines Francoist Spain's systematic campaign to woo the Arab countries, in the course of which even the regime's failure to form diplomatic relations with the Jewish state established in 1948 became a vehicle for improving Spain's relations with the Arabs.[2] On balance, this campaign appears to have been a successful one with respect to the mustering of Arab support for Spain's admission to various international organizations. Franco was only partially successful, however, in his efforts to foster economic cooperation, a sphere of potential development that the Madrid government did little to exploit. Finally, his hopes that hostility towards Israel and political and economic relations with the Arab countries would allow him to maintain control over northern Morocco proved illusory. He did manage to achieve a temporary respite from Arab nationalists' criticism concerning Spain's holdings in North Africa, but when the French decided to grant independence to their protectorate in Morocco, he had no choice but to follow their example.

NATIONALIST SPAIN'S AMBITIONS IN NORTH AFRICA

During the Civil War, the Nationalists were already emphasizing the 'shared interests' of Spain and North Africa. Spanish Morocco was the Nationalists' starting point and main base in the first stages of the uprising against the

Second Republic. Franco himself had been formed, as a soldier and a politician, by his experiences as an officer in Spain's Moroccan protectorate. Arriving in Morocco in 1912, he had spent most of the next 14 years there. In 1938, in the midst of the Civil War, he told the journalist Manuel Aznar: 'My years in Africa live with me with indescribable force. There was born the possibility of rescuing a great Spain. There was found the idea which today redeems us. Without Africa, I can scarcely explain myself to myself, nor can I explain myself properly to my comrades in arms.'[3]

In the early days of the rebellion, Franco enjoyed wide support in the Moroccan territory under Spanish control and used tens of thousands of hired Moroccan mercenaries in his army, although his campaign was described as a Christian crusade against the 'Red, atheist Republic'.[4] The first use ever made of the Moroccan forces on Spanish soil had been to suppress the revolutionary uprising of the Asturian miners in October 1934. It was General Franco's idea, and it served as an opportunity to assess the effectiveness of these forces. Their success in the mission made them an important element in the Nationalist forces now rising up against the Republic.

A mixture of pressure and incentives led many Moroccans – 60,000–70,000 – to join the ranks of the rebels and, during the Civil War, to cross with them the strait separating North Africa from the Iberian Peninsula. They were motivated mainly by the severe economic hardship then prevailing in the protectorate and the hope of earning good wages and some food. To this were added the techniques of forced enlistment by means of oppression and terror, bolstered by propaganda, that the rebels employed among the various tribes. That propaganda called on the Moroccans to join the campaign against the faithless for the greater glory of God, even though the religion in whose name Franco fought was anathema to them. It should be noted, too, that the Republic elicited no sense of loyalty in the local tribes, since it had not had time to implement any substantial reforms in the protectorate. During the Civil War, Franco used the Moroccan soldiers as cannon-fodder and psychological weapons. The atrocities perpetrated by these troops, encouraged by their Spanish commanders, wreaked terror and demoralization in the Republican camp.

At the same time, the rebel leaders appointed Colonel Juan Beigbeder as High Commissioner of the protectorate of Morocco. Beigbeder had had considerable administrative experience in Morocco and spoke Arabic. He was well acquainted with the area and with the local leaders and strove to implement a pro-Muslim policy by permitting autonomy in all religious matters and allowing the local nationalist parties a certain measure of freedom.[5] In 1938, a delegation of Syrian journalists visited Spanish Morocco and subsequently published articles lauding the Franco regime's cordial policy and its contribution to the development of the region. A few months later, the sultan's representative in the Spanish zone told Beigbeder that 'Franco had won the heart not only of Morocco, but of all of Islam'.[6] All the same, during that period, when maintaining order and stability in the area and ensuring the population's cooperation were so vital, Franco showed no readiness to make any real concessions or to accede to the Moroccan nationalists' demands for permission to set up an independent administration – in short, he would not do anything that might endanger or loosen Spain's grip on the place.

During World War II, Franco tried to exploit the Axis's first victories to strengthen his country's hold on North Africa. In June 1940, after France fell into German hands, his forces took over the international zone of Tangier – a commercially prosperous port city of strategic importance – and incorporated it into the administrative system of the Spanish protectorate in Morocco. Caution led him to characterize this proceeding as nothing more than a temporary administrative step motivated by the war. Since three of the major powers supervising Tangier – France, Britain, and Italy – were at war with each other, the Spanish government maintained that this was the only way Spain could guarantee the neutrality of the region and of its protectorate. The Falange greeted the move with enthusiasm, declaring that Tangier would remain Spanish forever.

During those same days of June 1940, Spain also considered invading French Morocco. This plan never came to fruition, however, just as nothing ever came of Nationalist Spain's hopes of a promise from Nazi Germany that in the event of an Axis victory Spain could establish an empire of its own. In the first stages of the war the rulers of Spain entertained the delusion that once a 'New Order' was established in Europe they would rule once more over Gibraltar (lost at the beginning of the eighteenth century), receive pieces of the French empire in North and West Africa (French Morocco and the Oran region in Algeria), and even expand Spain's rule in the regions around the Spanish Sahara and Spanish Guinea.[7] All these hopes were soon dashed, however, and in 1945, when the Allies' victory was complete, an international conference, to which Spain was not even invited, met in Paris to discuss Tangier's future. The conference decided that Spain must leave the city by October, and Franco was ignominiously forced to withdraw his forces from Tangier.[8]

A COMMUNITY OF INTERESTS

In the ensuing years of international isolation imposed on his regime, Franco deliberately and systematically strove to move closer to the Arab countries. In the Arab world he found, for the most part, conservative leaders and traditional, monarchic regimes that abhorred godless Communism and secular Western liberalism. He sought to benefit from the power of the Arabs' vote in the United Nations, to secure, through their friendship, Spain's position and interests in the Maghreb and to open the markets of Islam to Spanish exports. Accordingly, he portrayed his country as a friend to the Arabs, ready to help defend their interests.[9]

He succeeded in this, even though Spain still controlled Muslim territory. At the beginning of the 1950s, Spain's possessions in Morocco still included the protectorate in the north assigned to it by the accord it had signed with France in 1912. This consisted primarily of the Rif region, which was important to Spain as a line of defence from the south, as a source of iron ore, and as evidence that it was still a major European power and should be respected as such. (Throughout the twentieth century Spain has had trouble accepting the loss of its empire and its demotion to a third-ranking power.) Spain also saw in the protectorate a new theatre for its military operations, having lost in 1898 the remains of its empire in America and the Philippines. In addition to the protectorate, which was theoretically ruled by the sultan of Morocco, since the early modern period Spain had enjoyed complete sovereignty over the coastal cities of Melilla and Ceuta – the former having been wrested from the Muslims in 1497 and the latter taken from the Portuguese in 1688. It continues to hold both these enclaves to this day. In southern Morocco it ruled over the small territory of Ifni and, still farther south, the desert colony of Río de Oro.

Spain's growing ties with the Arab states at the end of the 1940s can be partly explained by the animosity that both Spain and the Arabs felt – though for different reasons – towards the Western countries, particularly Britain and France. Relations between Spain and France were tense and had gone through many crises in modern times, beginning with Napoleon's invasion of the Iberian Peninsula at the beginning of the nineteenth century and continuing up to the hostile policy of the Fourth Republic, which made France the Western power most inimical to Franco's regime. The division of Morocco into French and Spanish spheres of influence was an additional source of misunderstandings and friction. Spain always fretted that it was the loser by this partition; after all, no other European state was closer to the Maghreb geographically, ethnically, historically, and culturally. The relations between Spain and Britain were of course overshadowed by the latter's control of Gibraltar since the beginning of the eighteenth century. For the Spanish Nationalists this was an open wound, and at the beginning of the Civil War Franco was already calling for the return of the Rock of Gibraltar. The Arab nationalists had many reasons to criticize French and British imperialism in the Middle East and North Africa, as well as what they saw as encouragement of the Zionist movement.

Thus, a shared grudge against the Western powers, a shared fear of Communism, and the Arab countries' dispassionate attitude towards Fascism – the Arab world showed a notorious lack of sensitivity to the Jewish Holocaust and the horrors of Nazism – all made Hispano-Arab cooperation possible. The Arab countries also hoped to benefit from Spain's influence with the Vatican and in Latin America to promote their own interests. One instance of this was the Lebanese Foreign Ministry's appeal to Spain's representative in Beirut to try to change Argentina's position on the Palestinian conflict, which, he claimed, bordered on neutrality and might injure Arab interests. Only Franco's direct intervention, insisted one of the heads of Lebanese diplomacy, was likely to change Juan Peron's attitude.[10]

Another factor that facilitated the relationship was that the Arab countries, having just attained full political independence, wanted to display their sovereignty by developing a network of diplomatic, commercial, and cultural relations with as many states as possible. A certain solidarity had arisen as well from a growing feeling in both Spain and the Arab countries that they had been badly treated by the UN, in the one case through the international boycott imposed on the Franco regime and in the other through the resolutions that permitted the establishment of a Jewish state in Palestine and Israel's admission to the UN. On more than one occasion at the end of the 1940s, Arab and Spanish diplomats discussed the possibility that Madrid might try to mobilize the Latin American countries to support the Arabs and their demands for the return of the Palestinian refugees, as well as implement a liberalization programme in Spanish Morocco; in return, the Arab countries were supposed to support the proposal to lift the diplomatic sanctions on Madrid. In addition to these political factors, Franco's years in Morocco and what he had picked up of the Arabic language may have given him a certain nostalgic sympathy for the Arabs.[11]

In 1945, Franco had already proposed cultural cooperation to the Arab League (in public ceremonies he frequently appeared with his Muslim guard) and asked the Arab countries to take a friendly line towards Spain in the UN and other international frameworks. In June of that year, the Instituto de Estudios Africanos (Institute of African Studies) was established under the auspices of the Consejo Superior de Investigaciones Cientificas (High Council of Scientific Research) to promote research and publications on African subjects, particularly those pertaining to the Maghreb. Similar institutes, focusing on Hispano-Arab relations, were subsequently founded in Spanish Morocco as well.[12] In 1946 Franco amended a few aspects of his policy in Spanish Morocco in order to ensure Arab support. Although in February of the same year the representatives of the Arab states supported the UN resolution censuring Spain, by December, when most of the UN General Assembly voted in favour of imposing a diplomatic ban on Spain, the Arab states had changed their position; most of the Arab and Muslim delegates abstained.[13] In Arab capitals, newspaper articles stressed that Spain constituted no threat to world peace, that its political system was its own business, and that consequently the UN had no right to intervene in its internal affairs. In November 1947, when the General Assembly again debated the 'Spanish question', the same voting pattern repeated itself; Egypt, Iraq, Lebanon, Pakistan, Saudi Arabia, Syria, Turkey, and Yemen abstained. Madrid saw this as an important achievement.

Six of the Latin American states voted against imposing the ban on Spain in December 1946, and the number increased to eight the following year. Franco realized that Latin America and the Arab world represented his opportunity to break down Spain's international isolation, and he said so in a speech to the Spanish Parliament.[14] He invited the Secretary General of the Arab League to Madrid and began to make overtures to the Arab countries about establishing diplomatic relations and signing cultural agreements. To this end, the Foreign Minister, Alberto Martín Artajo, enlisted the aid of an expert on Arab affairs, Emilio García Gómez, who prepared a great deal of background material for the ministry and, at the beginning of 1947, led a cultural delegation on a tour of Egypt, Iraq, Jordan, Syria, and Lebanon. This delegation was supposed to expand cultural relations and turn them into a tool with which to promote political ties with the Arabs.[15] The Spanish press, which was closely supervised and completely controlled by the regime, was full of interviews with Arab political and diplomatic figures and editorials praising Hispano-Muslim relations.[16] Notable examples were the dailies *Informaciones* and *Arriba*, the Falange organ. The easiest place to demonstrate goodwill towards the Muslim world was, of course, Spanish Morocco, where Madrid could demonstrate an autonomous policy different from that of France. In April 1947 the Spanish High Commissioner, José Enrique Varela, met in Arcila with Sultan Mohammed V, and in September of the same year he inaugurated the great mosque of Melilla, taking the opportunity to affirm Spain's friendship for Islam.[17]

This policy of amity with the Arabs even had a special name in those days: m*ozarabidad*, a word that in Iberian medieval history was applied to the behaviour of Christians who, living under Muslim control, adopted the Arabic language and customs but retained their own religious faith. Nonetheless, in spite of all Spain's goodwill gestures in Morocco, Spanish rule there was an obstacle to *rapprochement* and the establishment of trust between Madrid and the Arab League states. Many North African exiles were concentrated in Cairo – including, notably, Abd el-Krim, the leader of the Rif war against Spain during the 1920s, and the Moroccan nationalist

Abd el-Khalek Torres. These exiles set up the Committee for the Liberation of North Africa, which, although mostly occupied with anti-French propaganda, also directed some of its barbs at Spain. An additional sore point was Spain's support for the internationalization of the holy places in Jerusalem, Bethlehem, and Nazareth, which conflicted with the policies of some of the Arab countries.

Franco found a warm friend in Jordan. By the summer of 1947 the two states had already established diplomatic relations, and King Abdallah declared that he was 'impressed by what General Franco [had] done for his country – the way he [had] routed the communist monster and maintained Spain's neutrality in the last war'.[18] In November, Spain established diplomatic relations with Iraq and Lebanon as well. Just before Israel's war of independence, Spain was displaying sympathy for the Arabs. Although the arms shipments that left the ports of Spain and ended in Arab hands were not large, they represented the beginning of Spain's arms-supply connection with the Arab countries, especially Egypt.[19] By the 1950s, Spanish arms sales to the Middle East were already more significant. Israel's hostile attitude towards Madrid and its support for the UN diplomatic boycott in May 1949 merely facilitated the increasingly close relations between the Franco regime and the Arabs – although at that stage the Spaniards had not yet given up trying to make friends with Israel. Right after the unsuccessful attempt in the UN to eliminate the boycott on Spain in May 1949, the establishment of diplomatic relations with Syria and the exchange of ambassadors between the two countries were announced in Madrid. A few months later relations were established with Saudi Arabia as well.

In May 1949, the Arab states changed their position from abstention to support for Franco's Spain when in the UN General Assembly they voted – in contrast to Israel – to cancel the ban on Spain. During that period, at least, the Arab League placed more importance on the 'Palestine question' – an issue in which Spain appeared to favour the Arab position – than on the 'North African question'. The members of the Arab League therefore decided to support Spain, and they did so again in the UN votes on Spain in the autumn of 1950, when the diplomatic ban on Spain was finally cancelled (although Spain was not allowed to join the world organization until 1955).

At the beginning of September 1949, when Spain was still suffering from international ostracism, the King of Jordan made an official visit to Spain. The Hashemite ruler had in fact been invited in 1947, but the war in Palestine, uneasiness in Egypt over the planned visit, and pressure from Moroccan exiles had led him to postpone the trip.[20] Nevertheless, Abdallah was still the first head of a foreign country to go to Spain on an official visit since the outbreak of the Civil War in 1936, and Franco took pains to welcome him with impressive ceremonies and a show of magnificence far in excess of the reception just given to him in London.[21] His visit was not as important as a visit from the American Secretary of State would have been, of course, but, as in Luis García Berlanga's film *Bienvenido Sr. Marshall* – in which a village pulls out all the stops in preparing for the arrival of the honoured guest – so the King of Jordan was greeted at the La Coruña port with a gun salute and ship sirens, a band, and thousands of people waving the flags of both nations. The Francoist propaganda machine had already had a great deal of experience in mobilizing great crowds to cheer a wanted guest, getting the media to sing the guest's praises, and preventing any expression of criticism or reservation.[22] Despite its dire economic situation, Spain spent huge sums on the Jordanian King's two-week visit. Franco's efforts to enhance the visit's importance were spurred by the fact that at the time an American squadron was visiting the port of El Ferrol – the first official visit by American battleships to Spain since World War II – while the debates in the UN General Assembly were just beginning at Lake Success.[23] The Spanish general wanted to show the world that the ban on his regime was crumbling.

Franco made sure that the King was taken to see the relics of Muslim Spain, wanting to show his guest that Spain could serve as a connecting link between the Muslim and Christian worlds. Abdallah was not invited, however, to visit Spanish Morocco, where the methods employed by the High Commissioner, General Varela, were provoking Arab criticism. Franco in fact granted various concessions to the Moroccan nationalist movement as long as most of its protests were directed against French rule, but every time the Moroccan nationalists seemed to be endangering Spanish interests their freedom of operation was reduced and strong measures were taken against them. The King of Jordan was allowed to meet in Granada with the caliph, the sultan's representative in Spanish Morocco, but only in the presence of General Varela – just to be on the safe side.[24] At the end of Abdallah's visit, a joint Spanish–Jordanian communique was issued reporting 'complete understanding between King Abdallah and Franco with regard to Middle Eastern affairs, the Communist threat, the Spanish administration in Morocco, and the future of Jerusalem and the holy places'.[25] For its part, the Spanish government announced a few gestures meant to benefit the inhabitants of Spanish Morocco. It agreed to provide aeroplanes for those desiring to make a pilgrimage to Mecca and to extend financial assistance to pilgrims who had trouble meeting the expense of the journey.[26]

The King's visit increased Franco's prestige in the Arab world, and after it others came to Spain as well: the regent of Iraq, the King of Libya, the son of the Sultan of Morocco, Lebanese and Egyptian ministers, and a whole series of political figures, administrative officials, and journalists from all over the Middle East and from the Arab League. These visits were a great boon to Spain's propaganda in both domestic and international quarters, since in the decade 1945–55 Spain was not exactly overrun with visiting dignitaries. They added sparkle to the regime's limited foreign relations in those years and managed to create for Spain an appearance of extensive foreign relations and for Franco the image of a leader of international stature.[27]

In May 1949, the month in which Israel voted against the Franco regime and just before Abdallah's visit, Spain announced to the government of Jordan its readiness to take in 1,000 Palestinian refugee children: 500 Muslims in Spanish Morocco and 500 Christians in Spain itself. These children, it explained, would be able to go to school there 'until they were given the opportunity to return to their homeland'.[28] By September of the same year, several hundred refugee children in Jordan, Syria, and Lebanon had been registered for the programme, and a special Spanish envoy went to the Old City of Jerusalem to coordinate the operation. Ultimately, however, the plan fell through, for various reasons. One of them was the opposition of Arab and North African nationalists, who did not want the children to be educated in conquered Muslim territory such as the Spanish protectorate in Morocco. There was also, however, a more concrete reason. Every child of Palestinian refugees received a food ration from the UN, which usually helped eke out the family budget; because of this, the refugees did not want to send their children to Spain. The Arab governments' reaction to the Spanish programme left Madrid with the impression that the Muslim states 'were not overly fond of the Arabs of Palestine'.[29] However, Spain made other humanitarian gestures with regard to the Palestinian Arabs that could be exploited for political and propagandistic purposes. In July 1949, for example, a shipment of medicines arrived in Beirut and was distributed to Palestinian refugees by the Spanish consul in Jerusalem. A month later, the ship *Plus Ultra* landed a cargo of clothing, medicine, and food in Port Said, Egypt, 'from Spanish Morocco to the refugees of Palestine'.

Cultural and friendship agreements helped cement the amity fostered by the state visits, the exchange of medals with various Arab leaders (the most notable example being the Order of Isabella the Catholic, which was awarded to King Farouk of Egypt, and the Order of Fuad I, given to Franco),[30] the pro-Spanish votes in the UN, and the expansion of diplomatic relations (even before the UN lifted the diplomatic ban on Spain, most of the Muslim countries already maintained full diplomatic relations with the Madrid government). Spain concluded accords of this kind with Lebanon in March 1949, a year after diplomatic relations had been established. It should be noted that the Catholic Maronites' dominant position in Lebanon contributed to the connection with Catholic Spain. Lebanon also hoped to benefit from Spain's influence in Latin America, where a considerable portion of its population had emigrated. The fact that thousands of emigrants returned from Latin America to Lebanon with a good grasp of the Spanish language and that Spain itself had a good-sized Lebanese community (particularly in the Canary Islands and Spanish Morocco) also helped strengthen the relationship.[31] Lebanese ministers visited Madrid, and in Spain the Maronite College was established for Lebanese students who came to complete their studies on the Iberian Peninsula.

During the second half of the 1940s Madrid directed special effort towards Cairo, which had become a centre for Spanish activity in the Middle East. At the time, it was also a centre of operations for North African and Middle Eastern nationalists, and the Arab League had established its headquarters there. The Egyptians themselves encouraged these activities as a means of winning a leading position in the Arab world. The Spanish delegation in Cairo accordingly focused on a wider field of endeavour than merely the relations on the Spain–Egypt axis; one of its goals was to establish contacts with other Arab states and organizations, primarily in the hope of enlisting support for Spain's position in the UN and other international forums, such as the Universal Postal Union. At the beginning of 1947, Spain did its best to defeat France's intention of preventing it from joining the Universal Postal Union, which was scheduled to open in May in Paris. Madrid asked the US administration to intervene with the French government on its behalf, but met with refusal. It accordingly focused its efforts on mobilizing support in the Latin American countries, especially Argentina, and in the Arab world, particularly Egypt. Despite the sympathy of these countries, however, Spain was not invited to the Paris conference. The international enmity against the Franco regime was then at its peak. Spain's good relations with Egypt were also reflected by the inauguration of the Farouk I Institute of Islamic Studies in Madrid by the Egyptian Education Minister in November 1950.[32]

Friendship and cultural agreements were also signed with Jordan (1950), Iraq (1951), Yemen (1952), Iran (1952), and Syria (1953). Spain also tried to improve its relations with Saudi Arabia, in view of the latter's importance in the Muslim world and the necessity of regular arrangements to allow the Muslims of the Spanish protectorate in Morocco to make the pilgrimage to Mecca.

Spain's economic relations with the Arab world developed along with the political connection. Up until the Civil War, the volume of Hispano-Arab trade was negligible. In fact, until then Spain had significant commercial ties with only four Arab states: Egypt, Saudi Arabia, Persia, and Libya.[33] During the Civil War and, subsequently, World War II, Spain's trade with the Middle East ceased almost completely. From 1946 on, however, Spain began to show great interest in economic cooperation with the Arab world, and this field indeed expanded steadily, although the political and propagandist aspect was the central element of Spain's relations with the Arab countries. Spain imported primarily cotton from Egypt and oil from Saudi Arabia and Iran. In the five years from 1948 to 1953, the Middle East's share in total Spanish imports approached ten per cent, but Spain's trade balance with the Islamic countries was negative; only 1.7–2.7 per cent of total Spanish exports found their way to the markets of the Middle East.[34]

On the list of Spain's principal trading partners in 1950, Saudi Arabia was sixth among the states from which Spain imported goods (61.7 million gold pesetas), climbing to fourth place the following year (91.2 million gold pesetas), where it was surpassed only by the United States, France, and Britain. Iran was in fifth place on the list in 1950 (62.9 million) but in 1951 dropped to ninth place (44.4 million). As for Egypt, it was only twenty-first on the list in 1950 (9.2 million gold pesetas) but rose to fourteenth a year later (31.6 million). The list of Spain's export destinations in those years, in contrast, shows a rather different pattern. Iran and Saudi Arabia did not figure at all on the list of the 25 principal states to which Spain exported goods in 1951, but Egypt was again in fourteenth place. Tangier was in ninth place and French Morocco in twenty-fourth.[35]

MARTÍN ARTAJO'S TOUR OF THE MIDDLE EAST

By April 1952, the friendship between Spain and the Arab countries was conspicuous, all the more so because the Western powers' status in the Arab world was declining: Britain, which was blamed for the existence of the state of Israel, was having trouble holding on to the Suez Canal; the French were facing growing unrest in North Africa, particularly in Tunisia; and the United States was already considered Israel's patron, despite its efforts to keep their relations low-key. While all this was going on, the Spanish Foreign Minister set off on a comprehensive tour of the Middle East.[36]

In his 1952 New Year's speech, Franco had declared that his country would continue its policy of supporting the Arab states. He mentioned that for hundreds of years Muslims and Christians had lived together on Spanish soil and spoke of Spain's historic role in both the Western and the Arab world. In another speech, delivered by national radio just before Martín Artajo's trip, the Caudillo presented Spain as a shining example of international cooperation, one that had taken upon itself a 'cultural mission', and he called on the peoples in whom religious feeling throbbed – such as Spain and the Arab countries – to make common cause against atheistic materialism. The foci of Spain's activity, said Franco, were on the

Iberian Peninsula with Portugal, in Hispanic America, and in the Arab world, which had a special place in its heart owing to the historical, spiritual, and blood ties between them.[37]

Martín Artajo defined his trip as a goodwill mission, an occasion to reciprocate the visits by the Jordanian King and ministers of various Arab states, and an expression of gratitude for Arab support in the UN and in other international organizations. The visit was also intended to demonstrate that the international boycott on Spain had lapsed, to create the appearance of an active, wide-ranging foreign policy, to ensure continued Arab support in international conferences, particularly for Spain's struggle to join the UN as a regular member, to portray Spain as a natural link and mediator between the Middle East and the Western powers, and to pacify Spanish Morocco. Among other things, Martín Artajo wanted to sound out the Arab governments on the Spanish idea of creating a defence alliance among the Mediterranean states, which would include, among others, the Arab and Iberian states – though not, of course, Israel. This alliance against the Soviet threat would complement the North Atlantic Treaty Organization (NATO), from which the Spanish dictatorship was excluded.[38] The importance that Spain attributed to Martín Artajo's trip and the almost personal commitment that Franco had made to his pro-Arab policy are indicated by the fact that the Generalissimo's only daughter, Carmen, and her husband, the Marquis de Villaverde, joined the Foreign Minister on the tour.

Martín Artajo's tour, the first visit by a Spanish minister to the Arab countries, lasted three and a half weeks (4 April–29 April 1952) and included six states: Lebanon, Jordan (including a visit to the holy places in East Jerusalem), Syria, Iraq, Saudi Arabia, and Egypt. The Arab capitals gave Martín Artajo an enthusiastic welcome. He, in turn, made speeches about the friendly relations between his country and the Arabs and about 'one blood flowing in the veins of Spaniards and Arabs, who share a single culture and a single destiny'.[39] The Spanish press was, of course, filled with triumphal rhetoric, and every day whole pages were devoted to coverage of the visit. Cinema newsreels showed shots of the various stops on the tour.

Officials in London, of course, were not very happy about the tour, fearing that Spain would try to exploit the difficulties Britain was having with Egypt over the questions of Sudan and the Suez Canal.[40] Israel, too, took a dim view of this new step in Hispano-Arab *rapprochement*. It was a far cry, however, from this to the note that the Spanish security services had passed on to the Foreign Ministry just before the trip, which read in part: 'given the method used by the English and the Zionists to rid themselves of people who might constitute an obstacle to their plans or create international difficulties for them, [this warning concerns] a possible attempt on the life of the Spanish Minister, to be carried out en route from Beirut-Damascus to Baghdad'.[41]

One of Martín Artajo's stops, coinciding with Holy Week, was Old Jerusalem, which he toured privately as a pilgrim, visiting the holy places on foot (Golgotha, the Holy Sepulchre, the City of David, the Pool of Shiloah, and so on). The Foreign Minister was instructed to keep away from all events organized in his honour, mainly to avoid creating misunderstandings concerning Spain's views on the status of Jerusalem. From Jerusalem he went on to Bethlehem and then Hebron, where he made a speech intended to explain that Spain bore no responsibility for the situation in Palestine, since it was not a member of the UN and had not taken part in the decisions concerning the fate of this territory in the Middle East.[42]

In the course of the Foreign Minister's tour and immediately after it, cultural and friendship agreements were signed with Egypt, Syria, and Yemen – thus completing a network of such accords that included most of the Arab countries. Subsequent to the tour, Jordan, Iraq, and Lebanon upgraded their legations in Madrid to embassies. These were the only concrete achievements of the visit – not counting, of course, the direct telephone lines between Beirut and Madrid, which Carmencita Franco inaugurated with a telephone call to her father. Nonetheless, the United States, which wanted to improve its standing in the Arab world, may have been impressed by the show of friendship between Spain and the Muslim countries and have assigned even greater importance to the need for a military treaty with Madrid. It is significant that Martín Artajo's departure from Spain almost exactly coincided with the arrival of a US military delegation charged with the task of negotiating with Madrid; many considered this timing a sign of Spain's intention to increase its bargaining power with the United States by means of the Arab factor.[43]

One circumstance that cast a pall on Martín Artajo's visit to the Middle East was Spain's colonial presence in North Africa. Many Arab newspapers, especially in Cairo and Baghdad, called on Spain to get out of Morocco if it wanted to remove an obstacle from the path to real friendship with the Arab world.[44] Before Martín Artajo's departure, Abd el-Khalek Torres and a few of his nationalist followers, who had been expelled to Tangier, were allowed to return to Tetun, the capital of the Spanish protectorate, to resume their party activities and to publish their newspapers – all to create a more relaxed atmosphere for the visit and to present Franco as a liberal statesman and friend of Islam. At the beginning of February the Spanish press had published a speech made by the caliph of Spanish Morocco to his subjects following a visit to Madrid and talks with Franco; the speech included positive remarks about Spain's policy in the protectorate. Martín Artajo was also accompanied by a high-ranking Moroccan officer, General Mohammed ben-Mezzian ben-Cassen, a Muslim who had fought with the Nationalists in the Civil War and had later held various commanding posts in the Spanish army, including the military governorship of Galicia. Although the Secretary General of the Arab League said that the problem of Morocco could be settled amicably, it was clear to everyone that Spanish rule over Muslim territories in North Africa constituted an obstacle to Madrid's relations with the Arabs.[45]

Not everyone in Spain was overjoyed by the display of Hispano-Arab friendship. Some observers expressed doubts about the economic and political basis of such an alliance, particularly in light of the divisions in the Arab world, while others disapproved of cooperation between an eminently Catholic regime and the Muslim world. This sense of uneasiness was bluntly expressed by the Archbishop of Seville, Pedro Segura, in a pastoral letter read in all the churches of his diocese. In it the cardinal argued that excessively close ties with countries holding a religious belief so far removed from Catholicism might cause believers spiritual confusion. Political or military cooperation was legitimate, but it should not entail identification with the moral or religious viewpoints of those countries, said Segura, in a direct reference to Franco's speech on the eve of Martín Artajo's departure for the Middle East. It should be recalled here that the Archbishop of Seville held extreme Catholic views and did not hesitate to attack either the neo-pagan behaviour of the Falange or certain actions taken by Franco himself. His fanatical Catholicism was more than once at loggerheads with the policy of the Holy See. Ten weeks before his attack on Franco's Arab policy, Segura had published a strong anti-Protestant pastoral letter in which he argued that the institution of religious freedom was an intolerable step that would lead to the disintegration of Spain.[46]

THE END OF THE MOROCCAN PROTECTORATE

In Spanish Morocco, the Moroccan nationalists were allowed greater licence – at least so long as most of their actions were directed against the French. The new High Commissioner, General Rafael García Valiño, instituted a more flexible policy than that of Varela (who had died in 1951).[47] The Spaniards took advantage of France's growing difficulties in Morocco and even secretly supplied rebels in the French zone with arms and money. Madrid sharply denounced the overthrow of the legitimate sultan, Mohammed V, his exile to Madagascar in August 1953, and his replacement by a puppet sultan, a docile elderly cousin by the name of Molai Mohammed ben-Arafa. This last step had been taken without any prior consultation with Madrid, to the Spanish government's open displeasure. Friday prayers in the mosques of Spanish Morocco continued to be recited in the name of the deposed sultan in recognition of his status as the true ruler. The anniversary of his coronation, 18 November, was celebrated with great fanfare that year. Franco expressed sympathy for 'the natural aspirations of the Moroccan people' and even encouraged autonomous Moroccan rule in the Spanish sector.

By these actions, Franco gave Spain the appearance of a progressive colonial power and a friend to the Arabs, in contrast to France and Britain, which suffered from their image as hated imperialistic powers. Ironically, in January 1954, the Spanish High Commissioner in Morocco declared that the world was threatened by two dangers: Communism and colonialism. The Spanish press also talked of the possibility of cooperation between Spain and the Arabs in their struggle against the control their 'common enemy', Britain, exercised over Gibraltar and the Suez Canal. However, Franco's policy afforded the Spanish protectorate only temporary immunity against the spreading nationalistic unrest in Morocco. By setting himself up as a defender of Moroccan nationalism against French colonialism, Franco did not leave himself a very wide margin for manoeuvre should France's policy change – and it did change, unilaterally, at the end of 1954, as successive governments in Paris strove to free their country from an irksome colonial burden.

At the beginning of 1956, the Moroccan nationalist ferment spread to the Spanish zone, which hitherto had been known as the 'happy region' (the situation in the Spanish protectorate continued calm for a long time, partly because, in contrast to the situation in the French section, there were not many settlers to cause tension in relations with the local residents). Spain's support for Moroccan nationalism – when it targeted the French – now boomeranged against Franco. He, however, preferred to blame the failure of his policy on the High Commissioner.

A few months previously, under pressure in Vietnam and Algeria, France had surprised the Caudillo again with a series of swift measures aimed at granting independence to the part of Morocco under its control. In September 1955, the sultan ruling by courtesy of the French, Mohammed ben-Arafa, left Morocco, and the legitimate sultan, Mohammed V, was restored to the throne. In December a Moroccan cabinet began to function in Rabat, and at the beginning of March 1956 France signed an agreement that granted independence to most of Morocco. These events sparked a wave of strikes and nationalist protests in the Spanish zone, and Franco was obliged to consent to independence for the Sharif kingdom, including the territory under Spanish control, by April 1956. Not even Spain's friendly relations with the Arabs could help him maintain control in Spanish Morocco.[48]

This was, of course, a bitter pill for the man who had won military glory in service in Morocco and who in the past had proclaimed his country's historical mission in North Africa. It was also the end of the dream of an African empire that Franco had cherished, especially during the early stages of World War II. The decision to let go of Morocco aroused disapproval in certain circles in Spain and in parts of the army, though it was vital to prevent an expensive and prolonged colonial war and serious damage to Spain's image as a friend of the Arab world. In any case, once Franco had made the decision, he carried it out with full fanfare, inviting the sultan to come to Madrid to make the official arrangements for ending the Spanish protectorate. The Caudillo wanted to present the abandonment of the protectorate – a step that in fact represented the failure of his Moroccan policy – as a victory and accordingly put all his propaganda resources into gear and mobilized the masses at his disposal. He himself delivered a speech expressing his happiness at handing over the Spanish zone to the sultan, the head of the independent new state of Morocco.[49] However, a few stumbling blocks remained in the relations between the two states; Spain retained possession of Ceuta and Melilla, Ifni, Cabo Jubi, and Río de Oro, and they were to overshadow its relations with Morocco for many years to come.

In general, Moroccan independence removed an important obstacle to Madrid's relations with the Arab countries. Spain, lacking diplomatic relations with Israel, was considered the western European country most friendly to the Arab states both up to Franco's death and afterwards, its traditional pro-Arab policy being one of the Francoist dictatorship's legacies to the newly democratic regime in Spain.[50] Under the governments of Carlos Arias Navarro, Adolfo Suárez, Leopoldo Calvo Sotelo, and – initially – Felipe González, the reluctance to establish full diplomatic relations with Israel continued, as did the fear of an angry Arab reaction to any *rapprochement* with the Jewish state. It was not until the institution of full relations between Madrid and Jerusalem in January 1986 that Spain's Middle Eastern policy achieved some degree of balance.

NOTES

1. On Francoist Spain's relations with Latin America during those years, see Raanan Rein, 'Francoist Spain and Latin America, 1936–1953', in Stein Ugelvik Larsen (ed.), *Was There Fascism Outside Europe?* (New York, forthcoming); Lorenzo Delgado Gómez-Escalonilla, 'Entre la hispanidad beligerante y la comunidad hispánica de naciones (1939–1953)', in Pedro Pérez Herrero and Nuria Tabanera (eds.), *España–América Latina: Un siglo de políticas culturales* (Madrid, 1993), pp.91–136.
2. On this subject, see Raanan Rein, *In the Shadow of the Holocaust and the Inquisition: Israel's Relations with Francoist Spain* (London and Portland, OR, 1997).
3. Quoted in Paul Preston, 'General Franco as Military Leader', in *Transactions of the Royal Historical Society*, 6th series, Vol.4 (London, 1994), p.24.
4. María Rosa de Madariaga, 'The Intervention of Moroccan Troops in the Spanish Civil War:

A Reconsideration', *European History Quarterly*, 22 (1992), pp.67–97; Shannon E. Fleming, 'Spanish Morocco and the Alzamiento Nacional, 1936–1939: The Military, Economic and Political Mobilization of a Protectorate', *Journal of Contemporary History*, 18, 1 (1983), pp.27–42; and Robert A. Friedlander, 'Holy Crusade or Unholy Alliance? Franco's "National Revolution" and the Moors', *Southwestern Social Science Quarterly*, 44 (March 1964), pp.346–56.

5. See Charles R. Halstead, 'A Somewhat Machiavellian Face: Colonel Juan Beigbeder as High Commissioner in Spanish Morocco, 1937–1939', *Historian*, 37 (Nov. 1974), pp.44–6; and Charles R. Halstead, 'Un "Africain" meconnu: Le Colonel Juan Beigbeder', *Revue d'Histoire de la Deuxieme Guerre Mondiale*, 83 (July 1971), pp.1–60.
6. See Norman J.W. Goda, 'Franco's Bid for Empire: Spain, Germany, and the Western Mediterranean in World War II', in this volume.
7. On Spain's imperialist ambitions, see José María de Areilza and Fernando María Castiella, *Reivindicaciones de España* (Madrid, 1941); José María Cordero Torres, *Misión africana de España* (Madrid, 1941); and Enrique Arquez, *El momento de España en Marruecos* (Madrid, 1942).
8. Charles R. Halstead and Carolyn J. Halstead, 'Aborted Imperialism: Spain's Occupation of Tangier 1940–1945', *Iberian Studies*, 7, 2 (Autumn 1978), pp.53–71; Graham H. Stuart, *The International City of Tangier*, 2nd edn. (Stanford, 1955), Ch.2.
9. On Spain's relations with the Arab world in those years, see 'Aspects of Spain's Arab Policy', 3 Dec. 1951 (US National Archives, Records of the Department of State, Washington, DC [hereafter NA], 752.00/12–351); María Dolores Algora Weber, *Las relaciones hispano-árabes durante el regimen de Franco: La ruptura del aislamiento internacional (1946–1950)* (Madrid, 1995); Benny Pollack, *The Paradox of Spanish Foreign Policy* (London, 1987), Ch.4; and Shannon Fleming, 'North Africa and the Middle East', in James W. Cortada (ed.), *Spain in the Twentieth-Century World* (Westport, CT, 1980), pp.121–54.
10. Madrid Embassy to State Department, 26 July 1948 (NA, 852.20210/7–2648); Griffis to State Department, 13 Sept. 1948 (NA, 752.82/9–1348); Cairo Embassy to State Department, 25 Feb. 1949 (NA, 752.83/2–2549); and Ruiz de Cuevas to Ministerio de Asuntos Exteriores [hereafter MAE], 4 Nov. 1948 (Archivo de la Fundación Francisco Franco, Madrid, Legajo 137/390).
11. S. P. Ben-Shmuel, 'Spain's Arab Policy' [Hebrew], *Hamizrach Hehadash,* 19 (1954), p.163; Consulate-General (Tetuan) to Public Record Office, Foreign Office Papers, London [hereafter FO], 4 Feb. 1947 (FO, 371/61523); Andrews to FO, 8 Sept. 1948 (FO, 371/73336); Marriott to FO, 8 Sept. 1948 (FO, 371/68382); Hanky to FO, 10 Jan. 1951 (FO, 371/96169); Francisco Franco Salgado-Araujo, *Mis conversaciones privadas con Franco* (Barcelona, 1978), p.227.
12. 'The Beginning of Spanish–Arab Friendship' [Hebrew], *Ha'aretz*, 5 Sept. 1949; Manuel Espadas Burgos, *Franquismo y política exterior* (Madrid, 1988), p.211.
13. On the resolutions concerning Francoist Spain, see A.J. Lleonart y Anselem and F.M. Castiella Maíz, *España y ONU* (Madrid, 1978–84), 3 vols. On the Arab countries' votes on the Spanish question, see María Dolores Algora Weber, 'La Liga Arabe ante "la cuestión espanola" en las Naciones Unidas: 1946–1950', in *Congreso Internacional sobre el Régimen de Franco: 1936–1975* (Madrid, 1993), Vol.2, pp.387–400.
14. Francisco Franco, *Discursos y mensajes de S. E. el Jefe del Estado a las Cortes Españolas, 1943–1961* (Madrid, 1961), p.102.
15. *Ha'aretz*, 29 Dec. 1946; 'Informe sobre envío de una misíon cultural al próximo oriente', 20 Feb. 1947 (Archivo del Ministerio de Asuntos Exteriores, Madrid [hereafter AMAE], R.2800/17).
16. Maffitt to State Department, 22 Feb. 1948 (NA, 852.00/2–2248); Emmons (Madrid) to State Department, 16 July 1948 (NA, 752.90B/7–1648).
17. Luis Suárez Fernández, *Francisco Franco y su tiempo* (Madrid, 1984), Vol.4, pp.344–45. On the Spanish protectorate in Morocco, see Víctor Morales Lezcano, *España y el norte de Africa: El protectorado en Marruecos (1912–1956)* (Madrid, 1986); and Miguel Martín, *El*

colonialismo español en Marruecos (1860–1956) (Paris, 1973).

18. *Ha'aretz*, 19 Sept. 1947.
19. On arms sales to the Arab countries during the 1948 war and on the one-sided pro-Arab reports in the contemporary Spanish press, see Rein, *In the Shadow*, pp.10–12.
20. *Ha'aretz*, 19 Sept. 1947; Suárez Fernández, *Francisco Franco*, Vol.4, pp.206–7; Dieguez to MAE, 15 Aug. 1949 (AMAE, R.2697/28); Troutbeck to FO, 13 Sept. 1949 (FO, 371/75315). Abdallah answered his Arab critics thus: 'Russia expresses antagonism towards Franco, just as it does to me. That's why Franco and I are effective and necessary to our countries. I am going to Spain because I want to see Franco, whom Russia hates, as it hates me.' *Ha'aretz*, 5 Sept. 1949.
21. *Ha'aretz*, 6 Sept. 1949; *Times*, 6 Sept. 1949. The Jordanian King's visit was extensively covered in the Spanish press. See, for example, *ABC*, 6–10 Sept. 1949. On the visit, see many reports in AMAE, R.2697/28, as well as Suárez Fernández, *Francisco Franco*, Vol.4, pp.343–4; 'Annual Political Report for Spain: An Estimate of the Situation in 1949', pp.42–3 (NA, 752.00/1–2650); Abdallah, King of Jordan, *My Memoirs Completed: 'Al-Takmilah'* (London, 1978), pp.60–61.
22. An outstanding example of the successful functioning of the propaganda apparatus could be seen during the visit of Eva Perón, wife of the President of Argentina, in June 1947. On that visit and the way it was exploited by the regime for purposes of propaganda, see Raanan Rein, *The Franco–Perón Alliance: Relations between Spain and Argentina, 1946–1955* (Pittsburgh, 1993), pp.53–64.
23. J. Lee Shneidman, *Spain and Franco 1949–1959* (New York, 1973), p.57; 'General Franco and the Arab Countries', an article translated into Hebrew from the French newspaper *Le Monde* and reprinted in *Ha'aretz*, 14 Oct. 1949.
24. Martín Artajo to the High Commissioner in Tetuan, 26 Aug. 1949, Varela to Martín Artajo, 28 Aug. 1949, and Martín Artajo to Varela, 30 Aug. 1949 (AMAE, R.2697/28); Howard to FO, 15 Sept. 1949 (FO, 371/75315).
25. 22 Sept. 1949 (NA, 852.00/9–2249).
26. *Times*, 20 Sept. 1949; 29 Sept. 1949 (NA, 852.00/9–2949).
27. José Mario Armero, *La política exterior de Franco* (Barcelona, 1978), p.54.
28. 11 Aug. 1949 (NA, 852.00/8–1149); Ben-Shmuel, 'Spain's Arab Policy', p.165; *Ha'aretz*, 24 Oct. 1947 and 5 Sept. 1949.
29. Martín Artajo to High Commissioner in Tetuan, 22 March 1950 (AMAE, R.4786/123); 'nota verbal' to the US Embassy, 25 Jan. 1951 (AMAE, R.4789/39).
30. Balfour to FO, 25 July 1951 (FO, 371/96170); 'Aspects of Spain's Arab Policy', 3 Dec. 1951 (NA, 752.00/12–351).
31. Ruiz de Cuevas to MAE, 13 March 1948 (AMAE, R.4783/73); *Arriba*, 17 Jan. 1948, and 17 and 21 Sept. 1948; *Informaciones*, 12 July 1948, 26 Aug. 1948; Memo of Conversation on the Relations of Lebanon with Spain, 13 May 1948 (NA, 711.52/5–1348); Emmons to State Department, 30 Sept. 1948 (752.90B/9–3048); report dated 18 March 1949 (852.00/3–1849); A. Hourani and N. Shehadi (eds.), *The Lebanese in the World: A Century of Emigration* (London, 1992).
32. Rein, *The Franco–Perón Alliance*, p.48; Aréstegui to MAE, 3 May 1947 (AMAE, R.4781/73); Bárcenas to Martín Artajo, 13 March 1950 (AMAE, R.4786); Balfour to FO, 25 July 1951 (FO, 371/96170).
33. For statistics on Spain's trade with these countries in 1934, see Ben-Shmuel, 'Spain's Arab Policy', p.157.
34. Ibid., p.165.
35. 'Annual Economic Review: Spain 1951', 6 May 1952 (NA, 852.00/5–652). The complete list can be found in Rein, *The Franco–Perón Alliance*, p.200. For figures on Spain's foreign trade in 1948–50, including trade with several Arab states, see 'Spain – Annual Economic Report for 1949', 6 March 1950 (NA, 852.00/3–650); 'Spain – Annual Economic Report for 1950', 30 March 1951 (NA, 852.00/3–3051). In 1953 there was an attempt to reduce the gap between pompous rhetoric and actual trade relations in the Hispano-Arab economic conference in Valencia. See *Le Monde*, 22 Jan. 1954 and 24 Feb. 1954; 'Semi-Annual

Review of Spain's Foreign Relations and Domestic Political Situation', 1 Feb. 1954 (NA, 652.00/2–154); and Witman to State Department, 23 Nov. 1953 (NA, 652.71B/11–2353).

36. Although Spain remained officially neutral in the conflict between Egypt and Britain, during those months the Falange newspapers unequivocally sided with Egypt; it also showed sympathy for Iran in the latter's disagreement with London. See 'Spain: Annual Review for 1951', 21 Jan. 1952 (FO, 371/101997). Spain embarrassed France around the same time by using its influence in Latin America to win support for the Arab countries' bid to put Tunisia's demand for independence on the agenda of the UN General Assembly. See Rockwell to State Department, 11 July 1952 (NA, 652.00/7–1152).
37. *Ha'aretz*, 2 Jan. 1952; Shneidman, *Spain*, p.96.
38. FO, 'Minutes', 23 April 1952 (FO, 371/102009); 'Tenemos la llave del Mediterráneo occidental', *Pueblo*, 27 March 1952; Rockwell to State Department, 11 Aug. 1952 (NA, 752.00/8–1152).
39. *Ha'aretz*, 15 April 1952. On Martín Artajo's trip, see the many reports in AMAE, R.3106/13 and R.4987/108. For the wide coverage in the Spanish press, see, for example, *ABC*, 4–30 April 1952.
40. Balfour to FO, 10 Jan. 1952 and 22 Jan. 1952 (FO, 371/102009).
41. 'Nota informativa de la Dirección Gral. de Seguridades', 6 March 1952 (AMAE, R.4987/108).
42. Terranova to MAE, 17 April 1952 (AMAE, R.4987/108); Furlonge to FO, 21 April 1952 (FO, 371/102009); *Ha'aretz*, 14 April 1952.
43. 'Spain: Annual Review for 1952', 16 Jan. 1953 (FO, 371/107668); *Time*, 28 April 1952, p.21; Shneidman, *Spain*, p.97; *Le Monde*, 6–7 April 1952; as well as *Ha'aretz*, 28 April 1952.
44. *Ha'aretz*, 15 April 1952; Crocker to State Department, 23 April 1952 (NA, 652.871/4–2352); Baghdad Embassy to State Department, 30 April 1952 (NA, 652.86/4–3052); and María Dolores Algora Weber, 'Realidades y contradicciones de la política árabe del franquismo: El viaje del ministro de Asuntos Exteriores Alberto Martín Artajo a Egipto y sus repercusiones en Marruecos', in Hipólito de la Torre (ed.), *Portugal, España y Africa en los últimos cien años* (Merida, 1992), pp.211–23.
45. Balfour to FO, 25 March 1952 (FO, 371/102009); Wesley Jones to State Department, 5 Feb. 1952 (NA, 652.71B/2–552).
46. *Le Monde*, 15 June 1952; *The Tablet* (London), 15 Nov. 1952; Rockwell to State Department, 11 July 1952 (NA, 652.00/7–1152); Suárez Fernández, *Francisco Franco*, Vol. 5, pp.90–92; Antonio Marquina Barrio, *La diplomacia vaticana y la España de Franco (1936–1945)* (Madrid, 1984), Ch.6.
47. Rafael García Valiño was one of the youngest and most capable Nationalist generals during the Civil War. 'García Valiño was regarded in some regime circles as a potential rival to the Caudillo. He had once declared that on the day that Franco died, he would turn up at El Pardo to take over.' See Paul Preston, *Franco: A Biography* (New York, 1994), p.642.
48. Franco Salgado-Araujo, *Mis conversaciones*, p.168; Fleming, 'North Africa', pp.137–8. On the Spanish protectorate in Morocco up until independence in 1956, see Víctor Morales Lezcano, *España y el norte de Africa: El protectorado en Marruecos (1912–1956)* (Madrid, 1986); Miguel Martín, *El colonialismo español en Marruecos (1860–1956)* (Paris, 1973); Antonio Marquina Barrio, *España en la política de la seguridad occidental* (Madrid, 1986), Ch.7.
49. Francisco Franco, *Pensamiento político* (Madrid, 1975), p.779; Franco Salgado-Araujo, *Mis conversaciones*, pp.170–73; Suárez Fernández, *Francisco Franco*, Vol.5, Ch.6; J.W.D. Trythall, *Franco: A Biography* (London, 1970), pp.244–6; Stanley G. Payne, *Politics and the Military in Modern Spain* (Stanford, 1967), pp.441–2; Shneidman, *Spain*, pp.141–6; José Luis de Arrese, *Una etapa constituyente* (Barcelona, 1982), p.52. In the course of his talks with John Foster Dulles in Washington in April 1956, Martín Artajo said: 'Our army fought for years in Morocco, creating blood ties, later sentimental ones. All the Generalissimo's authority was needed to talk of independence [for Morocco], which many – especially the military – viewed with apprehension' (AMAE, R.3599/41).
50. On Spain's relations with the Middle East and North Africa from the 1950s onwards, see Rein, *In the Shadow*, pp.178–92; José Mario Armero, *Política exterior de España en*

democracia (Madrid, 1989), pp.24–5, 66–7, 131–3, 140–41, 194–209, 220–22; Richard Gillespie, 'Spain and the Maghreb: Toward a Regional Policy?' in R. Gillespie, F. Rodrigo, and J. Story (eds.), *Democratic Spain: Reshaping External Relations in a Changing World* (London and New York, 1995), pp.159–77; and Antonio Marquina, 'La politica exterior de los gobiernos de la Unión de Centro Democrático', in Javier Tusell and Alvaro Soto (eds.), *Historia de la transición, 1975–1986* (Madrid, 1996), pp.182–215.

Spain's Input in Shaping the EU's Mediterranean Policies, 1986–96

ALFRED TOVIAS

The European Union's policies towards Mediterranean non-member countries in the past decade have rapidly evolved from being based on unilateral trade preferences in favour of these countries to focusing on financial aid, reciprocity, and non-economic items (political dialogue, cultural cooperation and so on). Spain is the UE member which has contributed most to this evolution, and it has much to gain from it. However, other policies, such as the creation of a border-free Europe, call for actions which affect Spain's relations with those countries and that it does not accept willingly, such as functioning as gatekeeper of the EU's southern borders.

Spain has not had traditionally what could be called a Mediterranean policy. It developed its so-called Arab policy in the 1950s, during the years of Franco's dictatorship, When in exchange for Spain's diplomatic backing in the Arabs' conflict with Israel, the Arab countries agreed to support the Franco regime in international fora. Rather than being the subject, it was the object of other countries' Mediterranean policies, among them that of the Six, the European Economic Community (EEC) that emerged in 1958. Whereas at its inception the EEC had no intention of having any such policy, it eventually responded to pressure from various Mediterranean countries by entering into preferential trade agreements in 1969–70 with Spain, Israel, Morocco, and Tunisia. With the inception of the EC's Mediterranean policy in 1972 Spain became part of it, but opted out in 1973–74, when it became clear that Franco's rule was coming to an end and that membership in the EC was almost within reach. Until then, Spain had been working discreetly with Israel in Brussels towards a revision of the 1970 preferential agreements that would take into account the effects on them of Britain's entry into the EC. Negotiations stalled in late 1973 because of the Yom Kippur War, and in early 1974 Spain parted ways with Israel. Envisioning the day when it would be a full member of the EC and benefit from the principles of the Common Agricultural Policy (CAP), including the EC's preference, Spain was no longer interested in revising the agreement, which had after all served its industry well. It applied to be a member of the EC in 1977, and negotiations with a view to membership started in early 1979 and continued until mid-1985. During that period, Spain fought tooth and nail but without much success for favourable treatment for its Mediterranean agriculture. The full benefits of the CAP were to be obtained by Spain after a transition period of ten years instead of the usual seven specified in the accession treaties for other types of agriculture, industry, and labour movements. These were also years of transition and consolidation for the new Spanish democracy, and the successive governments were extremely busy tackling the domestic agenda and the full integration of Spain into the international security and economic order devised by the Western world for Western Europe in the 1940s and 1950s (the EC, NATO, the Western European Union).

With the accession to power of the Socialist Party in 1982, the Ministry of Foreign Affairs was handed to Fernando Morán, a professional diplomat with his own conception of where the long-term interests of Spain lay. The Mediterranean was not an object of his attention. His focus was, rather, on the Maghreb, where he would succeed in moving away from the former policy of equilibrium towards Algeria and Morocco to a more global approach. Spain needed good relations with everyone now that the Maghreb was on its way to economic integration,[1] and development cooperation would in time become a component of its policy there. As for the eastern Mediterranean, the only problematic issue being discussed during Moran's tenure was the possibility of recognition of Israel and the establishment of diplomatic relations with it.

In July 1985, Prime Minister Felipe González formed a new government and appointed Francisco Fernández Ordoñez as Foreign Minister. The Prime Minister let it be known that with Spanish membership in the EC scheduled for 1 January 1986 a new chapter in Spain's foreign policy was about to begin. Unlike Morán, the new Foreign Minister was a pragmatist with no background in foreign affairs and, not surprisingly, from then on the Prime Minister occupied centre-stage in the design of Spain's foreign policies. He not only had a taste for it but brought to it a knowledge of European affairs accumulated in the course of his political career. Beyond this, from 1985 until 1992, as a combined outcome of Spain's entry into the EC, the perspective opened of the completion of EC's 340 million-strong internal market, and a drastic cut in the price of crude oil, Spain's economy boomed, leaving the Prime Minister with more time than before to devote to matters to which he attached particular importance, such as Spain's role in Europe.[2]

1986–89: CONSOLIDATING THE GAINS OF MEMBERSHIP

The years following Spain's entry into the EC were marked by an effort to learn the ropes of policy making in Brussels. It was felt that it would take time for Spain to achieve any real influence on EC decision making.[3] In non-EC matters, the key issue was to 'normalize' relations with the United States which in the eyes of the Spanish government meant progressively dismantling the US military presence on Spanish territory. On the Mediterranean front, the Spanish Foreign Ministry was relieved that Spain's establishment of diplomatic relations with Israel had not led to a backlash in relations with Arab countries. At that time, in the words of a Spanish expert,[4] Spain's Mediterranean policies were virtually limited to Ceuta and Melilla, the two enclaves that Spain had possessed in North Africa since the fifteenth century. In fact, until assuming for the first time the six-month presidency of the EC's Council of Ministers in early 1989, Spain maintained a low profile in the EC's foreign relations and in European Political Cooperation (EPC). There was a sense of modesty, but also of a clear intention to take advantage of membership and to send a message to everyone, including all the Mediterranean non-member countries, that Spain was a European country in the Mediterranean region rather than a Mediterranean country in Europe.

On the first point, Spain adopted the view, shared by the EC Commission itself, that the creation of a single European market by the end of 1992 would only widen the economic gap between poor and rich EC members and that this tendency should be offset by voluntary measures promoting more 'cohesion' within the community. This sentiment was echoed by González when he said that he favoured the creation of a social, economic, and cultural space in Europe and not merely an internal market.[5] Spain, backed by Greece, Portugal, and Ireland (and sometimes even by Italy), pressed the northern members of the Community to approve new aid to southern members. For instance, under Spanish pressure, the amount allocated to the three so-called structural funds in the EC's budget was doubled in 1988 in real terms from seven billion ECU to 14 billion ECU (calculated at 1988 prices), as part of the so-called 'Delors Package I',[6] representing about 27 per cent of EC expenditures and 0.3 per cent of the EC's domestic product. Later on, at the Edinburgh summit in 1992, a new agreement would be reached whereby not only would a new 'Cohesion Fund' be created but that funds would be doubled again over a period of five years until 1997.[7] The new Cohesion Fund, part of the Delors Package II, was to benefit states (not regions as in the Delors Package I) with a per capita income below 90 per cent of the EC's average, thus including Spain.[8]

On the second point, Spanish policy in Brussels regarding

Mediterranean non-member countries was rather short-sighted during the initial years of its membership. Spain tried to obtain new concessions from the Community that would not be extended to other Mediterranean countries, and failing this it objected to any concession that other EC members wished to confer on Mediterranean non-member countries. What was most important to Spain was that its agricultural products continue to receive preferential treatment with regard to those of Mediterranean non-members, maximizing artificial trade diversion in its favour. The negative effects would be concentrated on only a few countries: Morocco, Israel, Tunisia and Cyprus.

The effects of this philosophy may be seen from what happened between 1983 and 1988.[9] At the end of 1983, the first round of negotiations between the EC and Mediterranean non-member countries considered the possible effects of the expansion on the latter. This did not lead to a proposal from the Commission to the Council of Ministers until July 1985, and therefore no mandate was given to the Commission until November 1985, or more than two years after the original negotiations, which was, of course, too late for the EC to reach any agreement with Mediterranean non-members before Spain's entry. This delay, initiated by Italy with Spain's backing from the outside, succeeded despite Delors' desire, supported by the United Kingdom and the Federal Republic of Germany, to formulate an agreement before 1986. In March of that year the EC Commission asked for an additional mandate. This led to a new compromise, proposed by the (Dutch) President of the Council of Ministers on 17 April 1986, which was vetoed by Spain; for, before it would agree to the compromise, it wanted to make certain that Canary Island agriculture would be treated at least as well as that of the Mediterranean non-member countries.[10] Without entering into the ensuing negotiations between the EC and Spain, the latter's veto acted to block the development of the EC Mediterranean policy until October 1986. In answer to Moroccan charges that Spain's actions were aimed at increasing instability in North Africa,[11] Spain replied that it did not question the concessions included in the compromise of April 1986 and it only wanted to ensure that the Canary Islands would not suffer in comparison with Mediterranean third countries;[12] the real aim was to place the Canary Islands somewhere in between the Mediterranean countries and the Iberian Peninsula with regard to EC agricultural markets.[13] The background to the Spanish government's position was its fear that it had already accepted too many conditions during the negotiations for membership and that this might lead to domestic political problems. It was in this connection that the Spanish veto was aimed at obtaining new concessions for Canary Island agriculture.[14] The compensation being offered by the EC to satisfy Spain on this matter was not considered enough; it wanted new fishing rights from

France before it would withdraw its veto. When this had been agreed upon, Fernández Ordoñez himself told the Moroccan authorities that a compromise had been reached. This opened the way for renewed negotiations with the Mediterranean countries at the end of 1986, which resulted in agreements being signed by the parties involved (except for Morocco[15] and Yugoslavia) some months later. But here too Spain linked its signing of these agreements to the conclusion of negotiations on the Technical Adaptation Protocol, the agreement outlining Spain's adoption of the EC's Mediterranean policy agreements.

In sum, joint action by Italy and Spain had a substantial impact on the timing of the agreements and on their content. In the end, the final compromise agreed upon by the EC's Council of Ministers was that only 'traditional exports' by Mediterranean non-member countries would be preserved by the introduction of a system of tariff-free quotas on their agricultural exports to the EC. The system was conceived in such a way as to preclude static trade diversion against these countries regarding their exports of fruit and vegetables to the EC. The idea was clearly that any extra demand in EC markets would be picked up by Spanish farmers and not by their Mediterranean neighbours.[16] This meant in practice that Mediterranean countries would have to forget about fostering economic development on the basis of increased agricultural exports to the EC once Spain was given free access to EC markets. With hindsight, it can be said that the Spanish strategy of those years clearly paid off.[17] Exports of fruits and vegetables (not including citrus fruit) more than doubled in value terms from 163 billion pesetas to 367 billion pesetas between 1990, the starting date of the transition period for this kind of products, and 1994, when the full benefits of membership were put in place.[18] Citrus fruit exports also increased markedly, together with Greek exports, while Israeli exports have declined and Moroccan exports have stagnated.

Finally, regarding the orientation to be given to the Spanish presidency of the EC's Council of Ministers in the first semester of 1989, there were two major schools of thought in the Spanish administration. One wanted Spain to make its mark on EC's basic orientations,[19] while others felt that six months was too ambitious for a medium-sized country with limited resources and experience. In the end, this latter school of thought carried the day. Instead of Spain acting like the trouble-maker many EC old-timers expected it to be, it chose to assume a low profile, earning a reputation as a serious and enthusiastic European partner while completely rearranging its foreign policy priorities.[20] Spain sought mainly to advance its Latin America agenda. Among other things, it tried unsuccessfully to create a guarantee fund to help middle-income debtor countries (with Latin American countries in mind). Regarding Mediterranean-related issues, its foreign policy remained declaratory.[21] Its only notable action in the EC was helping to draft what later would become the Madrid European Council's Declaration of 1 June 1989, renewing the collective European position towards the conflict in the Middle East (a re-hash of the 1980 Venice Declaration). Beyond that, during Spain's six-months presidency an EC delegation visited the Middle East four times and a decision was made to double aid to the West Bank and Gaza Strip.

In fact, more than anything else, for Spanish diplomacy membership entailed the need to adjust to EPC mechanisms. As a Spanish scholar has put it,[22] it was necessary first to adapt Spanish foreign policy to the '*acquis politique*' and only then to seek the inclusion of Spanish priorities on the EPC agenda. Spain also had to adjust to the '*acquis communautaire*, regarding the Mediterranean, mainly based on trade agreements between the EC and Mediterranean non-member countries. Thus the concept of Mediterranean policy originating in the EC would replace Spain's traditional concept of an Arab policy. The Europeanization of Spanish foreign policy meant placing its relations with the Arab world in a European context. All this may explain why, three years after its entry into the EC, Spain's input in the shaping of EC foreign policy (except maybe with regard to Latin America) was negligible.

One more point regarding Spanish moves during this period: at the end of the first four years in which Jacques Delors presided over the EC Commission in December 1988, Spain succeeded in having a Spaniard, Abel Matutes (Spain's Minister of Foreign Affairs since 1996), placed in charge of the EC's relations with the Mediterranean and Latin American countries.[23]

1990–92: DEVELOPING THE TELESCOPE

Spain's attitude towards EC policies in the Mediterranean changed substantially after the second semester of 1989. Its incorporation into the EC brought the Community into closer geographical contact with the Arab countries and Africa, and this had tremendous implications in view of the intention to create, by 1993, a Community without internal borders. This new reality was encouraging many migrants from North Africa to penetrate the huge EC labour market through neighbouring Spain, where some of them remained. Migration increased in view of the harmonization or even just coordination of immigration and visa policies among EU member countries, which were expected to be more restrictive on average than in the past. In fact, illegal immigrants began arriving in Spain by boat as early as 1989. Of the 196 detained that year almost all were Moroccans.[24] The number of foreign residents in Spain had risen from 215,000 in 1981 to

425,000 in 1990. During this period 60,000 acquired Spanish nationality. Including illegal immigrants, the total number for 1990 was estimated to reach 625,000, and including new Spaniards 685,000, which still represented only 1.6 per cent of the total resident population, of which 0.8 per cent originated in non-EC countries (much less than comparable numbers in other EC countries). However, of the less than 200,000 illegal immigrants, about 46 per cent originated in Africa, particularly Morocco.[25] In fact, the latter represented only four per cent of the legal migrants from non-EC countries in 1989.[26] Under an amnesty programme in 1991, some 130,000 illegal immigrants came forward to regularize their presence.[27]

Thus, in a matter of years Spain had shifted from being a country from which people emigrated to a migrant destination, something which was by then the norm in the rest of western Europe. This explains why, according to various polls, Spaniards did not display any clear xenophobic tendencies in these early years of illegal immigration. And yet, very soon the government became aware that being part of the EC would require that Spain be more restrictive than before in controlling the movement of people across its borders. At first, it opted for half opening the door to immigrants. Neither the closure of frontiers nor the impracticable opening of Spain to the needy was being proposed.

Was this policy imposed by the EC? Clearly not. The regularization of illegal immigration was carried out by Spain unilaterally; the entry visa requirement for Maghrebian citizens imposed in 1991 was a measure that it would itself have taken sooner or later, although the official reason given was that it would adhere to the Schengen agreement among those EC members which wanted to eliminate internal barriers.[28] In fact, the Schengen agreement took effect in March 1995 and then only partially. Furthermore, it was under the 1989 Spanish presidency that the EC agreement on the joint policing of external frontiers, internal movements across frontiers, and cooperation on drugs, anti-terrorist measures, and tax evasion was reached.[29] Moreover, Prime Minister González expressed early support for the German Chancellor's idea of creating a European federal police. According to Baldwin-Edwards,[30] Spain found it expedient to conform to EC and Schengen arrangements even though these were difficult if not impossible to implement. Spain started pressurizing Morocco to readmit illegal migrants well in advance of any decision taken at the EC level. In fact, it was only at its meeting of 23 November 1995 that its Justice and Home Affairs Ministers resolved to insert readmission clauses in future agreements with third countries, whereby illegal aliens could be deported to those countries. Moreover, Spain asked for and received structural funds to build up its immigration infrastructure, which was practically non-existent at the beginning of the 1990s.

All this shows that the Socialist government of Felipe González willingly contributed to the containment of migration from the south without much pressure from Brussels. This applied even more to the Aznar's right-wing government that came to power in 1996. In fact, pressure sometimes seems to flow in the opposite direction, from Spain to other member states. Some Spaniards push for the development of an all-inclusive immigration policy. For instance, Joan Vallve, a member of the European Parliament, declared in a speech delivered at the Netherlands Association for International Affairs on 26 September 1997: 'I don't know if the north of Europe is aware of the Mediterranean question or on the contrary they believe that this problem concerns exclusively the southern states of the EU. Immigration is a European problem. It is necessary to develop the third pillar of the Maastricht Treaty to improve the authority of the Union in asylum and immigration policy.'

Interestingly enough, a number of Spanish officials in the Foreign Ministry and the Prime Minister's Office had been warning for years that these containment strategies would not work.[31] For them, the reason for migrating to the EC was not so much that the latter was operating as a magnet for potential migrants, but rather the dismal economic situation and high birth rates in the Maghreb. In any case, they correctly linked economic disparity and potential migration. Already in 1991 Miguel Angel Moratinos, then Deputy Director General for North Africa in the Spanish Ministry of Foreign Affairs, had argued that something had to be done to anchor North African populations. Spaniards like him began to understand better than before that the best way to counter undesirable immigration was to foster economic prosperity in North Africa. Under heavy pressure from the Spanish Commissioners in charge of the Mediterranean in Brussels, Abel Matutes and then Manuel Marín, in late 1989 the EC launched a revised Mediterranean policy which did not add much in terms of trade concessions (since Spain and other southern European countries did not want to hear about them[32]), but implied an important additional financial effort by the EC (greater by a factor of 2.7 than the financial package approved in the mid-1980s). In the trade domain, nothing of much significance was offered. The end of the transition period for the full elimination of duties on traditional agricultural exports of Mediterranean non-member countries was advanced by three years to 1993, but simply as a way of maintaining some parallels with Spain, which had been granted the same rescheduling some time before. The tariff quotas themselves would also be increased progressively until 1996 by 3–5 per cent – not significantly. The revised Mediterranean policy was in fact a minor victory for the southern countries over their northern neighbours, in that more aid would have to be distributed from Brussels without having to alter any element in the international division of labour around the Mediterranean, a subject that was 'taboo' for Spain.

The Gulf War in 1991 and the Algerian crisis in 1992 strengthened the belief in Spain that there was an urgency to engineering a rapid improvement in the economic situation in all of Northern Africa. Spain maintained that the fundamental problems of the Mediterranean were social and economic and that the creation of new security frameworks to bring peace to this part of the world had to be complemented by economic cooperation.[33] All this coincided with a better disposition of the United States towards EC actions to stabilize the situation in the Maghreb.

It was at this time that Spain began to develop what Carlos Zaldivar calls its 'telescope policy'. It realized that the situation on its immediate southern frontier (that is, northern Morocco, in particular Ceuta and Melilla) not only could not be separated from the situation in the Maghreb, but even had to take into account what went on in the eastern Mediterranean and the Middle East at large. In the words of Miguel Angel Moratinos, 'the Gulf crisis has accelerated the process of sociopolitical change there … to create prosperity and stability in the Maghreb is to assure peace and security in Spain ... to permit instability and underdevelopment in North Africa is to invest in crises and conflicts that, whether we like it or not, will be exported here'.[34] In the same vein, Spanish Foreign Minister Fernández Ordoñez visited the five Maghreb countries to indicate that Spain was eager to foster economic development in North Africa. However, it was clear from the outset that this was too important an economic task to be left to Spain alone. The EC (which by 1992 had become the European Union) had to be involved.[35] Thus, the Spanish Ministry of Foreign Affairs and the Prime Minister's Office had to convince others in Spain and in the EU that the Mediterranean was a unit for political action. Previously that unit had, for Spain and France, been the western Mediterranean, for Italy perhaps Egypt, for the United Kingdom its former colonies and mandates, and for Germany Turkey. None of the EU member countries had a Mediterranean policy. Only the EU had one, and it was 'only' a commercial one. At the same time, paradoxically, the EPC, developed since the early 1970s outside the EC's framework on an intergovernmental basis, had dealt almost exclusively with the Israeli–Arab conflict, much too much for Spain's taste.[36] Spain tried to demonstrate that the Mediterranean had an Islamic dimension, an energy dimension, an economic dimension, and a migration dimension. A global approach was warranted because trying to patch things up in one corner of the Mediterranean would be myopic. To be convinced of this one had only to look at the effects of the Gulf War all around the Mediterranean.

It is true, however, that Spain, along with all the EU's other members, had to accept an ancillary, mainly advisory role in the peace process of Israel and its neighbours, the latter being under the aegis of the United States in the wake of the Gulf War. Interestingly enough, however, perhaps presaging its later larger role in Mediterranean affairs, it was Spain which, at the urgent request of the United States, in May 1991 hosted the opening session of the peace process to the satisfaction of all the active participants, and in so doing acquired some prestige both for itself and indirectly for the EU.

The first real opportunity for Spain to show some leadership in putting together a 'package' to be sold to the EU's Council of Ministers was at the Lisbon summit in June 1992. The European Parliament (with strong Spanish backing) had refused to ratify the fourth financial protocol to the 1976 EC–Morocco agreement because of Moroccan violations of human rights in the western Sahara. As a result, Morocco had threatened not to renew the 1988 EU–Morocco fishing agreement, something which would have hurt Spain in particular. Fernández Ordoñez had been asked to report to the other EU Foreign Ministers in February 1992 on the political situation in the Maghreb, while the European Commission was to prepare a paper on the economic problems of the region. The Spanish Commissioner in charge of the Mediterranean at the time, Abel Matutes, proposed among other things the creation of a Euro-Maghrebi Development Bank, on the model of the European Bank for Reconstruction and Development. Fernandez Ordoñez presented the Maghreb as a 'time-bomb' which Europe had to disarm, in part through financial assistance.[37] But there was too much aid in the proposal to be stomached by Germany and the United Kingdom.[38] To make the proposal palatable to all EU members, the Spanish, Portuguese, and French Foreign Ministries came up with the idea of elevating the EU–Maghreb relationship to a new level by launching a 'Euro-Maghreb Partnership', with the aim of gradually creating among other things a free trade area between the EU and every Maghreb country by the year 2000.[39]

1993–94: DEVELOPING THE EURO-MED INITIATIVE

Already at the end of 1989, Felipe González warned during a visit to Morocco that the new neighbours to the east would be economic rivals and the dangers of EC foreign aid being diverted towards the east.[40] Spain itself was worried by a possible shift of potential investment to eastern Europe. These views were not without some justification; suffice it to recall here the launching by the EC in a matter of months, if not weeks, of the fall of the Berlin Wall in 1989 of emergency aid under the PHARE programme and the rapid conclusion of *ad hoc* trade arrangements with several eastern European countries, superseded in 1991 by more generous permanent agreements. Then there was the establishment in 1991 of the European Bank for Reconstruction and Development, in which EU countries played a key role. In fact, the revised Mediterranean policy analysed above was in a way a timid response to calls from Spain and other southern European countries to maintain some balance, if not symmetry, between east and south. But at this early stage this argument did not carry much weight. The strategic value of some key Mediterranean non-member countries (for example, Turkey) had sharply decreased with the end of the cold war, the real price of crude oil and gas had been falling continuously since the early 1980s and increasingly since 1985, and western Europe would in the future be less dependent on Arab oil given access to Central Asia and Russian sources of supply. In this respect, it became easier for Spain and other southern European countries to convince other EU countries of the urgency to act much more forcefully than in 1990.

González was among the European leaders who supported without hesitation and from the beginning the reunification of Germany proposed in 1990 by Helmut Kohl, the German Chancellor, but the collapse of the Soviet Union would have other consequences less to his liking. Some neutral countries (Sweden, Finland, and Austria) decided to apply for EU membership, something which would expand it to 15 members and pull its centre of gravity to the north. But this would at least be compensated by the fact that these were rich countries which could make a net contribution to the EU budget and thus maintain if not expand the 'cohesion' policies strengthened after Maastricht in 1992. González was much more cautious regarding Germany's view that a window of opportunity had been opened after the collapse of the Soviet Union for the EU to embrace its own neighbours to the east. Spain was afraid that the eastern expansion would undermine its position in the EU.[41] To buy time, Spain asked that before deciding about any expansion beyond the 15 there should be a further deepening of the EU. It also feared that too much energy would be devoted to the east and not enough to the Maghreb and southern Europe.[42] The obvious policy conclusion at that stage was that championing the Mediterranean cause in Brussels would avoid placing Spain in a peripheral position with the inevitable shifting of the EU's attention towards the east.

At the end of 1992, Spain could look back with pride at what it had achieved internationally as a middle-level power integrated into the EU: successfully managing the presidency of the European Council, hosting the Madrid Middle East Peace Conference of 1991, organizing the World's Fair in Seville and the Olympics in Barcelona in 1992. It was confident in its diplomatic clout and leadership capacity and felt that it could suggest new international projects to be launched by Brussels. At the same time, it sensed the need to act lest it be accused by its Arab neighbours of 'immobilism', of increasingly agreeing to do the 'dirty work' for the northern Europeans on its borders and discreetly offering logistical support to the US during the Gulf War.

Spain also had many ideas about what to do to improve the economic and social situation in Mediterranean non-member countries. Trade liberalization alone would not do; Europe had to help in the development of these countries by giving more funds.[43] Political reform was also needed. Europe had a role to play as it had at the time of democratic transition in southern Europe (including Spain) in the 1970s. One idea was to foster direct contacts between key European and Arab players in civil society. The inspiration came from the relative success of the Conference on Security and Cooperation in Europe (CSCE). As early as 1990 Fernández Ordoñez had proposed a Conference on Security and Cooperation in the Mediterranean that would adopt the CSCE's approach to security, humanitarian issues, and economic cooperation by confidence-building measures and by generating the process.[44] An international treaty would link all the aspects, as in the Helsinki Treaty. Only Italy had supported this approach; France had wanted an exclusive focus on the western Mediterranean and Germany; the United Kingdom and the Netherlands had been wary because they sensed that the United States would oppose such a project.[45] In any case, the Gulf War and the new Middle East peace process had rendered the idea obsolete. To succeed, Spain had to blend the CSCM idea with its own idea of a Euro-Maghreb partnership, which was much closer to the conventional trade policies conducted from Brussels since the 1970s. This would put the EU in the driver's seat, excluding the United States from the initiative.[46] Working in favour of this notion was that the EC had a long record of treating all the Mediterranean non-member countries as a group. Another advantage, already mentioned, was that in so doing Spain was helping to maintain the equilibrium of the EU's foreign relations. The drawback, as observed later on by the Arab side, was that from this point it would not be a real 'Euro-Mediterranean Initiative' but a 'European initiative for the Mediterranean'.

Internally, the Spanish Ministry of Foreign Affairs, now led by Javier Solana (replacing Francisco Fernández Ordoñez, who died in June 1992), from early on had to confront and disarm opposition to the economic part of the plan from the Ministries of Agriculture (which feared that Mediterranean non-member countries would not accept industrial free trade without any EU concession in agriculture) and Industry (which feared the transfer of labour-intensive firms from Spain to North Africa). Externally, France, Italy, and Portugal did not need to be convinced; a policy had to be devised that could be accepted by Germany, the pivotal player. For this, the government worked hand-in-hand with the Spanish Commissioner, Manuel Marín,[47] who presented a proposal in October 1994 for the establishment of a Euro-Mediterranean partnership to be submitted to the European Council in Essen in December 1994 and later to be discussed in more detail at a

Mediterranean ministerial conference. In the view of the Commission, which by law has the exclusive right to initiate legislation in the EC, the main elements of the new programme had to be (1) the creation of a Euro-Mediterranean free trade area by about 2010; (2) a doubling of the financial assistance drawn on the Community's own budgetary resources for the period 1995–99 (about 5.5 billion ECU); and (3) increasing technical cooperation (based on the experience drawn from the PHARE programme with central and eastern European countries).

In a press release, Marín did speak of 'anchoring' the Mediterranean non-member countries in a huge European economic space, presumably the expanded 15-member EU. In practice, and in relation to the revised Mediterranean policy of 1990, the Commission's idea was to have all these non-member countries give tariff- and quota-free access to manufactured products originating both in the EU and in other Mediterranean non-member countries. This was good but for the detail that the adjustment was to be made mainly by the Mediterranean non-member countries themselves, since industrial free trade prevailed in the direction south–north according to the cooperation agreements of the 1970s. On the EC's side, the Commission only 'asked' the member states to make additional effort in the agricultural domain. Again, as in the revised Mediterranean policy, the main additional contribution to be made by the EU was financial.[48] Economic provisions had to be complemented by 'a political dialogue' to cover 'soft' security issues as well as a 'cultural dialogue', both items modelled on the CSCE.

At the European Council meeting in Essen in December 1994, the Mediterranean became a priority zone of strategic importance for the EU, vindicating Spanish ideas of reestablishing some parallelism with eastern Europe, but not before Prime Minister González had threatened to block further moves towards an eastern expansion of the EU. His friendship with the German Chancellor was to play a key role in persuading Germany to change course. He presented his arguments well: Mediterranean non-member countries represented a market (even for Germany!) of 304 million people, compared with eastern Europe with only 116 million, and energy dependence on the former was 24 per cent of EC consumption, but only nine per cent for eastern Europe.[49]

Six months later at the European Council meeting in Cannes, the new project gained credibility when Felipe González reached an agreement with Kohl on the financial component of the Euro-Maghreb partnership. It is worth remembering that in the reference period 1992–96 Mediterranean non-member countries had been receiving one ECU for every five ECUs received by central and eastern European countries, a proportion that the United Kingdom and the Netherlands did not want to alter.[50] It is a measure of González's persuasiveness with Kohl that in the end the final package would alter this ratio to 5:3.5 for the whole of the period 1995–99 and not only at the end of the period, as the German Chancellor wanted. In the end, Spain would have realized its idea of launching from Brussels a multilateral pluri-annual development assistance programme for the benefit of the Mediterranean non-member countries, inspired by the PHARE programme and later to be called MEDA.

1995–96: THE BARCELONA CONFERENCE

Since the council meeting in Essen, it had been clear to Spain that there was a strategic opportunity to be seized. The three EU presidencies stretching from 1 January 1995 to 30 June 1996 would be in the hands of France, Spain, and Italy, in that order, all more or less in agreement about the importance to be given to the partnership. At the Cannes summit in June 1995 it was decided that a ministerial conference assembling the 15 EU countries and 12 Mediterranean non-member countries would take place in the second semester of that year under the Spanish presidency. It is not surprising therefore that the main drafting work for what was later to be called 'The Barcelona Declaration' was done by the Spaniards and the French, with some Arab input. Gillespie has found unmistakable signs of Spanish drafting and phraseology drawn from the Hispano-Moroccan friendship Treaty of 1991 (for example, the commitment to human rights and the right of each country to choose its own political, social, and economic system).[51] The choice of Barcelona as the site for the conference and the Euro-med Civil Forum which followed was for González a way of rewarding Pujol, the President of the Generalitat de Catalunya, for his backing of the Socialist minority government at the Cortes.

By all accounts, the Barcelona conference of November 1995 was a diplomatic success. In particular, Syria and Lebanon, which had decided to take part in the multilateral track of the peace negotiations in the Middle East since 1991, attended all the sessions together with Israel. As an outcome of the Oslo Process, the Palestinians were present as an independent entity, represented by Mr Yasser Arafat himself, in contrast to the Madrid conference of 1991. Moreover, the name of Barcelona was to be perpetuated by the creation of a 'Euro-Mediterranean Committee for the Barcelona Process' made up of senior officials of the EU and the 12 Mediterranean non-member countries concerned to oversee the implementation of the work programme. The conference was also a public relations success for the country and for Barcelona in particular, underlining the good relations of Spain with all sides (what the Spaniards call '*capacidad de convocatoria*'). As an early indication of what the 'civil society' aspect of the initiative was all about, the Generalitat de Catalunya, with the strong backing of the Spanish government and the European Commission and UNESCO, delegated the Catalan Institute of the Mediterranean in Barcelona to organize a 'civil forum' on 29–30 November and 1 December 1995. 1,211 persons representing nongovernmental organizations, such as chambers of commerce, unions, municipalities, and universities from 38 countries participated in a huge exercise of decentralized cooperation, proving the word 'partnership' or 'association' was not devoid of content. The civil forum and the ministerial conference which preceded it were linked by the Barcelona Declaration, which specified that the actions to be engaged in are to benefit not just the states and their regional and local authorities but also other actors of civil society. Concrete projects were to be presented by participants and worked out from the ground up. Last, but not least, it was decided to work towards institutionalization and continuity for the forum.

Two other conferences were organized around the Ministerial Conference: The Conference of Mediterranean Cities and the Alternative Mediterranean Conference, which tried to take a critical view as seen from the Third World of the ministerial conference and the partnership as conceived in the Barcelona Declaration. All this contributed to putting Spain on the map of Mediterranean policy making far beyond the six months of the Spanish presidency and in fact far beyond what had been contemplated by the Spanish presidency six months before.[52]

Various participants in the success would later be promoted to new tasks partly as an acknowledgement by governments and institutions of their previous work on Mediterranean-related issues. Foreign Minister Solana was named to the position of NATO Secretary General several months before the scheduled 1996 national elections, and Miguel Angel Moratinos was later named Special Envoy of the EU in the Middle East.

Alas, the Euro-Med initiative did not help the Socialist government much in electoral terms. Some observers saw in the Barcelona exercise a huge Spanish fiesta with fireworks, but more than anything else it was scandals and economic recession (unrelated to foreign affairs) which were the key factors in bringing down in mid- 1996 the government led by González since 1982. Quite unexpectedly, the government of José María Aznar decided to merge the North African Department at the Foreign Ministry with the Asia-Pacific Department, perhaps to signal a lower profile to be maintained in Mediterranean affairs in years to come. In any case, the new Prime Minister could not rely on the kind of majority in the Cortes which the Socialist government enjoyed until 1992 or on the experience used by Gonzalez to influence other European leaders.

CONCLUDING REMARKS

The EU policies towards the Mediterranean non-member countries in the past decade rapidly evolved from being based on unilateral trade preferences in favour of their industrial exports to focusing on financial aid, reciprocity in trade concessions, and non-economic factors (political dialogue, confidence-building measures, horizontal cooperation between NGOs, and so on). Spain is the EU member which has contributed most to this evolution, and it has much to gain from it. It has made the effort to shift from its exclusive focus on Morocco to the rest of Mediterranean non-member countries in order to convince other European member countries that the Mediterranean is an area of strategic importance for the EU and not just for its southern European members. However, other European policies, such as the creation of a border-free Europe, have called for Spanish actions less to its liking, such as functioning as the gate-keeper of the EU's borders. These actions might affect Morocco's relations with Spain in unexpected ways, and Spain does not seem willing to cooperate with the EU without some compensation (such as help in to financing its new policing operations).

It remains to be seen if the success of Spain's influence in the design and drafting of the Barcelona Declaration will stand up to economic logic or wither away. In the long run it seems absurd to keep European fruit and vegetable markets open for the almost exclusive benefit of Spanish farmers and simultaneously fund (with European taxpayer money via the EU budget) economic reforms in Morocco, Tunisia, and Egypt which exclude developing their agriculture, in which they have a comparative advantage. It would certainly make much more economic sense to use part of these funds to help Spanish, Dutch, and Italian fruit and vegetable producers adjust to a wider opening of EU markets to the competition of North African farmers.

In the realms of security and cultural dialogue, it remains to be seen if the northern and central European members of the EU will continue to be convinced by the analysis made by Spain and other southern Europeans and want to cooperate to make these two new areas of the EU's Mediterranean policy a success. Early indications since 1995 have been discouraging, for instance, the participation on the EU side in the several civil forums has so far been overwhelmingly Mediterranean. This is particularly worrying now that the achievement of economic and monetary union and the next EU expansion have become the paramount items on the EUs agenda for many years to come.

NOTES

1. J.A. Yañez Barnuevo and A. Viñas, 'Diez años de política exterior del gobierno socialista (1989–1992)', in A. Guerra and J.F. Tezanos (eds.), *La idea del cambio* (Madrid, 1992), p.106.
2. Between entry and 1991 it is estimated that about US $ 80 billion entered Spain, half of it in the form of foreign direct investment. Expansion not only meant easier access to EC and Portuguese markets than before but also reduced political risks. As a result, Spain found it easy to modernize its economy by massive import technology through foreign investment.
3. See, e.g., *El País Internacional*, 18 May 1987, which devoted an article to the alleged lack of coordination between different Spanish ministries, and between Spain's permanent delegation in Brussels and the Secretariat of State for the EC.
4. Interview with Carlos Zaldivar, former Director of the Research Department of the Spanish Prime Minister's Office, 22 Jan. 1998.
5. Speech presented to the Congress of Socialist Parties in the EEC, Cascais, Portugal, 5 May 1987.
6. Named for the then President of the European Commission, Jacques Delors, who had launched the single market project in 1985, just after being named to that position.
7. According to *The Economist* (25 April 1992, 'A Survey of Spain', p.8), EC aid to Spain would amount to some $ 7.5 billion a year for the period 1993–97.
8. K. Maxwell and S. Spiegel, *The New Spain: From Isolation to Influence* (New York, 1994), p.41
9. Here I draw extensively from A. Tovias, *Foreign Economic Relations of the European Community: The Impact of Spain and Portugal* (Boulder, 1990), pp.78–81.
10. *Boletín ICE*, No.2051, 22–28 Sept. 1986, pp.3057–60.
11. *El País*, 5 April 1987.
12. Confirmed in a conversation on 6 February 1998 with Pedro Solbes, former Spanish Minister of Agriculture and Finance, active in those negotiations.
13. *El País*, 22 Oct. 1986.
14. The concessions in question concerned 23 products, seven more than were included in the 1970 EC–Spain agreement. See Confederación Española de Organizaciones Empresariales, *Primer Año. Balance de la integración de ESPN* (Madrid, 1987).
15. Negotiations with Morocco lasted until mid-1988, because the latter linked issues such as fishing rights and the free passage of Moroccan trucks through Spain with the negotiations.
16. In the case of Tunisian olive oil a domestic system encouraging local consumption and the diversion of exports towards world markets was supported by the EC, to allow for trade diversion in favour of Spain.
17. Some sources contend that these policies are silently being pursued to this day. According to, for example, *The Economist*, 14 Dec. 1996, p.8, the Spanish Minister of Agriculture was fighting against changes in support payments for olive oil and resisting pressure to let more products from North Africa into the EU (for example, trying to postpone calendars of application of EC agricultural concessions in new agreements signed with Mediterranean non member countries in the context of the Euro-Med Partnership, initiated by Spain itself).
18. *El País*, 14 May 1995.
19. See *El País*, 3 June 1988, which indicated that Spain wanted to set itself at the British or German level and wanted to devote to the Spanish presidency as many resources as the latter, rather than as few as Denmark.
20. M. Salomon, 'Spain: Scope Enlargement towards the Arab World and the Maghreb', in F. Algieri and E. Regelsberger (eds.), *Synergy at Work: Spain and Portugal in European Foreign Policy* (Bonn, 1996), p.91.
21. For instance, see F. Fernández Ordoñez, 'Política exterior de España 1987–1990', *Política Exterior* (1987), p.15, where he cites the Mediterranean as the third priority of Spain's foreign policy, after Europe and Latin America.
22. K. Saba, 'Spain: Evolving Foreign Policy Structures, from EPC Challenge to CFSP Management', in Algieri and Regelsberger (eds.), *Synergy at Work*, p.181
23. Yañez Barnuevo and Viñas, 'Diez años de política exterior', p.113.

24. *The New York Times,* 18 Oct. 1992.
25. A. Izquierdo Escribano, 'The EC and Spanish immigration Policy', in A. Almarcha Barbado (ed.), *Spain and EC Membership Evaluated* (London, 1993), p.292.
26. J. Ibañez, 'La Política exterior española ante la immigración magrabi', *Papers*, 46 (1995), p.97.
27. *The Economist*, 25 April 1992.
28. Contrary to what was expected, Morocco did not criticize the Spanish move, probably because of a series of what were perceived as compensatory measures (for example, Spain's willingness to admit more legal migrants from Morocco, the Spanish Prime Minister's visit to Rabat, seen as a sign of confidence in the King of Morocco at a time of domestic turmoil there). Interestingly, Algeria retaliated, in turn requiring visas for Spanish visitors.
29. J. Story, 'Spain's External Relations Redefined: 1975–89' in R. Gillespie, F. Rodrigo and J. Story (eds.), *Democratic Spain: Reshaping External Relations in a Changing World* (London, 1995), p.47.
30. M. Baldwin-Edwards, 'The Emerging European Immigration Regime: Some Reflections on Implications for Southern Europe', *Journal of Common Market Studies* (Dec. 1997), p.630.
31. The number of illegal immigrants rose steadily after May 1991, when visas for Maghreb citizens were imposed.
32. Agriculture occupied still 10 per cent of Spain's labour force in 1993 and 4.3 per cent of its gross domestic product, down from 15.7 per cent and 7.4 per cent respectively in 1980.
33. Of course, and without much fanfare, part of the Spanish response was also to invest in rapid deployment forces and to strengthen anti-terrorist cooperation between the interior ministries of the area.
34. *New York Times*, 20 March 1991.
35. Interview with Miguel Angel Moratinos, former Deputy Director General for North Africa of the Spanish Ministry of Foreign Affairs, 4 Feb. 1998.
36. Ibid.
37. R. Gillespie, 'Spanish Protagonismo and Euro-Med Partnership Initiative', *Mediterranean Politics*, 2 (Summer 1991), p.5.
38. In the same vein, Spain, together with France, did not hesitate to oppose a proposal made by other countries in the EU's Council of Ministers to reduce EC aid to Algeria in the wake of the refusal by the regime in this country to accept the results of democratic elections.
39. A. Vascocelos, 'Portugal: Pressing for an Open Europe', in C. Hill (ed.), *The Actors in Europe's Foreign Poli*cy (London, 1996), p.276.
40. E. Barbé, 'Reinventar el Mare Nostrum: El Mediterráneo como espacio de cooperación y seguridad', *Papers*, 46 (1995), p.13.
41. A. Ortega, 'Spain in the Post-Cold War World', in Gillespie *et al.* (eds.), *Democratic Spain*, pp.182–4.
42. In 1993 the EC was devoting yearly 2.5 ECU of aid for each person in the Maghreb and 7 ECU for each Central and Eastern European. See ibid., p.193.
43. Manuel Marín, the Spanish Commissioner in charge of the Mediterranean since the end of 1992 best expressed this view when he said: 'Fundamentalism is not the result of the spread of Western values but the fact that these values spread and then cannot be satisfied. The way to stem extremism is to offer the people a real hope of prosperity', *Time Magazine*, 11 Dec. 1995.
44. Ortega, 'Spain in the Post-Cold-War World', p.192.
45. Gillespie, 'Spanish Protagonismo', p.35.
46. E. Barbé, 'The Barcelona Conference: Launching Pad of a Process', *Mediterranean Politics*, 1 (Summer 1996), p.26.
47. Interview with Miguel Angel Moratinos, former Deputy Director General for North Africa, Spanish Ministry of Foreign Affairs, 4 Feb. 1998.
48. Here the intervention of Spain was explicit when it declared that it wanted the EU to establish a kind of PHARE for the Mediterranean. See *Bulletin Europe* 6326 (30 Sept. 1994), p.10.
49. *El País*, 20 Nov. 1995.
50. E. Barbé and F. Izquiedo, 'Present and Future of the Joint Actions for the Mediterranean

Region', paper presented at the 2nd Pan European Conference on International Relations, Paris, 13–16 Sepy. 1995.

51. R. Gillespie, 'Spain and the Mediterranean: Southern Sensitivity, European Aspirations', *Mediterranean Politics*, 2 (Summer 1997), p.207.
52. See 'Comunicación' del gobierno sobre la presidencia Espanola del consejo de la Unión Europea', *Meridiano CERI*, 4 (1995), pp.20–30, where only two columns (of a document of more than 11 pages) out of three are devoted to the Mediterranean.

Spanish Foreign and Security Policy in the Mediterranean

ANTONIO MARQUINA

The Mediterranean has long been a priority of Spanish foreign policy. Since achieving membership in the European Community Spain has tried to attract the Community's attention to the Mediterranean and in particular to the importance of stability in the Maghreb. With the end of the cold war Spain and Italy launched an initiative for a conference on security and cooperation in the Mediterranean without success. Spain, in collaboration with France and Italy, drew the attention of the EC to the Maghreb, and negotiations of free-trade agreements were undertaken in Morocco and Tunisia, culminating in the Euro-Mediterranean Conference of Barcelona in 1995. At the same time, Spain supported dialogue and confidence building between the Western European Union and the Maghreb states and made an effort to interest NATO in the south.

The foreign and security policy of Spain during the Franco regime focused on the Mediterranean, and, more concretely, on the western Mediterranean. The traumatic decolonization of Morocco and Algeria's alignment the Soviet Union created the Spanish military concern about a possible threat from the south that was evident in the negotiations on United States bases in Spain during the 1960s and 1970s. Having made the transition from dictatorship to democracy, and begun to consider its NATO membership, Spain still had this potential threat from the south in mind. The army's exit without honour from the Sahara due to international support for the Kingdom of Morocco, Moroccan irredentism with regard to the Spanish cities of Ceuta and Melilla, Algerian pressures, and the Libyan–Moroccan pact resulted in the inclusion of this traditional threat from the south in the first Spanish joint strategic plans, which established the vital strategic objectives of the armed forces and the lines of action for achieving them.[1]

Under the Unión de Centro Democrático (UCD) governments beginning in the mid-1970s, the western Mediterranean remained a foreign policy priority. Relations with Morocco and Algeria were key relations among the Arab states. Spain's economic and cultural presence in the Arab states of the eastern Mediterranean, including Turkey, was very limited, but it maintained a certain degree of political influence there based on its refusal to recognize the state of Israel. With regard to Morocco and Algeria, a balanced policy was established during the presidency of Adolfo Suárez (1976–80), but this balance was abandoned in favour of Morocco during the presidency of Leopoldo Calvo Sotelo (1981–82). As part of the Western strategic design, especially during the first Reagan administration, Morocco began to receive preferential treatment. The process of gaining NATO membership for Spain also contributed to this alteration of the balance. Algeria was obsessed with the issue of the Sahara and early perceived the change in the Spanish position.[2]

The so-called balanced policy was criticized by the first Socialist government, which took office after the October 1982 general elections. The policy that the new government proposed was called 'global', favouring the creation of a Great Maghreb that would allow it to avoid choosing between Morocco and Algeria and to prevent the intervention of the superpowers in the area in support of Morocco or Algeria in a struggle for hegemony in the Mahgreb. The new Foreign Affairs Minister, Fernando Morán was looking for room to manoeuvre in the western Mediterranean, expressing, for instance, to his Algerian counterparts his interest in reducing the role of the non-Mediterranean powers in the area, suggesting the departure of foreign fleets, and considering the collaboration of Italy *non-grata* because of its military participation in NATO. The case of France was different because of its special situation within NATO and its weight in the European Community (EC). Nevertheless, the first trip abroad by Fernando Morán and President Felipe González was to Morocco. This was to prevent any possible conflict with Morocco influencing domestic policy, as had happened in the past.[3]

With regard to the eastern Mediterranean, Spanish policy did not significantly change. The state of Israel continued unrecognized in the first years of the Socialist government; Morán conditioned recognition on an advance in the resolution of the Arab–Israeli and Palestinian–Israeli conflicts. Spanish policy also remained unchanged with regard to the conflict between Iran and Iraq although to some extent favouring Iraq.

SPANISH MEMBERSHIP IN THE EUROPEAN COMMUNITY

The most significant change took place with the achievement of membership in the EC in 1986. Spain now had to recognize the state of Israel, but bilateral relations were maintained at a relatively low level to avoid offending the Arab states. They had supported the Franco regime in international fora in the most delicate moments of the debates over the decolonization of the Spanish territories in Africa, and especially over the Gibraltar issue, and good relations with them were still vital.[4]

Once within the EC, Spain focused on its area of traditional interest, the Maghreb. In this sense, Spain tried to promote European cooperation with the Maghreb, despite its limited relevance to European Cooperation Policy: these questions were analysed within the Middle East Group as a 'miscellaneous' item, in practice a '*domaine réservé*' of French diplomacy. Spain also insisted on the involvement of the European states in the resolution of the western Sahara conflict, supporting the line established by the UN with its peace plan. The majority of EC states considered this conflict to be resolved in favour of Morocco.[5] At the same time, Spain, France, and Italy began to examine Maghreb issues in an effort to create an *ad hoc* group within the ECP, renaming the Middle East Group the Maghreb and Middle East group. Thus, from October 1987 onward ECP declarations on Maghreb appeared. Moreover, Spanish–French and Spanish–Italian seminars on the western Mediterranean began, in order to formulate joint approaches and common policies.

When Spain assumed the presidency of the EC in the first semester of 1989, cooperation councils between the EC and the Maghreb countries were revitalized. The Arab Maghreb Union also received the support of the Twelve. During the French presidency in the second semester of 1989, a document prepared by Spain called *Europe and the Integration in the Maghreb* was approved within the policy planning framework. The European Council meeting in Strasbourg adopted a joint proposal by Spain, France, and Italy to revitalize the Euro-Arab dialogue that had been frozen since 1977. During 1990, however, EC interest in issues concerning the Mediterranean and the Maghreb noticeably declined. At the Open Skies Conference in Ottawa, Spain proposed establishing a Conference on Security and Cooperation in the Mediterranean (CSCM), and that proposal eventually became a Spanish–Italian initiative. During the second semester of 1990, the Italian presidency launched this plan as well as the 4 + 5 Initiative (Spain, Portugal, France, and Italy, plus Mauritania, Morocco, Libya, Algeria, Tunisia), which had a clear French stamp, and was the outcome of intense discussion among Spain, France, Italy, and Portugal that had begun years before.[6]

The 4 + 5 Initiative focused on north–south cooperation, although with a clear view to the globality and indivisibility of security in the Mediterranean. In the case of the Conference on Security and Cooperation in the Mediterranean, the Spanish authorities were interested mainly in applying the European experience to the Mediterranean area. In Europe the CSCE had been used for crisis management and reduction of the strained relations between the western and the Communist countries. In the

Mediterranean it was necessary to avoid the transfer of the tensions which characterized the east–west conflict and the rearmament in North Africa. The interests of the CSCM were to be the same as those of the CSCE: security, economic cooperation, and the human dimension, with economic cooperation being the most important. But the war between the coalition and Iraq sank this initiative. On 4 March 1991, a joint document from Spain, France, Italy, and Portugal was rejected. The United States had not liked the plan from the very beginning because of its military implications, and France had not been very receptive (the initiative not being French).[7] The priorities during 1991 were security arrangements in the Persian Gulf and the Arab–Israeli and Palestinian–Israeli conflicts. Thus, the Madrid Conference on the Middle East abandoned part of the mission of the CSCM.

The 4 + 5 Initiative (later on, with the inclusion of Malta, 5 + 5), was not a success either. During 1991 there were attempts to reorient it in the direction of the CSCM's objectives, beginning with the eastern Mediterranean, but these efforts were blocked by the Gulf War, the crisis in Algeria, and the sanctions against Libya for its terrorist attacks on the Pan-Am aeroplane over Lockerby, Scotland, and the French UTA plane. After this, the Spanish government returned its attention to the western Mediterranean. Because of the situation in Algeria and the crisis of the Arab Maghreb Union, Morocco thought that the latter should play a leading role in the EC's relations with the Maghreb. For Morocco, the crisis of the Arab Maghreb Union meant a reorientation of EC policy to the level of bilateral talks.[8] Taking as a pretext the negative vote by the European Parliament on the EC's Fourth Protocol with Morocco, Spain submitted a proposal to create a free trade area between Morocco and the EC. This bilateral approach was a step backward dictated by circumstances. On 17 February 1992 the EC Council of Foreign Ministers met in Lisbon and instructed Spain and the European Commission to make two reports, economic and political, on the perspectives of the relations between the EC and the Maghreb. The two reports, 'Europe before the Maghreb', by the Spanish Ministry of Foreign Affairs, and 'L'avenir des relations entre la Communauté et le Maghreb, Aspects économiques', by the Spanish Commissioner Abel Matutes, were generally well receive. On 6 April the Council asked the Commission to present a proposal based on political dialogue; economic, technical, and cultural cooperation, and the growing creation of a free-trade area. At the same time, the Commission adopted a communiqué from Matutes recommending a partnership between Europe and the Maghreb, and new instruments were created to this end. Some days later, on 1 May, Morocco and the EC concluded an agreement on fishing that was considered a first step towards this new economic, political, social, and cultural partnership.

On 27 June 1992, the European Council, meeting in Lisbon, issued a declaration on European Union (EU)–Maghreb relations prepared by the Spanish Ministry of Foreign Affairs. The EU reiterated its solidarity with the Maghreb states and its decision to contribute to the stability and prosperity of the Mediterranean area through partnership relations. Months later, in December 1992, the Commission submitted to the Council the guidelines for negotiation of an agreement with Morocco. The document excluded agricultural products, and Morocco considered it unbalanced. As a result the Council was unable to adopt such guidelines until December 1993, and at this point they were extended to Tunisia and, later, Israel.[9]

Spain also promoted the institutionalization of dialogue between the Maghreb states and other European institutions. Dialogue between the Western European Union (WEU) and the Maghreb states, following the model of the east European states, began formally in May 1993.[10] Besides this, in September 1992 Spain, France, and Italy began discussing the creation of forces to be available to the WEU. At first the idea was to create an air–naval force, but eventually the plan included land forces. Differences of approach with regard to land forces led to the development of two initiatives: EUROFOR and EUROMARFOR, the former a land-based rapid deployment force and the latter an air–naval force with amphibious capabilities. Both forces were officially proposed at the WEU ministerial meeting in Lisbon in May 1995. Apart from their use in trilateral operations, the established priority for operational use was WEU, NATO, and the United Nations. The creation of forces drew upon the experience of collaboration in military exercises such as Farfadet 92 in France, Ardente 93 in Italy, and Tramontana 94 in Spain, which showed the viability of air–naval–land cooperation among the three states. The missions designed for EUROFOR and EUROMARFOR were to be similar to these exercises.[11]

Regarding NATO, in 1993 Spain promoted a NATO approach to the Mediterranean in an effort to achieve greater stability in the area. For this, the lack of interest in France and Italy had to overcome, and, more important, the doubts of the United States and the UK. This new approach was reflected in a declaration by the heads of state at the NATO Brussels Summit in January 1994. The Spanish initiative was an important change; since the end of the cold war the PSOE and important sectors of the government had taken the position that the security problems in the Mediterranean were not military and therefore a non-military approach was required.[12] Spain and the other Mediterranean EC states also promoted contacts between the CSCE and the non-member Mediterranean states, as is reflected in the final document of the 1992 CSCE Helsinki conference.[13]

TOWARDS THE EURO-MEDITERRANEAN CONFERENCE OF BARCELONA

On 24–25 June 1994 the European Council, meeting in Corfu, asked the Commission to conclude agreements with Morocco and Tunisia in the coming year and gave guidelines to the Council of Foreign Ministers for a joint evaluation with the Commission of EU global policy towards the Mediterranean area and possible initiatives, with a view to calling a conference between the EU and the partner Mediterranean states on the political, economic, and social problems of the area. This was a significant step. Months later, on 25 October, the Commission submitted to the Council and to the Parliament a communiqué proposing a global aid programme for the Mediterranean of 6,300 million ECUs for the period 1995–99. This aid was delayed by dissension among the EU states. At the Cannes meeting of the European Council in June 1995 the financial package was finally approved, with the southern Mediterranean receiving 4,685 million ECUs. The Spanish position, and reflecting that of Felipe González and his links with Chancellor Helmut Kohl, was very important to this achievement. It guaranteed the Barcelona Conference, opening the way to a Euro-Mediterranean partnership, and made possible the initiative of fishing negotiations and the partnership agreement with Morocco (Tunisia signed the agreement on 12 April 1995).[14]

EU policy on partnership agreements with Morocco and Tunisia was disappointing for these states. For them, the liberalization of the economy meant substantial foreign aid and significant financial support. Industrial restructuring, the loss of incomes from custom duties, and the maintenance of the traditional flows of exports in the agricultural sector constituted the main problems. Morocco complained about the lack of reciprocity and negotiations with the two countries stalled. At the same time, the EU programme of financial aid had not yet been approved. The tension in the negotiations led Morocco to call for modifications of the 1992 fishing agreement, demanding a reduction in quotas and a halt to the increase in the number of fishing licences. This was a threat to Spain, because 90 per cent of the fishing fleet in Moroccan waters was Spanish. Spain also strongly opposed the opening of the fruit and vegetable market because of schedule issues: other EU states, such as France, could maintain other positions because of their different timetables.[15] The peace process in the Middle East had just started, and consequently the EU could no longer limit its thinking to the Maghreb; this too was a blow to Moroccan expectations.

The collapse of the CSCM initiative and the launching of the Middle East peace process induced Egypt to seek a principal role in planning a Mediterranean Forum. This initiative was supported by France and Italy, but

Spain initially favoured a broader proposal. The first meeting of the Mediterranean Forum was in Alexandria on 3–4 July 1994. Spain headed the political working group, Italy the cultural issues one; Egypt that of social and economic affairs, and Portugal held the senior officials group meeting. The meetings were held regularly, and Spain found this forum useful in important moments such as the launching of the Euro-Mediterranean Conference.[16]

THE SPANISH PRESIDENCY OF THE EU AND THE WEU

Once the basis for a new European approach to the Mediterranean region was established, Spain took the opportunity of its presidency of the EU and the WEU to advance Mediterranean concerns. In the case of the EU, it succeeded in developing a Euro-Mediterranean consensus. The efforts of the Spanish diplomats to get a consensus including the Arabs and the Israelis on a text devoted to political and security cooperation were remarkable. On 27–28 November 1995 the Euro-Mediterranean conference was launched in Barcelona, opening important perspectives. The Conference was a fundamental achievement in the foreign policy of the EU. Its notion of the partnership included not only economic aspects and a free-trade zone but also social, human, cultural, political, and security aspects. The Conference was simply a starting point, because the content of the first chapter of the Barcelona Declaration on the identification of a common area of peace and stability was not a security partnership. The creation of a shared-prosperity area was a serious challenge to the industrial framework of the southern Mediterranean countries, and, with regard to the development of human resources, the understanding of cultures, and exchanges between civil societies, the weak point was precisely the nature of civil society in the non-European countries other than Israel. The north–south migration movements did not have a correct focus according to the southern Mediterranean countries.

A working programme was adopted in *ad hoc* meetings of ministers, senior officials, and experts, exchanges of experiences and information, meetings between elements of civil society, and contacts among parliamentarians, regional and local authorities, and social partners. A Euro-Mediterranean Committee for the Barcelona Process was created for the meetings of foreign ministers and the role of the European Commission was spelled out.[17]

Within the WEU, Spain gave a new impulse to the dialogue with the Maghreb states. The Spanish criteria, widely shared by the NATO countries, were focused on the following points: The activities of the WEU were to be framed in terms of a broad, global concept of security to achieve stability in the Mediterranean region; in this context, the WEU was to deal with the military aspects while the EU would focus on the other aspects of a broad concept of security; the WEU was not to adopt an adversarial approach to supposed threats from the south. The objective was the creation of a dialogue with the aim of increasing mutual knowledge and understanding. The dialogue was to promote as a priority principles considered capable of contributing to the stability and security of the Mediterranean as a whole, especially the peaceful settlement of conflicts, transparency in military doctrines and activities, non-proliferation of weapons of mass destruction, and the sufficiency of conventional armaments.

During the Spanish presidency this dialogue was promoted, maintaining the structure created by the WEU Ministerial Council in Kirchberg and supporting broader cooperation with measures such as exchange visits of military officials, joint participation in exercises in UN peacekeeping operations, and the invitation of observers to military manoeuvres. In this context, measures were taken that involved the North African countries.[18]

There was also an attempt to involve NATO in this direction. Thus, in September 1994, at an informal meeting of the NATO Defence Ministers including the French Minister, Spain introduced a proposal for cooperation with certain North African countries. The proposal included the establishment of contacts to explain the goals and activities of the Alliance, the possibility of joint participation in humanitarian and peacekeeping operations, and the possibility of inviting military observers to Allied exercises in the Mediterranean. Later, on 25 November, the Atlantic Council approved a report on the relation of possible activities of the Alliance with regard to the Mediterranean non-NATO member states. Six days later, on 1 December, the NAC ministerial meeting assigned to the Permanent Council the task of developing the dialogue and preliminary contacts. Finally, on 8 February 1995, the NAC approved a document containing its recommendations: an explanation of the ends and goals of the Alliance, which included crisis management, humanitarian and peacekeeping operations, exposition of concerns and interests regarding Mediterranean security interlocutors, and exploration of the issues to be included in subsequent meetings. Contacts between the international secretariat and the states started on 24 February. The starting round included Egypt, Israel, Morocco, Mauritania, and Tunisia. Later, in November 1995, Jordan was invited to join. At the beginning of March, Spain began meeting with the ambassadors of these states and also with officials in their capitals. But the dialogue with NATO as well as in the WEU was soon limited because of the originally limited content of the dialogue (more in the case of NATO than in the WEU) and because of the blocking of the Middle East peace process by the new Prime Minister of Israel, Benjamin Netanyahu.[19]

In fact, at the beginning of 1996, on the eve of the electoral victory of the Popular Party, although certain problems remained, constructive progress in directing the attention of various fora on security towards the Mediterranean was remarkable.

THE POPULAR PARTY'S APPROACH

The José María Aznar administration has followed the same guidelines regarding the Mediterranean with some modifications. In the security field, the priority has been full military integration into NATO. This orientation, very clear in its electoral programme,[20] means first of all a lower profile for the WEU, in which Spain had formally been very active. As a result, and given France's traditional preoccupation with the containment of Germany in Europe, the Mediterranean dialogue within the WEU started to fade. Spain did, however, promote the intensification of the Mediterranean dialogue within NATO. The ministerial meeting at Sintra and the July 1997 NATO Madrid Summit established a new sort of meeting of the 16 NATO countries and each of the Mediterranean partners, creating coordination through the Mediterranean Co-operation Group and thus improving the prospects for confidence and understanding in the Mediterranean. Every Mediterranean partner will receive the same opportunities, but each will be able to determine the intensity and range of its commitment. The dialogue is intended to strengthen international efforts in order to broaden cooperation in other fora created in the Mediterranean. It calls for multilateral meetings on a case-by-case basis. Among the activities initially specified besides the political dialogue are participation in the NATO Scientific Committee and the gathering of information on the scientific activities of NATO, participation in seminars and conferences of mutual interest, participation in the NATO Defence College and in courses at the Oberammergau NATO school on arms control, verification, environmental protection, civilian planning for emergencies and European co-operation on security issues, participation in military co-operation in response to natural disasters and civil emergency plans, and the exchange of observers in military exercises. This dialogue does not, however, cover defence planning, and there is no plan for joint exercises as in the NATO Partnership for Peace.[21]

This plan is advancing more slowly than expected because of the cost of the partnership for the peace programme, which leaves few resources to be assigned to the Mediterranean, and the blocking of the Middle East peace process, hindering effective dialogue on military security in the Mediterranean. It is expected, however, that the current dialogue, which already includes important elements of cooperation, can arrive at some kind of partnership framework suited to the cultural and social character of the Mediterranean area. Consequently, Spain will try to incorporate more in this initiative and allow more resources for it. This proposal has a remarkable number of incentives for the southern countries. The Partnership for Peace has achieved great prestige because of its performance, especially in Bosnia; Spain hopes to be the forum for meetings between Morocco and Mauritania.

Spain's approach to NATO does not mean that it disregards the WEU and its dialogue with the Mediterranean partners. It considers it unacceptable to transfer to NATO the security and political dialogue contained in the first chapter of the Barcelona Declaration, with its important elements of hard security. Furthermore, it wants to preserve and enhance the Euro-Mediterranean Conference as a forum in which the Arab Mediterranean countries (with the exception of Libya) and Israel can participate together. Initiatives such as EUROFOR, EUROMARFOR, and the Spanish–Italian amphibious force are specifically Mediterranean and are assigned primarily to the WEU. It is Spain's position that the WEU needs to be included in the European Union. With regard to the Organization for Security and Cooperation in Europe (OSCE), the new Spanish government has continued to insist on the necessity of promoting dialogue with the Mediterranean states as stipulated in the Lisbon Declaration of 1996.

NATO, the WEU, the OSCE and other fora must, however, be complementary to the Barcelona Process. The three aspects of that process are not moving forward at the same rate: progress on economic, social, cultural, and human aspects is quite good but there is less progress on political and security matters. The problem is lack of confidence and slow convergence due mainly to differences in approach. As the Barcelona Declaration itself points out, the Barcelona Process is not intended to replace other processes of conflict resolution, such as the Middle East peace process, but in the field of security could contribute significantly to the Middle East peace process if peace is achieved in the Mediterranean area. The Charter of Stability and Security, for instance, could contribute substantially to completing the network of international guarantees that would require peace. In any case, the Spanish government believes that the EU must play a broader role in the peace process.[22]

FOREIGN POLICY PRIORITIES

Spain has gradually extended its policy to the eastern Mediterranean. Its interest in establishing a larger commercial presence and increasing its investments in Turkey have become clearer under the Popular Party government, and it has also sought to enhance its presence in Egypt.

Relations with Israel have dramatically increased in every way since the establishment of diplomatic ties in 1986. With regard to the Gulf countries, an increase in the Spanish presence has been observed only in Iran. In other countries with major oil reserves, such as Iraq, the Spanish government's position has been to wait and see. The interests in Iraq, Iran, and the Caucasus, and infrastructure building and industrial equipment of Spanish oil companies are important here. Nevertheless, the main focus of interest for Spanish foreign and security policy continues to be the Maghreb.

Traditionally, the stability of Morocco was considered essential to Spanish security, but the situation in Algeria has also occupied the foreground since the military coup that interrupted the electoral process. Spain recognized that the Algerian problem could not be resolved by military means, that the corruption of the military regime and its disrepute among the people would impede any unilateral solution. It saw negotiation among the political forces which rejected terrorism as necessary to resolve the conflict. But the conflict in Algeria had its impact in the Mediterranean. An Islamic state in Algeria was considered disruptive not only for the Maghreb, but for the Middle East as well, and thus ultimately such considerations finally conditioned the policies of the European states. To this we must add the special consideration of France for its former colony, the impact on France of the change to an Islamic-oriented political regime, and the consequent flow of refugees. In the end, Spain and other countries, such as the United States, had to accept the political line that France established; support for the San Egido platform was abandoned. The Popular Party government took a more pragmatic line, supporting the political reorganization designed by the Algerian military and economic establishment. The interests of Spanish companies such as Gas Natural pushed it in this direction, and in 1992 a significant increase in Spanish investment in Algeria could be detected.

In the case of Morocco, Spanish policy during the past ten years has created a network of economic relations that helps to reduce the traditional conflicts that have overshadowed bilateral relations. The agenda is extensive and includes military collaboration. Morocco is the main recipient of Spanish financial cooperation, and Spanish investment there is the greatest in North Africa. Relations with Morocco were institutionalized at a high level with the signing of a treaty of friendship and cooperation in Rabat on 4 July 1991. The treaty contains such general principles as respect for international law, sovereign equality, non-intervention in internal affairs, restriction of the threat of use of force, peaceful settlement of disputes, cooperation in development, respect for human rights, and dialogue and cultural understanding. Because of this, the treaty establishes the framework for bilateral political relations, financial and economic cooperation,

cooperation in development, cooperation on defence issues, cooperation on culture and education, and consular and legal cooperation. The importance of this treaty is two-fold. It both structures relations with Morocco and makes them more predictable. It also constitutes a model for relations with Algeria and Tunisia. A similar treaty was in fact signed with Tunisia on 22 October 1995.

Spain also supports Morocco's pursuit of a special relationship with the EU, and, since the signing of the EU–Morocco free-trade agreement on 26 February 1996, has supported Morocco in exploring the possibilities of cooperation with the EU and facing the challenge of adapting its productive sector to a free trade area. The Moroccan claim to Ceuta and Melilla – a point of possible friction – is to some extent frozen. Spain is confident of a peaceful future succession in Morocco. In the case of Tunisia, Spain has tried to enhance its presence there and since the signing of the treaty of friendship and cooperation Spanish investments have increased.

Spain is trying to obtain more room to manoeuvre in the context of the new economic opportunities created by the free-trade area. This is the philosophy underlying its approach to the rest of the Maghreb countries. The question is how to support the stability of these states through mainly economic measures. The defence and promotion of human rights are limited in view of the instability of these countries; to press them excessively on this point is considered likely to exacerbate their problems in a moment of transition. But this feeds the perception of an excessive pragmatism, especially when the priority seems to be economic stability rather than the political stability that is essential for the attraction of investments.

CONCLUSION

Spain has made an important effort to make the United States, the EU, and European organizations aware of the problems of the Mediterranean countries. Its main focus has been the Maghreb and the western Mediterranean, but the CSCM and the Euro-Mediterranean Conference of Barcelona have made broader approaches to the achievement of stability in the Mediterranean. Spain recognizes the impossibility of acting effectively alone in the European organizations. In most cases its achievements have been the outcome of joint efforts with France and Italy. Sometimes, however, Spain has acted almost alone, for example in attracting the interest of NATO to the Mediterranean since 1991.

Spanish policy will continue to focus on directing the attention and resources of the various European organizations towards the Mediterranean. For this, it will need not only to cooperate with France and Italy, but also to enhance its presence in the eastern Mediterranean, where possible divergences of interests between Europeans and Americans and important areas of instability are apparent.

NOTES

1. See in this regard, Antonio Marquina, *España en la politica de seguridad occidental, 1939–1986* (Madrid, 1986), Chs.7 and 9; idem 'Spanish Foreign and Defence Policy since Democratization', in Kenneth Maxwell (ed.), *Spanish Foreign and Defense Policy* (Boulder, CO, 1991), pp.19–63.
2. Antonio Marquina, 'La política exterior de los gobiernos de la Unión de Centro Democrático', in Javier Tusell and Alvaro Soto (eds.), *Historia de la transicion 1975–1986* (Madrid, 1996), pp.182–216.
3. Antonio Marquina 'La evolución de la política de seguridad española (1982–1992)', in Rafael Calduch (ed.), *La politica exterior espanola en el siglo XX* (Madrid, 1994), pp.369–89.
4. Regarding Spanish decolonization, see Antonio Marquina, 'La política exterior de España 1939–1975', in José Andres Gallego (ed.), *Historia contemporánea de España*, 13, 3 (Madrid, 1995), pp.447–623.
5. Carlos Echeverria, 'Origen, evolucion y perspectivas de la cooperación entre la Comunidad Europea y los países de la Unión del Magreb Arabe', in Antonio Marquina (ed.), *El Magreb: Concertación, cooperación y desafíos* (Madrid, 1993), pp.221–43.
6. Antonio Marquina, *El flanco sur de la OTAN* (Madrid, 1993), pp.66–9.
7. Ibid., p.68.
8. Ibid., p.69.
9. Antonio Marquina, 'The European Union Negotiations on Partnership-Building Agreements with Morocco and Tunisia', in Antonio Marquina (ed.), *Confidence Building and Partnership in the Western Mediterranean. Issues and Policies for the 1995 Conference* (Madrid, 1996), pp.31–45.
10. See the content of this dialogue in Carlos Echeverria, 'WEU approach to the North African Countries', in Assembleia da Republica, *Os problemas de securança no Mediterraneo ocidental* (Lisboa, 1995), pp.31–7.
11. Javier I. Garcia, 'Setting up the Common European Defense: Western European Union and the Mediterranean', in Marquina, *Confidence Building and Partnership in the Western Mediterranean*, pp.79–103.
12. See Antonio Marquina, 'Mediterráneo e sicurezza nell'ottica spagnola', *Relazioni Internazionali*, 34 (1995), pp.45–6.
13. See *Cumbre de la Conferencia sobre la Seguridad y la Cooperación en Europa* (Madrid, 1992), section 10 of the Helsinki Summit Declaration.
14. See Marquina, 'Mediterrano e sicurezza', pp.44–5
15. See Marquina, 'European Union Negotiations', pp.36–42.
16. Appearance of the Minister of Foreign Affairs, Javier Solana, before the Commission for the European Union, Madrid, 2 March 1995.
17. *Conferencia Euromediterránea*, Barcelona, 27 y 28 de noviembre de 1995 (Madrid: OID, 1995).
18. Marquina, 'Mediterrano e Sicurezza', p.45.
19. Antonio Marquina, 'Los desafíos en el Mediterráneo', in *La cumbre de Madrid y el futuro de la Alianza Atlántica* (Madrid, 1997), pp.27–43.
20. See Partido Popular, *Con la nueva mayoria, Programa electoral* (Madrid, 1996), pp.220–56.
21. See e.g. Jette Nordan, 'The Mediterranean Dialogue: Dispelling Misconceptions and Building Confidence', *NATO Review*, 4 (1997), pp.26–9.
22. 'Conferencia del Señor Ministro en Institut Catala de la Mediterránia d'Estudis i Cooperació', Barcelona, 16 Feb. 1998.

List of Contributors

Michael Alpert holds the Chair of Modern and Contemporary History of Spain in the University of Westminster. He has published widely on the Spanish Civil War. His most recent book is *A New International History of the Spanish Civil War* (London, 1994). His research on the Jews of Spain is the subject of the forthcoming book: *La ley en que espera vivir y morir: Criptojudaísmo e Inquisición en la España del XVII y XVIII siglo* (Madrid, in press).

Shannon E. Fleming is employed by the US Social Security Administration. He is a specialist in nineteenth- and twentieth-century Spanish North African history and has written a number of articles on this topic. He is also the author of *Primo de Rivera and Abdel-Krim: The Struggle in Spanish Morrocco, 1923–1927* (New York, 1991).

Fernando García Sanz is Senior Researcher in Contemporary History at the Higher Council of Scientific Research (CSIC) in Madrid. His research has covered the history of international relations, of Spanish foreign policy and, in particular, the history of Italy and its relations with Spain. His latest publications include *Historia de las relaciones entre España e Italia. Imágenes, Comercio y Política Exterior (1890–1914)* (Madrid, 1994); *Juan Pérez Caballero y Ferrer, ¿Una nueva diplomacia en la estela del '98?* (*Historia Contemporánea*, 1996); *I 'Paesi latini' e le crisi coloniali di fine Ottocento* (Foggia, 1998). He is the editor of *Españoles e italianos en el mundo contemporáneo* (Madrid, 1990), and *Italia e Spagna: crisi di fine secolo e lo Stato liberale* (Roma, forthcoming 1999). He is currently preparing a monograph on the Western Mediterranean during World War One.

Norman J.W. Goda is Assistant Professor of History at Ohio University. His publications include *Tomorrow the World: Hitler, Northwest Africa, and the Path Toward America* (College Station, 1998) and articles in the *Journal of Contemporary History*, *International History Review* and the *Journal of Modern History*. He is currently studying the diplomacy of war crimes justice.

Antonio Marquina is a Professor of International Relations and Security Studies in the Faculty of Political Sciences of Complutense University, Madrid. He is the author or editor of *Confidence Building and Partnership* *in the Western Mediterranean* (Madrid, 1996), *Elites and Change in the Mediterranean* (Madrid, 1997) and *Las migraciones del Norte de Africa a España y la Unión Europea: Tareas para una política de asociación* (Madrid, 1997).

Ricardo Miralles teaches contemporary history at the University of the Basque Country. His publications include: *El socialismo vasco durante la Segunda República* (Bilbao, 1988), *Equilibrio, hegemonía y reparto: Las relaciones internacionales entre 1870 y 1945* (Madrid, 1996) and *Juan Negrín: El hombre necesario* (Las Palmas de Gran Canaria, 1996).

Stanley G. Payne is Hilldale Jaume Vicens Vives Professor of History at the University of Wisconsin Madison. His most recent books are: *Franco y José Antonio: El extrano caso del fascismo español* (Madrid, 1998), *El primer franquismo* (Madrid, 1998), *A History of Fascism 1914–1945* (Madison, 1995), the edited work *Identidad y nacionalismo en la Espana contemporánea: El Carlismo 1833–1975* (Madrid, 1996), and the co-edited books *La guerra civil* (Madrid, 1996) and *España y la Segunda Guerra Mundial* (Madrid, 1997).

Raanan Rein is Senior Lecturer in Spanish and Latin American History at Tel Aviv University. He is the author of many articles and several books, among them *The Franco–Perón Alliance: Relations between Spain and Argentina, 1946–55* (Pittsburgh, 1993) and *In the Shadow of the Holocaust and the Inquisition: Israel's Relations with Francoist Spain* (London, 1997). He is also the editor of *Estudios Interdisciplinarios de América Latina y el Caribe*.

Octavio Ruiz-Manjón is Professor of Contemporary History at the Complutense University, Madrid. He has published many articles on turn-of-the-century Spanish Republicanism and is now working on an intellectual portrait and updated biography of Fernando de los Ríos. He is editor of several books on Spanish contemporary history, among them *Los nuevos historiadores ante la guerra civil española* (Granada, 1990) and *Los significados de 1998* (Madrid, in press).

Ismael Saz is Professor of Contemporary History at the University of Valencia, where he also serves as chair of the department. He has written extensively on Fascism, Francoism, and international relations. He is the author of *Fascistas en España* (Madrid, 1980 in collaboration with Javier Tusell) and *Mussolini contra la II República* (Valencia, 1986). He has also edited two volumes, *Repensar el feixisme* (Afers, 1996) and *España: La* *mirada del otro* (Ayer, 1998), and is currently working on a book entitled *El fascismo* that will be published by Editorial Hipotesi of Barcelona.

Susana Sueiro Seoane is Professor of Contemporary History at the National University of Education at a Distance. The main lines of her research are Spanish foreign policy in the first third of the twentieth century and Spain as a colonial power in North Africa. On these subjects she has published a book entitled *España en el Mediterráneo: Primo de Rivera y la 'cuestión marroquí' 1923–1930* (Madrid, 1993), as well as numerous articles.

Nuria Tabanera García is Professor of Spanish American History and Foreign Affairs at the University of Valencia. Her main contributions are on Spanish emigration and exile to the Americas, the political relations between Spain and Latin America, and the political history of Argentina in the nineteenth and twentieth centuries. Her publications include *Ilusiones y desencuentros: La acción diplomática republicana en Hispanoamérica (1931–1939)* (Madrid, 1996), and, with P. Pérez, *España–America Latina: Un siglo de políticas Culturales* (Madrid, 1993).

Alfred Tovias is Associate Professor in the Department of International Relations and Deputy Director of the Helmut Kohl Institute for European Studies of the Hebrew University in Jerusalem. He is chairman of the Israeli Association for the Study of European Integration. He is the author of *Tariff Preferences in Mediterranean Diplomacy* (London, 1977), *Foreign Economic Relations of the European Community: The Impact of Spain and Portugal* (Boulder, 1990), and the co-author of *The Economics of Peace Making: Focus on the Egyptian–Israeli Situation* (London, 1983).

Index

Books of Related Interest

Politics and Policy in Democratic Spain

No Longer Different?

Paul Heywood, *University of Nottingham* (Ed)

'Spain is different' was a favourite tourist board slogan of the Franco dictatorship. Is Spain still different? This volume provides an original series of analyses of how politics in democratic Spain has developed since the remarkable success of the transition to democracy. The book reflects on the transition to democracy and reviews some key features of Spain's subsequent democratic development. It then goes on to look at the policy process and questions many of the prevailing interpretations in Spain. This volume lends weight to the argument that Spain is no longer 'different', at least not in the sense associated with the tourist slogan.

Largely the work of Spanish scholars, it looks at the functioning of Spain since the introduction of democracy and more particularly since the Constitution of 1978.

248 pages 1999
0 7146 4910 4 cloth
0 7146 4467 6 paper
A special issue of the journal West European Politics

In the Shadow of the Holocaust and the Inquisition

Israel's Relations with Francoist Spain

Raanan Rein, *Tel Aviv University,*
translated by **Martha Grenzeback**

This book analyses the reasons for the failure of all efforts to establish diplomatic relations between Israel and Francoist Spain from the late 1940s to the mid-1970s. Based on research in four countries, it uncovers the political discussions and the diplomatic moves of each country as well as the mutual images common in Spain and Israel, and their influence on both public opinion and policy makers. In the late 1940s the Francoist dictatorship was eager to form ties with the new Jewish state. At that stage it was Israel who rejected any *rapprochement* with Franco. In the mid-1950s, however, Israel became interested in cultivating a closer relationship with Madrid. Now it was Franco's turn to say 'no'. Only in January 1986 did Spain's Prime Minister Felipe González and Israel's Labour Prime Minister, Shimon Peres, sign the agreement to establish full diplomatic ties between the two countries.

288 pages 1997
0 7146 4796 9 cloth
0 7146 4351 3 paper

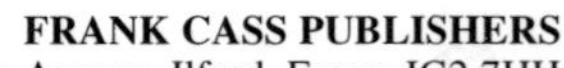

Newbury House, 900 Eastern Avenue, Ilford, Essex, IG2 7HH
Tel: +44 (0)181 599 8866 Fax: +44 (0)181 599 0984 E-mail: info@frankcass.com
NORTH AMERICA
5804 NE Hassalo Street, Portland, OR 97213 3644, USA
Tel: 800 944 6190 Fax: 503 280 8832 E-mail: cass@isbs.com
Website: www.frankcass.com